"Bringing together the best experts in the business, *Generating and Sustaining Nonprofit Earned Income* offers up critical advice and insights to help even the most experienced social entrepreneurs improve upon enterprise performance. A critical addition to any practitioner resource library."
　　—Jed Emerson, lecturer in business, Stanford Business School, and senior fellow,
　　　　William and Flora Hewlett Foundation, David and Lucile Packard Foundation

"We live in a world that begs for the creation of new models of economic justice and opportunities. This book provides valuable information supporting the efforts of nonprofit entrepreneurs to succeed in creating and operating ventures that are both sustainable and replicable while meeting economic and societal needs. Go for it!"
　　—Ben Cohen and Jerry Greenfield, cofounders, Ben & Jerry's

"Nonprofit ventures have few of the traditional supports that are available to other types of organizations. Straddling the for-profit and nonprofit cultures, they inhabit a world not officially recognized where roadmaps do not exist. Life on the thin strip between one land and another is always a precarious existence, full of trials and tribulations, but also charged with opportunity. This book provides the best thinking to help nonprofits capitalize on that opportunity."
　　—Bill Shore, chairman, Community Wealth Ventures

"State-of-the-art advice from a stellar collection of experienced voices in the field of nonprofit social venturing. Nonprofit managers, students of social enterprise, philanthropists, and social venture competition entrants, take note: you need to read this book."
　　—Catherine H. Clark, director, Research Initiative on Social Entrepreneurship, and
　　　　faculty adviser, Global Social Venture Competition, Columbia Business School

"You've got questions? This book has the answers. It is thorough, practical, and chock-full of practitioners' wisdom. It's a great resource."
　　—Edward Skloot, executive director, The Surdna Foundation

"You wouldn't take a long trip without a plan. Neither should you start an earned income venture for your nonprofit organization without this book. Having been there myself, I can say with great confidence that this book will provide the framework for the planning, launch, and operation of a successful and sustainable nonprofit enterprise. Whether you are an investor, manager, or board member, you need this book to guide you on what can be a very challenging but rewarding journey."
　　—Gary G. Mulhair, managing partner, Global Partnerships,
　　　　and past president and CEO, Pioneer Human Services

"This book cuts through the rhetoric about social enterprise. It provides clear and sober advice as well as practical tools for navigating the launch, challenges, and financing of mission-driven businesses."
　　—Betsy Biemann, associate director, The Rockefeller Foundation

To further illustrate the concepts discussed in this collection, readers are invited to review the business plans of several nonprofit ventures that entered the 2002–2003 National Business Plan Competition for Nonprofit Organizations, a program of the Yale School of Management– The Goldman Sachs Foundation Partnership on Nonprofit Ventures.

The business plans are available FREE on-line.

If you would like to download electronic versions of the business plans, please visit www.josseybass.com/go/nonprofitearnedincome

Thank you,

Sharon M. Oster
Cynthia W. Massarsky
Samantha L. Beinhacker

GENERATING AND SUSTAINING NONPROFIT EARNED INCOME

ABOUT THIS BOOK

Stephanie Bell-Rose
President, The Goldman Sachs Foundation

This book is dedicated to those on the cutting edge of the growing field of nonprofit enterprise and is an outgrowth of our wonderful partnership with two outstanding organizations, the Yale School of Management and The Pew Charitable Trusts—leaders in their respective fields of education and philanthropy. The program born from this union, The Partnership on Nonprofit Ventures, has sought to educate nonprofits about business enterprise, serve as a mechanism for capitalizing promising profit-making ventures with financial support, and provide intellectual capital to build the practice of social entrepreneurship in the nonprofit sector at-large through its comprehensive website and signature event, the National Business Plan Competition for Nonprofit Organizations. Our goal in supporting this program has been to supply not just financial support, but also intellectual capital—the greatest resource of our firm. The resulting collaboration, blending business, academic and philanthropic expertise, defies traditional boundaries between sectors and provides new resources in response to an unmet need in the nonprofit field.

At The Goldman Sachs Foundation we have embraced nonprofit enterprise as an effective means to foster innovation and generate positive social impact. It is an effective catalyst for creative thinking and problem solving in the social sector and a powerful tool for educating and motivating both socially committed business leaders and business-minded nonprofit leaders.

It is our hope that this book will provide nonprofit leaders with concrete lessons to assist their organizations in establishing and running income-generating ventures. This book also aims to improve substantially the quality and dissemination of information about successful business planning and operations. We hope that the lessons learned will have positive long-term effects on the professionals building their business enterprises in the charitable sector and the students taking their skills into the marketplace. We trust that the educational tools presented here will help nonprofits generate more of the financial resources necessary to solve the complex problems of our world today.

GENERATING AND SUSTAINING NONPROFIT EARNED INCOME

A Guide to Successful Enterprise Strategies

Editors
Sharon M. Oster, Cynthia W. Massarsky,
and Samantha L. Beinhacker

Yale School of Management–
The Goldman Sachs Foundation
Partnership on Nonprofit Ventures

Foreword by
Bill Bradley
Former U.S. Senator

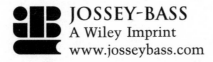

JOSSEY-BASS
A Wiley Imprint
www.josseybass.com

Published by Jossey-Bass
A Wiley Imprint
989 Market Street, San Francisco, CA 94103-1741   www.josseybass.com

Jossey-Bass books and products are available through most bookstores. To contact Jossey-Bass directly,
call our Customer Care Department within the U.S. at 800-956-7739, outside the U.S. at 317-572-3993,
or fax 317-572-4002.

Jossey-Bass also publishes its books in a variety of electronic formats. Some content that appears in print
may not be available in electronic books.

The publisher and the author make no representations or warranties with respect to the accuracy or
completeness of the contents of this work and specifically disclaim all warranties, including without
limitation warranties of fitness for a particular purpose. No warranty may be created or extended by
sales or promotional materials. The advice and strategies contained herein may not be suitable for every
situation. This work is sold with the understanding that the publisher is not engaged in rendering legal,
accounting, or other professional services. If professional assistance is required, the services of a competent professional person should be sought. Neither the publisher nor the author shall be liable for dam-
ages arising herefrom. The fact that an organization or Web site is referred to in this work as a citation
and/or a potential source of further information does not mean that the author or the publisher en-
dorses the information the organization or Web site may provide or recommendations it may make.
Further, readers should be aware that Internet Web sites listed in this work may have changed or disap-
peared between when this work was written and when it is read.

Credits are on page 312.

Library of Congress Cataloging-in-Publication Data

Generating and sustaining nonprofit earned income: a guide to successful enterprise strategies / editors
Sharon M. Oster, Cynthia W. Massarsky, and Samantha L. Beinhacker ; foreword by Bill Bradley.
    p. cm.
  Includes index.
  ISBN 0-7879-7238-X (alk. paper)
  1. New business enterprises.   2. Nonprofit organizations.   I. Oster, Sharon M.   II. Massarsky,
Cynthia W., date.   III. Beinhacker, Samantha L., date.
  HD62.5.G46 2004
  658'.048—dc22

                                                                        2004003741

Printed in the United States of America
FIRST EDITION
HB Printing   10 9 8 7 6 5 4 3 2

CONTENTS

TABLES, FIGURES, AND EXHIBITS

TABLES

FIGURES

EXHIBITS

FOREWORD

Bill Bradley
Former U.S. Senator

The revenues of the nonprofit sector are a little over $700 billion per year: $500 billion in fees, $200 billion in contributions. The sector controls more than two trillion dollars in assets. It has complex funding and its organizations are diverse, often spanning many geographies. It is, in a very real sense, a force to be reckoned with and to be acknowledged in American life in a way that has not been the case to date. Roughly half of our nation's hospitals and colleges and universities are nonprofits. The nonprofit sector accounts for the vast majority of our civic and social service infrastructure.

Just look at what the nonprofit sector has done in America over the years—it has led the drive to create everything from the polio vaccine to Sesame Workshop to a nationwide 911. It has protected endangered species, played a crucial role in bringing down apartheid and rebuilding civil society in Eastern Europe, demined war zones across this world, cared for aged patients and the homeless, provided help for schools—and the list goes on and on.

So, there is a great deal to be proud of for those of us who have worked in the nonprofit sector. At the same time, there's still a lot more to do. If we simply look out at the world, we see 650 million children who live on less than a dollar a day, about 42 million Americans who don't have any health insurance, and about 14 million children in America who still live in poverty, and our education system continues to fail many. Biodiversity is still endangered, AIDS remains a grave and growing health threat worldwide, and diseases that we thought we had taken off the list a long time ago, such as tuberculosis and measles, have come back to show us they're resistant to the kinds of things we've done up to this point.

There are tremendous challenges for the nonprofit sector that are more daunting today in a time of economic crisis than ever before. Of course, the non-profit sector has always done more with less, but these days we're being tested for our creative and strong organizational abilities. I would suggest that at a time in which we've seen the federal budget go in three or four years from surpluses that seemed to extend all the way to the horizon to deficits that seem to extend all the way to the horizon, the nonprofit sector has an even more important role to play as we think about dealing with the basic issues of our society and about the prob-lems that confront the world.

That brings us to this book's topic: nonprofit revenue generation, which I'd like to put into a broader context of the social capital market.

Let me start by saying that raising funds for nonprofits has never been easy or efficient. In fact, when McKinsey & Company's Nonprofit Practice recently studied the social capital market, we found that it lacks the four characteristics of an efficient market: cost-efficient processes, a robust information flow, value-driven allocation, and flexibility and responsiveness.[1] Let's look at each of these in turn.

The nonprofit sector lacks cost-efficient fundraising processes. For instance, in the for-profit capital market, costs of raising capital consume just 2 to 4 per-cent of funds raised. In the social capital market, however, the costs of raising cap-ital consume roughly 18 percent of funds raised. Such costs stem largely from the market's tremendous diversity and fragmentation; both nonprofits and funders have to search among many alternatives to find the one that meets their needs.

The nonprofit sector also lacks the second characteristic of a dynamic market—a robust information flow. The for-profit market has an active industry of infor-mation sources to assist funders and investors, as well as common accounting standards. In contrast, in the social capital market it is difficult to access clear, re-liable data regarding returns on potential investments due to difficulty in quanti-fying social returns and the lack of standardized performance data. In addition, the social capital market fails to embrace a uniform standard of accounting and reporting, and there remains a relative dearth of credible, widely adopted infor-mation to guide funding decisions.

The social capital market fares just as poorly on the third characteristic: a value-driven allocation process. In the for-profit market, investment decisions are linked to performance success. In the social capital market, returns—in this case social returns—are difficult to quantify or measure. In this market there are no standard measures of performance success, and investment decisions are often based on criteria other than financial or organizational performance and potential social impact (such as institutional loyalty, desire for recognition, appeal of a friend, and so on).

Finally, the social capital market is neither flexible nor responsive. In the for-profit market, investors are able to withdraw funds from low-return investments (often at a loss) and redistribute them to higher return investments. In the social capital market, however, contribution decisions are largely final and irreversible. Moreover, funding is often restricted, short-term, programmatic, and reliant on the funding schedules of donor institutions.

So, what shall we make of all this? Can we as funders, investors, and non-profit leaders do anything to improve the way the social capital market works? As funders and investors we should take the time to channel our resources into the most effective organizations. And I think it's reasonable to ask each nonprofit to say how it measures its impact on the problem it is supposed to be attacking, to report results, and to have the CEO of the nonprofit attest to the accuracy of those results.

Also, as nonprofit leaders we should attempt to reduce the costs of fundrais-ing by finding alternative and more efficient ways to generate revenue, and that is what this book is all about.

Many of you have already begun to do this. According to Lester A. Salamon's recent report, "The State of Nonprofit America,"[2] between 1977 and 1997 the revenues of America's nonprofit sector increased by 144 percent after adjusting for inflation, nearly twice the 81 percent growth rate of the nation's economy—and 47 percent of that revenue growth came from a growth in fee income. And we're talking not just about the usual suspects here—health care and education nonprofits—but also about social services and arts and culture organizations. In fact, the social services sector saw almost a 600 percent increase in the amount of fee income during the twenty-year period from 1977 to 1997, and fee income rep-resented 35 percent of that sector's total revenue growth during that time.

Of course not all of this fee income comes from business-type ventures—some of it comes from fees charged to traditional clients for services rendered—but a lot of it does. The IRS reported a 35 percent increase in the number of charities reporting "unrelated business income" between 1990 and 1997—and as we all know, none of the ventures that are defined as related to the nonprofit's mission are even included in this number.

The ventures started by nonprofits are as varied and as innovative as anything in the private sector. For example:

- Nonprofits with expertise in everything from training parents to advocate on behalf of their children to working with former drug addicts have started con-sulting practices to advise other nonprofits.

- Child care and senior citizen centers are taking advantage of excess capacity in their kitchens and adapting their culinary skills to create catered meals for private and corporate events.
- Alcohol and drug treatment programs are marketing their expertise and services to corporate employee assistance programs.
- Environmental conservation organizations are leveraging their brands and knowledge in many ways—from certifying the lumber sold by large home-repair companies to offering high-end, expertly guided trips to lands they protect.
- Community development and social service agencies that help the economically disadvantaged are running a variety of businesses, from landscaping to manufacturing to clerical operations, and providing decently paying jobs for their clients in the process.

While we applaud those organizations that have launched revenue-generating efforts, we should also recognize that nonprofit enterprise is not for everyone. It's risky business, and nonprofits must consider not only the financial risks but also the potential impact of the enterprise on the organization's commitment to its mission, on its brand and reputation, and on its organizational health. Launching a business enterprise can be a real cultural and organizational shock, and organizations should not make the decision lightly.

This book will provide you with important information on the prerequisites for success, including fit with your organization's mission and distinctive expertise, a skilled management team, board and staff buy-in, market demand, and many other elements. Whether you are a nonprofit practitioner, academic or student, funder or investor, I believe that this information will help you make the right decision for your organization and give you access to the expertise and knowledge you need to get going.

Notes

1. Bradley, B., Jansen, P., and Silverman, L. "The Nonprofit Sector's $100 Billion Opportunity." *Harvard Business Review,* 2003, *81*(5), 94–103.
2. Salamon, L. M. (ed.). *The State of Nonprofit America.* Washington, D.C.: Brookings Institution Press, in collaboration with the Aspen Institute, 2002.

PREFACE

Sharon M. Oster
Cynthia W. Massarsky
Samantha L. Beinhacker

Much literature on the subject of entrepreneurship begins by talking about Joseph A. Schumpeter, an Austrian who wrote in the early part of the twentieth century. This economist saw innovation and entrepreneurship as the central agents of a capitalist society—as providing new ways of producing and organizing the production that upset the business models of the past while simultaneously creating new value for society. Schumpeter referred to this as the process of creative destruction. For him, this creative process was exclusively private sector oriented. Indeed, in Schumpeter's recital, it was the lure of profits that fed the fires of entrepreneurship, giving rise to successive waves of monopolists, each of whom extracted profits in his or her turn, before eventually being toppled by another more rapacious contender.

In today's world of high technology and a more global economy, this picture is ever more compelling as the half-life of firms shrinks. But from our perspective this story does have one critical missing element. In this twenty-first-century world we have increasingly come to appreciate the possibilities for a new kind of entrepreneurship—social entrepreneurship—in which innovative and energetic individuals, driven by prospects of social rather than individual gains, develop new goods and services, new delivery methods, and new organizational forms all directed toward solving social problems, some of which have been with us for centuries.

Many of the social entrepreneurs of this new world are found *between* the sectors— people who work in nonprofit organizations but seek to begin earned-income ventures to create new revenue sources and enliven their organizations in a range of ways. Indeed, during the course of administering the National Business Plan Competition for Nonprofit Organizations of the Yale School of Management–The Goldman Sachs Foundation Partnership on Nonprofit Ventures, we have found extraordinary organizations and people with exceptional ideas. For example, we have discovered people in the community economic development area who have ideas for employing displaced or disabled workers in manufacturing new products with a clear market niche. We have encountered a group of computer-savvy nonprofit entrepreneurs acting as canny middlemen between software companies with an interest in donating their products, and nonprofits in need of computer software, and we have learned about two arts institutions that have come together to leverage one of their greatest assets, theatrical costumes, to launch a costume rental company.

But earning income from commercial ventures is often no easier than generating donations. The failure rate for small businesses (for-profit as well as nonprofit) is extraordinarily high. For nonprofits that are moving from a focus on serving client needs to filling customer demand, the leap can be large indeed. This book aims to aid you in making that leap, and then to facilitate the learning that emerges to help you apply it in practice.

The material contained in this book stems from the Partnership on Nonprofit Ventures' First Annual Conference and Awards Ceremony held in May 2003, where most of our contributors held master classes or served as panelists at workshop sessions. The goal of the Partnership on Nonprofit Ventures' educational forums such as our annual conference, as well as our signature program, the National Business Plan Competition for Nonprofit Organizations, is to provide both intellectual capital to nonprofit entrepreneurs on the strategies involved in implementing a profitable enterprise, and financial capital needed to fund and sustain an earned-income venture. In the world of nonprofit ventures, there is no other single venue that offers nonprofits access to both of these key ingredients.

A Note About Language

In the past ten to fifteen years, the field has spawned a glossary of new terms to describe the practice of generating earned income. For example, a number of terms, from *social enterprise* and *affirmative business* to *nonprofit business venture* and *nonprofit enterprise,* are commonly used to describe the practice. Although the terminology may be a matter of question, the concept is not. For our purposes, this book uses the term adopted by the Partnership on Nonprofit Ventures and refers to all types of nonprofits engaged in generating earned income, as opposed to contributed income, as *nonprofit enterprises.*

Intended Audience

In this book, we have encouraged each author to provide concrete lessons to assist nonprofit organizations desiring to navigate their way out of the "funding trap" and at the same time to engage readers in a conversation about sound business planning strategies that can significantly benefit their organizations' internal capacity and financial health.

There are three key audiences for this book. The primary audience is top management within a nonprofit organization who are intent on securing new ways to help sustain their organizations. Having invested in studying the feasibility of nonprofit enterprise for their organizations, these senior executives are eager to learn and incorporate the best practices and strategies to build and grow their ventures. The book's orientation toward the real-world execution of nonprofit enterprise will guide the decision making of senior nonprofit executives and give them the necessary resources to lend their ventures the best chance of success.

The second audience for this book is academics at business schools and other graduate programs, and the students they teach (including recent undergraduates as well as professionals returning to school to obtain advanced degrees). For business school students and others studying social entrepreneurship, this book demonstrates both theoretical concepts as well as real-world situations that will hone their practice of analysis and business planning.

The third audience for this book is current and potential funders of nonprofit enterprise as well as board members of nonprofit organizations. Potential funders, investors, and board members are seeking information about the strategies that nonprofits employ to generate revenue and are looking to identify and disseminate sector-building practices to help build the field.

This book offers practical skills and strategies for getting started with the business planning and implementation of your nonprofit enterprise. We encourage readers to absorb the contents that are most appropriate for their stage of business development, and to revisit chapters as they progress in their ventures in order to correct course and discover new strategic directions.

Overview of the Contents

The book is divided into three sections. Part One details key issues in business planning for nonprofit enterprise and covers essential steps in business planning. In Chapter One, J. Gregory Dees lays out cautionary words about the challenges, costs, and risks associated with nonprofit business ventures and provides careful guidance on writing and implementing a business plan for a nonprofit enterprise.

In Chapter Two, Paul Connolly lays out the foundation for getting started and describes how to build organizational capacity to support earned-income activity. In Chapter Three, Jeffrey A. Sonnenfeld, and Maxwell L. Anderson offer expert advice on leadership development strategies and shed light on the various expertise and skill sets that are needed to run a successful business venture. In Chapter Four, Christopher Lovelock demonstrates various methods for conducting research and identifying the target market for a nonprofit venture. Sharon M. Oster, in Chapter Five, delivers practical tips on how nonprofits can price the products and services they offer. In Chapter Six, William H. Heritage Jr. and Timothy J. Orlebeke offer a primer on the legal and tax considerations in nonprofit enterprise. In Chapter Seven, Katherine M. O'Regan explores the complex governance issues raised both for the parent nonprofit organization and for the nonprofit enterprise and recommends the best ways to oversee a nonprofit enterprise.

Part Two features an array of information on finding and attracting capital—perhaps the greatest challenge faced by an organization seeking to launch a nonprofit enterprise or expand an existing one. Chapter Eight, compiled by David Bornstein and The Goldman Sachs Foundation, gives information on an array of financial tools and other resources that are available to nonprofit business ventures. In Chapter Nine, Amy Solas and Adam M. Blumenthal help bring the business plan to potential funders; describe effective ways to develop clear, concise, and persuasive investor presentations; and point out common weaknesses in nonprofit pitches to raise capital. Richard Steckel, in Chapter Ten, offers another model of nonprofit enterprise, providing concrete lessons on how to develop strategic alliances with for-profit corporations. In Chapter Eleven, Kristin Majeska describes the emerging field of high-engagement funding and presents the challenges and opportunities of this funding model. Lee Davis and Nicole Etchart, in Chapter Twelve, provide an overview of the unique challenges and opportunities for financing and supporting nonprofit enterprise in the context of emerging international markets.

Part Three highlights issues related to turning your business plan into action. Clearly, developing and writing a business plan, getting agreement and approval, and launching the enterprise are enormous accomplishments. But the job of implementing the plan is often much more difficult and fraught with complex challenges and decisions. This section alerts readers to what lies ahead and offers important lessons and practical advice on launching your venture.

In Chapter Thirteen, Patricia Caesar and Thomas Baker explain the fundamental principles of implementing a business plan. They present specific lessons on testing and validating product concepts, setting pricing and revenue expectations, putting the right metrics and measurement systems in place, assembling the right team and internal resources, and managing board involvement. Kim Alter, in Chapter Fourteen, underscores the importance of diligent contingency planning as a critical ingredient in successful enterprise development and provides guidance on the key issues experienced during implementation of a nonprofit enterprise. In Chapter Fifteen, Dennis Young highlights some of the trade-offs that nonprofit management and boards face when planning and implementing their business ventures and suggests an economic model for decision making. In Chapter Sixteen, Stephanie Bell-Rose provides guidance on the value and challenges associated with tracking performance benchmarks. Rick Aubry, in Chapter Seventeen, presents the issues involved in ramping up a nonprofit enterprise and *going to scale.*

From business planning to capital raising to implementing your business, this book provides practical, concrete models and examples for all the key aspects of building and growing a nonprofit enterprise. We hope it will become a reference for you and, like the business plan itself, part of your everyday working environment.

ACKNOWLEDGMENTS

This collection was accomplished through the Herculean efforts of everyone involved. Most of the material contained in this book stems from the First Annual Conference and Awards Ceremony of the Partnership on Nonprofit Ventures held in May 2003, where many of the book's contributors taught master classes or served as panelists at workshop sessions. We greatly appreciate all the chapter authors for agreeing to the tight deadlines for delivery of materials and for providing such a fine product.

The program that inspired this book is, as its name suggests, truly a partnership. We believe that a significant measure of the success of the program comes from the competitive strengths of our two funding partners and our founding institution.

The Pew Charitable Trusts was the brainchild of the program, having commissioned the feasibility study that led to the development of the first-ever National Business Plan Competition for Nonprofit Organizations as a way to provide targeted guidance and resources to nonprofits most capable of launching and operating revenue-generating business ventures. The Goldman Sachs Foundation has also proved to be an excellent fit for The Partnership. Goldman Sachs has provided a number of people who have used the skills they normally apply to large-scale business deals to the analysis of our somewhat smaller-scale nonprofit ventures. We have benefited from having Goldman Sachs executives on our board, as our evaluators, and at the conference as presenters. The hands-on quality of

The Goldman Sachs Foundation itself has improved our product at numerous stages along the way.

The Yale School of Management has had since its founding a mission of educating leaders for business and society. Since 1993, *U.S. News & World Report* has consistently ranked the Yale School of Management number one in nonprofit management among the nation's graduate management programs. Importantly, the emphasis of the nonprofit management program is precisely on the kinds of nonprofit ventures on which The Partnership is centered. At Yale, students are taught the importance of rigorous business skills in managing in all of the sectors. The Business Plan Competition, which emphasizes the social payoff to careful and hardheaded business planning in launching ventures in the nonprofit sector, resonates strongly with the message of the Yale School of Management. The extraordinary fit between the Yale mission and The Partnership comes home to us in seeing the involvement of the Yale School of Management alumni. For the arduous work in evaluating the business plans, more than five hundred School of Management alumni have volunteered their efforts, and many have participated in our conference and contributed to this volume as well.

We are especially grateful for the pro bono efforts of McKinsey & Company, under the direction of Lynn Taliento in the Firm's Nonprofit Practice, who have offered their expertise in analyzing a portion of the nonprofit ventures that entered the Competition. For all this we are extremely grateful.

Stanley Garstka, deputy dean of the Yale School of Management and cofaculty director of the Partnership on Nonprofit Ventures, has provided invaluable guidance and support to the program and to this book. We recognize and applaud the efforts of our indefatigable program assistant, Betty Velazquez, who performs her job seemingly effortlessly. Bridget Gillich, program coordinator, lends critical support to our efforts as well. We wish to thank our editor, Johanna Vondeling, and others at Jossey-Bass for guiding the vision, preparation, and production of this book.

Finally, we wish to recognize the incredible efforts of the thousands of nonprofit entrepreneurs who are the source of our inspiration.

February 2004

Sharon M. Oster
New Haven, Connecticut

Cynthia W. Massarsky
Tenafly, New Jersey

Samantha L. Beinhacker
Englewood, New Jersey

THE EDITORS

Sharon M. Oster is Frederic D. Wolfe Professor of Management and Entrepreneurship, director of the Program on Social Enterprise at the Yale School of Management, and co-faculty director for the Yale School of Management–The Goldman Sachs Foundation Partnership on Nonprofit Ventures. She is a specialist in competitive strategy, microeconomic theory, industrial organization, the economics of regulation and antitrust, and nonprofit strategy, and has consulted widely to private, public, and nonprofit organizations. She currently serves on the board of directors for such corporate institutions as Health Care REIT, Transpro, and Aristotle, as well as on nonprofit boards at Yale University Press, New Visions, and Choate Rosemary Hall.

Oster received her doctoral degree from Harvard University and a bachelor of arts degree from Hofstra College. She has written extensively on the regulation of business and competitive strategy. Her book *Modern Competitive Analysis* (Oxford University Press, 1999), used widely at management schools, integrates a broad range of views in its analysis of management strategy and emphasizes an economic approach to strategic planning. Her first book, *Strategic Management for Nonprofit Organizations* (Oxford University Press, 1995), takes the same economic approach to managing nonprofit organizations.

Cynthia W. Massarsky is no stranger to nonprofit organizations and nonprofit enterprise, having worked in the field for more than twenty-five years. During the last thirteen years she has operated CWM Marketing Group, a management consulting firm specializing in marketing and new business development in the nonprofit sector. She has also provided various services, including feasibility studies and grantee evaluations, to philanthropic foundations.

Massarsky is currently co-deputy director of the Yale School of Management–The Goldman Sachs Foundation Partnership on Nonprofit Ventures. Her list of clients is diverse, including organizations such as Save the Children, Bank Street College of Education, the Association of Junior Leagues International, AmeriCorps, the Ford Foundation, Wellesley College, Nonprofit Finance Fund, the National Endowment for the Arts, The Pew Charitable Trusts, AmFAR, the U.S. Fund for UNICEF, and The Rockefeller Foundation. Prior to founding her own firm, Massarsky worked with Scholastic, Marlo Thomas's Free to Be Foundation, the Foundation Center, and New Ventures, a consulting firm that guided nonprofits in exploring and initiating earned-income ventures.

Massarsky earned a bachelor's degree from Simmons College and an M.B.A. from Cornell University. Widely published, she is author of "Business Planning for Nonprofit Enterprise," a chapter in *The Nonprofit Entrepreneur,* edited by Edward Skloot and published by the Foundation Center in September 1988; coauthor with Loren Renz of *Program-Related Investments: A Guide to Funders and Trends,* published by the Foundation Center in April 1995; author of "Enterprise Strategies for Generating Revenue," a chapter in *The Jossey-Bass Handbook on Nonprofit Leadership and Management,* by Robert D. Herman and Associates (1994); coauthor with Samantha L. Beinhacker of "Nonprofit Enterprise: Right for You?" (*Nonprofit Quarterly,* Fall 2002); and *Enterprising Nonprofits: Revenue Generation in the Nonprofit Sector,* published by the Yale School of Management–The Goldman Sachs Foundation Partnership on Nonprofit Ventures (2002).

Samantha L. Beinhacker is co-deputy director of the Yale School of Management–The Goldman Sachs Foundation Partnership on Nonprofit Ventures. She is also managing partner of the management consulting firm Langbaum Associates. The firm specializes in new business development, strategic planning, and organizational capacity building. Her consulting experience includes assisting the management of nonprofit, public, and private-sector corporations in developing new business concepts; conducting strategic planning sessions; writing marketing and communications plans; designing and conducting business plan research; creating, developing, and evaluating public relations and advertising materials; and providing management capacity development support. Her clients include The Pew Charitable Trusts, The Rockefeller Foundation, New Jersey SEEDS, YWCA of New York City, Verizon Corporation, and Fortune Brands, among many others.

Beinhacker earned a bachelor of arts degree, *magna cum laude*, in history from Tufts University and a master's degree in U.S. women's history from the University of Wisconsin. She is coauthor, with Cynthia W. Massarsky, of "Nonprofit Enterprise: Right for You?" (*Nonprofit Quarterly*, Fall 2002); and *Enterprising Nonprofits: Revenue Generation in the Nonprofit Sector*, a Yale School of Management–The Goldman Sachs Foundation Partnership on Nonprofit Ventures study commissioned by The Pew Charitable Trusts (2002).

THE CONTRIBUTORS

Kim Alter is founder and principal of Virtue Ventures LLC, an international consulting firm specializing in social enterprise, small business, and corporate social responsibility. An "MBA with a social conscience," Alter has endeavored for more than fifteen years to bring business practices and tools to nonprofit organizations, engendering their sustainability through earned-income and capacity building. Her clients include the United Nations Development Programme, the Inter-American Development Bank, the World Bank, Save the Children, Counterpart International, and Ashoka, among many others. Her work has taken her to more than thirty developing countries worldwide, including Central Asia, where she is currently working on an eighteen-month contract to support the financial sustainability of civil society organizations in the region. She is author of *Managing the Double Bottom Line: A Business Planning Guide for Social Enterprises* (Pact, 2000) and its accompanying workbook; *A Social Enterprise Typology: Contextualized in Latin America* (Virtue Ventures and Inter-American Development Bank, October 2003); and numerous articles and other publications. She was a founding member of Social Enterprise Alliance, a network membership organization. She holds an M.B.A. jointly from Boston University Brussels (Belgium) and Vrij Universiteit Brussels. She currently resides in Almaty, Kazakhstan, and Washington, D.C.

Maxwell L. Anderson is author of dozens of articles and monographs on art and museums. He received a doctoral degree in art history from Harvard

University in 1981. He was subsequently assistant curator at the Metropolitan Museum of Art and has been director of three of the leading art museums in North America, most recently New York's Whitney Museum of American Art. He has taught on the faculties of Princeton University and the Università di Roma, and served as a leadership fellow at the Yale School of Management for the 2003–04 academic year. His commitment to collaboration among museums has led him to Capitol Hill to advocate for international conventions and treaties permitting the free circulation of artworks internationally and for national bills in support of the arts. Past president of the Association of Art Museum Directors, he is at work on a book titled *The Quality Instinct*, an exploration of how some people become connoisseurs of art.

Rick Aubry is president and executive director of Rubicon Programs Incorporated, a nonprofit organization providing services to more than four thousand homeless, very low income, and disabled men and women annually. Aubry has served as director of Rubicon since 1986, overseeing the growth of the agency from $980,000 to nearly $16 million in annual revenues in 2002. The agency now generates more than $7 million of its revenues from businesses that have low-income, disabled, and formerly homeless people as their primary employees. In 2002 Aubry was appointed lecturer in management at the Stanford Graduate School of Business (GSB), where he is also a faculty affiliate of Stanford's Center for Social Innovation. He is a graduate of the inaugural Stanford GSB Executive Program for Nonprofit Leaders, and his work at Rubicon has been cited in the *Harvard Business Review*, the *Brookings Institute Journal*, the *New York Times*, and *Enterprising Nonprofits* (J. Gregory Dees, Jed Emerson, and Peter Economy, eds., John Wiley & Sons, 2001). Aubry earned his bachelor of arts degree from Syracuse University, his master's in psychology from West Georgia University, and his doctoral degree in psychology from the Wright Institute in Berkeley, California.

Thomas Baker is senior consultant with Marks Paneth Strategy Group in New York. He has more than twenty years of experience managing successful businesses in print and online publishing, broadcasting, entertainment, and education. As founder and long-time general manager of the *Wall Street Journal Online*, he helped it grow into the largest paid news and information site on the Web. Previously he also served as marketing manager for Carnegie Hall in New York, overseeing its advertising, communications, and subscriber programs. He has degrees from Princeton University and Columbia Business School.

Stephanie Bell-Rose is president of The Goldman Sachs Foundation, a $200 million international corporate foundation whose mission is to promote excellence and innovation in education and to improve the academic performance and life-long productivity of young people worldwide. Previously she served as foundation counsel and program officer for public affairs at the Andrew W. Mellon Foundation, where she directed legal affairs and designed funding programs and research initiatives in education, immigrant policy, race and opportunity, and Latin American development. Born in Brooklyn, New York, Bell-Rose earned an associate's degree in business from Harvard College, a juris doctor degree from Harvard Law School, and a master's in public administration from the Kennedy School of Government. As a recipient of Harvard University's Rockefeller Fellowship, she spent a year in Caracas and Mexico City studying urban development in Latin America. Keenly interested in education and economic progress in the United States and abroad, Bell-Rose currently serves on the boards of the Barnes Foundation and Harvard University's Hauser Center for Nonprofit Organizations, and is a member of the Council on Foreign Relations, serving on the Chairman's Advisory Council and the Executive Leadership Council. She has received a congressional citation for her work on behalf of children, a leadership award from the Westchester Children's Association, and the Fay Prize from Radcliffe College. Her most recent publication, "The Corporate Role in Developing Leaders: From the Sideline to the Frontline," appeared in the winter 2002 issue of the *College Board Review*.

Adam M. Blumenthal, a 1989 graduate of the Yale School of Management, took the post of first deputy comptroller and chief financial officer for the city of New York in 2002. In this position, working for Comptroller William C. Thompson Jr., he has responsibility for the capital markets functions of the comptroller's office, including management of the city's $80 billion pension fund, issuance of public debt, and budget and economic analysis of the city of New York. As part of his pension fund responsibilities, he has significantly increased the funds' economically targeted investment strategies. From 1989 to 2002 he held numerous positions with American Capital Strategies, including CFO, president, and vice chairman. During his time at American Capital, the firm grew from a boutique investment-banking firm specializing in employee buyout and economic development transactions to a $1 billion market cap finance company. Blumenthal has also served as advisor to both the Argentine government and the Congress of South African Trade Unions.

David Bornstein specializes in writing about social innovation. His first book, *The Price of a Dream: The Story of the Grameen Bank* (University of Chicago Press, 1996) was selected as a finalist for the New York Public Library Book Award for Excellence in Journalism. He is also author of the recently published *How to Change the World: Social Entrepreneurs and The Power of New Ideas* (Oxford University Press, 2004). His articles have appeared in the *Atlantic Monthly* and the *New York Times,* and he co-wrote the PBS documentary *To Our Credit* (1998).

Bill Bradley is a managing director of Allen & Company, LLC. Additionally, he is chief outside advisor to McKinsey & Company's Nonprofit Practice. From 1997 to 1999 he was a senior advisor and vice chairman of the International Council of J.P. Morgan & Co., Inc. During that time he also served as an essayist for "CBS Evening News" and as a visiting professor at Stanford University, Notre Dame University, and the University of Maryland. Bradley was a candidate for president of the United States in 2000. He served in the U.S. Senate from 1979 to 1997, representing the state of New Jersey. Before serving in the Senate, he was an Olympic gold medalist in 1964 and a professional basketball player with the New York Knicks from 1967 to 1977, during which time the Knicks won two world championships. Bradley holds a bachelor of arts degree from Princeton University and a master's degree from Oxford University, where he was a Rhodes Scholar. He has authored five books on American politics, culture, and economy.

Patricia Caesar is president and CEO of the Marks Paneth Strategy Group (MPSG), a company dedicated to developing strategic business plans for nonprofit organizations, foundations, and corporations. MPSG uses a unique and comprehensive approach to business planning, including plan development, funding and financing, buy-in and transition, implementation, and performance assessment. MPSG also provides a broad range of capacity-building services, including organizational development, governance, fundraising and financing, marketing communications, program and product development, and executive search. A graduate of Brandeis University, Caesar received a master's degree in administration and organizational development from Columbia University, where she was a Ford Foundation fellow in the Program for Educational Leadership. She is a member of the board of directors of Facing History and Ourselves National Foundation; Collaborative for Academic, Social and Emotional Learning; and the Greyston Foundation.

Paul Connolly is senior vice president at TCC Group (formerly the Conservation Company), a twenty-five-year-old firm with offices in New York and Philadelphia and full-time staff based in Chicago. He leads the firm's nonprofit practice and serves on its board of directors. The TCC Group provides management consulting, strategic planning, and evaluation services to nonprofit organizations, private foundations, and corporate citizenship programs. Connolly provides consulting services to nonprofits and grantmakers and serves on several nonprofit boards. He is coauthor with Carol Lukas of *Strengthening Nonprofit Performance: A Funder's Guide to Capacity Building* (Wilder, 2002). Connolly received a master of arts degree in public and private management from the Yale University School of Management and a bachelor of arts degree from Harvard University.

Lee Davis is a cofounder and CEO of NESsT, an international organization dedicated to supporting social enterprise in emerging market countries, particularly through the NESsT Venture Fund, a philanthropic investment fund supporting a portfolio of social enterprises in Central and Eastern Europe and Latin America. Along with NESsT partner Nicole Etchart, Davis is coauthor of several books on social enterprise and venture philanthropy, including: *Get Ready, Get Set: Starting Down the Road to Self-Financing* (Santiago, Chile: NESsT, 2003) and *Profits for Nonprofits* (Budapest, Hungary: NESsT, 1999). He is currently editing NESsT's forthcoming book *Not Only for Profit: Innovative Mechanisms for Philanthropic Investment*, an analysis of innovative investment mechanisms for supporting social enterprise. In 1996–1997, he authored *The NGO-Business Hybrid*, a seminal study on nonprofit enterprise activities in thirteen countries, while a research fellow at the Johns Hopkins School for Advanced International Studies, where he also served as a professorial lecturer in social change and development, developing and co-teaching the first graduate-level course on social enterprise in the developing world. He holds a master of arts degree from Johns Hopkins University and a bachelor of arts degree, *magna cum laude*, Phi Beta Kappa, from Connecticut College.

J. Gregory Dees is faculty director of the Center for the Advancement of Social Entrepreneurship at Duke University's Fuqua School of Business. Prior to coming to Duke he served as the Miriam and Peter Haas Centennial Professor in Public Service and as founding codirector of the Center for Social Innovation at Stanford University's Graduate School of Business. For five years Dees also served as entrepreneur-in-residence with the Ewing Marion Kauffman Foundation's Center for Entrepreneurial Leadership. He spent most of his academic career at the Harvard Business School, where he helped launch the Initiative on Social Enterprise. In 1995 he received Harvard Business School's Apgar Award for Innovation in Teaching for his new course, "Entrepreneurship in the Social Sector." He previously served on the faculty at the Yale School of Management and worked as a management consultant with McKinsey & Company. In 1996 he interrupted his academic career for two years to work on economic development in central Appalachia. He holds a masters degree in public and private management from Yale University and a doctoral degree in philosophy from Johns Hopkins University. He has written extensively on social entrepreneurship and is coeditor, with Jed Emerson and Peter Economy, of *Enterprising Nonprofits* (Wiley, 2001) and *Strategic Tools for Social Entrepreneurs* (Wiley, 2002).

Nicole Etchart is cofounder and CEO of NESsT. Along with NESsT partner Lee Davis, Etchart is coauthor of several books and publications on social enterprise and venture philanthropy, including *Get Ready, Get Set: Starting Down the Road* *to Self-Financing* (Santiago,Chile: NESsT, 2003) and *Profits for Nonprofits* (Budapest, Hungary: NESsT, 1999). She is currently editing NESsT's forthcoming book *Risky Business: The Impacts of Merging Mission and Market,* which provides the results of a multiyear research effort to document the effects of social enterprise on some fifty nonprofits from fifteen countries. She has more than twenty years of experience in international development, nonprofit management, and civil society development, having held executive positions with international organizations working in the United States, Africa, Asia, and Latin America. Etchart holds a master of arts degree from the Nitze School of Advanced International Studies at Johns Hopkins University, and a bachelor of arts degree, *magna cum laude,* Phi Beta Kappa, from Tulane University. She was born and currently lives in Santiago, Chile.

William H. Heritage Jr. is a shareholder and director of the Grand Rapids, Michigan, law firm of Wheeler Upham, P.C., which was established in 1883. Formerly General Counsel of Rapistan, Incorporated, Heritage has concentrated his practice in the areas of corporate, taxation, and business law. He received his undergraduate degree from Duke University in 1966 and a master's degree (1969) and juris doctor degree (1970) from the University of Virginia. A member of the Business Law Section of the American Bar Association (Nonprofit Organization Subcommittee) and the State Bar of Michigan (Business Law and Taxation Sections), he has represented numerous tax-exempt organizations for more than thirty years.

Christopher Lovelock is an adjunct professor at the Yale School of Management and principal of Lovelock Associates. A leading authority on service management, he has worked with service companies and nonprofit organizations in many settings, including museums, health care, higher education, and public transportation. His distinguished academic career includes eleven years at Harvard Business School and visiting professorships at the International Institute for Management Development in Switzerland, INSEAD (formerly known as the European Institute for Business Administration) in France, and the University of Queensland in Australia. He has also held short-term appointments at the University of California, Berkeley; Stanford University; and the Massachusetts Institute of Technology and has given seminars on six continents. His research and teaching emphasize success factors in service-driven organizations, including the need to integrate the marketing, operations, and human resource functions. A prolific and award-winning author, Lovelock has written or coauthored more than one hundred cases, sixty articles, and some two dozen books; his latest is *Services Marketing,* Fifth edition (Prentice Hall, 2004). Earlier books include *Public and Nonprofit Marketing* (with Charles Weinberg, John Wiley & Sons, 1984) and *Product Plus* (McGraw-Hill, 1994). He has been honored by the American Marketing Association's Award for Career Contributions to the Services Discipline, a *Journal of Marketing* best article award, and *Business Week*'s European Case Award. He holds a master of arts and bachelor of communications degrees from Edinburgh University, an M.B.A. from Harvard University, and a doctoral degree from Stanford University.

Kristin Majeska is founder and president of Common Good Ventures (CGV), which enables nonprofits to improve their performance dramatically, leading to greater social returns (more jobs created, more hungry children fed, more family farms saved, and so on) and greater long-term financial self-sufficiency for these organizations. To accomplish this goal, CGV combines philanthropic dollars with long-lasting business consulting partnerships focused on accountability and results. CGV has partnered with eight social enterprises since 2000, and Majeska was recently recognized by Mainebiz as "one of the twelve people shaping the future of Maine's economy" for CGV's success at helping nonprofits "work smarter." In 2003, CGV's nonprofit partners together served more than thirty-five thousand people. Majeska founded CGV after spending a year as a Farber Fellow with the Roberts Enterprise Development Fund. There, with the support of the Phalarope Foundation, she ran the San Francisco City Store, a social enterprise that employed at-risk youth and formerly homeless adults. Majeska authored the chapter on customer understanding in *Enterprising Nonprofits* (Dees, and others) and has contributed to many other publications in the field. Prior to moving into the social enterprise arena, she was a principal of Mercer Management Consulting, an international strategy consulting firm. She is a graduate of the Stanford Graduate School of Business, where she was co-coordinator of the Public Management Program, and of Carleton College.

Katherine M. O'Regan is associate professor of public policy and associate dean of faculty and academics at New York University's Robert F. Wagner Graduate School of Public Service. O'Regan teaches courses in microeconomics and program evaluation. She researches issues and programs affecting the urban poor, including transportation, employment, and isolation problems, and segregation and performance in the New York City public schools. Currently she is examining a collection of board governance issues among nonprofits in New York City. She has been a visiting scholar at the Federal Reserve Bank of Boston and the Brookings Institution, and has consulted for such organizations as the U.S. Department of Housing and Urban Development, the Connecticut Department of Human Resources, and the Community Development Venture Capital Alliance. Among her board activities, she is on the Research Advisory Council for the National Center for Nonprofit Enterprise. O'Regan received her doctoral degree in economics from the University of California, Berkeley.

Timothy J. Orlebeke is a shareholder and director of Wheeler Upham, P.C., a Grand Rapids, Michigan, law firm that was established in 1883. A significant portion of his practice is the representation of nonprofit entities engaged in a variety of for-profit activities through their parent organizations, subsidiaries, and for-profit entities, frequently involving tax credits and other incentives related to real estate development. He has also served on the boards of several nonprofit and tax-exempt organizations, and has held public office as a city commissioner and as a board member of the regional transportation authority, among others. Currently he serves as president of the Kent County Housing Commission, a public housing authority. Orlebeke received his undergraduate degree from Calvin College in 1974 and his law degree from Wayne State University in 1978. He is a member of the Real Property sections of the Michigan and Grand Rapids Bar Associations.

Amy Solas has more than fifteen years of experience in financial communications and related fields, including extensive international experience. As president of Solas Communications International, Inc., she advises financial sponsors, investment banks, and operating companies on capital-raising communications, new business development, and investor relations. Before launching her consulting practice she was a vice president in J.P. Morgan's Latin American Investment Banking and Corporate Communication groups. Previously Solas was with the financial communications consultancy Ogilvy Adams & Rinehart (now Ogilvy Public Relations). She started her career at the *New York Times*. She holds a bachelor of arts degree from Georgetown University and an M.B.A. from the Yale School of Management.

Jeffrey A. Sonnenfeld is professor and associate dean for executive programs at the Yale University School of Management as well as founder, president, and CEO of the Chief Executive Leadership Institute of the Yale School of Management. This institute, the nation's first "CEO college," offers scholarly research on top leadership, corporate governance, and unique leadership education through scholarly research and peer-driven educational programs. Previously Sonnenfeld spent ten years as a professor at the Harvard Business School. His research, publications, and consulting work address issues of CEO succession, board governance, and corporate culture. Sonnenfeld's research has been published in eighty scholarly articles, and he has authored five books, including *The Hero's Farewell: What Happens When CEOs Retire* (Oxford University Press, 1988), an award-winning study of CEO succession. His most recent *Harvard Business Review* article, "What Makes Great Boards Great," has received widespread acclaim. His work is regularly cited in the national media and he is a regular commentator for the *Wall Street*

Journal, the *New York Times,* CNBC, Fox News, CBS, PBS, and NPR. Professor Sonnenfeld received his bachelor of arts, M.B.A., and doctoral degree in business administration from Harvard University.

Richard Steckel has an international reputation as a consultant and speaker on nonprofit social enterprise and for-profit strategic corporate citizenship. Since 1984 he has developed earned-income strategies for more than two hundred for-profit and nonprofit organizations. Before founding the consulting firm AddVenture Network of which he is president and CEO, he was executive director of the Denver Children's Museum, where he introduced innovative ideas that made the museum a national model of the earned-income approach to fundraising. He is coauthor with Robin Simons and Peter Lengsfelder of *Filthy Rich: Turning Nonprofit Fantasies into Cold, Hard Cash* (Ten Speed Press, 1989); coauthor with Robin Simons, Jeffrey Simons, and Norman Tanen of *Making Money While Making a Difference: How to Profit with a Nonprofit Partner* (High Tide Press, 1999); and coauthor with Jennifer Lehman of *In Search of America's Best Nonprofits* (Jossey-Bass, 1997).

Dennis R. Young is professor of nonprofit management and economics at Case Western Reserve University and founding CEO of the National Center on Nonprofit Enterprise. From 1988 to 1996 he was director of the Mandel Center for Nonprofit Organizations. He is founding editor of *Nonprofit Management and Leadership* and past president of the Association for Research on Nonprofit Organizations and Voluntary Action. He is author of many scholarly articles and author or editor of several books on nonprofit organizations, such as *The Music of Management* (Ashgate Publishing, 2004); *Effective Economic Decision-Making for Nonprofit Organizations* (The Foundation Center, 2004); and *Economics for Nonprofit Managers* with Richard Steinberg (The Foundation Center, 1995).

GENERATING AND SUSTAINING NONPROFIT EARNED INCOME

PART ONE

KEY ISSUES IN BUSINESS PLANNING FOR NONPROFIT ENTERPRISE

CHAPTER ONE

PUTTING NONPROFIT BUSINESS VENTURES IN PERSPECTIVE

J. Gregory Dees

It has become quite popular for nonprofit organizations to start business ventures. As more and more nonprofits compete for limited pools of philanthropic and government support, the prospect of an additional source of earned income becomes increasingly appealing. Income from a business venture is particularly attractive because it comes without the restrictions commonly attached to grants and major donations. The interest in these ventures is not limited to funding. Many nonprofits are finding that business ventures can serve as effective methods for addressing their social objectives. For instance, a homeless shelter may start a retail bakery to generate funds and provide a live business setting within which the shelter's residents can develop their job skills.

This current experimentation with nonprofit business ventures is, on the whole, a promising development. Creative and judicious use of these ventures can position social sector organizations to accomplish much more than they could by relying only on the limited philanthropic and government resources they are able to attract. In the past, many nonprofits missed worthwhile opportunities to serve their missions effectively and generate funds for their organizations because they did not seriously consider the range of earned-income ventures that might be appropriate

The author thanks his colleague and frequent writing partner Beth Battle Anderson for her valuable suggestions on this chapter.

for them. Their increased willingness to cross sector boundaries gives social entrepreneurs new tools for accomplishing their objectives.

Nonetheless, it would be a mistake to think that nonprofit business ventures are always beneficial. Nonprofit leaders should not jump on this bandwagon without understanding and addressing the challenges, costs, and risks of taking the ride. Making money with business ventures is more difficult and can take much more time and capital than many people realize. If it were easy to create wealth through new businesses, we would not see such high business failure rates. Even when a nonprofit venture succeeds financially, it could pull the parent organization and some of its most valuable resources, such as senior management time, away from the core mission. In some cases, the financial benefits will not be worth the hidden costs to the organization. When the venture also has a social purpose, as many nonprofit ventures do, managing to serve both purposes well increases the degree of difficulty and quite often increases the costs of the venture. Making sure that a business venture is a worthy undertaking for a nonprofit is not an easy process. It requires a firm understanding of the economics of the venture, the market it aims to serve, the competition trying to serve that same market, the direct social impacts of the venture, and any indirect costs or tensions it might create for the parent.

The best way to understand and address all the relevant factors is by developing a business plan for the venture that combines rigorous analysis, creativity, and action-based learning. Conducting a thorough venture planning process significantly increases the probability that the venture will serve the parent organization well, allowing venture managers to anticipate important challenges and avoid common mistakes. It is crucial to stay focused on the ultimate bottom-line, cost-effective mission impact throughout this process.

Combining Rigorous Analysis, Creativity, and Action Learning

Developing a venture that is likely to have a positive net impact on the performance of the parent organization is no easy task. The best place to start is with a business planning process that blends a rigorous analysis of the potential opportunity with creative thinking and action-based learning. Crafting a compelling business plan is a powerful learning experience that should lead to clearer expectations and a more viable venture than would otherwise occur. It forces the venture leaders to do their homework before the parent makes a major irreversible commitment. A comprehensive planning process forces the proponents of a venture to articulate its objectives clearly in the context of the parent's mission, to define the venture's products and target market, to conduct a realistic assessment of demand and buyer behavior, to create cost and revenue projections that are plausible, to determine the amount of investment likely to be needed until the venture becomes self-sufficient, to craft a creative and compelling strategy, to articulate and test the key assumptions behind the strategy, and to set realistic financial and social expectations as the venture develops. The insights gained in the planning process increase the chances for success. They may also convince the leaders to walk away from a venture that is not likely to yield sufficient benefits to justify the costs. If the business plan sets realistic goals for venture performance, it also provides a tool that the venture leaders can use to manage expectations as the venture develops. Producing a strong plan has the added benefit of helping the venture leaders attract resources to get the venture off the ground. It makes it possible to define the kinds of social and financial returns that can be offered to investors.

Rigor is essential to this process. If entrepreneurial nonprofit leaders do not subject their new venture ideas to a fact-based, analytic planning process, they run the risk of moving prematurely or making costly strategic mistakes. Rigorous analysis is not enough, however. It must be accompanied by creativity. The analysis is bound to uncover unexpected complications, challenges, and problems. Creativity is needed for designing and redesigning your venture to address these issues. Even with a rigorous analysis and creative venture design, it is not possible to know for sure how a venture will work until you try it. Uncertainties will remain. As a result, business ventures are continual works in progress. They evolve and sometimes change radically based on experience in the marketplace. This means that the rollout plan should be designed to promote action-based learning in a timely way so that changes can be made before too much time and money have been wasted.

You will no doubt hear that many new ventures succeed without a business plan. This is true. Planning does not come naturally to many action-oriented entrepreneurs. What you do not hear about are the large number of ventures that fail for reasons that could have been addressed in a good planning process. A team can climb a mountain without a map or any particular plan for the ascent, but their chances of reaching the summit in a timely fashion are greatly increased if they have a map and a plan that are grounded in knowledge of the terrain they will have to cross. Of course the team cannot control or even predict with certainty important weather conditions, and landslides may have destroyed trails that were previously available, but with a map and a plan it is better positioned to make adjustments when difficulties are encountered. In the same way, a well-crafted business plan increases the probability of a venture's timely success, especially when it takes the parent organization into unfamiliar territory. It is worthwhile even if the details of the plan have to be changed along the way.

Developing a business plan for a nonprofit venture is not exactly the same as developing a business plan for a traditional business venture. If it were, we would not need this book. Nonprofit leaders starting new ventures could simply read any of the dozens of very good books already available on business plans and enter traditional business plan competitions. The main difference is that nonprofit ventures are first and foremost a means to help the parent organization serve its social mission. The business plan must be structured with that in mind. If the plan makes clear how the venture will help the parent organization directly or indirectly improve its mission performance, it should provide proponents of the venture with ammunition to persuade key stakeholders (both internal and external) that this is a good thing to do, not for the money alone but for the mission. After all, the mission is presumably the glue that holds the stakeholders together.

Conducting a Thorough Venture Planning Process

Venture planning, if done right, is a demanding process. For more than twenty years I have been involved in business strategy and venture planning as a consultant, teacher, and researcher. For the past decade I have been able to focus my work on social entrepreneurship. I have a broad perspective on social entrepreneurship that is not limited to launching business ventures, but many of the organizations I have studied and written about are nonprofit organizations exploring this avenue. Through this work I have identified a number of challenges and mistakes that are commonly made in the venture creation process. The following recommendations are designed to help nonprofit leaders address the challenges, avoid the common mistakes, and increase the chances that their ventures will succeed in serving or supporting their organization's social mission.

Identify Suitable Venture Opportunities

The first step in developing an attractive venture opportunity is coming up with an idea. Too often nonprofit leaders will see what others are doing and want to copy it. "If their drug rehab program can run a moving business, why can't we run one with residents from our drug rehab program?" Or they spot some market trend and want to jump on the bandwagon. "Look at all the Starbucks! Why can't we start a high-priced coffee shop?" Some of these ideas may well work, but chances of success increase when nonprofit leaders focus on opportunities that have a natural fit with their organization's resources, assets, capabilities, clientele, and mission. These factors can serve as the basis for a competitive advantage. A theater group with a large stock of costumes is better positioned to enter the costume rental business than to open a restaurant. As you look for suitable opportunities, keep in mind intangible assets, such as relationships and reputation. The point is to identify opportunities that the parent organization is well positioned to pursue and that will be seen by key stakeholders as natural extensions of its operations.

Assess Organizational Openness and Readiness

Many nonprofits are not ready to launch and run businesses, especially when the businesses require new skills, behaviors, and values. The time demands can be tremendous and the learning curve dangerously steep. Even when the opportunity fits well with the parent organization's capabilities, program staff in the parent organization may resist the venture, perceiving it as competing with them for scarce internal and external resources. The new venture may require methods of operation that are antithetical to the values of the parent. One social service organization reported a tension between the loan officers in its new microlending operation who were trying to collect loan payments and the social workers assisting the same clients. The new venture may even require higher compensation levels as you compete with businesses for management talent. This can also be a source of tension with core program managers. Be realistic in assessing the fit of the new venture with your culture and in identifying potential points of tension. Chances of success are greater if your organization is ready, willing, and able to take this on. Of course, some level of tension is tolerable and may even be a good thing, but too much conflict between the new venture's values, methods, and skill requirements and those of the parent organization can be costly, undermining the value of the venture.

Be Clear About the Venture's Objectives

Many nonprofit ventures are launched with a certain amount of ambiguity about the objectives. Will the venture serve the mission directly? If so, how? And how can we measure its success on this dimension? What kind of social impacts are expected and by when? Is the venture primarily designed to be a source of funds for the parent organization? If so, how much funding is it reasonably expected to generate? When will it begin generating funds? What investment is required to get it to that point? Rough objectives and measures should be defined from the beginning of the venture planning process and revised along the way based on what the venture team is learning. In the process it is especially important to define the kind of minimum thresholds that the venture must meet to be worthwhile. These thresholds are akin to a "hurdle rate" in business. If the venture does not look like it will get over the hurdle, it should not be pursued. Because social impact is often hard to measure or convert to dollar equivalents, the process for nonprofit ventures cannot be as mechanical as it is in business, but minimum targets can be set through a judgment process. Rough minimums can be set by comparing the expected impacts created by the proposed venture with what could be accomplished if the same time, energy, and money were used for other purposes.

Define, Research, and Test the Venture's Value Propositions

For any venture to succeed it has to create attractive value propositions for all the key stakeholders. A value proposition describes an exchange in terms of what the stakeholders in question must give or give up and what they get in return. An attractive value proposition is one that, in the eyes of the stakeholders involved, creates value, in the sense that stakeholders get something more valuable to them than what they have to give. So far we have focused on the value proposition for the parent organization. This is the ultimate test from the parent organization's point of view. However, in order to be successful over a significant period, the venture must be able to create attractive value propositions for other key stakeholders as well.

From a business point of view, the value proposition for customers is most important. The key question is whether customers will believe that the venture offers them enough value to make it worth all the costs of doing business with it. The value created for customers must be assessed relative to their next best alternative. This is what links market and competitor analysis in the business plan. Competitor analysis is all about determining the alternative value propositions that competitors offer customers now, and how competitors might change their propositions as a result of your entry into the market. Venture founders often make several mistakes in assessing the attractiveness to customers of their value proposition. Because the nonprofit sector is heavily needs driven, nonprofit entrepreneurs sometimes mistake need—something important that is lacking—for demand—the ability and willingness to pay. In some communities, the need for day care is high but the demand is low because those who need it cannot pay enough to cover the cost of supplying it. Alternatively, demand for large sport utility vehicles is high, but the actual need for the capabilities they offer may be low. The ideal is to find an opportunity with both high need and high demand, but in the end demand is what matters most from a business point of view. Another mistake is to think too narrowly about competition, including thinking only about those competitors who offer exactly the same products or services. A competitor is anyone who can deliver a comparable value to customers. Look at it from the point of view of a customer making a decision. What alternative would you consider? An environmental group that wants to offer river rafting trips should focus not only on rafting competitors, but also on other activities that might appeal to the same target market in exchange for their vacation time and money. Another common mistake is to consider only price in thinking about what customers give up. Often it is not enough to be competitive on price. Other factors, such as location, convenience, responsiveness, loyalty (to existing suppliers), switching costs of changing to a new supplier, perceptions about quality, and more, may play key roles in driving customer behavior. Again, the key is to look at the decision from a potential customer's point of view.

Entrepreneurs often conduct surveys to help them predict customers' buying decisions. Often these surveys are poorly designed and solicit only opinions rather than gather data about past behavior. Asking "How much do you pay on average for a loaf of freshly baked whole wheat bread?" is better than asking "Would you pay $3 for a loaf of freshly baked whole wheat bread that is made by homeless people trying to better their lives?" What someone has done is a much better predictor of future behavior than what they say they will do. Opinion surveys are particularly problematic when it comes to testing the willingness of customers to purchase a socially beneficial product or to do business with a socially oriented firm. It is natural for respondents to give answers that make them look good. Again, it is best to focus on behavior. Ask when they last used social criteria in actually making a purchase, then follow up for details. People may still misrepresent their past behavior in order to look good, but this is less likely than misrepresenting future intentions. The best information will come from a test market or pilot in which actual buying behavior is measured and analyzed.

The heart of the business plan, particularly the sections on the market, the competition, and the strategy, are all about demonstrating that the venture will present an attractive value proposition to its intended customers. Other value propositions that should be assessed carefully are those for the venture's work force and for any investors (philanthropic or commercial) that might be needed. People drive the success of any venture, and the ability to attract the right people can be a crucial factor in the venture's success. In the case of ventures that employ clients of the parent organization for training purposes, the workforce value proposition is where the social value is created. The clients, such as homeless shelter residents, may not have very attractive employment and training alternatives, making it easy to convince them to participate. However, some ventures may provide more valuable training and be more inherently appealing than others. Because the staffing model is related directly to serving the mission, the venture development team should pay special attention to how the venture creates value for these clients and work to increase that value where possible. If outside investors are needed, it will be important to understand the kind of value, social or financial, they want to get out of the investment. Deals need to be structured to reflect the different interests and values of these potential investors.

Be Fair and Thorough in Allocating Costs

Many nonprofit ventures look good financially only because of hidden subsidies from the parent organization. Proper allocation of costs is crucial and often not done very carefully, largely because it is no simple matter, especially when costs are shared between the new venture and the parent organization. The most common mistake is not to allocate the cost of senior management time. This is often a scarce and valuable resource, and its value needs to be reflected in the costs of the new venture. In an ideal world, this time would be sold to the new venture based on its opportunity costs, not on executive salaries. The issue is what that time is worth to the parent organization. For instance, if senior management could raise $100,000 a year in the time they devote to the new venture, this is the true value (cost) of that time to the parent organization. The venture should have to cover this much just to make the parent organization whole. Of course few organizations will go through an honest assessment of opportunity costs. In any case, a fair share of senior executives' salaries should be allocated to the new venture based on the time they devote to it.

A related mistake is to assume that if the new venture is purchasing something from the parent organization, this constitutes additional financial benefit for the parent. This is rarely the case. Consider a nonprofit arts center that owns and occupies a building in a downtown shopping district. It launches a gallery to sell art in the ground-floor space. The gallery venture agrees to pay the parent organization $2,000 per month for the store and storage space. Does this represent an additional $24,000 financial benefit for the parent? No, it does not. The space has a fair market value, particularly if it could be leased to some other retail business. If $2,000 per month is the fair market value, then this is an appropriate cost for the gallery and should not be treated as a financial benefit to the parent organization, because the parent could receive the same revenue from leasing the space to anyone else. At most the parent organization saves the expense of finding another tenant. If the parent could charge a higher price to another tenant, say $3,000 per month, then the $24,000 in rent paid by the gallery actually represents a $12,000 annual loss to the parent organization, not a gain at all. It masks a hidden subsidy. New ventures need to be charged the full fair-market value or opportunity value for any services or resources they are using from the parent organization, and no more (for IRS purposes). Only if the parent could not realize any other benefit from the shared resource should these transfer payments be treated purely as incremental cash flow from the venture to the parent organization. Fair cost allocation can be tricky, but it is worth a serious effort if the parent organization wants to understand the true value of the business venture.

Use Cash Flow, Not Revenue or Profit, as the Measure of Financial Impact

It is fascinating how many people simply look at business ventures as means to diversify their revenue streams. They seem to miss the obvious point that if the incremental revenues do not exceed the incremental costs of running the venture, the venture will be a net drain on the parent organization. They will actually have to raise more money to subsidize the venture, quite possibly at the expense of more mission-oriented programs. Imagine a $3 million dollar agency that is totally dependent on grants launching a new venture that will generate $1 million in new revenue per year but actually cost $1.2 million to operate. The agency's revenue is certainly more diversified, with nearly 24 percent of its budget coming from earned income ($1 million out of $4.2 million). But not only does the executive director have to spend valuable time overseeing the launch of a new venture, but she also has to raise not $3 million a year but now $3.2 million to keep all her other programs operating at the same levels and the venture alive. The diversification does not ease the organization's fundraising burden or make it less vulnerable to cuts in donor funding. This kind of subsidy makes sense only if the new venture provides sufficient direct mission impact to justify the additional fundraising and the time commitment by agency management.

A more common and potentially devastating mistake is to assume that the parent can take all the profits out of the business venture once it becomes profitable, or that its subsidy is limited to operating losses. One of the most painful but important lessons many entrepreneurs learn is that profits are not the same as free cash flow. Free cash flow is cash that is produced by the venture that is not needed for its continuing operations. Free cash flow is what you can take out of the business without harming its ability to operate. Many businesses, especially growing businesses, require that a large portion of any profits be reinvested in the business. How many companies do you know that pay out 100 percent of profits as dividends to shareholders? Very few, if any, could afford to do this while keeping their companies strong. It is true that once a venture stops growing, its cash needs decline significantly and the tables turn. To use an old business consulting expression, if the venture is a success, it may become a cash cow that can be milked. However, achieving this point can take much longer than most people expect. Even if the venture gets there, it might be wise to reinvest some of the cash it generates in looking for the next business idea, because this once-profitable business may well decline. New competitors may enter the market. New technologies may create better value for customers. Customer tastes may change. Few businesses can be milked forever; only a safely invested endowment lasts forever. This is why it is crucial to understand the cash dynamics of the venture you are starting and to manage cash carefully.

Every business plan needs a detailed projected cash flow statement to supplement the income statements and balance sheets. The cash flow statement will show how much cash the venture needs as it grows and when the venture can realistically expect to generate cash for the parent organization. It is not uncommon for new ventures to require cash infusions for years, especially as they grow. In addition to covering the loss in year one, the parent organization may need to put in another $50,000 to cover working capital needs. The expected profit of $100,000 in year two may not be enough to cover the cash needed to grow in year three, requiring a small cash subsidy even though the business is profitable. The projected $2 million in revenue and $200,000 in profits in year three may yield only $30,000 in free cash that the parent can extract from the venture without harming plans for year four. It may be five or more years before a successful business reaches a steady state in which free cash flow equals or exceeds its profits. Struggling businesses may never get there. Of course this is just an illustration. The cash dynamics of every business are different. They depend primarily on working capital needs, such as inventory and accounts receivable, on payment terms with major suppliers, as well as on additional required investments in space, furniture, and equipment as the business grows. Available financing from leasing companies, banks, or others may offset the venture's internal cash needs, but these methods of managing cash flow have a cost and may be hard to secure for a young nonprofit venture. This is an area in which it pays to understand the details of the business. Do not assume that you can take the profits out and use them for mission-related purposes. You could be in for a major disappointment. From the parent's point of view only free cash flow is available and this is what should be counted in deciding whether the venture is worthwhile.

With this in mind, do not expect a quick financial fix from a business venture. New ventures are not promising for organizations in need of emergency financial aid. Even with promising business ventures, it can take years and significant investment to reach the point at which the venture is creating cash that can be used to support the parent organization. It typically takes a very healthy parent organization, perhaps with a sympathetic funder, to launch and build a business venture to the point of self-sufficiency. Even then, business is risky and market conditions are constantly changing. The parent organization should not expect the venture to generate cash in perpetuity without requiring major reinvestment from time to time.

Recognize That Negative or Low Cash Flow Can Be Justified by Direct Social Impact

Another mistake that nonprofit leaders make in evaluating venture possibilities is to focus too much on financial performance, forgetting that the only rationale for the venture to begin with is to improve the mission performance of the parent organization. Generating cash is only one way to do this. Direct mission impact is another. A mission-related venture might be worthwhile even if it needs an ongoing subsidy. Cost-effective performance may justify the subsidy. Consider a bakery that is created as a training ground for homeless people to learn job skills. Even if it needs to be subsidized, it may be the most efficient and effective way to accomplish the training and place people in jobs. The net subsidy per participant could be lower than a comparable classroom-based job-training program, and working in the bakery could be a more effective way of preparing participants for real jobs. The central question is, Could the parent organization achieve greater social impact by allocating the same resources to another approach? If not, then the subsidy is justified. This is an important concept for funders, as well as for entrepreneurial nonprofit leaders, to embrace. Just because the venture is structured as a business does not mean it must be profitable to be worthwhile. It just has to be the best use of scarce philanthropic and management resources. Of course in the best of circumstances a nonprofit venture will create both effective mission impact and significant free cash flow to be used to support other programs, but this wonderful combination is relatively rare. When a venture creates direct social benefits, these must be factored into the assessment and given proper weight.

Plan for a Staged Launch in Order to Test Assumptions and Resolve Uncertainties

Starting and running a successful business of any kind requires passion, commitment, persistence, and flexibility. It is a common mistake to forget about the flexibility. Most business ideas evolve significantly as they are tested in the marketplace. This is because no amount of research will resolve all the key questions about the venture. Key uncertainties will remain. The plan will make assumptions that need to be tested. Entrepreneurship, at its best, is a form of action learning. The rollout plan for a venture can often be structured to enhance the action learning and to make sure that key assumptions are tested before major irreversible commitments are made. Of course some businesses, such as Federal Express, cannot be launched without a major commitment of resources, but most business launches can be staged with significant investment coming in once core assumptions have survived a market test. This is the idea behind pilots and so-called beta tests. Entrepreneurs commonly blend action, analysis, and creativity as they refine their ideas. This process can be designed in a strategic way to test the most crucial and uncertain assumptions first. Entrepreneurship experts commonly recommend that the rollout of a new venture should proceed in stages, with milestones or checkpoints built in to indicate when core assumptions will have been tested and some uncertainties resolved. This is one of the most powerful risk management tools for entrepreneurs because each untested assumption presents a risk for their original business model. New venture creation is a process of discovery and continuous adaptation to the realities of the marketplace. If nonprofit leaders want to enhance their chances of success, they will stage their ventures and test their assumptions.

Balance a "How Can" Mind-Set with an Objective Assessment

Most of the mistakes discussed thus far cause nonprofit leaders to pursue unwise ventures or to pursue ventures in unwise ways. Another kind of mistake is abandoning a venture idea without sufficient effort to make it work. New ventures are inherently risky, and it is easy for critics and doubters to find reasons not to take the risks. Yet most successful entrepreneurs have been persistent in the face of adversity and skepticism. It is important not to give up on a venture prematurely, but stubborn commitment to a bad idea can also be a disaster. The key lies in adopting a "how can" mind-set, then balancing that with objective judgment. Instead of asking, "Can we make this venture work?" successful entrepreneurs ask, "How can we make this venture work?" Each nonprofit venture should have a champion who adopts this mind-set and has the creativity and knowledge to apply it well. Venture champions are constantly on the lookout for solutions to problems and ways of overcoming barriers that arise in the planning process or in the early stages after launch. Their job is to make the venture work from the point of view of the parent organization. Of course the venture champion should not be given final decision-making authority about whether the parent organization will support the new venture. A review board that can objectively assess the venture as the champion designs and redesigns it would be better positioned to make the decision. This review board should involve parent organization staff or board members, as well as outsiders with relevant expertise or crucial resources. In this way the parent organization can benefit from the persistence and "how can" mind-set of a venture champion and still assess the venture in a rigorous and objective way.

Staying Focused on the Ultimate Bottom Line

Nonprofit leaders considering new business ventures must be able to answer one fundamental question: Is this venture going to be worth the investment of time, energy, and funds it will require? Despite all the popular rhetoric about a "double bottom line" for social ventures, nonprofit leaders have only one ultimate bottom line by which to measure a venture's worth. In the end, it all comes down to mission. Money is simply a means to an end. No amount of profit can make up for failure on the social side. It is an input into the process, not a bottom line on the same level as mission impact. *A venture is worthwhile only if it is an efficient way to serve or support the parent organization's mission performance.* This ultimate bottom line can be served directly by integrating mission-related objectives into the new venture, indirectly by using the venture as a cost-effective way to subsidize worthwhile mission-related programs of the parent organization, or by creating both direct mission impact and indirect benefits. Nonprofit leaders should ask whether, from a mission perspective, a venture is the best way to spend and invest the organization's scarce resources and use its abilities to mobilize resources. Improving social performance is the only legitimate reason for a nonprofit to make any significant investment in a new venture.

Many nonprofit venture plans place too much emphasis on profits as the measure of success and neglect the social impacts. The architects of these plans seem to lose sight of the ultimate bottom line for a nonprofit parent organization. Profits are neither necessary nor sufficient for a venture to be a success with regard to social impact. An exclusive focus on profits is shortsighted for three reasons touched on earlier in this chapter. Let me review them because they are important.

First, *nonprofit business ventures can generate sufficient direct social benefits to justify their existence even when they are not profitable.* Consider the example of a homeless shelter starting a bakery to train and employ shelter residents. This could be a cost-effective way to help them become more employable, even if it loses some money each year. It may be both cheaper and more effective than alternative job readiness or skill training programs. It may be worth subsidizing this kind of venture. A nonprofit venture plan should identify the direct social impacts created by the venture and assess the cost-effectiveness of using the venture to generate these impacts. This can make potential investors comfortable with the financial losses projected for the venture.

Second, *a profitable venture may still be a very inefficient way to generate funds for the parent organization.* As we have seen, even profitable ventures may not generate free cash flow, in which case they make no financial contribution to the parent organization. But more important is that even when the venture does generate free cash flow, it may be a very costly way of raising the amount of cash it creates, considering the investments of time, scarce human resources, and start-up capital required. Philanthropic fundraising might be a cheaper and easier way to generate the same amount of money. It may not be as sexy as a business venture, but it may be a more sensible path to mission impact. When the primary benefit created by a venture is cash for the parent organization, a persuasive business plan will make the case that this particular venture is a cost-effective way to generate these funds.

Third, *generating profits simply to sustain the parent organization may not be sufficiently inspiring to important investors and other key stakeholders.* Most nonprofit ventures, even those undertaken only for financial gain, require below-market-rate capital, as well as other forms of in-kind or financial support from suppliers, distributors, and other partners, who are often, at least in part, socially motivated. For many of these stakeholders, the financial sustainability of a parent organization is not a sufficiently meaningful goal. It is too abstract when compared to the mission impacts that the parent nonprofit was created to serve, whether it is protecting biodiversity, increasing economic opportunities for disadvantaged populations, reducing hunger, fighting crime, enriching lives through the arts, or any of the other social objectives that move people to create and support nonprofit organizations. From a management point of view, financial benefit is certainly important, but it does not have the same inherent value as mission-related social impact, and it does not motivate people in the same way. Failure to convert a venture's profit into desirable social impact undermines the appeal of the venture and wastes the profit. It can strengthen a venture plan considerably to show how the funds created by the venture will be used to improve the parent organization's social impact, illustrating why, in social terms, the venture is important. Clear and meaningful links to social results create a much more compelling plan, and they should. Society is better off when resources flow to nonprofit organizations that can best use them to produce social impact.

Of course, assessing potential new ventures in terms of likely net impact on mission performance requires a complex judgment that weighs the expected positive and negative effects of the venture. On the positive side is the direct social impact likely to be created by the venture itself, plus the impact created by the mission-related activities that are supported by the surplus funds generated by the venture, along with any other benefits that strengthen the parent organization. These other benefits can be hard to articulate or demonstrate, but they are important to recognize. It may take a deliberate effort to make sure they are captured. Starting a business venture may lead the parent organization to strengthen its capabilities in a number of areas, such as marketing, cash flow management, operations, strategy, and more. The key will be making sure that these skills are transferred from the venture team to the rest of the parent organization. The very process of creating a venture plan could force the parent organization to engage in a healthy overall assessment of its various programs from the point of view of both financial strength and mission importance. If handled correctly, the venture could also serve as a rallying point for staff members who are excited about exploring something new, and it could demonstrate to prior supporters that the parent organization is serious about securing its financial future and creative about serving its mission.

On the negative side is any reduction in mission impact caused by diverting valuable resources to the venture, along with any undesirable side effects. This side of the equation is even harder to assess in concrete terms but should not be neglected. It includes the opportunity costs of using resources for this venture that could have been used for other productive purposes. For instance, if the venture requires a day per week of the parent organization's executive director's time, it is important to think about how that time might have been spent to create social impact or even to generate funds from other sources. Is this venture a worthwhile use of that valuable time? This side of the equation also includes subtle and un-intended effects, such as potential harm to the parent organization's credibility or reputation, tensions between staff of the new venture and staff performing core mission functions, political complications that might arise, and harm to others in the community. If a homeless shelter starts a bakery in a neighborhood that has plenty of bakeries already, it may simply drive the family-owned bakery down the street out of business. This alone may not be a sufficient reason to abandon the venture, but it could well be a good reason to consider other options. When the op-portunity costs and other negative effects are honestly assessed, pursuing a par-ticular business venture could be a serious mistake from a mission point of view, even if it is expected to make a positive financial contribution. The net effect is what matters. A rigorous venture assessment will take all these factors into ac-count, focusing on the ultimate bottom line of mission impact.

Conclusion: Practicing Social Entrepreneurship

This chapter has argued that nonprofit ventures should be viewed from the per-spective of their contribution to the parent organization's ability to serve its social mission. They can contribute to cost-effective mission performance either by cre-ating direct social impact or by providing resources to support core programs of the parent organization. Through a rigorous and creative business planning process nonprofit leaders can assess venture ideas from a mission point of view and improve the chances that their business ventures will prove worthwhile.

Nonprofit ventures are quite popular right now, and perhaps for good reason. It appears that they have been underused in the past and opportunities have been missed. Many people identify nonprofit business ventures with social entrepre-neurship. Before closing, it is important to emphasize that business ventures are only one way that nonprofit leaders can be entrepreneurial in serving their social missions.

Successful social entrepreneurs will use the most effective structures, strate-gies, and funding mechanisms to achieve their social objectives. Social entrepre-neurship should not be seen as a funding strategy, and it should not be tied to the idea of business ventures. The concept of entrepreneurship goes much deeper than that. At its heart, entrepreneurship is about establishing new and better ways to create value. The eighteenth-century French economist who popularized the term, Jean-Baptiste Say, put it slightly differently when he said that entrepreneurs shift resources into areas of higher productivity and yield. What distinguishes social entrepreneurs is their focus on creating social value. They measure productivity and yield in terms of social impact. They help us find better ways to use resources to improve the world in which we live. When ventures serve this purpose, social entrepreneurs will pursue them. Otherwise they will use different organizational strategies and structures. They will not be shy about using philanthropic and government resources when they are appropriate and available. They do not see donor dependency as a disease, nor do they see earned income as a panacea. They recognize the strengths and weaknesses of both forms of revenue. Despite popular conceptions, neither form is inherently more reliable or sustainable than the other. Businesses fail all the time, and many donor-dependent nonprofits have been around for many decades, even centuries. Social entrepreneurs look for the strategy, structure, and funding mechanisms that are most likely to ensure effective and efficient social performance given specific mission objectives and a particular operating environment. Business ventures should be approached from this more comprehensive entrepreneurial point of view.

CHAPTER TWO

BUILDING ORGANIZATIONAL CAPACITY

Paul Connolly

Increased competition, greater demand for services, and decreased public and foundation support are leading many nonprofits to consider increasing earned income activities in order to become less reliant on philanthropic and government support. Yet nonprofit ventures do not happen in a vacuum. As Jed Emerson, former president of the Roberts Enterprise Development Fund, has noted, "At the end of the day, the organization is the vehicle through which social entrepreneurs and other practitioners are doing their work."[1] Indeed, the organizational context can make or break a nonprofit business venture. This chapter explains what nonprofit organizational capacity is, how to build it for successful nonprofit ventures, and what the critical resources are for supporting capacity building and earned-income ventures.

Organizational Capacity and How It Is Built

Any nonprofit organization needs to have some basic infrastructure or capacities in place in order for a nonprofit venture to succeed. *Capacity* is an abstract term

Parts of this chapter were adapted from Connelly, P., and Lukas, C. *Strengthening Nonprofit Performance: A Funder's Guide to Capacity Building.* Saint Paul, Minn.: Amherst Wilder Foundation, 2002. Used with permission.

that describes a wide range of capabilities, knowledge, and resources that non-profits need in order to be effective. What makes an organization effective? According to Grantmakers for Effective Organizations, it is "the ability of an organization to fulfill its mission through a blend of sound management, strong governance, and a persistent rededication to achieving results."[2] Organizational capacity is multifaceted and continually evolving. Figure 2.1 depicts the six interdependent components of nonprofit organizational capacity, all of which interact with the external environment and are necessary for high performance: mission, vision, and strategy; governance and leadership; program delivery and impact; strategic relationships; resource development; and internal operations and management. These interdependent factors all contribute to the health and performance of a nonprofit organization. The model also suggests continual interaction between the organization's external environment and its internal components.

FIGURE 2.1. COMPONENTS OF ORGANIZATIONAL CAPACITY.

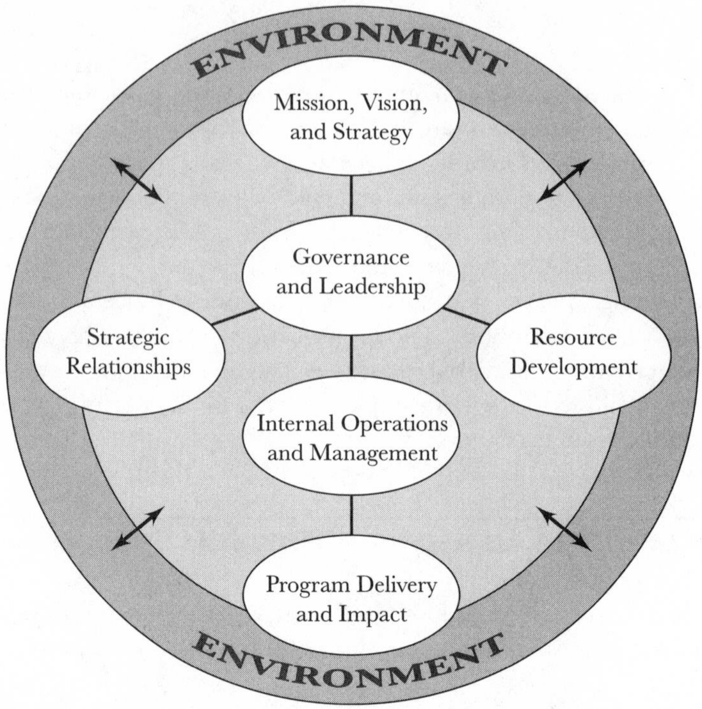

Source: Adapted from Paul Fate and Linda Hoskins, *Organizational Assessment Guides and Measures* (St. Paul, Minn.: Wilder Center for Communities, 2001). Used with permission.

Mission, vision, and strategy. The organization has a vital mission and a clear understanding of its identity. It is able to articulate its values clearly. It is involved in regular, results-oriented, strategic, and self-reflective thinking and planning that align strategies with the mission, values, and organizational capacity. The planning process involves stakeholders in an ongoing dialogue that ensures that the organization's mission and programs are valuable to the constituency it serves.

Governance and leadership. Members of the organization's board of directors are engaged and representative, with defined governance practices. The board effectively oversees the policies, programs, and organizational operations, including review of strategic goal achievement, financial status, and executive director performance. The organization is accomplished at recruiting, developing, and retaining capable staff and technical resources. Its leadership is alert to changing community needs and realities.

Program delivery and impact. The organization operates programs and conducts activities that demonstrate tangible outcomes and impact appropriate to the resources invested. Programs are high quality and well regarded. The organization utilizes program evaluation results to inform its strategic goals. It understands community needs and has formal mechanisms for assessing internal and external factors that affect the achievement of goals.

Strategic relationships. The organization is a respected and active participant and leader in the community and maintains strong connections with its constituents. It participates in strategic alliances and partnerships that significantly advance the organization's goals and expand its influence. It communicates well with external audiences.

Resource development. The organization successfully secures support from a variety of sources to ensure that its revenues are diversified, stable, and sufficient for its mission and goals. The resource development plan is aligned with the mission, long-term goals, and strategic direction. The organization has high visibility with key stakeholders and links clear, strategic messages to its resource development efforts.

Internal operations and management. The organization has efficient and effective operations and strong management support systems. Financial operations are responsibly managed and reflect sound accounting principles. The organization utilizes information effectively for organizational and project management purposes. Internal communications are effective and the organization's culture promotes high-quality work and respectful work relationships. Asset, risk, and technology management are strong and appropriate to the organization's purpose.

Each of these components serves a critical role in the organization's overall effectiveness. Mission, vision, and strategy are the driving forces that give the organization its purpose and direction. Program delivery and impact are the nonprofit's primary reasons for existence. Strategic relationships, resource development, and internal operations and management are all necessary mechanisms to achieve the organization's ends. Leadership and governance are the lubricant that keeps all the parts aligned and moving. All of these components are affected by the environment in which the organization exists.

Adaptive capacity—the ability of a nonprofit organization to monitor, assess, and respond to internal and external changes—is critical for any nonprofit organization, and especially for one that is pursuing a nonprofit venture that requires marketplace interactions. It entails explicating goals and activities and the underlying assumptions that link them, evaluating organizational and programmatic effectiveness, and flexibly planning for the future. Adaptive capacity also encompasses improving the level and quality of creating strategic alliances, collaborating and networking with others in the community, and increasing the extent to which a nonprofit organization shares knowledge with colleague organizations.

Before pursuing an earned income activity, a nonprofit organization should consider conducting an organizational assessment to take stock of its organizational capacity and determine its readiness to pursue a venture. (Community Wealth Ventures, Development Training Institute, the Leader to Leader Institute, Inno-net, the Management Center, the Maryland Association of Nonprofits, and the Nature Conservancy all have organizational assessment instruments available.) Leaders of the organization can conduct a self-assessment or use an outside consultant to perform the assessment. In any case, the organizational assessment will help identify areas that need strengthening before the organization embarks on its venture. After the venture is up and running, it will inevitably influence the various components of organizational capacity. An organization can conduct an assessment periodically to track its development progress.

When assessing nonprofits and planning strategies for strengthening capacity, one needs to examine each component separately, in relation to the others, and within the organization's overall context. Organizations operate as complex systems in which a change in any one part of the system affects other parts and the functioning of the whole. In addition, a variety of factors can influence an organization's needs at any time, including the following:

- Age and developmental stage of the organization
- Size of the organization
- Type of work the organization does
- Cultural or ethnic identity of the organization
- Environment in which the organization functions

These factors require capacity-building activities that are uniquely tailored to the organization and the venture. For example, an adolescent organization may need to focus on building administrative systems and formalizing programs, while a mature organization may need to eliminate red tape, streamline operations, and edit programs. Similarly, if a mature or stagnant nonprofit organization pursues a start-up enterprise, it may have adequate systems in place to support it, but there may be a culture clash between the start-up venture and other, more established programs. On the other hand, a new nonprofit organization may need to develop its infrastructure first, before it is ready to launch an enterprise.

Strengthening Organizational Capacity for Successful Nonprofit Ventures

The six main keys to strengthening organizational capacity for a successful non-profit venture are described here. Examples of nonprofits that need to focus on each area are included.

1. *Clear vision and goals.* Both the organization and the venture need to know where they want to go and what the expected outcomes are. The organization also needs to have clear expectations about the double bottom line of "mission" and "money." For example, a community development corporation has a good initial track record for a new revenue-generating venture. But the overall vision of the organizational leaders has become blurry as the group has expanded quickly, primarily by responding to opportunities as they have arisen. To ensure the enterprise's continued success, the organization's vision and the venture's relation to it need to be clarified.

2. *Solid business plan.* The organization and the venture need to have strong business plans that are based on reliable information about market needs, competition, and core competencies. A nonprofit organization, for instance, wants to expand its venture for selling quality reading glasses in India. The organization needs to create a business plan for the venture for franchising and replication.

3. *Strong and stable board, management, and staff.* Effective organizations and ventures require talented people. The board and staff need to have business expertise and be patient, willing to take risks, and tolerant of changes to the organizational culture. A public interest advocacy organization is already successfully operating a project that sells geographic information system mapping services to other non-profits. The group wants to grow this business. To do so, it needs to hire more specialized staff and enhance the governance oversight function for the project.

4. *Integration of earned income activities with other programs.* To succeed, an earned income venture needs to be an organizational priority that is incorporated with the rest of the organization's programs. An international nongovernmental organization (NGO) has established a thriving income-generating business for selling publications, but that business is treated with suspicion as a separate business-oriented entity by the advocacy and education programs at the parent organization. The NGO needs to integrate its publishing, advocacy, and educational programs to maximize organizational effectiveness.

5. *Effective operations and management information systems.* Nonprofit ventures require the technological capacity to track data and account for goods, services, and finances. A Latino community-based organization that seeks to empower low-income Mexican immigrants has a solid business plan for manufacturing customized medical scrubs to generate earned income, yet in order to launch the enterprise effectively, it needs first to develop a management information system to control inventory and track daily sales.

6. *Good evaluation system.* By evaluating the performance of a venture, a nonprofit organization can document impact and social return on investment and determine how to do a better job. A rehabilitation center that serves people with disabilities is running a successful operation that packages and distributes unique die-cut greeting cards and gift tags. To expand this nonprofit enterprise, the organization needs to develop an evaluation system that documents the social impact of the enterprise.

A nonprofit organization can use this list to take stock of its readiness to pursue a venture and identify capacities it needs to develop. The nonprofit does not need to have all of these ingredients in place before pursuing a venture, but it does need to be aware of these components and have plans to improve the critical areas in order to enhance the venture's potential for success.

Critical Resources for Supporting Capacity Building and Earned-Income Ventures and How Nonprofits Can Tap Them

There are two main resources for supporting earned-income ventures: capacity building assistance and money.

Capacity-Building Activities

Capacity-building refers to activities that strengthen a nonprofit organization and help it better fulfill its mission, including, among other activities, strategic planning, technology upgrades, operational improvements, and board development.

Exhibit 2.1 shows the wide variety of types of capacity-building activities. The ones that are most important for nonprofit ventures include business planning, market research and strategy, and financial systems improvement.

Nonprofit managers and trustees usually work on their own to improve organizational performance by planning on an ongoing basis, providing stronger management and oversight, hiring new staff, training staff, upgrading systems, acquiring new equipment, and renovating and purchasing facilities. Indeed, much

---

EXHIBIT 2.1. CAPACITY-BUILDING ACTIVITIES.

Governance and Leadership

- Leadership development
- Board development
- Executive transition

Mission, Vision, and Strategy

- Strategic planning
- Scenario planning
- Organizational assessment
- Organizational development

Program Delivery and Impact

- Program design and development
- Evaluation

Strategic Relationships

- Collaboration and strategic restructuring
- Marketing and communications

Resource Development

- Fund development
- Business planning for revenue-generating activities

Internal Operations and Management

- Human resource management and training
- Financial management
- Operations
- Technology and information systems
- Facility planning
- Legal issues
- Volunteer recruitment and management
- Conflict resolution

---

organizational development work is a sensitive inside job that the organizations themselves must do on their own. Often, however, nonprofits turn to outside individuals and groups—capacity-building providers, including researchers, writers, publishers, trainers, educators, facilitators, and consultants—to support their organizational capacity-building needs. These providers assist nonprofits through referrals, research, publications, education and training, peer exchanges, convening, and consulting.

Referrals. Frequently, nonprofits need to be directed to resources that can help them address organizational challenges and opportunities, including useful Web sites, written materials, workshops, courses, and consultants, as well as to other nonprofits that have faced similar challenges.

Research. Research related to nonprofit management and governance can help researchers develop models and tools for nonprofit leaders to use. Researchers can also assess the effectiveness of the performance of an organization or venture and of various capacity-building activities.

Publications. There are many publications—both in print and increasingly online—related to nonprofit management and governance and nonprofit enterprise. These include practical, hands-on, how-to guides and journals filled with checklists and sample forms, as well as academic journals and books that report on research and explain theories and concepts. Nonprofit staff and board members can apply knowledge gleaned from these materials to their own situations to enhance the effectiveness of their organizations and ventures.

Education and Training. Organizational capacity-building efforts address the needs of the individuals who staff an organization. Training and educational opportunities enable employees, trustees, and volunteers to develop skills to help them do a better job managing, overseeing, and supporting their organization and venture. Offerings can range from brief, one-shot seminars to year-long, university-based courses. While some seminars are led by an instructor who imparts knowledge within a set curriculum, others are coordinated by a facilitator who helps people within an organization or from different organizations share with and learn from one another. Increasingly, distance-learning opportunities are being offered online. Whatever the format, adults learn best when there is a clear agenda with specific goals and when there is an opportunity to apply new skills and concepts to real-life, work situations.

Peer Exchanges. Peer exchanges—including roundtables, case-study groups, and learning circles—are based on the premise that participants can be both teachers and learners. To be most successful, peer exchanges need a skilled facilitator, a safe environment in which participants can express and modify their beliefs, and a balance of structure and flexibility. Peer exchanges can lessen the isolation of participants, help them become more self-confident, and heighten their awareness of diverse views and alternate solutions.

Convening. The term *convening* refers to various nonprofits coming together in one setting. Nonprofits have considerably more power to influence funding trends, the context for nonprofit enterprises, complex community issues, and developmental challenges when they band together. Convening can facilitate joint action. Meetings allow nonprofit leaders to learn from one another, collectively set agendas, and organize joint efforts. Conferences and forums can enable nonprofit executives to plan ways to increase the effectiveness of their organizations and fields and enhance their communities, as well as advocate for policies that can increase their nonprofits' efficiency and impact.

Consulting. *Consulting* is a broad term that describes a wide array of relationships between a nonprofit client and a professional advisor, whether an independent consultant, nonprofit management support organization, or private consulting firm. Consulting roles vary depending on the consultant's style and background, the needs of the client, and the type of project. In some cases, a consultant acts primarily as a directive expert, conveying information and prescribing solutions related to programs, organizational development, or specialized areas such as accounting, marketing, or business planning. In other situations, a consultant plays the role of a facilitator, guiding a process and collaboratively helping the client to reflect on options and make decisions. More consultants are serving as coaches to nonprofit executives by offering new ideas and perspectives, asking challenging questions, and helping to process information and adapt behavior. Consulting engagements are most successful when the advisor and client agree on goals and strategies, have clear mutual expectations, share a commitment to making change, and dedicate adequate time to the effort.

Funding for Ventures

Funders are interested in investing in building the capacity of nonprofits for earned income ventures for a variety of reasons, including the desire to enhance program impact, increase nonprofit sustainability, and leverage philanthropic dollars. While some foundations, such as the San Francisco-based Roberts Enterprise Development Fund, have long track records and deep experience in investing in nonprofit business enterprise, others, such as young venture philanthropies, are just beginning to make investments in this area.

Funders invest in nonprofit enterprises by providing grants and capital financing to support nonprofit enterprises, by providing direct management assistance to nonprofit organizations, by supporting capacity builders and intermediaries that provide assistance to nonprofit ventures, and by making grants to researchers and educators involved in the field of social entrepreneurship. Funders provide different types of funding for different stages of venture development, and they also expect a higher degree of performance measurement and accountability.[3] Increasingly, funders are providing a combination of funding and management assistance to support nonprofit ventures. The Fannie Mae Foundation and the Eugene and Agnes E. Meyer Foundation, for example, supported a cohort of eight executives to meet regularly through a peer exchange to discuss the feasibility of developing ventures. The foundations then provided funding to support some of the planned income-generating activities.

Conclusion

The organizational context of a nonprofit venture cannot be ignored. For a non-profit enterprise to thrive, some fundamental organizational infrastructure needs to exist. When planning to start or expand an earned-income activity, a nonprofit needs to take stock of and strengthen its organizational capacity to increase the venture's potential for success.

Notes

1. Roberts Foundation. *Social Purpose Enterprises and Venture Philanthropy in the New Millennium.* Vol. 2: *Investors Perspectives.* San Francisco: The Roberts Enterprise Development Fund, The Roberts Foundation, 1999, pp. 217–223.
2. Grantmakers Evaluation Network and Grantmakers for Effective Organizations. *High Performance Organizations: Linking Evaluation and Effectiveness.* Report from the 2000 Grantmakers Evaluation Network and Grantmakers for Effective Organizations Conference, Kansas City, Mo., Mar. 2000, p. 2.
3. For more on the different types of funding needed by nonprofits at different stages, see Emerson, J., and Carttar, P. *Money Matters: The Structure, Operations and Challenges of Nonprofit Funding.* Boston and San Francisco: Bridgespan Group, 2003; Emerson, J. *The U.S. Capital Market: An Introductory Overview of Developmental Stages, Investors, and Funding Instruments.* San Francisco: The Roberts Enterprise Development Fund, The Roberts Foundation, 1998.

CHAPTER THREE

LEADERSHIP STRATEGIES FOR MANAGING A NONPROFIT ENTERPRISE

Jeffrey A. Sonnenfeld and Maxwell L. Anderson

The precedent-setting challenges and cultural tensions required for the successful launch of a nonprofit business mean that good intentions and great need can be derailed by inadequate leadership. Planning for and implementing a nonprofit business require more than a few good ideas. It also requires an individual who has strong leadership skills and a passion to bring the ideas to fruition. The project champion must be able to summon the participation of key decision-making staff within the organization and, given the financial means, the influence and authority to move the venture forward. Much has been written about effective leadership in voluntary organizations and nonprofit institutions, but little has been said about executives charged to lead both the nonprofit and a fledgling business venture. This chapter outlines a few of the necessary characteristics and skill sets.

The specific management challenges associated with operating a nonprofit enterprise extend to what a nonprofit executive might face in operating the parent organization and vary from those that a for-profit manager might experience. These challenges include the difficulty in bringing the board along to support the business venture, problems related to balancing mission with a financial focus, cultural issues, succession planning, and finding and retaining management staff. This chapter highlights these key challenges and presents a variety of management strategies that have been developed to address the operational issues associated with running a nonprofit enterprise.

Characteristics of a Nonprofit Leader

Research conducted by the Chief Executive Leadership Institute points out five characteristics of an effective nonprofit executive: authenticity, personal dynamism, recognition and appreciation, goal setting, and boldness.[1]

Authenticity

Nonprofits have extremely high expectations for their CEO on the dimension of authenticity. The CEO needs to start by earning the trust of the organization so that together the organization and the CEO will be able to take the kinds of risks associated with new business ventures; and the CEO has to show that he or she is well anchored in the core of the enterprise and in the world that it represents. Research suggests that the CEO need not be an anthropologist or a physician, but he or she must understand the fundamental purpose of the nonprofit and have a proven track record. The CEO must also be connected through networks and knowledge.

But authenticity goes beyond the CEO's professional expertise—it also has to do with believability and integrity. That their CEO is seen as credible is especially important to nonprofits, for unlike many private sector companies, nonprofits have to prove and reprove their legitimacy every day, because it is so easy to carelessly detract from the legacy that had been handed down to them. It is important even for a newer nonprofit to be able to clarify what the organization fundamentally stands for.

In short, nonprofit enterprise initiatives can move the institution into unfamiliar domains, thereby making the personal model of leadership essential. In 1995, one month into Adelphi University's centennial year, the faculty voted 131 to 14 to demand that their president, Peter Diamandopoulos, resign. The new mission to enhance the school's educational pedigree had questionable nonprofit enterprise priorities. Diamandopoulos defended his new business direction by stating, "I am a businessman and I invest money in stocks and bonds. I invest money buying houses. I invest money buying art for the university and other things that enhance the elegance of the institution."[2]

This new mission was showcased through a spacious office and a plush Manhattan apartment full of work by artists such as Picasso, Calder, and Miro. A mammoth salary package placed this commuter-college president among the ranks of highly compensated for-profit CEOs and garnished him with luxurious perks. Meanwhile, despite high-profile splashy advertising campaigns about a new campus mission to upgrade the school, conditions deteriorated; student enrollments declined by 25 percent, course offerings were reduced, staff were laid off, student activities were cancelled, and library acquisitions dried up.[3]

Perhaps the most infamous recent example of the violation of authenticity was in the creation of United Way's side businesses under William Aramony. These new businesses resulted in fraud and the misdirection of funds to support the sordid personal life of former chief Aramony. After twenty-two years as CEO, Aramony was forced to resign in 1992. He was convicted in 1995 and sentenced to prison for spending $1.2 million of the nonprofit's money on vacations, travel, and perks for himself and friends. Aramony was released in 2001 after serving a seven-year term.[4]

The fundamental credibility of the United Way system was badly damaged at that time and donations fell off sharply. Now, three CEOs later, the 2,100 autonomous United Way chapters around the United States must still address the Aramony scandal during their fundraising campaigns.[5]

Yet such credibility challenges at the United Way continued even after Aramony's departure. In fact, during his first year on the job, new United Way CEO Brian Gallagher had to ask for the resignation of the president of the National Capital Area chapter, Norman Taylor, over the use of funds there. Gallagher stepped into his new position in the fall of 2001, soon after the September 11 terrorist attacks, just in time to respond to the public outrage over the United Way's alleged diversion of funds intended for the victims of that disaster. Seeing how the American Red Cross's CEO Bernadine Healy lost her position over the controversial similar allocation of $950 million from philanthropic extensions after September 11, Gallagher acted swiftly to release funds according to donor wishes and quickly established his own credibility and trust in the United Way.

Personal Dynamism

The second characteristic of an effective nonprofit executive is personal dynamism. In the world of nonprofits, the goal of a leader is often not to be a custodian of stability, but rather to be a catalyst for change while at the same time taking on an illustrious, rich legacy. Both creators of new institutions and change agents of established institutions must excite others through their personal accessibility and by the inspiring images they paint.

For example, as CEO of the American Museum of Natural History, Ellen Futter assumed control of a staid enterprise best known for its aging displays and fiscal conservatism and quickly decided not to rest on the 130-year legacy she had inherited. Futter conducted a survey of natural science literacy that produced such alarming results that she quickly gained millions of dollars from NASA and the state of New York. She built alliances with major industrialists and then challenged new corporate sponsors and board members to envision the museum's role in making New York City "the Capital of the Universe." Through a continuing stream of two hundred forums, fundraising speeches, and employee rallies she was able to get her institution to reach for the stars. In 1996 she demolished her museum's beloved Art Deco Hayden Planetarium to rebuild with unrivaled technological sophistication the Rose Center for Air and Space for $210 million, increasing the museum's size by 25 percent. On top of this, Futter revamped the museum's work on biodiversity and added lively exhibits on such topics as body piercing, diamond mining, pharmaceuticals, and the dinosaurs of Jurassic Park, leading to a 43 percent increase in attendance and a doubling of the endowment in five years.[6]

Such an extensive overhaul is the rare triumph. It is more likely that many of a new leader's constituents will identify with the status quo of their institution and not be interested in revitalization, fortification, or change efforts. Instead, they will be very much vested in avoiding change and maintaining the status quo. Often they are attracted to nonprofits because in theory such organizations don't have the volatility of the world of commerce. But a leader has to be ready for change.

The consequences of such clashes are well mapped out by Thomas Hoving in his book *Making Mummies Dance: Inside the Metropolitan Museum of Art*. Hoving describes the powerful resistance of traditionalists to his efforts to transform his elitist institution into a more populist, business-oriented enterprise over the stormy decade in which he led the Met. He describes virulent infighting and intrigues during battles with Robert Lehman, Ed Koch, J. Paul Getty, Jacqueline Kennedy Onassis, and other opinion leaders over his blockbuster exhibits and other controversial commercial moves such as gift shops in galleries, external promotional banners, disposing of donated artwork for cash, and leasing the galleries for private parties.[7]

Through personal dynamism a leader makes change more understanding and palatable, and hopefully more participatory. But accessibility goes hand in hand with personal dynamism. Leaders must make themselves available, wander around, hear and listen both in large groups and in one-on-one forums. They must intimately know their hospital, their school, their social action agency, and thus not be mannequins propped up behind podiums reciting rehearsed paeans about an institution they know only in theory. When they talk they must vividly convey the imagery of the institution, anchored in what the institution genuinely stands for and in ways that are tangible and inspirational.

Accordingly, Futter was quick to acknowledge the legacy and goodwill of traditional loyal donors and visitors. Thus it was no accident that she retained the name of the original beloved Hayden Planetarium even though it was demolished and rebuilt on the footprint of the original. Futter commented, "Change and repositioning of an institution are not foremost about marketing; it comes last.

You need to have something to market. Marketing is all about institutional vision and strategy. Know where you are and where you're going. You must understand what is sacrosanct to external audiences. You must acknowledge nostalgia."[8]

Another inspirational example of personal dynamism is Marsha Johnson Evans, now head of the Red Cross of America, where she fortified the noble mission of her organization following the tainted blood supplies scandals and allegations of misdirected funds intended for families of September 11. In her prior position as head of the Girl Scouts of America, Evans, an admiral in the U.S. Navy, repositioned the Girl Scouts from being focused on cooking, camping, and their profitable cookie venture by developing new programs to expand membership and make the organization more contemporary. These programs—with names such as GirlSports, Girl Scouting Beyond Bars (for girls with mothers in prison, thus taking the organization to more than twenty prisons), Money Smarts and Camp CEO, and computer education programs—have dramatically changed the focus of the organization.

In addition, through these programs and the diversity program entitled Girl Scout: For Every Girl Everywhere, Evans achieved the highest participation in thirty years, with membership growing to 4.7 million. She also created the Girl Scout Research Institute for research and pubic policy information on the healthy development of girl scouts as they mature. Evans's own visits to Girl Scout chapters are legendary and she was known for regularly attempting to recruit her seatmates on airplanes to become members of the Girl Scouts' 860,000 adult volunteers. In fact, she sparked a 17 percent increase in adult volunteers over the five years of her term, before departing for the Red Cross. All of this activity was wrapped around other tangible rebranding changes, such as a campaign stating that the Girl Scouts was the place "where girls grow strong," and the bold popular change in the design of the Girl Scouts uniform.[9]

Recognition and Appreciation

A third dimension of solid leadership is the use of recognition and appreciation. A leader of nonprofits has to pull a lever of empathy much more than does a leader of a for-profit, who can often buy his or her way out of poor leadership with a lot of cash. It's not generally the case that people can be retained and motivated with extraordinary cash incentives. There are ways to reward people who have taken risks and failed, or taken risks and succeeded, and it is critical to share that knowledge by developing internal recognition programs that reference these individuals, or by finding ways to decorate people and show them deep appreciation. In addition to celebrating the dedication and imagination of volunteers, Marsha Johnson Evans launched the Girl Scouts' National Woman of Distinction Award, which celebrates prominent women leaders across sectors.

Goal Setting

The fourth characteristic of an effective nonprofit leader is goal setting or expectation setting. Nonprofit leaders need to show that they can make a difference, and that they truly are comfortable with the organization they have inherited. They need to raise the level of aspiration and reach for more than what they were handed when they walked into the institution. They need to communicate the notion that this place will be different because they are there, and that they are going to make a significant contribution and not just feed off of the reflective glory of their predecessor. Futter displayed this characteristic in asking her museum constituents to envision a national knowledge-building mission that would be great for the city of New York. Similarly, Evans modeled such aspirations in encouraging the Girl Scouts to think of preparing its members for female role models in society while reaching underserved communities.

When James Firman took over leadership of the National Council on Aging (NCOA) in 1995, he was convinced that more frugal management practices, partnerships with industry, and better marketing of core services could save the organization from near insolvency. The NCOA now enjoys a substantial annual surplus and offers an array of new services, such as the Web site BenefitsCheckUp.org for alerting seniors to public benefits for which they may qualify.

Similarly, when Ray Empson, an attorney and former clothing CEO, assumed the leadership of Keep America Beautiful, he did not accept the status quo. Instead he saw natural opportunities to partner with industry over toxic waste and litter issues while exciting the larger public in his organization's mission. In 2002, the Great American Cleanup was their largest event ever, mobilizing more than 2.3 million volunteers in fourteen hundred communities and all fifty states.

Boldness

The fifth and last dimension of effective nonprofit leadership is a certain element of boldness. The initiative of the leader often must stir the organization in critical ways. This means that the leader takes chances at his or her own inspiration rather than letting market forces back him or her to the wall. The leader's boldness, however, must not be fearless risk taking; instead, it must constitute a thoughtful amount of courage.

In his twenty-three years as director of the National Gallery of Art in Washington, D.C., J. Carter Brown never seemed to select the easy route but instead flourished on bold, controversial moves. The I. M. Pei Wing, for example, was widely criticized, as was his endorsement of Maya Lin's Vietnam Memorial, although both were later celebrated as masterpieces. During his reign the museum's operating budget grew from $3 million to $52 million and the endowment from $34 million to $186 million. Most controversial of all were his crowd-pleasing, mass-oriented blockbuster exhibitions like Treasure Houses of Britain, which opened with a shimmering social whirl, including a visit from Prince Charles and Princess Diana; Treasures of Tutankhamun; Matisse in Nice; and Circa 1492: Art in the Age of Exploration. Brown successfully increased the gallery's collection by more than twenty thousand works of art and elevated the National Gallery to one of the most important collections in the world.[10]

Jean Picker Firstenberg demonstrated similar courage in the face of controversy as CEO of the American Film Institute (AFI). She took many bold strides as head of the only national arts organization devoted to film, television, and video. She launched major annual high-profile awards ceremonies to recognize accomplishments in film and television, an international film festival, special "one hundred best" programs celebrating great works by category, critical film preservation programs, and partnerships with public schools, and she created the AFI's own campus for its conservatory and other AFI activities. With no mandate forcing such initiatives and with controversy surrounding each of these successful moves, Firstenberg's personal courage was necessary to launch these efforts and guide the AFI through each stage of development.

The Challenges of a Nonprofit Executive Leading a Nonprofit Enterprise

An effective leader of a nonprofit enterprise must have the ability to do three things well. First, he or she must be able to set compelling goals for the enterprise in tandem with the organization's existing goals to ensure that they are carefully aligned with the mission of the organization and its governance structures. The nonprofit manager charged with operating a nonprofit enterprise must be able to negotiate the long process of arguing about and agreeing on what matters most to the organization, including the creation of side ventures. Second, the leader must be able to achieve those goals through a collective effort rather than by making it a solitary act, and others in the organization must be able to take pride in the progress toward those goals. Finally, the nonprofit leader must be able to communicate the success of the venture and reinforce that success over time so that people feel they are part of the dreaming, achieving, and celebrating. Many challenges, however, stand in the way of such ambitious goals for leadership. Here we examine a few of the more salient issues that can get in the way of nonprofit entrepreneurs.

Mission Conflict

A challenge that often faces the nonprofit executive is how to bring along those who won't share the collective dream, for undoubtedly there will always be some and there is likely to be strong resistance to change when launching a business venture. The resistance to the blockbuster exhibits at the Metropolitan Museum of Art is an example of this tension. Other times, staff may wisely detect a succession of goals that depart from the original mission. Some people wondered whether the National Foundation for Infantile Paralysis, a nonprofit organization founded in 1937 and dedicated to fighting polio, should have continued after the success of the Salk and Sabine vaccines eradicated polio, or whether the group reformulated as the March of Dimes was right to evolve into a broader mission.

The debates over mission need not become a collective nightmare. The legitimacy of critics must be respected, but critics must also be shown the need for change. The executive must learn to incorporate the kind of diplomatic skill sets that are needed for effective conflict management. While Marsha Johnson Evans dramatically expanded the Girls Scouts' contemporary mission, she did not denigrate the valued legacy of selling cookies, camping, and cooking. In fact, in her last year at the Girl Scouts, 2.4 billion cookies, or two hundred million boxes, were sold.

Sometimes it is hard to make sweeping changes in personnel in ways that might best benefit the institution, so a great deal of diplomacy is required at times to keep dissident professional staff or unhappy trustees moving ahead in constructive ways. Indeed, the institution benefits from diverse views rather than forcing those who hold them into unhappy, conspiratorial alliances. A challenge here is that, unlike a significant number of for-profit boards, many nonprofit boards regularly see board members "working" staff and staff members "working" boards. This causes agendas to arise that can undermine what the CEO is trying to accomplish. These people are not evil conspirators or destructive personalities, but they have a different set of beliefs. If such a controversy becomes public, it can hurt the organization's mission and frighten away donors.

At the same time, staff unrest can be a helpful failsafe for the board; therefore, access to professional staff is critical. This was evident in the justified outrage over United Way and American Red Cross diversion of donor funds away from the intentions of donors in the aftermath of the September 11 tragedy. Seizing the moment to create new offerings to capture public concerns and help underwrite longer-term initiatives can come off as opportunism and deception.

The nonprofit leader doesn't need to encounter surprises with the board. He or she needs to have a finger on the pulse of all external constituencies in the conflict management equation.

Another challenge that nonprofit executives might face when leading a business venture is the larger question of the compass they use in the decisions they need to make day-to-day. If they are distracted by the allure of a return on investment as the primary benefit for initiating an enterprise rather than focusing on the value of the organization's social mission, then that mission can be diluted. The CEO of a nonprofit enterprise needs to keep the vision very clear in his or her mind even if deputies (such as COOs or CFOs) are in place to see that the institution is well positioned for commercial and financial success.

Succession Planning

Leadership succession is a challenging issue and of paramount importance to the executive leading a nonprofit enterprise, for research has shown that without a project champion, a venture can flounder.[11] Historically, most senior nonprofit leaders grow up within the institution as generalists. They do a considerable amount of good-soldier service within their own institution and then rise up. Historically, we have not seen a tremendous amount of management flow between nonprofit organizations. Yet recently we have begun to witness quite a bit of fluidity of leadership talent in the nonprofit sector.

This pattern is not unlike what is seen in the private sector, where the number of years of executive tenure in a Fortune 500 firm has shrunk to just under three years. This volatility has dramatic consequences for nonprofit organizations when boards are looking for a successor to their CEO. They very often run to the other side of the deck and look for someone with skills that seem to be wanting in the predecessor. In these instances they usually end up not being satisfied in the long run with the gradient of success, and they tend to run back in the other direction next time. Adjudicating performance and making decisions about succession are much like a governance tennis match. Often too a board falls in love with a person but does not agree on the metrics of success for the organization. Having clearly defined goals rather than buying the hype of the individual addresses the central issue: What is the culture of the institution and what does this culture require in a leader?

Identifying and Recruiting Strong Leaders

Some nonprofit institutions have a historic insularity with a legacy of "taking care of their own." Some are more loyalty based than truly meritocratic, and staffing needs are fed by their internal organizations. These institutions are classified as "clubs." A second type of institution maintains a system in which specialists are rewarded; these kinds of institutions are called "academies." In academy-like organizations, a considerable amount of institution-specific house knowledge is built up. Either one of these systems attracts people who are security oriented. If the intention of the enterprise is to build that sort of culture, then that's the appropriate kind of recruitment and staffing. All institutions need to be sure, however, that they are providing people with the stability, the predictability, and the reliability of that more conservative institution.[12]

By contrast, many nonprofit managers lack business and entrepreneurial skills required to launch or otherwise grow successful ventures, and the churn of an enterprise is significantly greater than what might be experienced in a traditional nonprofit organization. Therefore, it is critical to pay solid attention to recruiting strong managers who have the requisite financial background and tolerance for risk. In this situation, rewards and opportunity might be offered as bait to secure the appropriate talent. These "baseball team" systems must be very strong at recruiting because they will lose the risk-embracing people if they don't reward them quickly. Also, if financial incentives aren't offered to retain them, a succession of highly compelling assignment opportunities must be provided.

Regardless of which of these cultural systems an institution falls into, the recruiting message has to be honest and aligned with the organization's cultural values. The recruiting culture needs to match the enterprise's goals, and if that enterprise is changing the organization's culture, it will shake up those who were recruited in the past.

Identifying strong leaders sometimes means attracting people who are stronger than the senior leaders in the institution. The first thing that the very young Henry Ford II did was to hire a General Motors vice president who had been passed over for a promotion to teach him how to run his auto company. Michael Dell did the same thing by hiring a septuagenarian who had been a brilliant technology entrepreneur to help him run his company. But that takes a lot of confidence, and a nonprofit leader has to feel that hiring people to complement his or her own skills will not be considered a character deficiency. In fact, such confidence could be perceived as a strength rather than a weakness.

Board Governance

One of the enormous issues facing a nonprofit executive leading a business venture is the issue of the size of the board. Generally, the size of corporate boards is not a problem; they typically number between half a dozen and a dozen people. There are only a few examples of very large bank mergers where the board had more than a dozen people, and that was transitional. Conversely, some nonprofit boards have been enormous, with several hundred people participating. This was one of John Seffrin's first challenges when he stepped in as CEO of the American Cancer Society. As the first public health professional to run this enormous community-based voluntary health organization with 2,400 local units, two million volunteers, and more than two hundred board members, Seffrin helped guide the board to reduce its size by two-thirds while tightening its mission to emphasize prevention and research support for early-career scientists. Jim Firman at the National Council on Aging similarly inspired his board to cut its size by two-thirds. Other nonprofit boards delegate decisions to smaller sets of trustees and executive committees. The risk with this method is that it typically disenfranchises the rest of the board members and makes them quite uncertain about their role.

We have also seen the development of "vanity boards" where fallen leaders from another sector come to reclaim the pulpit they've lost in their other world. Another equally pernicious issue of the for-profit board is the heavy reliance on marquee names. The lure of such people, of course, is access to their financial resources and personal networks. They often maintain gateways to influence and connections that are vital, but one of the dangers is that these individuals will not pay attention to the business matters facing the venture because, due to other commitments, they are unable to provide the needed diligence. In fact, frequently these marquee names are just the ones who don't have the time to roll up their sleeves and look under the hood to make sure there is an engine there. For example, the fraud and waste during William Aramony's later days as CEO of United Way occurred despite the fact that his board had such experienced executives as the CEOs of IBM and JC Penney. Ironically, other boards tend to trust that due diligence has been guaranteed because such gilded names are on the board.

Another example of such abuse of marquee names is the saga of the bankrupt Foundation for New Era Philanthropy scandal in which highly respected, honorable financial leaders such as Sir John Templeton, Julian Robertson, and William Simon were duped into endorsing a new philanthropy led by John Bennett Jr., who was actually the creator of a $135 million philanthropic pyramid scheme. Bennett promised to double the amount of a donating institution's gift in six months from the funds of anonymous wealthy benefactors. In reality, however, Bennett used incoming donations to pay off his double-your-money commitments while at the same time diverting large sums for his personal use and for-profit enterprises. Relying on the credibility of such names, dozens of churches and colleges and universities invested their funds in this fraudulent enterprise. After the collapse of the scam, Bennett was found guilty of eighty-two counts of fraud and sentenced to a twelve-year prison term.[13] As with Aramony of United Way, the board at New Era was not doing its job, despite the expertise and prominent reputations of its members.

Another critical dimension of board governance is the need to foster a culture of open dissent that encourages board members or the CEO to raise uncomfortable and problematic issues in a safe environment. The dangers of what Yale political scientist Irving Janis labeled "groupthink" makes it hard for concerned board members to voice their dissent. As one well-known director told us, "No one wants to be seen as the skunk at a lawn party."[14] Yet dissent is not disloyalty.

It is vitally important to have this dialogue especially if the venture being proposed is something that is anathema to the nonprofit's mission. Together the board and CEO must look very hard at the issues and decide whether the venture will reinforce the mission or destroy it. Controversy is crucial to turning that rock over all sides. One technique is to encourage various board members to take positions of advocacy in order to challenge initial views and not just rubber-stamp things. Also, the CEO should not feel a personal *raison d'etre* with the cause he or she is advancing to avoid defeat, meaning that they have just lost a vote of confidence, as in Parliament.

A tactical approach to nurturing this type of culture is for the CEO to sketch out the pros and cons so that the issues can be openly raised, then tossed around. A second tactical approach is to have one-on-one meetings with board members to the extent possible, to test out their interest in advance of full board consideration. Naturally a person with a powerful voice or dominant profile could take the discussion on an unproductive track and upset all the careful consideration that has been done in advance. But the conversation must deal thoughtfully with the downsides and the potential of any idea and make clear to the governing authorities that the CEO has thoroughly considered the challenges and understands the necessary next steps.

Conclusion

Boards should stop expecting their leaders to be messiahs, and leaders should not resent the diligent participation of the board. The expectations of all parties unfold over time and are not well defined at the beginning of the employment relationship. Conflict should be considered not failure of character but a predictable situation. There should be periodic process renegotiations between boards and their CEOs to be certain that evolving definitions of trust, mastery, and expectations are resolved. As Clark Kerr said in 1967 upon his dismissal by Governor Ronald Reagan as president of the University of California, "I leave here the same as when I entered—fired with enthusiasm."[15] It is hoped that boards and their CEOs can minimize such despair when launching and operating a nonprofit enterprise.

Notes

1. Agle, B., and Sonnenfeld, J. "Dimensions of Charisma as Properties of CEO Dispositions: Perceptions of the Top Management Team." Paper presented at the National Meeting of the Academy of Management, Las Vegas, Nevada, 1992. See also Sonnenfeld, J. "Three Cheers for Charisma." *Wall Street Journal,* Nov. 12, 2002, p. B-2.
2. Editorial Desk, "The Plundering of Adelphi." *New York Times,* Oct. 14, 1995, p. 18.
3. Leatherman, C. "Adelphi President Is Under Fire." *Chronicle of Higher Education,* Nov. 3, 1995, p. A–23.
4. "Charitable Seductions." *Time,* Oct. 1994, p. 27; Sinclair, M. "William Aramony Is Back on the Streets." *Nonprofit Times,* Mar. 1, 2002, p. 1.; Jones, J. "Old Board to Select New One at Troubled United Way." *Nonprofit Times,* Nov. 1, 2002. p. 5.
5. Shepard, C. E. "United Way Head Resigns Over Spending Habits." *Washington Post,* Feb. 28, 1992, p. 3.
6. Singer, N. "Planetarium Hollywood: Out of This World." *New York,* Feb. 21, 2000.
7. Hoving, T. *Making Mummies Dance: Inside the Metropolitan Museum of Art.* New York: Simon & Shuster, 1993.
8. Singer, "Planetarium Hollywood."
9. Judge, P. C. "How Will Your Company Adapt?" *Fast Company,* Dec. 2001, pp. 135–138.
10. Conconi, C. "Remembering J. Carter Brown." *Washingtonian,* June 2002.
11. Massarsky, C. W., and Beinhacker, S. L. "Nonprofit Enterprise: Right for You?" *Nonprofit Quarterly,* Fall 2002, pp. 50–55.
12. Sonnenfeld, J., and Peiperl, M. "Career Systems Typologies and Strategic Staffing." *Academy of Management Review,* 1996, *13*(4), 588–600.
13. Putka, G. "Pennsylvania Seeks to Freeze New Era Assets." *Wall Street Journal,* May 17, 1997, p. A–3; Carnes, T. "New Era's Bennett to Prison: How Could a Little-Known Christian Business Executive Defraud Charities of $354 Million While Claiming to Do God's Work?" *Christianity Today,* Oct. 27, 1997.
14. Sonnenfeld, J. "What Makes Great Boards Great?" *Harvard Business Review,* 2002, *80*(9), 106–113.
15. Hechinger, G. "Clark Kerr, Leading Public Educator, Dies at 92." *New York Times,* December 2, 2003, p. B–32.

CHAPTER FOUR

TARGETING THE MARKET AND DEVELOPING A MARKETING PLAN

Christopher Lovelock

Now that you've identified your product or service and done your preliminary research into the market, it's time to get down to the business of developing a marketing plan that will allow you to launch your product or service successfully. But a word of caution is in order: nonprofit organizations hoping to generate income from new ventures start with the odds stacked against them.

The sad fact is that most new products and services fail. Although no comprehensive data are available relating solely to nonprofits, research shows that the overall failure rate for new consumer products is 95 percent in the United States and 90 percent in Europe. New goods and services targeted at business-to-business markets also face high failure rates. Although large established companies can usually survive an occasional failure, small organizations with limited resources are quite vulnerable and may even be dragged under by an unsuccessful venture. Careful planning and a disciplined approach to market targeting, however, can improve the chances of success.

Why do so many new offerings fail in the marketplace? There are a variety of reasons. Sometimes senior executives push through a favorite idea without reference to customer requirements or the size of the potential market. When customers see no significant benefits in a new product or service, relative to existing offerings, they are unlikely to change their established purchasing behavior. Even when the basic idea is good, a new offering may fail commercially if it is poorly designed, incorrectly positioned in the marketplace, not advertised effectively, or overpriced. Difficulty in obtaining support from distributors or other intermediaries is another cause of failure. Finally, the launch of new products may be derailed when competitors fight back more strongly than expected.

The fact that even highly sophisticated companies with large budgets, good reputations, and substantial marketing expertise can run into difficulties and experience substantial losses suggests that launching a new venture is fraught with difficulties and offers no guarantee of financial success. Nonprofits are not immune to these problems so should approach the task of developing and marketing a new venture with caution.

Added Complexities for Nonprofit Ventures

Many observers have commented on the difficulties faced by nonprofits in trying to adopt a marketing orientation. Typically their mission statements give priority to societal rather than financial goals. The "product"—if such a term is used at all—is often imbued with a certain nobility and may be viewed as unique, even when it is not. Programmatic activities are rarely expected to recover all associated costs from users or clients; instead, operating deficits are covered by grants, donations, income from endowment funds, or tax revenues. And there's often tension between mission achievement and customer satisfaction, at least in the short term.

These nonprofit perspectives and priorities are very different from the market-driven model of profit-oriented ventures, where the mission is to make money, competition is taken as a given, and achieving customer satisfaction is seen as a key objective. If the revenues from a product or service fail to cover costs within a certain period after initial launch, then hard-headed economic considerations mean it will be withdrawn from the marketplace.

Nonprofit managers wishing to start an earned-income venture must be prepared to adopt a new mind-set and a new way of doing business that may clash with existing approaches.

Improving the Chances of Success

The keys to competing successfully in the challenging environment surrounding the launch of a new venture include skills in marketing research, strategy, and execution—areas in which many nonprofits have traditionally been weak. But the chances of success can be improved by developing a well-thought-out marketing plan in which special attention is paid to targeting the right market. These same skills continue to be needed after the launch in order to ensure continued success and profitability. Moreover, the fact that a strategy has been successful in the past does not necessarily mean that it should remain unchanged in the future.

In this chapter we walk you through the steps involved in developing a marketing strategy for *new offerings* (a term we use to represent both goods and services) that are designed to generate a positive revenue stream for your organization. We present key tools and concepts, using a variety of examples to highlight their practical application. In particular, we relate the experience of one organization, Parrett Paper, a for-profit venture of the nonprofit Rochester Rehabilitation Center, through a series of case extracts that are keyed to different steps in the planning process.

Our approach may look simple, but you're likely to find that actual execution is hard work. In particular, we emphasize the use of marketing research and rigorous thinking to generate insights into how the market might be segmented and to understand the nature of the existing competition. Access to relevant, credible information helps managers to make better decisions. At any stage in this process you may conclude that it is not worth proceeding further with a particular project, at least in its current form. Disappointing though that might be, it is certainly better than rushing ahead poorly prepared and ultimately facing an expensive failure.

The Role of a Marketing Plan

A marketing plan is part of a broader business plan that includes finance, operations, and human resources. But marketing should be the driving element because it focuses on generating income by meeting the requirements of customers, who usually have alternative choices. The planning process should provide a systematic way of analyzing the market for a new offering and help you to evaluate the organization's strengths and weaknesses in what is often a highly competitive environment. Effective planning should ensure that the chosen strategy is based on facts instead of conjecture, involves a careful appraisal of alternatives rather than a rush to judgment, and reflects an objective perspective as opposed to personal preferences. The planning process should involve a systematic, coherent, step-by-step process and allow sufficient lead time to gather and interpret needed data.

The marketing plan should identify what types of customers your organization will target and describe how your product or service will be differentiated from the competition, how it will be priced and distributed, and how it will be promoted to target customers. The plan should set realistic sales goals and relate anticipated revenues to the costs of achieving them, recognizing that building volume to the point where profitability is achieved will take time and that sustaining and increasing volume requires satisfied customers.

Approaching marketing in this way allows for the application of frameworks that can help managers identify both market opportunities and key risks. The written plan ensures that everyone is reading, as it were, from the same sheet of music and can make timely and informed decisions. When putting things in writing you must document the facts and assumptions on which goals and strategies are based, avoid ambiguity, and provide an explicit plan of action, identifying the resources that will be needed. A written plan, which will need to be updated at yearly intervals, facilitates communication and coordination between different members of the team. There is no single format for such a plan, but a suggested approach, structured as a series of questions, is shown in Exhibit 4.1.

Facing a Marketing Challenge at Parrett Paper

In the winter of 2001, the managers of The Out-Source (TOS), a division of the non-profit Rochester Rehabilitation Center, decided to purchase the operations of a former customer, Parrett Paper. TOS, whose mission is to provide job training and meaningful work to people with disabilities, had twenty-five years of experience in supplying low-tech manual labor on a contract basis to companies in the Rochester, New York area.

Parrett's product line consisted primarily of all-occasion cards and gift tags featuring zoo animals, pets, dinosaurs, and farm animals, each with a brief description of the depicted animal. TOS employees had earlier worked for Parrett Paper for several years, stripping cards from large sheets and assembling them for sale. However, despite achieving annual revenues of $350,000, Parrett became moribund in 1996 following the death of one of its owners, who had been responsible for all marketing activities. Six years later, the surviving owners of Parrett Paper—who had subsequently pursued other interests—offered to sell TOS the firm's name, inventory, custom designs, dies, and artwork, at a significant discount to its value.

TOS provided manufacturing labor and custodial maintenance services to some twenty major clients and contributed $3 million in earned income to Rochester Rehabilitation Center. Parrett Paper was seen as an attractive addition to this operation, providing an internally controlled source of work with potential for future growth. After six years of dormancy, however, Parrett Paper had a line of products but no sales. To relaunch the products, its new management needed to assess the size and composition of the market, evaluate the competition, identify target customers, select retail intermediaries, and develop pricing and promotional strategies that would generate sufficient sales revenues to cover all costs and ultimately generate profits that Rochester Rehabilitation Center could use to support additional mission-related services.

EXHIBIT 4.1. MARKETING PLAN FORMAT.

Where are we now? (Situation analysis)
- External
  - Market analysis: size, trends, segmentation, customer purchasing behavior
  - Supplier and distributor analysis
  - Competitor analysis: sales, market share, strengths and weaknesses
- Internal
  - Objectives of new venture
  - Our strengths and weaknesses (relative to new venture)
- Summary of problems and opportunities

Where do we want to go? (Marketing program goals at specific points in time)
- Competitive standing
- Sales targets
- Financial results: revenues, profits
- Market share

How are we going to get there? (Marketing strategies)
- Positioning
  - Target segments
  - Competitive differentiation
  - Value proposition: distinctive benefits
- Marketing mix
  - Core product, supplementary services, and delivery systems
  - Price and trade terms (if selling through intermediaries)
  - Marketing communication: advertising, personal selling, promotion, and so on

What resources are needed? (Marketing budget)
- Resources: money, people
- Allocation
- Analysis of costs relative to anticipated revenues

What do we need to do? (Marketing action plan and schedule)
- Detailed breakdown of activities required
- Responsibility by name for executing specific activities
- Activity schedule in milestone format
- Tangible and intangible results expected from each activity

Are we moving toward our destination? Do we need a course correction? (Monitoring system)
- Ongoing situation analysis
- Intermediate and final measures of performance
- Variances between goals and actual performance

Steps in the Marketing Planning Process

As shown in Exhibit 4.1, creating a marketing plan involves consideration of six broad topics. Although the process may appear straightforward, maximizing the chances of success requires a rigorously objective approach, including the willingness to undertake in-depth research and analysis. The steps in this process are iterative and interactive rather than purely sequential.

This chapter focuses on how you can develop answers to the following questions: Where are we now? Where do we want to go? How should we position our venture in order to get there? The discussion is organized around the following steps: internal analysis, market analysis and segmentation, competitive analysis, and positioning strategy. From these steps should emerge a marketing action plan that targets specific market segments, offers features that distinguish your product or service from that of the competition, and articulates a value proposition that will appeal to customers in the segment or segments you have targeted. Coverage of marketing-mix strategies, budgeting, action plans, and monitoring systems lies beyond the scope of this chapter. Included, however, is a brief overview of the role of marketing research.

Internal Analysis

A marketing plan should begin with a review and analysis of your organization's current situation and an objective assessment of its strengths and weaknesses relative to the goals of the new venture and its requirements for success. The factors that make a nonprofit successful in achieving its core mission are not necessarily helpful for achieving success in a for-profit venture, because the two businesses are often radically different from each other. Consider an art museum that wants to make money from the retailing of gifts. The museum is in the business of conserving and displaying artworks, encouraging inquiry, and heightening public understanding and appreciation of these works. Its expertise is centered around preservation, research, exhibit display, education, management of visitor flows, and facilities management. Few of these strengths will carry over to a retail operation, a competitive business where the criteria for success include skills in store layout, product selection and merchandising, pricing, Web site and catalog design, and direct mail operations.

Realistically, nonprofits need to be brutally honest about their strengths and weaknesses as these apply to new ventures. The marketing plan you adopt should play to your organization's strengths and either find ways to avoid its weaknesses or define methods of overcoming them.

Managers at TOS saw the acquisition of Parrett Paper as a way to serve its mission of offering suitable employment for disabled clients. TOS believed that associating Parrett products with its nonprofit status and mission might provide competitive differentiation, add appeal for customers, and give it an advantage in obtaining distribution through other nonprofits, such as the gift shops operated by zoos and museums.

Among TOS's relevant strengths was a management team that excelled at the manufacturing process and operations management—necessary criteria for success as a subcontractor to local businesses. Hence, assembling Parrett greeting cards from its huge existing inventory would be easy—TOS had done it before. The hard part would be marketing and distribution, an area in which TOS lacked experience. So the management team recruited an informal board with industry experience to provide needed advice.

Although Parrett was able to link its mission to its for-profit venture, not every organization can do so. Many nonprofits believe their mission is so noble that customers will immediately see the products of its for-profit ventures as superior to competing alternatives. Perhaps customers will make a single purchase as a form of donation, but unless the product in question meets their expectations for quality and value in exchange for their money, the chances of their making repeat purchases are slim. The Girl Scouts could never have achieved long-term success with their cookies if the cookies were seen as overpriced and not very tasty.

Moreover, some organizations are likely to find that publicizing their core mission can actually be disadvantageous for a for-profit venture. Hard-headed customers may view nonprofit entrepreneurs of a seemingly unrelated business as inexperienced amateurs and thus ill-equipped to provide high-quality products and services. For example, consider a nonprofit that seeks to rehabilitate ex-convicts and provide them with meaningful employment. One of its profit-making ventures is a house-moving business, but it cannot promote its underlying mission to prospective customers for fear that revealing its workers' criminal backgrounds would immediately discourage people from using its services.

The analysis of internal strengths and weaknesses serves as an important screening process for the appropriateness of a proposed venture. How well matched with the requirements for success is your organization's financing, reputation, values, and staff capabilities? An honest and complete assessment of your organization's resources will aid you later in deciding which customers to serve and which product benefits to emphasize, and in articulating your market positioning to customers.

Many nonprofits with distinctive physical facilities—including museums, aquariums, theaters, botanical gardens, and historic houses—seek to generate additional income by renting out these facilities for private events such as corporate functions, alumni reunions, and weddings. If handled well, this strategy can generate a significant revenue stream. In Boston, for example, the Museum of Science netted about 4.5 percent of its total income in 2002–03 by hosting 350 events.

However, Ed Able, president of the American Association of Museums, while admitting the potential benefits of such rental ventures, highlights some serious concerns and constraints, including the appropriateness of the space itself, the need to protect the collections, and policies that exclude rentals to groups that would be incompatible with the values or mission of the institution. Staffing for events may involve use of volunteers who are not always available for extra service. Rentals may be limited to periods when the facility is not normally open to the public. "I'm always a museum first. I'm not going to change my schedule to accommodate rentals," says one museum administrator, according first priority to the institution's core mission.

Market Analysis and Segmentation

If you decide that the proposed venture is compatible with your organization's mission and that you possess or can develop the skills needed to conduct the proposed venture, the next step is to scope out the potential market for the product or service you propose to offer. Key questions include the volume and value of demand for this type of product, how the market is segmented, and the nature of anticipated future trends.

Parrett Paper learned from a 1998 report that the value of the U.S. greeting card market was growing steadily and that sales were predicted to reach $8.3 billion by 2002. Data published on the Web site of a national trade association, the Greeting Card Association, however, showed that unit sales of cards had matured and revenue growth was primarily a function of higher card prices. Although people of all ages and types exchanged cards, women made more than 80 percent of card purchases. More than half of all sales were accounted for by seasonal greeting cards, with the balance consisting of cards for special occasions such as birthdays and anniversaries as well as get well, thank you, and sympathy cards. Growth was taking place in cards sold for everyday use rather than in holiday cards. Card prices varied widely, with most retailing in the $1.50 to $4.00 range. Outside this range there was growing demand for less expensive cards. Many customers were willing to pay more for quality and differentiation, so cards featuring special techniques, intricate designs, and heavier stock could command higher prices. The report noted the growing volume of electronic greetings but viewed these as complements rather than as replacements to paper greeting cards.

Understanding Market Segmentation. A market segment is a group of current or prospective buyers who have certain characteristics in common, reflecting personal (or corporate) characteristics, needs, purchasing behavior, or consumption patterns. Exhibit 4.2 highlights some widely used segmentation variables.

No organization can hope to succeed by being all things to all people. The secret lies in developing distinctive offerings that can be targeted at specific segments of the market. In many instances, marketers create segments based on multiple variables. Figure 4.1 shows a hypothetical example in which a nonprofit organization has divided the market for its products into segments based on three variables—gender of the purchaser (male or female), the purchaser's household income (three levels), and the region of the United States in which the purchaser lives (four geographic regions)—to create twenty-four possible segments. To focus its efforts, the organization might target women from households with income in

EXHIBIT 4.2. EXAMPLES OF SEGMENTATION VARIABLES.

Consumer Characteristics
- Demographics, such as age, education, family status, income, job, housing, ethnicity, language
- Geography, such as zip code of home or work location; urban vs. suburban vs. rural, climate
- Psychographics, such as attitudes, opinions, values, lifestyle

Business Characteristics (End-User or Intermediary)
- Firm size
- Number of employees
- Industry (instead of the outdated SIC codes, use the new NAICS codes: *U.S. Department of Commerce, North American Industry Classification System—United States.* Washington, D.C.: National Technical Information Service, 2002.)
- Locations of factories, offices, stores
- Corporate values and priorities

Benefits Desired from Use of Product or Service
- Selection criteria will vary according to nature of offering

Purchasing Behavior and Consumption Patterns
- Volume of purchases
- Frequency and scheduling of purchases
- Distribution channel used
- Price sensitivity and need for credit
- Purpose for which product is used
- Number of regular suppliers

excess of $80 thousand and confine its efforts to the northeast and mid-Atlantic states.

Criteria for Market Segmentation. What's the best way to segment the market? First, you must choose segmentation characteristics that are measurable so you can estimate the number of prospective customers in each segment and the value of their purchases. Second, from a practical standpoint, it should be possible for your organization to reach customers within the identified segments efficiently; this means the ability to use communication and distribution channels that specifically target these segments. The next criterion is responsiveness. For sales to take place, customers within a given segment must respond favorably to distinctive marketing strategies. Researching the experiences of other businesses can reveal valuable lessons. Your organization is probably not the first to target a given market segment, so learn from the successes and failures of others. Finally, the segment should be large enough, in terms of purchasing power, to generate a significant volume and value of sales for your organization, even if you obtain only a small market share.

FIGURE 4.1. MARKET ANALYSIS EMPLOYING MULTIPLE SEGMENTATION VARIABLES.

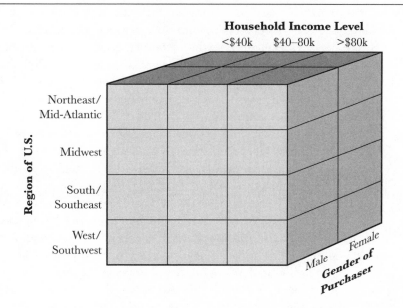

Parrett's initial review of existing research found that broadly based ways of segmenting the enormous greeting card market included purchaser demographics (for instance, females versus males), purpose of greeting (seasonal event, birthday, wedding, and so on), price sensitivity, and willingness to send electronic cards by e-mail instead of paper ones by postal mail. It decided to examine purchasing behavior to see where people bought cards.

Target Segments and Niche Strategies. A target segment is one that a business elects to serve because it fits with the firm's capabilities to match or exceed competing offerings, is sufficiently large to offer adequate sales potential even in the face of competition, and (in a for-profit context) will support pricing strategies that should generate sufficient revenues to yield a profit after covering all attributable costs. In what are known as niche strategies, businesses target segments with distinctive needs and purchasing patterns and seek to serve them better than anyone else could. These segments are often too small to be of interest to major marketers, but a specialized supplier can succeed by tailoring product features and marketing strategy to the characteristics and requirements of the segment in question.

Segmenting Distribution Channels. Although some products can be sold directly—Girl Scouts come to your door to sell cookies, Goodwill sells items through its own retail stores, and sheltered workshops often contact local businesses directly in search of contracts—many goods and services are more easily sold through intermediaries. Manufacturers wishing to serve distant markets must choose between selling directly through orders received by mail, phone, or Internet and selling through retail and wholesale intermediaries. Relatively few businesses can afford to attempt both routes. Even when a service is delivered directly, the selling task itself may still be assigned to intermediaries, often (but not always) in exchange for a commission.

For instance, nonprofits wishing to rent out space for events often find it is more efficient to market themselves to wedding planners and event managers, who can then offer their own clients an array of possible locations, rather than trying to market directly to betrothed couples and other end users.

The Visiting Nurse Associations (VNAs) of America, a trade association for more than 150 locally based VNAs across the nation, has documented a number of turnkey, revenue-generating concepts that its members can implement in their local communities. One of these ideas is a service to provide specialized treatments, such as infusions or wound care or physical therapy, for patients who have ongoing treatment needs while they are on vacation. This service is designed for VNAs located in vacation areas. Implementing this concept requires a VNA to market the service to local hotels and lodging establishments, encouraging them to advertise this option as a fee-based service for guests.

Parrett Paper learned that the vast majority of greeting cards were sold through retail channels. These included big outlets like mass merchandisers, drugstores, and supermarkets that were interested only in dealing with large suppliers who would provide financing of high-volume purchases. According to an industry report, the "Big Two" card marketers, Hallmark and American Greetings, dominated sales through these major chains, which accounted for 55 percent of all sales.[1] So Parrett turned its attention to sales through smaller retail outlets in the U.S. such as the country's 73,250 gift stores and 7,973 card shops (which accounted for 34 percent of all sales), 21,049 bookstores, and other small retail outlets, including gift stores at museums and other visitor attractions. From the Museum Store Association, Parrett learned that there were about 1,800 museum gift stores in the United States, including those at zoos and aquariums.

Competitive Analysis

Competitors exist in almost every market. But it's important to recognize that competition may take one of three main forms:

Direct competition. This consists of a similar or very close substitute to your own product or service. Directly competitive offerings are usually marketed in a broadly similar fashion. For instance, an airline offering service from Boston to New York faces direct competition from several other airlines.

Indirect competition. This is a feasible alternative that meets the customer's needs in a similar way while remaining different on several dimensions. Instead of flying, Boston–New York travelers can also take an Amtrak train, ride a bus, or drive a car.

Generic competition. This involves an altogether different approach. In this case, the product or service solves the same needs but in different ways and is typically supplied by an organization in a different industry. Instead of traveling to New York for a business meeting, an executive could choose to organize a video conference instead.

Even if an airline serves routes on which there are no competing carriers, it would be a mistake to define itself as just serving the air travel market. Instead, it needs to see itself as being in the transportation business. By digging deeper and thinking about the needs that travelers are trying to satisfy, an airline marketer will recognize that many individuals in the important business travel segment are going to meetings and that video conferencing has become an increasingly acceptable substitute for many discussions and presentations that previously required face-to-face contact.

Nonprofits often see their offerings as unique and make the mistake of ignoring the threat of indirect and generic competition. The issue is not how the organization sees its products or services but how prospective customers see them and what alternatives they are willing to consider that might meet their needs.

How can you determine the nature of the competition for your offering? A first step is to define the geographic scope of the market in which you intend to promote your product, because this market may constrain the alternatives available to prospective buyers. The next step is to consider possible competitors in terms of the three broad categories we've just discussed: direct, indirect, and generic. Here you have to start thinking creatively about the benefits your product or service offers and consider what alternative ways exist to deliver these. Research can then help you identify and profile potential competitors in each category. After analyzing the competitors' profiles, it is possible to rank the competition according to the level of threat presented, such as the similarity of products and superiority of appeal, expertise, and resources.

From a published study, Parrett Paper learned that Hallmark Cards and American Greetings each commanded 42 percent of the greeting card market, with the balance accounted for by a number of much smaller firms.[2] The Big Two concentrated their strategy on pushing cards into mass market retailers where they could anticipate large sales volumes, so they often neglected small, specialized retail stores. Through further research, including visits to trade shows, Parrett Paper obtained details of many small suppliers of greeting cards, among which it identified four firms whose cards had some features similar to its own.

Selecting a Market Position and Developing a Value Proposition

Having assessed your own organization's strengths and weaknesses, gathered insights into the nature of competition, determined market size and trends, determined how the market might be segmented (especially in terms of customer needs and preferences), and identified the characteristics of different intermediaries, you are now ready to make decisions on how to position your new offering in the marketplace. Figure 4.2 shows how the different steps in the analytic process are linked. As you can see, this is an iterative process rather than a purely sequential one. The outcome is a decision to offer a product or service whose features and pricing will appeal to prospective customers in the chosen target market segment or segments because they appreciate its value and perceive it as offering distinctive advantages over competing alternatives.

FIGURE 4.2. POSITIONING A PRODUCT IN THE MARKETPLACE.

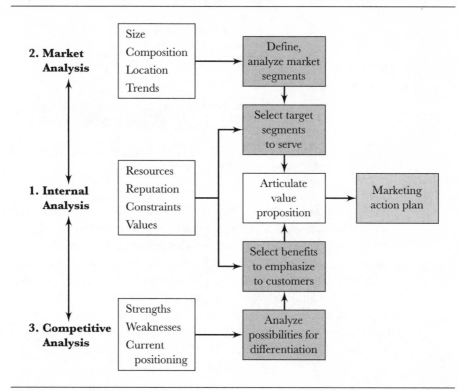

Prioritizing and Targeting Market Segments

Your research may reveal a number of possible market segments to target. So the final task is to rank those segments according to their attractiveness and your organization's ability to serve them. A useful tool for this task is the strategic planning grid in Figure 4.3, which allows you to rate each segment according to its market attractiveness on one axis and its fit with organizational strength on the other.

Market attractiveness should be rated using insights from the market and competitive analysis such as market size, growth rate, customer requirements, nature of distribution channels, and competitor characteristics. Organizational strengths should be rated using factors from the internal analysis such as financial requirements, managerial expertise, production capabilities, and compatibility with mission. The ideal segment is one that not only represents a very attractive market opportunity but also fits well with your organization's own strengths. The risks will mount if the fit is not as strong or the market potential is less attractive. As displayed by the grid, the darker the cell, the lower the chances of success.

FIGURE 4.3. STRATEGIC PLANNING GRID.

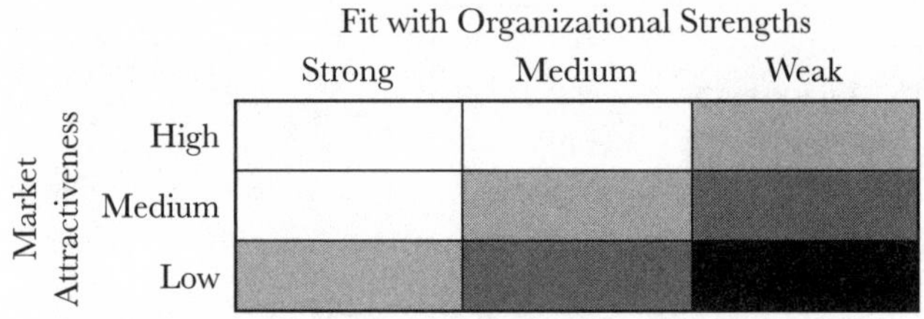

Fit with Organizational Strengths

Market Attractiveness	Strong	Medium	Weak
High			
Medium			
Low			

Source: Kotler, N., and Kotler, P. *Museum Strategy and Marketing.* San Francisco: Jossey-Bass, 1998. This material is used by permission of John Wiley & Sons, Inc.

As a small business, your venture faces both opportunities and threats in selecting a market position. The main risk is of offering a "me-too" product with no distinguishing characteristics to market segments that are already served by stronger, more established suppliers. Conversely, by selecting a small segment that you can serve better than your larger competitors can, you may be able to avoid the risk of provoking an aggressive competitive response. But keep in mind that some positions in the market are not worth targeting. There may be insufficient demand (who wants an expensive but low-quality product?) or the costs of serving the segment may be too high. Do the research and analysis to find out.

Through disciplined analysis, Parrett Paper quickly eliminated much of the huge market for greeting cards from further consideration. It knew it could not afford to compete with Hallmark and American Greetings, who dominated large retail networks and controlled five-sixths of the market. Although this still left substantial sales opportunities for the remaining, relatively small players, Parrett Paper recognized that the appeal of the animal-themed cards in its large inventory was limited mostly to children and people with interests in specific animals. In both instances, women would be the most likely purchasers. Because the cards contained no messages, they were more suited for special occasions than for the large seasonal markets. There was little point in targeting Parrett Paper's high-quality cards at price-sensitive customers, because the necessary low prices would only depress margins; and with only limited resources and few marketing skills in house, Parrett Paper could not afford to contact a wide array of outlets.

Value Proposition

When articulated through marketing communications, the summation of what the product or service stands for is known as a value proposition.

Parrett Paper states its value proposition as follows: "Our cards are unique in both subject matter and design; our die-cut images give more reality to the animal figures, and the cards include an educational message. Since Parrett Paper cards are simply designed and very colorful, they are appealing to both adults and children. Because of our unique, quality cards and our first-rate customer service, Parrett Paper is attractive to a wide range of retail outlets. However, our animal cards are especially attractive to zoos, aquariums, museums, and other specialty retail shops."

To ensure that your offering has the distinctive features that customers will value, you will have to analyze the benefits sought by prospective purchasers in specific segments. Nonprofit organizations often excel at recognizing and responding to urgent human needs, but have much less experience with understanding and addressing the needs of the typical consumer. Although your product or service must meet basic needs, you should focus on understanding how consumer desires differ among various market segments and, in the light of your analysis, decide which segment offers the best match.

To make a profit, your organization must target prospective customers who are willing to pay more for your product or service than it costs you to produce and market it. The fact that people appreciate a product's features doesn't mean they will pay any price to get it—there are limits to what people are willing and able to pay. Customers in some segments, however, can and will pay more. If you work for an organization dedicated to serving low-income clients, don't fall into the trap of charging too little. Nonprofits often underestimate the costs of marketing, overestimate the number of prospects, and underprice their products. A rigorous market segmentation process should help you avoid these mistakes. Sharon Oster discusses pricing strategies in depth in her chapter in this volume.

With one or more target segments selected and a well-defined value proposition in place, the next step is to develop and implement a marketing action plan for your product or service, including pricing, distribution, and communication efforts; however, a detailed discussion of developing and implementing an action plan lies beyond the scope of the current chapter.

Parrett Paper's management team concluded that its best chance of success lay in positioning itself as a niche marketer, targeting its high-quality, animal-themed cards (each of which contained educational information about the animal depicted) at customers who visited gift shops in children's and natural history museums, aquariums, and zoos. This meant that its distribution strategy could focus on a set of stores that was relatively easy to identify and contact.

Because each card contained an educational message about the animal depicted on the front, Parrett Paper's merchandise met the IRS requirement for exempting these nonprofit institutions from paying income tax on the retail profits from selling them. Further, Parrett Paper believed that the managers of these nonprofit stores were more likely than those in regular stores to appreciate the mission of Rochester Rehabilitation Center and give Parrett Paper a chance. Recognizing that cards can be damaged on store racks, especially in low-volume stores, the firm decided to add a cellophane sleeve around each card. This sleeve saved the stores from the cost of having to throw away damaged cards and helped to distinguish Parrett Paper from competing suppliers. Although museum stores constituted the primary target segment, Parrett Paper also established contact with other prospective purchasers through participation in trade shows and development of catalogs for mailing.

The Role of Marketing Research

Throughout this chapter we have emphasized the importance of undertaking research and analysis before making strategic decisions. Yet nonprofits are often hesitant to invest significant resources in conducting market research studies. Apart from the cost and time involved, staff and board members are sometimes concerned that responding to pressure from the marketplace will alter the organization's mission. They may believe they know what is best for the organization and even naively conclude that customers are sure to feel as passionately about the organization and its offerings as they do. Unfortunately, the latter situation is rarely the case, particularly in situations where the organization is seeking to launch a for-profit venture.

A nonprofit may initially attract some customers for its for-profit venture because of its basic mission, but customers will return only if they are fully satisfied with the offering. The challenge is to recognize that customers often see things differently, reflecting their distinctive needs and preferences. Market research data can help you profile prospective customers and understand their needs and desires. This information can provide the direction you need to allocate resources efficiently and choose wisely among seemingly plausible options in shaping product and service features, targeting the most promising segments, selecting the optimal distribution channels, avoiding head-to-head contests with stronger competitors, and developing appropriate pricing and communication strategies.

Market research is also useful for monitoring the progress of your product or service in the marketplace following the initial launch, and for answering such questions as How satisfied are our customers? How do intermediaries feel about our products? Has there been any response by competitors? What changes do we need to make in product or service features? Should we revise our pricing policies or adopt a different approach to selling and promotion?

Sources of Market Information

Unlike major corporations, most nonprofits do not have large budgets for market research. Understanding and recognizing the limitations of each type of market research is essential in order to use management's time and your organization's money most effectively. Research has value only to the extent that the resulting information enables managers to make better decisions about how to market their products or services.

In other words, it is not worth investing resources to collect information that is "nice to know" but will have no impact on decision making. To justify such investments, it's also important to relate the level of spending more to the incremental value anticipated from making a better decision. For example, it would be unwise to commission a market research study costing $5,000 that is expected to improve sales revenues only by $3,000. Additionally, information must be timely because receiving information too late in the game can result in a wasted investment.

Information for marketing decisions can come from either primary or secondary sources. Primary data is information that is gathered for the purpose of making a specific marketing decision, such as a survey of prospective customers. By contrast, secondary data is information that was collected earlier for other purposes but can be used to solve the problem at hand. Because secondary data is more readily available, marketing research usually begins here. Primary sources may be used later as the need for more specific information becomes necessary.

Because secondary information already exists, it has several advantages over primary data. First, secondary data is readily available and can be obtained quickly, sometimes directly from the Internet. Second, it is often less costly to collect than primary data. Although some published reports are sold at a price, much secondary data, including many government statistics, is available free of charge. The disadvantages are that secondary data, having been collected for another purpose, may lack the desired precision and be out-of-date. But even when it is incomplete or inconclusive, secondary data may help to clarify potential new research needs and save you from having to reinvent the wheel. A good place to start is a topic search through an Internet search engine such as www.google.com.

Parrett Paper was able to gain quickly a good understanding of the greeting card market from a review of external secondary data sources. These sources included several published reports, including one from the Greeting Card Association. Visits to the Web sites of existing suppliers were also helpful, and useful information was obtained from the Web site of the American Zoo and Aquarium Association. Parrett Paper also learned a great deal from attending regional trade shows across the country. Participation in these shows served both marketing and research purposes. At these shows, Parrett

Paper displayed its products and promoted them to prospective purchasers. It was also able to examine competitive offerings and learn about the preferences and purchasing behavior of different types of consumers and stores from conversations with store representatives.

After one year a review of internal records showed that Parrett Paper had generated revenues of $56,415 during 2002 on a base of 255 outlets. These sales included both cards and gift tags. Card sales to the zoo, aquariums, and museum store niche accounted for 30 percent of all revenues. Other key sources of sales were small gift shops and the Container Store, which was a substantial purchaser of Parrett Paper gift tags.

Based on 2002 benchmarks, Parrett Paper set ambitious sales goals for future years, seeking to achieve profitability by 2004. In the meantime, it reported that card assembly had provided work for six employees of The Out-Source during 2002.

Conclusion

New ventures start with the odds stacked against them. You can improve your organization's chances for success through intensive screening of proposed new products and services to weed out ideas that are unlikely to work or that represent a poor fit with the organization's skills. Objectivity and realism are essential ingredients to this exercise. If you decide to launch a new offering, you will need to develop a research-based marketing plan that reflects a disciplined approach to market and competitive analysis. In particular, you should focus your marketing efforts by targeting customers in one or more carefully chosen market segments and by learning as much as you can about what they are looking for, what their buying criteria are, and how they purchase. If target customers are best reached through intermediaries, then you will have to research the needs and expectations of these businesses too. Your challenge will then be to differentiate your offering from competing alternatives so that your venture can meet customers' needs, preferences, and expectations better than anyone else's.

Notes

1. "Greeting Card and Stationery, 2002—Greeting Card and Stationery Report: The Market, the Industry, the Trends." Stevens, Pa.: Unity Marketing, 2002.
2. *The U.S. Greeting Card Market*. New York: Packaged Facts, 1998.

CHAPTER FIVE

PRICING GOODS AND SERVICES

Sharon M. Oster

Earned income ventures inevitably involve pricing some kind of good or service. For some organizations, this is their first experience with pricing. This chapter explores some of the strategies for pricing goods and services of nonprofit enterprises. As will be shown, the fact that these goods or services are offered through nonprofit enterprises creates challenges that are absent from free-standing commercial ventures, and we will explore these as well.

Setting the Stage

There are three broad categories of issues to consider in setting prices. First are the ideological questions: Is it suitable for your organization to charge a price for something? Is it culturally appropriate to charge a price for something? In considering an earned income venture, answering these ideological questions is the first hurdle. Second are some practical issues. My favorite example of these involves swing sets in the park. When my children were little, we often used to go to the park. On occasion, all the swings were occupied by other small children. Many of you undoubtedly have had the same experience. If like me you were an economist and in that park, the main thing you would be thinking as you stood there is, "If they only charged a price for swinging, one of these children would get off sooner." But of course charging a price per hour to swing is typically not very practical. Often the park is empty and the ticket taker would have nothing to do; when people do come to the park they often come empty-handed, and so on. As it turns out, in many parts of the nonprofit world, as in parks, it simply is not practical to charge a price for something. So, in starting an earned income venture, the practicality of pricing is an important consideration.

Finally, the third set of issues involved in pricing are the business-oriented economic issues. This chapter concentrates on this set of issues, though we do not avoid completely either ideology or practical matters. Within economics we focus on three questions. The first is the simplest: If you have a good or service, how do you think about setting a price? In particular, we explore some of the simple economics of determining the right price for a good or service, including both theoretical aspects and practical techniques.

We then move to a somewhat more sophisticated set of pricing issues: Under what circumstances should prices vary by customer type or product version? Consider the situation of the Benhaven Learning Network, a new earned income venture developed by a school for autistic children in Connecticut. The Learning Network offers consulting services to public school systems in Connecticut for working with autistic children in a classroom setting. At present Benhaven Learning Network charges a fixed, constant price to all school districts, yet Connecticut is a highly diverse state, with some of the wealthiest cities in the nation and some of the poorest. Should Benhaven price-discriminate among the school districts it serves, charging different prices to different sites? In what kinds of situations can an organization charge some segments of its audience one price and other segments a different price? What techniques can be used by an organization seeking to implement differentiated prices? Under what conditions do more complex pricing structures help or hamper an organization's mission?

Finally, we explore the conditions under which one might create collections of goods and services, bundle them together, and price that bundle. We look at both bundles of similar or related goods—such as a series of concerts—and bundles of rather disparate goods, such as hotels bundled with airfare. Why do organizations create bundles? When are they revenue enhancing? What are the practical issues involved? Consider an arts organization that produces a season of concerts. Should it create a miniseries combining Mozart with Bartok? Mozart and Schubert? Or no miniseries at all? Should New York's Guggenheim Museum sell a pass to its Soho site bundled with a ticket to the midtown museum? When should an organization bundle over time, for instance, by creating membership products that allow individuals to use the services of the organization as much as they want for a single fixed fee? These are complicated topics and we lay out some of the most important considerations, providing examples as we move along.

Setting the Right Price

In instituting a price for something that was previously given away or in raising an existing price, the first principle to consider is the relationship between the quantity sold and the price charged. In most circumstances, if an organization raises its price for a good or service, it will sell a little bit less of it. This observation is at the core of what economists have to say about prices. When prices go up, volumes sold decline. The harder question, and the one that will matter in finding the right price, is just how much that volume will go down. The answer to this central question, to what extent do customers respond to price increases or decreases, involves an idea that economists call *elasticity*. The price elasticity of a product in a market is a measure of how responsive the customers in that market are to a price change. As it turns out, whether it is a good idea from a revenue generating point of view to raise or lower prices depends on elasticity. For an unresponsive or inelastic market, price increases are attractive because, faced with higher prices, few customers leave, so the organization generates higher fees from an only slightly diminished clientele. With an elastic market, price increases "cost" the organization too much in terms of lost customers. So, the heart of the economic theory of the right price is knowing the shape of the demand curve. The economic theory of pricing says that demand curves slope down; that is, demand decreases as price increases. The hard part is figuring out how much they slope down.

Fortunately there is some guidance about what one might expect the shape of the demand curve to be. Consider a situation in which a nonprofit has just begun a new venture. The El Puente Community Development Corporation is a small nonprofit in El Paso, Texas, that focuses on the plight of workers displaced by the movement of manufacturing facilities from the Texas border to Mexico. One of their new earned income ventures is Diseños Mayapán, a manufacturing facility that employs displaced workers to make medical scrubs. How should El Puente think about setting a price for those scrubs in order to meet their goal of establishing a viable profit-making venture?

Prior to EL Puente's entrance into the market, many of the health care providers they hope to service were purchasing from other suppliers. In general, whenever a new good or service enters the market, people must be convinced to buy the product rather than whatever they were buying earlier. Similarly, whenever an organization raises the price for an existing product, it must hope that customers remain loyal. Thus, the first task in thinking about price setting is to evaluate the substitutes available. It is for this reason, among others, that there is always a prominent section in business plans that describes the competition. That section lays the groundwork for determining price elasticity; it helps answer the question of what potential and actual customers will do when faced with a new set of prices. The greater the number of substitutes and the more closely they resemble your product, the stronger will be the price response.

A second feature of a product and its market that affects elasticity is the demographics of the user base. People are not equally price-sensitive. On average, for a given good or service, people of higher incomes tend to be a little less responsive to a price increase than people with less income. Scojo Foundation is a New York-based nonprofit whose mission is to improve the health and welfare of disadvantaged populations, particularly with respect to their eyesight. The Foundation's current business venture proposes selling nonprescription reading glasses to the visually impaired in various provinces of India. Because potential consumers are not equally price sensitive, Scojo's plan sets different prices for clients according to province, in part to exploit differential elasticities associated with different economic levels.

Note, however, that a nonprofit's high-income customers are not necessarily willing to pay any price for a good or service. Even the wealthy care about prices. Yet another product feature that influences elasticity is the essentiality of the product or service. From the customer's point of view, the more essential something is, the fewer substitutes there are for it outside of the product class. As a result, unless there are good substitutes within the class, price increases are likely to stick. This suggests that arts organizations, even with some local monopoly power, will likely have more trouble with price increases than organizations with similar power in the health care arena, all else being equal, because people are less likely to find satisfactory substitutes or options for health-related purchases than for art-related ones. Consumers interested in art can more naturally shift their demand to other forms of entertainment than can consumers of health care. In the case of El Puente, for most of the health care providers in the potential customer base, scrubs are an essential item. As a result, in setting prices, El Puente can focus its attention on other producers of scrubs. In the absence of such direct competitors, prices are likely to be relatively inelastic.

A fourth factor affecting elasticity is the period under scrutiny. Reactions immediately after a price change may not be the same as longer-run responses. Consider consumer reaction to an increase in the price of gasoline. The short-term response has been found to be very modest. But for price increases sustained over a longer period, elasticities are higher because people are able to make adjustments in their work and living patterns, for example. Stockpiling behavior can also cause elasticities to be misread. Suppose El Puente experimented with a large price cut for its scrubs. The immediate response might be quite large as hospitals stock up on scrubs. But El Puente would be quite misled if they did not realize that part of the week's sales would be offset by lower sales in the future as hospitals used the inventories they acquired. A price decrease can move demand across time, as opposed to simply increasing the steady state level. In other words, when we have a sale on a good or service, we may simply increase the amount that people buy now but reduce their future purchases by an equal amount. In such a situation the price decrease yields no net gain for the organization. While inventory build up is less likely in the service businesses that many nonprofits are in, there are still some examples with which to be concerned.

Before we proceed to more practical techniques for determining elasticity, there is one last observation to make: *Cliff-edge effects* occur when prices go from zero to a small number. A number of for-profit dot-com firms have experienced these effects, as have many nonprofits when they begin to charge a fee for their goods or services. The early evidence seems to be that customers' purchasing declines or stops completely when sellers charge even a small amount where they had charged nothing before. Once customers are used to paying even a modest fee, however, increases in that fee may create little response in customer behavior.

Let's turn now to the more practical issues: How does an organization like El Puente decide just what price to charge for its scrubs, given the general predictions about elasticities that it develops? The first task is to consider the competition. What products similar to yours are out there and at what price are they being sold? Some nonprofits face less local competition for the programs they offer because there may not be other organizations providing the same product in the same geographic area and there may be few substitutes. One rarely sees the "four-gas-stations-on-the-corner" pattern in nonprofits that one observes in for-profits. Moreover, on average, nonprofits tend to be more differentiated than for-profits, and this also mutes price competition. Conversely, looking at nonprofit enterprises, one can see the many gas stations on the corner. The competition, then, translates into more price sensitivity than the typical nonprofit parent is accustomed to experiencing.

What can one do to set correct prices other than examine the competition? Another possibility is to experiment over time. In this arena, as with many things in life, it is easier to go down than to go up. The general intuition is simple: if you get people used to a low price, you just make them mad if you raise the price; but if you start them with a high price, you can encourage them to think they are getting a bargain by lowering the price. The main exception to this rule is in what economists have come to call network businesses, in which being first with customers gives a firm a long-lived edge in the business. If building an early base in the business is important, starting low and raising prices as you increase your customer appeal may be a better strategy. Otherwise, start a tad high and come down.

It is also possible to experiment over space. A number of businesses offer similar products for sale in different places. Organizations can use test markets to see empirically what the elasticity is, remembering to be careful that the different areas are close enough to each other in customer profile to make the lessons transferable. In the U.S. for-profit world there are cities that serve as test markets again and again because they are thought to represent the "typical" American city. For nonprofits with a broad geographic reach it is useful to think a little about whether there is a neighborhood or market segment in which experimenting would yield transferable lessons.

Finally, experimenting with related products can be very useful. Consider the arts organization running a music series in which the works of different composers are offered. To determine elasticity here, try raising or lowering the price of the Mozart but not the price of the more contemporary, unknown piece. See what can be learned about the price sensitivity of the rest of the product mix from small increments of change. Ultimately you will likely find that a search for optimal prices is a trial-and-error process, conducted with guidance.

Thus far we have focused on setting prices by looking at the demand side of the market—how much people are willing to pay for a given good or service. But of course costs will matter as well. In fact, many sellers begin by looking at the cost side and then asking whether customers will pay a price high enough to cover all the costs of production. In beginning here the hardest task is to make sure that you are considering the "right" costs in price-setting.

The key cost-side feature of price setting for a new product is to ensure that the price of the new product or service at least covers the incremental cost of producing it. What do we mean by incremental cost? For most goods or services, production requires some added workforce and raw materials; these are part of the additional or incremental costs that must be covered. They are also called variable costs, because they are based on the number of goods or services produced. To the extent that any of the other organizational assets—such as space or use of a van—are diverted to this new use when they could profitably be used in an alternative activity, the cost of these organizational assets must be considered too. Conversely, for costs that are truly fixed—executive director salaries or insurance, for example—a new product does not have to cover a portion of these costs to nevertheless be worthwhile. The following example helps to demonstrate this concept.

The National Foundation for Teaching Entrepreneurship (NFTE) is a New York-based nonprofit that teaches entrepreneurship to inner-city young people to improve their academic and life skills. NFTE offers a series of programs, including some directed at teaching the teachers. Each of the programs is priced to cover the instructional cost, including workbooks, teachers, rental space, and so on. Conversely, though all require some attention from Steve Marriotti, the executive director of NFTE and his team, there is no attempt to apportion equally the overhead costs related to him. Instead, the demand-side factors we described earlier are used to determine how much above the incremental costs NFTE can set its prices. In this way, some goods or services offered for sale by an organization will make a large contribution to overhead costs, and others will help less. Again, as long as incremental costs are covered, new goods or services will help the economics of the venture.

Before turning to a discussion of price structures, it is useful to remind ourselves of some of the complexities of pricing in the nonprofit world—complexities that involve both the mission of the nonprofit and its multiple revenue sources. The discussion thus far has focused on choosing price levels by taking into account the number of customers lost at varying levels. Yet regardless of how strategic a nonprofit is in raising prices, some consumption will be lost, and the loss of these customers may differentially affect the nonprofit. Typically, the standard commercial venture asks itself a simple profit-maximizing question: How many people have I lost relative to the revenue increase I've gotten from raising the price to the people who stayed? This is a very simple calculation and undergirds the discussion thus far in this chapter. For firms with most costs structures, if one raises the price by 10 percent and loses 5 percent of customers, that is a good deal profitwise. But consider the nonprofit that is raising the fee it charges for one of its program-related services. For this nonprofit, losing that 5 percent may be too much.

Why might the nonprofit be different than the for-profit on this matter? First, there are mission-driven reasons, particularly if the clients lost are especially in need. Nonprofits often care about who they serve, not just how many. Clients who drop out may have adverse effects on their communities as a whole. Recent experiments on user fees for medical treatments in less developed countries have at times resulted in substantial losses in use; for interventions around contagious ailments such as vaccinations and worm medications, a loss in patients may create multiplicative adverse effects in later periods.[1]

Second, raising the fee for a product or service and subsequently losing customers may have effects on other revenue streams of the organization. Some grantmaking organizations use volume as an evaluation metric. Here, even if price increases result in only a small client drop, the nonprofit may end up with a revenue reduction on the grant. Note, however, that in some cases funders actually create incentives for the imposition of user fees. Consider the situation of the Stanley Isaacs Neighborhood Center in New York City. The Center offers meals to seniors and receives a percentage of the cost of each meal from the city of New York. The Center suggests a voluntary donation or fee of $1 toward the cost of each meal. The city of New York expects that the Center will raise $25,000 toward the cost of the meals, and if it does not, that sum is pulled out of city monies that are allocated to the Center. So, the earned income side of the nonprofit can have either positive or negative multiplier effects once funders are considered.

An additional complication comes from the cost side of the operation. Thus far the discussion has focused on revenues, but of course what really matters is profitability in terms of price setting. For organizations with substantial fixed costs, losing a few customers costs more than expected in that it limits the organization's ability to spread fixed costs across all its clients or customers.

Finally, there may be crowding-out effects. As nonprofits increase their earned income, funders and donors may begin to cut back their own contributions. One of the places these effects occur is in private school tuition where a subset of the potential donors is current parents who are experiencing large tuition increases. In most parts of this country, private school tuition has outpaced inflation in the last decade and there has been no diminution in demand. Yet some of the same parents who are willing to pay high tuitions are reducing their voluntary contributions—and that means, of course, that raising the tuition is not as attractive as it would be in a single-revenue-source organization.

We turn now to consider price structures. The next section explores the ways in which differentiating a price structure can ameliorate some of the problems of customer loss while simultaneously enhancing venture revenues.

Differentiated Prices

Economists use the rather unfortunate term *price discrimination* to refer to any situation in which an organization sells identical goods to different people for different prices. Such discrimination is the lifeblood of many nonprofits, allowing for a form of cross-subsidization that serves both the ideology and the economics of those nonprofits. This section describes the theory behind such price discrimination, and some techniques for implementing it.

Consider the problem we described earlier as the downside of raising prices: losing customers. Now suppose we construct a way to charge different prices to different people. What do we want to do? The economic answer is simple: identify those people who are price inelastic and raise their prices, while leaving unchanged the prices facing more elastic demanders. Employing this strategy yields the seller more revenue with fewer lost clients than a strategy with a more modest price increase to everybody. Note that there is also a potential mission gain because many nonprofits value client use, particularly in the arts and education, and this price discrimination will help to preserve use. Furthermore, it is often the case that again the people who are most inelastic are the people with the most resources, so there are potential redistribution benefits as well. On the positive side, then, price discrimination allows for increased revenues, with lower customer losses and some positive redistribution. The one fly in the ointment, as we will see shortly in our discussion of real discrimination techniques, is a perception of unfairness that may crop up.

What are the keys to designing a discriminatory price structure? From an economics perspective, the key requirement for an effective pricing structure is to prevent arbitrage. That is, we must prevent the customers who buy our product at one price from reselling it to the customers targeted for a higher price. In the case of the reading glasses sold by Scojo in India, discussed earlier, one potential barrier to the organization's articulated strategy of charging different prices in the different provinces is the possibility of itinerant salespeople cropping up, buying glasses in the low-price provinces, and reselling them in the higher-priced areas. From an ideological and political perspective, price discrimination works best if it is at least somewhat voluntary either because it has been connected to the mission or because it results from self-selection. Again, fairness will be key here. In the following paragraphs we describe examples of each method.

In practice there are a number of ways in which price discrimination occurs. In education, discrimination based on ability to pay is common. At private universities like Yale, with need-blind admissions policies whereby students are accepted regardless of their ability to cover the full price of admission, the price of a year's education can vary from close to zero to more than thirty thousand dollars. In these schools, all families that want a tuition discount fully disclose their financial situations (their income and assets), and this information is used to generate a price. Imagine a similar situation at the Bronx Zoo. The zoo understands fully that the ability of its patrons to pay varies widely. Suppose we required people who came to the Bronx Zoo gate to bring their tax forms to see what admission fee they would be charged. That's the way the zoo at Yale is organized. Parents bring their 1099s to the gate and the Yale admissions people say, "For you, the price is $2,000, and for you it'll be $34,000." In fact, in premier U.S. colleges, Gordon Winston and David Zimmerman have found that more than half of the tuition increases in the last couple of decades have been redistributed to people who are most capable of absorbing the premium value.[2] From an economics perspective, the nice feature of this discrimination plan is that the higher income people are also likely the most inelastic demanders! The consequence of the price discrimination is a full class with high revenues (but not the highest possible revenues, because some pay less than full price).

What allows Yale to price-discriminate in this way? Preventing arbitrage is easy: admission to a school is not transferable. You can't trade your acceptance to Harvard to somebody else. One of the impediments to ticket-oriented organizations in using price discrimination is precisely the arbitrage opportunities: the individual who buys a cheap ticket to the Mozart concert can resell it, a possibility that fore-closes the symphony's opportunity to sell higher-priced tickets. For education—and indeed for many services—transference is more difficult and thus price discrimination is somewhat easier to implement.

To make this kind of individual-by-individual price discrimination work, or-ganizations also have to be able to identify people by their ability to pay. Schools can do this, though it is a time-consuming process that makes sense only if the in-dividuals are already being scrutinized and if the volume of customers is relatively low. For the Bronx Zoo, sorting through the financial forms at the zoo's gate is an impractical idea, even if one could prevent ticket resale. Conversely, for some or-ganizations group membership is a reasonable proxy for ability to pay. For example, it may be possible for the zoo to offer lower discounts to schools that are outside New York City than they offer to New York public schools because schools out-side New York might not otherwise come or buy, given the additional transporta-tion costs associated with the purchase. When it comes to price discrimination, thinking outside the box is a very useful exercise.

We turn now to the issue of fairness in this form of discrimination. In the case of college tuition, there has clearly been some backlash. Parents seeking tuition aid often argue, for example, that if they save up money to pay tuition, they are penalized for it because they will get less aid. For the colleges, discrimination is difficult in part because the slope is steep and the levels of payment at the top are quite high indeed. So what can organizations do to try to make this form of dis-crimination easier to swallow? One answer clearly involves an attempt to connect the price discrimination to the broader educational quality, to make the case that attracting a diverse group of kids from all economic backgrounds is central to the educational product that is being delivered to all of the students. For a school to manage price discrimination successfully, it is important to sing this song. Many schools also point out that even at the top end of the price scale, students typically are not paying the full cost of their education, though calculating the true full costs of an education is rather difficult. Of course, in the case of the premier colleges and preparatory schools, it is helpful that the overall demand for these services is so high.

A second form of price discrimination is based on category of payer. The medical profession has honed this form of discrimination to a fine art. The price to a given patient for an appendectomy at a specific hospital on a specific day, for example, depends on who is paying. There is one price to an HMO, another price to Medicaid or Medicare, a third price to a private insurer, and a fourth to any-one unfortunate enough to have to pay out-of-pocket. These fees all result from elaborate bargaining processes in which the hospitals try to judge, payer by payer, price elasticity. Note again that the service is not transferable and that the deals are made with relatively large buyers so there are relatively modest transactions costs in setting up the discriminatory apparatus. In the medical arena, the fact that it is mostly third parties (government or insurers) who pay the fees helps to reduce the political backlash of claims of unfairness, though in recent years the government has become restive when it does not get the lowest rates.

The final form of price discrimination involves offering closely related versions of the product or service with the intention of reaping substantially higher profit margins on some versions than on others. This form of discrimination is an imperfect one because the products or services sold are not identical. Nevertheless, since the intention is to use the product or service variations to help exploit differential elasticities, it is useful to discuss it here. In the literature this form of discrimination is sometimes called *versioning*.

The cleanest example of how versioning works is from the software arena. Consider a firm that has developed a data management program with many bells and whistles. Making that program available, with all of its features, to all customers costs nothing. Nevertheless, most firms producing programs offer not only the full-featured version but a stripped-down edition. The two versions are offered at widely different prices. The key in this process is to make sure that the bells and whistles left in the better model are essential to the inelastic user and matter little to the more elastic user. For example, a data management program may come with a larger or smaller capacity, a feature that helps sort business users from student users. An accounting program may or may not include modules for depreciation, again discriminating small from larger businesses. Note that the entire function of the multiple versions is to allow the software firm to segment its market, thus generating large revenues from the higher priced clients without losing the patronage of the more elastic customers. If you can figure out how to add something to your product that will be very appealing to one segment of your population and not really matter in the least to another segment, this feature can be used effectively to price-discriminate. Moreover—and this is also important in terms of viability—the price discrimination will be self-imposed by clients.

In the nonprofit world, arts organizations are longtime users of versioning. For example, consider health facilities in social service organizations, such as Jewish Community Centers. Many offer standard equipment in their fitness centers for all members and additional amenities (such as trainers, private showers, towels, and so on) in their executive fitness centers for an added membership fee. Or to use another example from the arts world, how much do you pay to go to a concert? It depends. Are you seeing it on a Wednesday night, Tuesday night, or Thursday afternoon? Are you sitting in the back row, front row, or middle row? Were you given a fancy brochure? Is someone sprinkling stardust in your hair while you watch? There are many versions of a given concert and all cost different amounts.

In some cases, of course, the price differences reflect scarcity. Here, arts organizations are using a form of yield management that is used by the airline industry, where customers are attracted by lower prices to flights that have excess capacity and that the airline would like to fill. In part, theaters are using prices to drive customers from Saturday night to Wednesday night. In other words, these organizations are using pricing to increase the overall yield by enticing customers to move to "versions" where demand is not as strong. But what is also happening is that products are being designed with the relative elasticities of various customers in mind.

The versioning form of price discrimination has another feature that helps make it work: on the whole, it is voluntary. That is, individuals effectively choose which piece of software to buy or where to sit in the concert hall or when to go to the theater. Even when theater tickets vary in price depending on whether they are bought early or at the last minute, and even though we can then have two people sitting side-by-side who have paid quite different prices, there is some recognition by clients that this allocation is reasonably fair.

We have now provided some sense of the widely different forms that price discrimination can take, and we have recognized that for many nonprofits such discrimination is a central part of strategic price setting. We turn now to a related form of pricing known as *bundling*.

Bundled Prices: Membership and Series

There are two broad types of bundling to consider. First, an organization may wish to sell, as a bundle, unlimited rights to use its services or products. Typically we think of this bundle type as *membership rights*. Memberships that come with use rights are common in museums, for example, as well as in a range of private-sector organizations such as health clubs and golf clubs. A second form of bundling involves the selling in one package of two or more different products otherwise sold separately. Bundles may vary from quite related products, say a series of concerts, to quite disparate products, such as a museum trip and Coca-Cola.

Consider first the membership market. Memberships are, of course, in part a device for developing a donor community. But for some organizations membership actually plays another role as well. It provides a reduced per-visit price to local customers who are likely to be most price sensitive. Once one has bought a membership, admission is free. Why is this form of membership so good for museums? First of all, museums have excess capacity, so if members visit ten times a year rather than five times because it costs them nothing once the fixed fee is paid, that creates no incremental cost for the museum. Indeed, from a mission perspective the increased visitation is a good thing. Rule one, then, is that free-use memberships are especially useful for organizations with zero incremental costs of service.

These memberships have other useful features as well. They discriminate against tourists, who tend to be the more inelastic users. Most tourists will not visit a city often enough in a year to make a membership worthwhile, but once they have paid to come to a destination city, they are likely relatively inelastic in terms of their per-day visit fees. Few art-loving visitors from Asia are likely to give up a visit to the Metropolitan or Getty Museum because the admission fee is too high. In this way, a modest membership fee coupled with a high daily rate exploits the elasticity differences in the two populations.

Museums have another feature that make memberships especially useful, a feature that has only recently been analyzed by economists. Consider the health club market. Recent work suggests that if you actually look at most health club memberships, they are not a good value given use rates. Most individuals would be economically better off if they simply paid on a per-use basis. So why do people buy these memberships? A recent article offers two possibilities: On average people have unrealistic expectations for themselves (that is, they expect to use the club often), or they know they are weak and they buy memberships to try to induce themselves to exercise more.[3] In any case, customers will embrace memberships for these virtuous goods. Behavioral economists define virtuous goods as product and service attributes that are particularly attractive to the consumer's sense of self. Museums are exactly the type of product that people like to think of themselves consuming. In making the calculation just described, most people will overestimate use rate and thus be willing to pay more for a membership than they should. For nonprofits selling less virtuous goods, memberships may be less attractive as a pricing strategy.

For this form of membership to make sense, the nonprofit should also be selling a good or service that individuals wish to consume reasonable quantities of at a zero price. Health clubs and general art museums both have this property. For a more specialized museum, or the zoo, optimal use for most people may well be only a few times per year. For these products, this form of quantity-based membership program is not likely to work.

There are clear applications of this bundling principle outside the art sector. For many job training programs, clients are expected to pay a modest fee, both for cost-recovery and to demonstrate commitment to the program. The lessons we have just described suggest that, wherever possible, fees for the whole program should be tendered ahead of time. Clients are more likely to be willing to pay for the employment training before the arduous training begins, and having made the prior investment, clients are more likely to follow through with the training.

This discussion of memberships and bundling also points to some lessons in setting the right membership price. For low-end memberships, the rate should be set with an eye toward expected use. Nonprofits should be strategic in recognizing that for many people memberships are a tool for extracting a sale price and not principally a means of donating funds. And nonprofits should recognize that a premium can be extracted for virtuous goods.

Bundling is increasingly common in both the nonprofit and for-profit worlds and can serve a range of purposes. Consider now the second form of bundling—selling two or more products together.

Consider the example of a nonprofit organization that operates a live radio station on which there is all-day reading to people who are visually impaired. The station is transmitted through a one-knob radio, given at quite low rates to people who become members of the program. To supplement revenues from the membership fees, the organization runs a fundraiser, a guide dog walkathon in which people with guide dogs walk around the track, paying per mile. The organization encourages people with normal vision to walk as well, also for a fee. When the organization tried to raise the per-mile price, it found that it differentially lost its blind walkers. The solution? Station members—all of whom were visually impaired, because otherwise the station was of little interest—were given a preferred rate; in other words, membership and the walkathon were bundled. Here the bundling served as a form of price discrimination, done quite cleverly, without taking anything away from the dignity of the population—another important element in price discrimination schemes.

Bundling disparate products together can also serve a second function, one that I call "putting a vitamin pill in the middle of a treat." For example, for many concertgoers, later classical music, particularly the more atonal pieces, is less appealing than Mozart or early Beethoven. To the extent that this is in part due to lack of exposure, one solution is to insert more modern work into the middle of a more standard program. In many situations, both for-profit and nonprofit, bundling is done as a way to develop markets for the long run, coupling new products with more established brands. In the for-profit arena, coupons to a new product are sometimes offered with the purchase of more well-established brands, in a variant of the bundling method. Nonprofits may well find that offering discount coupons or reduced fees for new offerings to their existing customers will create new customer patterns.

Finally, bundling can also serve to increase an organization's ability to extract revenue from a market by effectively flattening the demand curve somewhat. Suppose an organization is selling two products, perhaps a Jazz concert and a Chinese Opera. Assume that there is plenty of seating capacity and that the potential audience is such that some fraction would pay a lot for jazz but very little for the

Chinese opera, while the other half has the reverse preferences. Given these disparate tastes, the organization can choose to charge a very low price for both events, hoping to attract the full audience to both. Or it can choose to set rates high, sell only to the fans of the event, and have a half-empty theater. Bundling offers a third option. The theater can offer a package or bundle for the two events to two types of patrons, at a price that is just under the sum of the value of the two concerts. While the patrons look quite different when we think about the concerts as individual items, their willingness to pay for the bundle will look quite similar. They will differ only in which of the two events gives most value to the bundle for them. As a general matter, bundling together rather different products may be revenue enhancing for organizations that have ample capacity and are trying to serve disparate populations.

Conclusion

Nonprofit organizations often approach pricing with something akin to embarrassment; managers know it is an important part of raising revenues but remain concerned about the effects of price on service use. This chapter has provided some guidance in setting prices with an eye to both revenue enhancement and mission.

In many cases the two sides of revenue enhancement and mission are reinforcing and not at war. Given the centrality of price setting to fees-for-service and new earned income ventures, it is useful to add a brief word on some of the other attractive features of pricing. There are a number of side benefits from charging fees that are not always appreciated in the sector. Charging a fee can, for example, help control congestion. One of the problems commonly seen in a number of nonprofits is a slavish adherence to low prices, resulting in crowded conditions that degrade the quality of service to all clients. In addition, there is strong evidence in the psychological counseling arena, for example, that forcing people to pay a little bit means they have more of a stake in what you're doing. For many nonprofits in the helping services, client empowerment may be very important. Pricing can help remind people that they are consuming something that is valuable and that they ought to do their part in making sure it has some kind of an impact. Charging a price can also empower staff to think about clients as customers.

In many ways, the complexity of the nonprofit world allows for much more creativity in designing pricing than does the for-profit world. In exploring this terrain, there are a few final lessons to keep in mind. First, in setting and charging prices it is essential to distinguish between client need and customer demand. As a nonprofit organization you may well see the need among your clients for a particular good or service, but you will not generate any revenue unless there is an associated demand or willingness to pay. Second, in setting prices it is essential to distinguish between demand for the good or service overall and demand for your own organization's version of that good. Many nonprofits likely have far fewer competitors for their core programmatic activities than they have for their earned income ventures. Finally, strategic pricing can offer nonprofit organizations a range of benefits in addition to revenue generation—benefits that they can realize with careful thought about the complex missions they seek to achieve.

Notes

1. Kremer, M., and Miguel, E. "Worms: Identifying Impacts on Education and Health." *Econometrica*, forthcoming.

2. Winston, G., and Zimmerman, D. "Where Is Aggressive Price Competition Taking Higher Education?" Williams College Working Paper, Williamstown, Mass.: Williams College, 2000.

3. Della Vigna, S., and Malamadier, U. "Self-Control in the Market: Evidence from the Health Club Industry." Working Paper. Cambridge, Mass.: National Bureau of Economic Research, 2002.

CHAPTER SIX

LEGAL AND TAX CONSIDERATIONS

William H. Heritage Jr. and Timothy J. Orlebeke

When you have defined your business purpose and commenced essential business planning steps such as identifying your target market, developing product and delivery costing estimates, and estimating required human material resources, it is appropriate to analyze the legal and tax considerations of your new venture. Sensible decision making about the form of your business organization will help to avoid future problems of various kinds and greatly increase the likelihood that the planned venture will succeed. Success in this context means creating benefits for a nonprofit entity without causing concomitant adversity that undercuts the parent organization's tax-exempt status or its community standing or otherwise interferes with the organization's central purpose. The legal structure of a business can affect the tax-exempt status of the parent organization, the taxability of its profits, the extent of control retained or lost by the parent organization, and even the business's community image. The choices your nonprofit makes for the venture should be informed by these considerations, and also by your parent organization's goals and values. This chapter presents and discusses legal and tax issues that arise when a nonprofit entity forms and operates a business venture. The

The authors would like to thank their client, the Inner City Christian Federation (ICCF), for the opportunity to write this chapter, which came about in great part because of the creation of ICCF's mortgage business and subsequent entry into the Partnership on Nonprofit Venture's National Business Plan Competition for Nonprofit Organizations.

goal is to provide information that will help you adopt the strategy most likely to meet your organization's specific needs.

Profitable Activities by Nonprofits

Nonprofit, tax-exempt corporations exist not to make money but to fulfill one of the purposes recognized by federal law as justifying their tax exemption. Initially, then, it seems incongruous to discuss how tax-exempt nonprofits should deal with taxation of their profits. Under state and federal tax laws, however, as long as a nonprofit corporation is organized and operated for a recognized tax-exempt, nonprofit purpose and has secured the proper tax exemptions, it can take in more money than it spends to conduct its activities. The nonprofit terminology for this condition is an *excess of revenues over expenses*. In other words, without forming another business entity, a nonprofit can make a profit, depending on the source of that profit. Whether or not a nonprofit's income is taxable depends on whether the activities are related to the nonprofit's tax-exempt purpose and whether they are "regularly carried on" according to the Internal Revenue Code's definition of the phrase. This is a matter not of choice but rather of law and regulations. (For more detail, see the section called "A Word About Terminology and Definitions" near the end of this chapter.)

Tax-Exempt Revenues from Related Activities

Tax-exempt nonprofits often make money as a result of their activities and use it to cover expenses. In fact, this income can be essential to an organization's survival. As long as a nonprofit's activities are related to its purpose, any profit made from them is not taxable. An activity is ordinarily considered substantially related (that is, not unrelated) to the corporation's exempt purposes if it contributes to the accomplishment of those purposes other than through the production of income. An art museum, for example, may produce nontaxable profit from selling reproductions of its own art, either in its own museum shop or through catalog sales. That same shop, though, may be taxed on income it produces from the highly profitable sale of unrelated local souvenirs. The income-generating activity is not substantially related simply because the nonprofit needs the funds that it generates and will put them toward charitable purposes or because it occurs side by side with a qualified tax-exempt enterprise.

Revenue from related commercial activities can be used by the nonprofit for general or specific funding needs but may not be used for the benefit of officers, directors, or other principals of the nonprofit other than in the form of legitimate and reasonable salaries.

Making a Profit from Unrelated Business Activities

Sometimes nonprofits make money in ways that are not related to their nonprofit purposes. While nonprofits can usually earn unrelated business income without jeopardizing their nonprofit status, they have to pay corporate income taxes on it, under both state and federal corporate tax rules. Generally the first $1,000 of unrelated income is not taxed, but the remainder is.

A nonprofit that operates a regular trade or business unrelated to its tax-exempt purposes is taxed on these business earnings, known as Unrelated Business Taxable Income (UBTI).[1] The definition of UBTI contains numerous exceptions that may be relevant to the nonprofit, including the following:

- Activities in which nearly all the work is done by volunteers
- Activities carried on primarily for the benefit of members, students, patients, officers or employees (such as a hospital gift shop for patients and employees)
- Sales of merchandise that has mostly been donated to the nonprofit (such as a thrift store)
- Rental or exchange of mailing lists of donors or members, and distribution of items worth less than $5 as incentives for donating money (such as stamps or preprinted mailing labels)

In addition, the very definition of UBTI may offer relief to a nonprofit seeking to avoid imposition of tax on its business revenues. An unrelated business or trade is any trade or business that is regularly carried on and not substantially related to the corporation's exempt purposes. The activity is "regularly carried on" if it is conducted at a frequency and with a continuity comparable to the commercial activities of for-profit ventures. In other words, unless the business activity is a type that is excluded from the definition of unrelated business, a nonprofit's commercial income may be taxed as unrelated business income if the business activity is regularly carried on and is not substantially related to exempt purposes.

Thus, for example, a nonprofit tax-exempt developer of low-income housing may, without incurring tax on unrelated business activity, accept a one-time donation of a house that it then rehabilitates and sells on the open market for a substantial profit. The activity in question is not subject to tax on UBTI because the rehabilitation and sale of homes to the general public is not an activity that is "regularly carried on" by the exempt organization. The result would be completely different if, on a frequent and ongoing basis, the organization received donated properties, rehabilitated them using the tax-exempt organization's resources, and sold them for a profit.

In addition, certain types of nonprofit income are excluded from UBTI unless the income is debt-financed. Categories of UBTI excluded income include the following:

- Dividends, interest, payments with respect to securities loans and annuities, and royalties
- Most rents from real property
- Insubstantial rents from personal property leased with real property
- Gain from the sale of capital assets
- Certain research income

Nonprofits that are corporations pay tax at the corporate income tax rate, and the trusts and estates rate applies to foundations that are trusts for UBTI income. A nonprofit that does not engage in an unrelated trade or business need not concern itself with UBTI, although determining which activities are unrelated is not always a simple matter. For additional information about UBTI, consult Internal Revenue Service (IRS) Publication 598, *Tax on Unrelated Business Income of Exempt Organizations.*[2]

Reasons for the Use of a Subsidiary for Profit-Making Activities

As noted earlier, a nonprofit may conduct certain insubstantial or occasional unrelated profit-making activities without creating tax liability or jeopardizing its tax-exempt status. It is not necessary to establish a separate taxable entity for such activities. However, a nonprofit may choose to create a taxable subsidiary through which to conduct unrelated activities, especially if those activities would otherwise become substantial and thereby jeopardize the nonprofit's exempt status. Although the IRS does not define what it means by "substantial," a nonprofit might want to consider creating a subsidiary if the income generated by its unrelated activities exceeds approximately 15 to 20 percent of its organization's revenue.

There are other, nontax reasons why a nonprofit might want to function through more than one entity and thereby create a subsidiary for its business venture. These reasons relate to organizational accountability, growth of the business, staffing, desirability of a joint venture, and issues of control and liability.

Organizational Accountability

A nonprofit's board of directors, its contributors, and the general public expect that a nonprofit organization will adhere to its mission. Because of this, a nonprofit operating a business venture may want to avoid giving even the appearance of tainted activities or a weakening commitment to the organization's primary purposes. A separation of nonprofit and for-profit functions may ensure that contributors are not misinformed or confused about the exempt organization's main pursuits, thereby helping to preserve its image, ability to fundraise, and other activities. This consideration may be relevant even when the for-profit activity arguably falls outside the definition of UBTI, or within one of the exceptions discussed earlier. It is also the case that a nonprofit that directly operates a for-profit activity may face increased scrutiny from the IRS, which generally wants to ensure that its for-profit activities comply with the charitable purposes of the exempt organization. As such, the organization needs to reflect appropriately any sharing of personnel, facilities, or resources between its for-profit and nonprofit operations. To minimize any threat to its exempt status, especially when net income is likely to be significant, the nonprofit might prefer to relegate the income-generating activity to a for-profit subsidiary.

Planning for Growth

Even though a for-profit activity may not legally demand that a new entity be formed, if the nonexempt activity requires, or may over time require, a substantial devotion of management time and attention, or a significant number of employees, conducting the for-profit activity through a separate entity may prevent diversion from the nonprofit's principal activity. At some point this diversion potential not only may damage the nonprofit's ability to address its stated corporate purpose, but also may jeopardize its tax-exempt status. This risk can arise incrementally and over time so that a nonprofit's incidental and occasional profit-making venture becomes, in a sense, too successful and begins to demand so much attention that it actually changes the organization's focus away from its core values and places the entity at risk in a number of ways. Careful initial planning, including the development of a realistic business plan, will help the nonprofit recognize that the success of its venture may ultimately overwhelm the parent organization, and the parent may thus desire to form a subsidiary organization despite the modest and manageable size of the venture in its early stage.

Staffing Needs and Desirability of Joint Ventures

A taxable entity has more flexibility in the area of compensation than does a nonprofit. Particular nonprofits may place explicit or implicit caps on employees' salaries to reflect the culture of the organization or to keep high salaries from discouraging outside contributions. Within a for-profit entity, such limits often do not apply. When compensation can help attract or retain the talent needed to run a separate activity, an organization might set up a for-profit subsidiary. It may also be that proper management of the for-profit activity requires a kind of expertise not generally present in the ranks of the nonprofit or in the officers or board, and the need for that expertise may lead the nonprofit to consider a joint venture.

Often a joint venturer may be able to bring unique and proprietary talent, resources, and know-how to the collaborative effort. Were it not for the nonprofit's willingness to venture or partner with the commercial entity, each organization and, indeed, the public at large might be denied the results of joined assets and resources.

In addition to the staffing considerations just mentioned it may be useful for other reasons for a nonprofit to enter into joint ventures with individuals or for-profit entities. Some new enterprises require substantial capital outlays. In those situations a nonprofit may want to hand off the cost of developing programs to a for-profit partner in exchange for giving up a share of the resulting revenues. By creating or partnering with a for-profit entity, a nonprofit can allocate shares of ownership relatively easily. For the for-profit partners, taxable status increases the likelihood that management of the activity will be directed toward maximizing profit.

There is also the intangible advantage that a business venture might be taken more seriously if organized as a for-profit business, joint venture, or both. Such partnering may especially assist a nonprofit that does not have the necessary internal business expertise to ensure the enterprise's success.

A clearly separate for-profit venture that begins as a partnership with one or more for-profit organizations may be easier to sell successfully in the open market as well. For example, certain ventures may create attractive short-term opportunities. Running an enterprise for decades, however, is not always in the long-term interest of the nonprofit organization as a whole. Thus, a nonprofit might raise capital, act as a partner or shareholder for a short time, and then sell the venture.

In joint ventures between exempt and taxable participants, an important IRS concern is that impermissible private benefit might result. Accordingly, the IRS carefully screens such joint ventures and looks for evidence that the exempt participant controls the enterprise in a way that protects its primary exempt purpose. In some transactions, before giving clearance, the IRS calls on the exempt organization to make a guarantee, such as meeting an environmental condition or dedicating a percentage of revenues to services to low-income individuals.

Using a taxable vehicle for the nonprofit's investment can eliminate the need for such close scrutiny, although it raises other issues, many of which have been touched on here. For example, for-profit joint ventures often raise questions about how expenses are allocated between partners and about how compensation is paid to staff who are dually employed. In addition, recent changes to the tax laws limit a nonprofit's ability to exclude certain income. Under the revised law, a tax-exempt organization must report as income all interest, rents, and royalties paid by taxable subsidiaries in which it directly or indirectly owns more than a 50 percent stake. Thus, economically equivalent transactions can produce different tax results. For example, to exclude royalties from licensing arrangements, the non-profit must take a passive role and let the for-profit partner regulate the activity. By contrast, to exclude income from a joint venture with a taxable partner, the nonprofit must retain control over the activity.

Control Issues

Joint ventures that converge the mission and economic interests of nonprofits and commercial partners offer numerous and diverse opportunities to tax-exempt entities. Such alliances are particularly well-suited where special business expertise or much needed initial capitalization can be offered by the for-profit entity. In the planning of a for-profit venture, tax-exempt entities must exercise caution to make certain that they establish and maintain sufficient control over the joint venture so as to assure that it is operated in a manner consistent with the charitable purposes of the tax-exempt partner, and that undue benefit is not conferred on commercial participants. The nonprofit entity should make sure that the joint venture is not structured or operated in a manner that would constitute an undue benefit to its for-profit partner or other for-profit entities. A tax-exempt corporation that is a prospective partner in a joint venture (whether organized as a limited liability company, partnership, or corporation) must take care to structure the joint venture, and the nonprofit's role therein, in a manner that minimizes the risk that the nonprofit's participation might put the organization's tax-exemption in jeopardy or generate unexpected, unrelated business income.

Even if the tax-exempt corporation's participation in a for-profit joint venture is only a small part of the tax-exempt entity's total activities, the nonprofit organization should exercise a level of control over the venture's operational issues that will ensure that the venture operates to further the tax-exempt organization's charitable purposes. This is particularly true in the case of limited liability companies or joint ventures structured as partnerships. With such pass-through entities, the IRS attributes the acts of the partnership (or limited liability company) entity as being the actions of the joint venture partners.

Liability Concerns

Not all business ventures by nonprofits succeed. By separating activities into different corporations, a nonprofit can sometimes take advantage of the limited liability laws that apply to individual corporations. Bankruptcy laws can make it easier to abandon a failed venture; the ability to contain lawsuits helps protect other parts of the nonprofit. It is also important to note that the protections for directors serving for-profit corporations are distinctly different from those for volunteer directors of nonprofit organizations. Nonprofit directors currently enjoy potential federal and state-level protections for their service; but not directors in the for-profit arena. Careful examination of your state's protection and indemnification provisions for profit-motivated corporate directors is encouraged.

Choosing the Right Business Entity

What business form should the nonprofit choose for its profit-making subsidiary? To illustrate the various options, consider the following example. A tax-exempt housing developer wishes to encourage home ownership by its core constituency of low- and moderate-income clients. Through a contractual relationship with a consortium of local banks it has for several years successfully processed mortgage applications and serviced the resulting loans. It now wishes to form its own mortgage brokerage in order to generate revenue that can be used both to support its established programs and to facilitate the delivery of mortgage financing to the unconventional borrower. Let's look at the options available to this housing developer and determine which of them will meet the nonprofit's needs most appropriately.

One of the first decisions to make when establishing a profit subsidiary is to determine what form the business organization should take. Some of the tax-related considerations about the relationship between the two organizations were raised earlier. Several others must also be weighed in making this decision: liability, administrative and legal complexity, continuity and transferability of interest, number and type of investors, and income tax considerations. Final decisions about the form of your business, however, should be made only after a thorough review with your lawyer and accountant.

By their nature, some forms of business are better suited than others to tax-exempt profit-making ventures. Although you will see that the corporation, limited liability company, and limited partnership are the business forms most likely to suit a nonprofit's entrepreneurial venture, we discuss others as well.

Sole Proprietorship

The simplest form of business organization is the sole proprietorship. Ownership of this type of business is by an individual in his or her name. This business form is very simple in the sense that there is a single owner who operates the business personally. The sole proprietor typically files an assumed name certificate with the county clerk's office and, in most cases, does not even get a separate tax number but instead merely uses his or her social security number. Because a proprietorship is owned by a "sole natural person," this form of organization permits very little structural and continuing involvement by the nonprofit (for example, appointment of board members). As such, it is probably not the best selection for the housing development example, and usually not an appropriate business form for most nonprofit enterprises as well.

General Partnership

The next least complex form of for-profit entity is the general partnership, a business owned by two or more persons. The general partnership has the same unlimited liability features as the sole proprietorship. That is, there is no limitation on the liability of the partners individually, and individual partners are also liable for the business liability of the partnership.

Unlike the sole proprietorship, however, the general partnership is legally a separate entity from the individual partners. The partners may be any combination of individuals, partnerships, corporations, or other entities. The general partnership has a separate taxpayer identification number. Typically it must file a certificate of co-partnership with the local county clerk, but it need not file anything with the state. The general partnership is operated on a consent basis by the partners, who have a private agreement as to their voting rights and their rights to the partnership assets. It is recommended that these agreements be in writing.

For tax purposes, profits and losses are passed through the partnership and treated as profits and losses of the individual partners. This pass-through taxation feature can be problematic for some nonprofits depending on circumstances. In addition, because most often the nonprofit will wish to create more separation from its profit-making venture than this form of business allows in order to avoid incurring unnecessary liabilities and the risk of jeopardizing its tax-exempt status, in general this business form, like the sole proprietorship, is considered a less appropriate choice than other forms for nonprofit enterprise.

Corporation

There are many circumstances in which it would make good sense for a tax-exempt organization to pursue a profit-making venture through a for-profit corporate subsidiary. As discussed previously, the relationship between the parent organization and the subsidiary must be structured and maintained while keeping in mind that creation of a controlled subsidiary organization increases the likelihood that the nonprofit will receive, and be taxed on, UBTI. Balancing that concern with the parent organization's desire to control its new venture is sometimes difficult, and yet with careful structuring it can be accomplished.

The corporation is the form that many businesses take, although limited liability companies are becoming increasingly popular (these will be discussed shortly). A corporation is created by filing articles of incorporation with the designated state agency or bureau. Because the corporation is a separate legal entity, it has a separate taxpayer identity. Any licenses or governmental authorizations necessary to operate the business must be secured in the name of the corporation.

Once it is organized, the corporation owns the business assets. The persons who organized the corporation frequently become the shareholders, who in turn select the directors. The directors then elect or appoint officers, who operate the business for the corporation. Personal liability is limited to the shareholders' investment in the corporation unless they take or fail to take action that results in personal liability.

Some states authorize so-called directorless corporations, which are operated much like a proprietorship or general partnership. This type of corporation has no board of directors and the executive functions are given to an individual. The result is the limited liability protection of the corporation and the ease of operation of a proprietorship. For nonprofits, this option should be avoided, however, because of the need to maintain legal and effective control over subsidiary operations, especially when commercial co-owners are also involved.

If the nonprofit parent decides that the business will take corporate form, it must make a number of additional decisions, including how the corporation will be treated for tax purposes and how much control the parent nonprofit will exert over its subsidiary.

The C Corporation. A regular or C corporation is subject to federal income tax. A C corporation is taxed on its profits, and its shareholders are taxed only on dividends. Traditionally, many small businesses have been C corporations because they have no intention or ability to pay dividends. The owners take their money out of the corporation in the form of compensation for services. (If the amount of compensation paid to the owners becomes excessive in the view of the IRS, however, some of the income may be reclassified as dividends, resulting in taxation at both the corporate and shareholder levels.)

If C corporation is selected as the form for the subsidiary, the subsidiary itself will be taxed on the income from its activities, but dividends paid by the taxable subsidiary to the exempt parent organization will generally not be UBTI. In addition, the subsidiary will pay corporate rates on its net taxable income according to the prevailing federal structure. The current structure is shown in Table 6.1. According to the table, the first $50,000 of profit is taxed at the rate of 15 percent. The more burdensome 34 percent rate does not apply until net taxable income figures exceed $100,000. Only net taxable income, after allowed expenses,

TABLE 6.1. CORPORATE INCOME TAX RATES.

Taxable Income More Than (in $)	Taxable Income Not More Than (in $)	Tax Rate (%)
	50,000	15
50,000	75,000	25
75,000	100,000	34
100,000	335,000	39
335,000	10,000,000	34
10,000,000	15,000,000	35
15,000,000	18,333,333	38
18,333,333	—	35

is subject to taxation. There are therefore many tax and operational planning opportunities to record expenses and thus reduce the amount subject to tax.

In addition, the tax-exempt parent organization of a taxable subsidiary should be aware that for all such subsidiaries in which the parent nonprofit holds more than a 50 percent ownership interest (this sort of entity is called a *controlled subsidiary organization*), the tax-exempt corporation's receipt of rent, royalties, interest, and other types of income may be taxable as UBTI. This is in contrast to the usual rule, under which a tax-exempt corporation's receipt of rent, royalties, interest, and similar kinds of passive income is not taxable as UBTI, provided that such income is received from an entity unrelated to the tax-exempt corporation. Once again, planning and strategic organizational decisions may avoid adverse tax results.

The S Corporation. Another business form, the S corporation, is taxed like a partnership. Profits (and losses) are passed through and treated as income to the shareholders. Thus there is no tax at the corporate level, but tax is imposed at the shareholder level. The rules governing S corporations require that there be only one class of capital stock, and that only individuals, estates, and certain trusts may be shareholders. The tax status of an S corporation, therefore, is typically not available to subsidiaries of nonprofit corporations.

Regarding issues of control, the nonprofit organization can create and substantially influence its for-profit corporate subsidiary by simply holding all of the subsidiary's issued and outstanding voting stock. By doing so it retains the power to articulate the corporation's purposes and to elect and remove the entire board of directors. The parent corporation, as the sole shareholder, can maintain control of the subsidiary and at the same time allow it to operate as an independent entity under the direction of its own board of directors. The new organization is nevertheless an independent organization with its own board, officers, and employees. Its board selects officers who are responsible for executing the policies of the board. These officers do not report to the parent organization, but they are accountable to the parent-appointed board. In turn, the board of the subsidiary is accountable to the parent nonprofit as its sole shareholder.

Because corporations have long existed and are in widespread use, the ways in which corporate entities must interact in order to maximize control by the nonprofit but still avoid adverse tax consequences have been well-developed. Creative and careful use of the corporate business structure allows the parent organization to create a wholly owned for-profit subsidiary that will substantially benefit the nonprofit without generating UBTI. The relationship between a nonprofit parent and its for-profit corporate subsidiary can be depicted as shown in Figure 6.1.

In the earlier example of the nonprofit wishing to form its own mortgage brokerage, the subsidiary can indirectly benefit the nonprofit parent by devoting a portion of the profits from its operations to the more expensive and difficult origination of nonconforming loans. If the relationship has been structured so that the subsidiary is a separately operated and managed independent organization, the subsidiary may also pay dividends to the parent organization without those dividends being considered unrelated business income. The subsidiary may also make charitable contributions to the parent organization, subject to the IRS limit on contributions by corporations of 10 percent of the company's taxable income. At a later

FIGURE 6.1. RELATIONSHIP BETWEEN A NONPROFIT BOARD AND ITS FOR-PROFIT SUBSIDIARY.

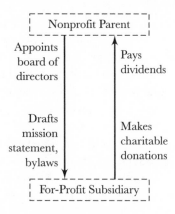

time the successful corporate subsidiary may raise capital by selling additional shares of stock, or the parent organization may sell some of its stock and use the proceeds to further its own charitable purposes.

Limited Partnership

A limited partnership is formed by one or more general partners and one or more limited partners. Usually the general partner or a party whom the general partner designates provides the operating management, and the limited partners are passive investors. The limited partners' liability is limited to the amount of their investment. Filing requirements vary by state, but usually the limited partnership must file a limited partnership certificate with the appropriate state-level agency. In most cases, the sale of limited partnership interests involves securities law considerations that are essentially the same as those involved with selling stock in a corporation. These securities law problems may not arise or may easily be avoided if the limited partnership is a small business partnership with only a few participants who are actively involved in the business.

A nonprofit may form a limited partnership because it needs investor participation from individuals or entities that demand the protection of limited liability and wish only to be passive investors. For example, tax credits of various kinds are valuable to some sophisticated individual and corporate investors whose only interest in the nonprofit's profit-making venture is the receipt of those credits. The nonprofit may serve as the general partner or, more commonly, form a for-profit corporate subsidiary to do so. This ownership structure easily permits the investors to stay passive and uninvolved, and allows the nonprofit to completely control the entity's operations. The structure of the limited partnership could be as shown in Figure 6.2.

FIGURE 6.2. STRUCTURE OF A LIMITED PARTNERSHIP.

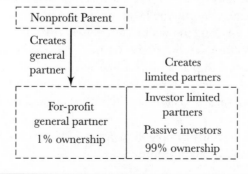

Limited Liability Companies

The limited liability company (LLC) is a relatively new form of business organization in the United States, although it is used widely in Europe and Latin America. Every state has adopted authorizing statutes for forming an LLC. The model uniform statute, however, has not been widely embraced and there are widespread differences among the state laws.

The LLC combines the operating and management flexibility of a partnership with the limited liability of a corporation. The owners of the LLC are its members. Generally LLCs are taxed as partnerships, meaning that income is passed on to the members to report and pay applicable taxes on. If the nonprofit itself is the member, it may elect to have the LLC taxed as an entity rather than as a partnership in order to avoid the attribution of UBTI to the parent organization.

An LLC need not have annual meetings, a board of directors, officers, or stock certificates. The mode of operation is set out in a private agreement just as with a partnership. The LLC enjoys the tax advantage of an S corporation in that profits are presumptively taxed to the owners but not to the LLC. There are, however, no shareholder qualifications as with an S corporation, and therefore an LLC may work well for nonprofits under appropriate circumstances.

To qualify for noncorporate (pass-through) tax treatment, an LLC may have only two of the following four corporate characteristics: (1) continuity of life, (2) centralized management, (3) limited liability, and (4) free transferability of interest. Limited liability is typically available, so organizers of an LLC may choose only one of the three remaining features if they wish to obtain the tax advantage of an LLC. Choosing more than one additional characteristic will result in the LLC having three corporate characteristics and being taxed as a C corporation.

An LLC can be a workable alternative to a wholly owned corporate subsidiary in a jurisdiction that permits the LLC to be owned by a single member. Because the LLC entity typically requires less organizational maintenance than does a corporation, it may be appealing to nonprofits and nonprofit enterprise. As described, LLCs do not, for instance, typically require boards of directors, periodic meetings documented with minutes, officers, or complex annual filings. For a nonprofit seeking to own but not closely control a for-profit venture, the LLC may be an attractive alternative to the corporate subsidiary. It can also replace a limited partnership as an investment vehicle for passive sophisticated investors. Because, however, enabling legislation differs meaningfully from state to state, it is most appropriate to consult with skilled tax and legal advisers before choosing this entity.

The following example illustrates an effective use of an LLC by a nonprofit parent and its business venture.

A nonprofit medical clinic seeks to relocate to a better location so it can more effectively accomplish its purpose of providing subsidized medical care to a low-income population. The clinic wishes to rehabilitate and occupy a building within the core city area, thereby providing easier access for its primary constituency. Acquiring a building and properly outfitting it as a medical facility requires an outlay of capital that is far more than the organization has or can raise. A local bank, however, is interested in acquiring the tax credits that are available through a federally certified historic rehabilitation. The amount that the bank is willing to pay for the right to receive those credits provides enough funding so that the organization can undertake the proposed building rehabilitation.

The nonprofit entity then forms an LLC. The LLC's operating agreement provides that the bank will own 99 percent of membership interests and the nonprofit's for-profit subsidiary corporation will own the other 1 percent. The agreement also provides that the nonprofit's subsidiary will manage and control the operations of the LLC, thereby permitting the bank to benefit from its investment while the nonprofit retains (through its subsidiary) day-to-day control of the enterprise. The operating agreement's provisions may also permit the nonprofit to acquire the bank's membership interest at some later date and for a reasonable market value. The same relationship could be accomplished through the use of a limited partnership, with the bank holding all the limited partner interest and the nonprofit controlling the general partner.

Terminology and Definitions

Nonprofit entities and their commercial counterparts are certainly often similar to each other, but there are distinct differences not only in their regulatory climate but also in their structure and operation. In some instances, the differences may appear to be cosmetic or subtle, but they should be understood nonetheless to be vitally important in both their potential and their restraints on such organizations. When planning a for-profit venture, it is important to grasp the fundamental business and tax realities of various forms of business.

Nonprofit Entities

Not all nonprofit entities are tax-exempt. Tax-exempt entities typically result from both organizational structure and qualification for and compliance with a rigid set of prerequisites established in the Internal Revenue Code. This chapter assumes that an existing tax-exempt entity, or one that will exist, wishes to engage in for-profit activity without losing its tax-exempt status. Adherence to the principles and practices described here is fundamental to acquiring and maintaining tax-exempt existence.

Almost always a nonprofit entity will be the creature of a state authorized statute. In the United States (unlike in Canada), very few organizational entities are authorized by federal law. Exceptions to federal or nationally authorized entities include banks, credit unions, congressionally mandated commissions, and so on.

At the entity organizational level, nonprofits are typically organized as either trusts or corporations. In the first half of the twentieth century, charitable trusts were often the organizational form for nonprofit foundations and functions. In the latter half of the twentieth century, and in part as a manifestation of the movement toward business characteristics in the nonprofit world, the corporate form has become more prevalent.

Whether they are trusts or nonprofit corporations, nonprofits are created and controlled by their governing instruments. A charitable trust is governed by a trust agreement or declaration of trust. A corporation's governing instrument is its articles of incorporation that are filed with the appropriate state agency. For non-profit corporations, bylaws are also an essential part of internal management.

The most important provision in the governing instruments of a tax-exempt nonprofit charitable organization is its purposes clause. Federal tax law governs tax-exempt status and requires that a tax-exempt charitable entity be organized and operated exclusively for religious, charitable, scientific, public safety testing, literary, or educational purposes. In addition, nonprofit organizations may be organized for purposes set forth in the Internal Revenue Code, such as business leagues, credit unions, cemetery companies, group legal services, and so on. One critical difference between nonprofit tax-exempt organizations and their commercial counterparts is the content set forth in the articles of incorporation pursuant to various Internal Revenue Code requirements for being a tax-exempt organization. Not only is the purposes clause subject to certain mandatory content, but there must also be provisions in the governing instruments (articles of incorporation and bylaws) that set forth prohibitions against private inurement, carrying on substantial lobbying activities, or participating in political campaigns. In addition, for Section 501(c)(3) charitable organizations, there must be a provision in the governing instruments specifying how the entity's assets are to be distributed if the organization is dissolved.

Nonprofit corporations may typically be organized on either a membership or a stock basis. The choice between these two foundation options is often controlled by whether the organization is to be managed by its members or by a board of directors. Nonprofit organizations are typically organized for perpetual existence. In addition, nonprofit corporations often do not contain detailed provisions on shareholder rights, proxy provisions, oppressive corporate acts provisions, and many other items that are often necessitated by the diverse ownership interests of a commercially functioning organization.

Nonprofit entities that seek to be recognized as exempt from federal taxation must file IRS Form 1023, Application for Recognition of Exemption Under Section 501(c)(3) of the Internal Revenue Code. The exemption application is not required if the nonprofit entity is a public charity and normally has gross receipts of $5,000 or less in each tax year or if the nonprofit is a subordinate organization covered by a group exemption letter. If Form 1023 is filed within fifteen months after the nonprofit entity's creation, its tax-exempt status will be effective retroactive to the date of organization. The application should be filed by the end of the fifteenth month after the month in which the articles of incorporation were filed or the trust agreement was executed.

Any business activity that is or will become a substantial economic function of a 501(c)(3) nonprofit corporation must be related to the nonprofit's exempt purposes. *Related* means directly or vitally supportive of the nonprofit achieving its exempt purposes. *Substantial* is typically defined as exceeding approximately 15 percent to 20 percent of the nonprofit's time or gross revenues.

If the business activity is not related to achieving tax-exempt purposes, many legal and tax counselors recommend that the business be conducted in a taxable for-profit subsidiary or joint venture. Otherwise, the nonprofit risks losing its tax-exempt status. The fact that the revenue generated is used to support the corporation's other charitable or educational activities does not make the business activity related. Profits from related businesses are not taxed. Profits from unrelated businesses are taxed at normal corporate income tax rates.

In summary, a nonprofit entity may be a trust or, more likely, a corporation created at the state level. The creation of the nonprofit corporation follows the requirements of each state's unique enabling statute, but typically involves the filing of articles of incorporation, the preparation of bylaws, and obtaining a federal tax identification number. In addition, where public solicitation of support is anticipated, many states have charitable organization registration laws that require organizations engaged in charitable solicitations to register with the appropriate state agency. The filing of organizational documents and creation of a nonprofit entity does not automatically endow the entity with a certain tax status. Tax status is a separate decision and registration process. Many nonprofits never seek tax-exemption and therefore operate as nonprofit entities but are subject to normal rules of taxation. Others pursue registration with the IRS as a tax-exempt entity and by doing so elect to be subject to a regimen of mandated restrictions on both their organization and function.

For-Profit Organizations

The organizational options for for-profit entities are much more varied than those typically utilized by nonprofit organizations. Once again, organization is accomplished at the state level pursuant to authorizing statute. Also, as is the case with nonprofits, organizational format choices do not automatically confer certain taxation status. In the for-profit sector, the taxation decisions are not tax-exempt versus taxable; all for-profit entities are taxable organizations. The decisions in the profit arena focus have to do with deciding at which level taxable income will be recognized. Some for-profit entities (typically corporations) are taxed at the organizational level at which the income is earned; others pass through the income to their owners, who report and pay the taxes at their respective applicable rates.

As mentioned earlier, the tax ramifications for a nonprofit undertaking a business venture are important matters. In addition, liability, financing, and other concerns have to be considered. For the many reasons already discussed, a nonprofit may find it desirable to form a subsidiary to conduct the business even though it may not be legally required to do so.

Decisions about such issues of corporate structure need to be reviewed as new circumstances arise and as the corporation and its business develop. Initially it may be appropriate to undertake a business within the nonprofit. As the business develops, as its management or capital needs change, or as the potential liability it represents increases, transferring the business to a subsidiary corporation or other for-profit entity may become necessary.

Conclusion

For some time there has been increasing convergence between some nonprofit organizations and the business world. Indeed, many nonprofit entities have conducted their tax-exempt missions through practices and procedures that closely parallel, if not mirror, the conduct of similar businesses by their for-profit entity counterparts. Questions about how commercial the operations of a tax-exempt entity's operations may be without jeopardizing its tax-exempt status have been litigated for years. Clearly there are notable general similarities between nonprofit and for-profit hospitals and health care systems. There are also nonprofit, tax-exempt entities in direct competition with one another in the marketplace in such diverse economic sectors as travel, media and entertainment, testing and evaluations, printing and publications, and many more. These examples of competitive convergence are not new, and many of them have helped to develop the form and content of the evolving commercialization of the nonprofit landscape.

In recent years, a number of tax-exempt organizations have pursued related activities that would normally qualify for tax exemption as for-profit, taxable enterprises. For example, a nonprofit, tax-exempt corporation may find that to fulfill its corporate mission it would be useful to engage in an activity that is outside the general range of activities for which it was organized and is operated. This activity is sometimes carried out within the existing organizational structure and other times as a separate subsidiary or joint venture. Some examples have been presented in this chapter. Other examples include a testing service creating a separate entity to address industrial opportunities, a university opting to create a for-profit research program, a hospital packaging software for commercial sale, or a housing group participating in a consortium to build low-income housing. Depending on the facts, the revenues derived from such activities may be of a kind not generally treated as exempt from taxation. Nevertheless, the nonprofit may believe that engaging in the business activity will further and better achieve its exempt purposes, promote public awareness, or provide similar ancillary benefits.

This chapter has identified some of the legal, tax, and business concerns that may arise from a nonprofit's decision to embark on a profit-making venture. Through the use of the principles and ideas presented here, and through careful, thoughtful application of the other business strategies discussed in this book, a nonprofit may successfully support its primary purpose by venturing into the for-profit realm.

Notes

1. For purposes of clarification, Unrelated Business Taxable Income, or UBTI, refers to income that is taxed because it is unrelated; Unrelated Business Income Tax, or UBIT, is the actual tax imposed. In other words, UBIT is generated by UBTI.
2. Internal Revenue Service, Department of the Treasury. *Tax on Unrelated Business Income of Exempt Organizations.* Pub. 598. Washington, D.C.: Internal Revenue Service, Department of the Treasury [http://www.irs.gov/pub/irs-pdf/p598.pdf], rev. Mar. 2000.

CHAPTER SEVEN

NONPROFIT VENTURES
AND GOVERNANCE ISSUES

Katherine M. O'Regan

As nonprofits consider undertaking activities that earn income (either in addition to meeting mission or quite distinctly as a revenue source created to support the mission), they should also be thinking through issues of governance. Income-generating endeavors have two distinguishing themes, both of which have governance implications: first, such activities are not purely about mission (in some cases they are almost unrelated to the primary mission of the organization); second, they may be activities in which there is great competition, possibly even from for-profit organizations. As such, the goals and associated oversight structure for such activities may differ from those of other aspects of the nonprofit. Furthermore, the existence of these activities within or related to the nonprofit may raise broad governance issues for the overall nonprofit, not just for the earned-income enterprise. This chapter is specifically about the governance side of such enterprises, about how to think through the issues they raise both for governance of the existing parent organization and for how to best oversee the nonprofit enterprise to increase the likelihood of its success.

Although quite a bit is known about nonprofit governance generally—from data on how boards are typically structured and notions on why this might be so,

The author thanks Sharon Oster for her guidance, specifically on the corporate governance issues, and Anita Sharma for her research assistance.

to best-practice suggestions and personal and anecdotal experiences—the specific issue of governance when a nonprofit expands into an earned-income venture is relatively uncharted territory. This phenomenon is new enough that no body of evidence exists on what has been tried and on how various approaches have fared.

This means that there is essentially no systematic research that can be used as a direct guide. There are, of course, the experiences of individual organizations, and not surprisingly, each has taken a somewhat different approach. Just as the specific governance characteristics differ across nonprofits by context, life-cycle, and so on, the governance structure of new ventures, whether they are kept inside the parent nonprofit or spun off as a separate entity, will also differ.

Rather than prescribe a particular outcome or formula, this chapter will help you frame your thinking about the governance issues associated with such ventures. It will do so by presenting a series of analytic steps designed to help an executive director and board narrow the range of governance options that are consistent with the parent organization's goals and capacities, and it highlights some key issues for each of these options. The chapter begins by considering the environment and goals of the new venture, two key dimensions of designing appropriate and effective governance structures. The characteristics of the venture's environment and goals are considered in light of their governance implications. The chapter then considers some specific governance issues typically raised by such enterprises, such as thinking about subsidiaries and whether a separate entity should be non-profit or for-profit, and ends with specific practices of good governance.

Mission and Context of the Venture

While reading this chapter, executive directors should ask questions about two aspects of governance: How does this new enterprise affect governance issues for the existing nonprofit overall? And what governance structures will best support the new enterprise? The composition, size, and even role of your board reflect certain needs of your organization: to protect the mission for various stakeholders, to provide operational skills for specific aspects of the organization (particularly early in the life cycle of an organization), and to garner resources (through board members who can play a role in this, personally and in their networks). In each of these cases, the specific nature of the organization and its mission fundamentally drive the range of stakeholders and the skill sets and resources needed on the board. As you undertake a business venture, your organization is engaging in activity quite different from what it has done in the past, which might require changes in your expectations for your current board, other changes in governance structure (board committee structure, internal reorganization), or even the establishment of a separate entity. So, to start, focus on clarifying the venture's mission. Because the most important characteristic of a successful board is its members' shared understanding of the mission and nature of the organization, a successful board strategy should include mechanisms for clarifying the board's common understanding. This chapter proposes mechanisms to help you do just that.

Mission Statement

To start, develop a mission statement for the venture itself, distinct from that of the parent organization. This statement generally goes beyond the business plan, making quite clear the main goal of the activity, and should be created in partnership with the board. Like all mission statements, it helps the organization clarify for itself and for others the goals of the venture and lays the foundation for measuring success.

As an example, consider the following text from Benhaven's Learning Network, a nonprofit agency that provides services for people with autism that is now branching into consulting and technical assistance for public school systems' special education programs (emphasis added):

> The mission of Benhaven's Learning Network (BLN) is *to support school system personnel in developing their capabilities to serve students with autism effectively.* BLN's distinguishing characteristic is the range of services provided as well as the availability of in-district technical support. By starting the consulting practice, Benhaven, Inc. greatly enhances the scope of its mission, affecting many more students than it ever could in its own facilities. *The new venture will also provide a financial contribution to the overall organization and give professional development opportunities to Benhaven, Inc.'s staff.*

While this paragraph is contained within the agency's business plan, its benefit is that it succinctly summarizes the mission of the venture. It specifically states that the mission is "to support school system personnel in developing the capabilities to serve students with autism effectively." Placing this statement right at the beginning of the plan highlights that the prime objective of the enterprise is to further the organization's social mission, not to raise revenue. After then clarifying how it will accomplish this mission, two additional objectives are mentioned: financial contribution to the overall organization and professional development opportunities to staff. These objectives help clarify that the revenue side of the enterprise is part of its mission, and an additional objective.

Having established a mission statement for the enterprise, there are two key attributes to assess when thinking about governance for the venture. Specifically, the *prominence* of the existing organization's mission is the *raison d'être* for the new venture and the basis on which the enterprise gets resources. The first of these attributes pushes the organization to go beyond the mission statement and to be quite explicit about trade-off between mission and money.

Motivation Assessment: Mission Versus Money

To help a board think concretely about the relative importance of competing objectives, an exercise, a "motivation assessment," summarized in Figure 7.1, has been developed. The height of the rectangle in the figure represents the portion of an organization's purpose that is motivated by mission on the one hand and money on the other. A diagonal divides the area in half, with the space above the diagonal representing the prominence of mission and the area below representing the importance of money. A large number of the activities undertaken by the typical nonprofit are 100 percent about mission so the organization would fall to the far left of the figure. At the other end of the spectrum, where the motivation is purely about profit (money), is where for-profits are likely to be encountered.

Now, consider where your enterprise would be on the figure. An earned income venture is likely to fall not as far to the left as the parent nonprofit would fall. But how far from the left would it be? In the Benhaven example, mission is mentioned before money, but the financial benefits are mentioned second. This suggests that the enterprise is somewhere in the middle, not clearly aligning with the pure mission of the parent organization, but far from activities motivated purely to raise revenue.

When taking the board through such an exercise, it is important that the focus be on the motivation of the enterprise rather than on its outcome. The issue is not whether the activity will generate revenue but whether the revenue is the primary motivation. If mission is the purpose, if resources were not a constraint, the activity would be undertaken regardless of its ability to generate income. For example,

FIGURE 7.1. MOTIVATION ASSESSMENT.

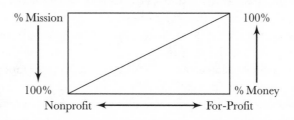

while a museum may generate revenue through patrons' entrance fees, letting people into the museum, not the fee itself, is the purpose of this activity. Were revenue secured completely independently of attendance, a museum would still desire to open its doors to the public, providing access to its collection. Were no revenue made, however, from some of the museum's ancillary activities—its gift shop sales, for example—it seems unlikely that it would wish to continue such activity.

This exercise will help clarify the relative importance of these dimensions in more concrete terms than the mission statement does. Being concrete about the importance of the income-generating aspects of the enterprise at the start is important for several reasons. First, it provides a more concrete means of measuring performance, and this should be established at the start and referred to regularly. Second, it highlights how closely related the main mission of the enterprise and that of the parent organization are. If they are far apart, a lack of congruence between the focus of the parent nonprofit and that of the enterprise is suggested. This lack of closeness has implications for many aspects of the organization, but of greatest interest here are the governance issues. The further to the right the enterprise is in the box in Figure 7.1, the more likely it is that its existing governance needs to be reevaluated, and possibly realigned or changed.

Finally, as an organization moves from the left to the right in the figure, it may well be changing the context in which it operates, or what can be called its resource competition, considered next.

Competition and Context for Earning Income

Although most nonprofits operate in competitive environments, the nature of that competition may well differ from the competition they will encounter in their for-profit enterprises. The board can be a key mechanism for competing for donors, contracts, even staff. As such, its composition no doubt reflects the role it plays in securing such resources. But some of the activities that nonprofits undertake in income-generating ventures compete quite differently for resources, most likely by competing for customers. In addition, in many cases this "product" competition may be against for-profit firms, a rather different set of competitors.

What does this mean for governance? When boards provide the network through which resources are garnered, the larger, more diverse boards of the typical nonprofit may well be an asset. But for earned-income ventures, value in the marketplace may be the primary means of competing successfully, in which case, rather than furnishing specific networks, a more important job for the board might be providing specific skills that are needed to compete for customers. To the extent that the new enterprise operates in different markets from the original organization, or in the same market but along different dimensions, there may be gaps between the skills on the existing board and those needed for going forward.

Let us assess the resource competition environment for Benhaven. In fact, Benhaven is competing against a limited number of other organizations (there are only three others in a growing and underserved market) and it is operating in a similar environment (same school systems) as the parent nonprofit. It is also providing services that rely on the same sort of expertise—indeed, they use the same staff—as the parent organization's activities. Furthermore, its thirty-five-year history in this arena suggest some reputation benefits to the enterprise from its close affiliation with Benhaven. In this case, it is possible that the exact same networks and skills are needed for both efforts. Along this dimension there may be great congruence between the existing governance and future needs. Alternatively, if competition in the enterprise occurs along different dimensions, it is possible that the business needs somewhat different skills than exist on the current board.

The largest gap is likely to occur when a nonprofit is moving from its existing market to a new activity that competes for resources against a new set of players, particularly if those players are for-profits. In this case, analysis might reveal that the enterprise has a very different activity than the parent organization is designed to do well or that the board is designed to oversee. As with mission incongruence, this lack of fit needs to be addressed. There are two possibilities. One possibility is to assess carefully the gaps between what the organization has and what it needs and make changes in the existing organization. The second possibility is to create a separate entity and design the organization and board to suit it. The latter option is considered here first.

Creation and Features of Subsidiaries

There are various motivations for creating a separate entity for a venture, and these motivations suggest adopting particular structural features for the organization itself and its governance structure. The rest of this chapter lays out three typical motivations for separation, draws some immediate implications for organizational form (that is, nonprofit versus for-profit), and provides specific details for good governance practice.

Reasons to Consider Creating a Subsidiary

As mentioned, there are several reasons that a nonprofit organization might consider setting up a separate entity for a venture, which could be put into three general categories.

To Protect the Organization's Tax Status. One reason for a nonprofit to consider creating a separate entity is that the proposed activity is expected to generate substantial revenue. Depending on the size of this revenue relative to the overall income of the organization, the venture could put at risk the nonprofit status of the entire organization. Of course nonprofits are permitted to earn income. However, if the income is greater than $1,000, an ongoing activity, and unrelated to the organization's tax-exempt purpose, the organization must pay the unrelated business income tax (UBIT). If, however, such activity becomes "substantial" compared to the nonprofit's other activities, it threatens the organization's tax-exempt status. The IRS has not defined *substantial,* but one rule of thumb that is discussed in the literature is one-third of an organization's income. In this case, separating the new enterprise into its own organization may protect the parent nonprofit or provide some assurance to its board and funders. Finally, it is worth noting that the existence of the subsidiary does not exempt the nonprofit from the UBIT (depending somewhat on the form of the income), but rather protects the nonprofit status.

If revenue generation is the motivation for separating the activity, there are also implications for whether the entity itself will be a nonprofit or a for-profit. Unless they can be related to another social mission, large revenues not connected to mission may require setting up a for-profit subsidiary.

To Protect the Organization's Assets and Reputation In addition to concerns about nonprofit tax status, stakeholders and staff might have concerns about other risks that such a new enterprise might entail. One of these risks is that the venture potentially threatens the reputation and assets of the existing organization. By creating a legally distinct subsidiary, an organization can protect its assets from financial liabilities and claims created by the new venture. It is also possible for this separation to provide protection from actions or outcomes from the venture that can be harmful to the parent organization's reputation. In Chapter Six of this book, William Heritage and Timothy Orlebeke provide a clear overview of the legal options and associated issues.

To Address Internal Management Issues. A third concern that might push an organization toward choosing a subsidiary structure is, in addition to the preceding *external threats,* a collection of *internal* management issues. These issues arise primarily from the distance between the mission and context of the enterprise and the mission and context of the parent nonprofit. The first issue is concern with mission drift. If the mission of the enterprise differs enough from the original mission of the parent organization, it may take on a life of its own within the parent organization. Consequently, it may drain resources from the parent organization and pull it toward succeeding at the enterprise rather than in its original mission. Many nonprofits have already experienced such tension as the pursuit of a particular funding source has pulled the organization in competing directions. Alternatively, if the new venture is put elsewhere, the parent nonprofit's focus is not in jeopardy. At the same time, the importance of the new activity is highlighted by establishing its own organization.

A second internal issue that might be minimized by creating a separate entity is cultural conflict that might otherwise arise if the venture is kept in-house. The venture is an entrepreneurial activity, requiring board members and staff who are themselves entrepreneurial. To the extent that the new activity competes in a market and needs to foster a market-oriented spirit in order to compete well, the orientation of the associated staff—indeed the venture's entire approach—might be in direct conflict with that of the overall organization. A related third internal issue may be an associated compensation clash. The staff associated with such work might be compensated differently than other staff members, creating internal management problems.

To the extent that mission drift is an issue, the answer to the question of whether the subsidiary would more appropriately be designed as a nonprofit or as a for-profit depends on the nature of the venture's mission. Going back to the motivation assessment of the enterprise, activities that have mission as their primary motivation but whose mission differs from that of the parent nonprofit may still require the independence achieved through separation. In such a case, a separate nonprofit gives a clear enough distinction. If the purpose, however, is primarily income, the activity may compete more effectively, and send the desired external signals, if established as a for-profit enterprise. If internal culture or compensation clashes are the issue, this would suggest that the subsidiary might benefit from a for-profit structure.

Authority for Establishing the Board

When creating a subsidiary, the parent organization has ultimate control. For a nonprofit subsidiary, this means the parent is essentially the sole voting member; for a for-profit entity, the parent owns the stock. The parent retains the right to elect and remove the entire board of directors of the subsidiary. The purpose of this control is to hold the subsidiary accountable for its performance while protecting the parent from financial liability for the actions of the subsidiary. That protection holds, however, only if there is genuine separation. If the parent exerts excessive control (which can be done by commingling funds, interchanging employees, using common letterhead, sharing office space, and so on), this legal protection is compromised, according to the legal doctrine of *alter ego*. The corporate veil can be pierced because the entities are not indeed independent.

For our purposes, there are two important points here. First, one way to compromise the independence of the subsidiary is to have too much overlap between boards. For the subsidiary structure to accomplish its goal of separation (and protection), the boards need to be primarily independent. This leads to the second point. It is through the board rather than through any other direct-reporting relationship or through continued overlap of board members that the parent organization exercises its authority. The selection of these directors is therefore key. Establishing a well-composed and well-structured board is a critical component of the subsidiary's success, which we turn to next.

Creating a Good Board

The same forces that lead an organization to establish a new venture as a separate entity also come into play in designing the subsidiary's board. As already noted, some ventures are best suited to be for-profit entities, others to be nonprofit. Regardless, these activities generate earnings, are entrepreneurial in nature, and may benefit from insights gleaned from for-profit boards. So we begin with some themes from current practices in the corporate sector.

Corporate Boards and Good Governance

There are several ways in which corporate boards differ from those of nonprofits, and these aspects must be considered when designing a new board for your venture, particularly if the new organization will be for-profit. Nonprofit boards on average have twenty members,[1] with many boards being much larger than this. It is not uncommon for a large nonprofit board to have forty members (as does the Boston Museum of Fine Arts) or more (the Boston Philharmonic has one hundred board members). For-profit boards, conversely, tend to be smaller, averaging eleven people for Fortune 1000 companies.[2] This smaller size is touted as a positive feature in the practitioner literature as potentially increasing personal accountability, and research does find that corporate board performance deteriorates with larger boards.[3] Yet there is little evidence that the larger size of nonprofit boards is detrimental to their functioning, which may be directly related to some key differences in the roles of these boards. While best-practice literature suggests that smaller boards are better, almost no empirical work has been done on this question. In fact, O'Regan and Oster primarily find evidence of benefits from size, such as increased likelihood of board members both giving personally to the organization as well as attending meetings.[4] The main reasons that nonprofits have larger boards than corporations do are that nonprofit boards represent a wider range of stakeholders, have more extensive networks to tap, and possibly need to cover a wider range of roles. Hence, some of the potentially offsetting benefits that nonprofits experience because their boards are larger don't appear to occur for corporate boards. So, when determining the size of the board for the new venture, keep in mind more than whether the subsidiary is for-profit or non-profit; consider also the underlying justification for size. If the new enterprise is nonprofit but competing for resources through its product or service rather than garnering resources through its board, then at least one benefit from having a larger board—namely, its more extensive network to tap for resources—is not likely to materialize. The size of the board should be determined by its role, not simply by its sector of activity.

Corporate boards may in part be smaller because of an additional difference between these sectors, namely that corporate board members are compensated for their work. There is an expectation from the corporation that in exchange for this compensation, the board members will show up for board meetings and come pre-pared. Also, any corporate board member who attends fewer than 75 percent of meetings must be noted in the annual report, adding quite a deterrent to absen-teeism. In addition, corporate board members are not reelected by the other board member, as with nonprofits, but by the shareholders. And unlike nonprofit boards, where term limits are common, corporate boards typically have no term limits and board members tend to serve for long periods—in some cases for the remainder of their lives. A final reason that corporate boards may be smaller than nonprofit boards is that their role is much narrower, focused on the fiduciary monitoring and evaluating of the CEO.

One more way in which corporate boards have traditionally differed from those of nonprofits is in their inclusion of a significant number of "insiders," or in-dividuals who are also employed at the company. This is quite different from non-profit boards, where staff involvement typically is limited to the executive director. The strong presence of insiders on corporate boards has long been criticized, and there is a growing research literature documenting the negative effects of this prac-tice. This feature of corporate governance has been most criticized in various as-sessments of recent governance scandals and has been among those addressed in various commission recommendations and in the 2002 Sarbanes-Oxley Act.[5]

This issue points to an interesting aspect of current reform efforts. Some of the features recommended for board governance of publicly traded companies already exist in the nonprofit sector, specifically board independence, chair inde-pendence, and term limits. Even the noisiness of nonprofit boards is being her-alded as a good practice for corporate boards to adopt.[6] These reforms also point out actions that both sectors need to take to promote good governance. The Sarbanes-Oxley Act notes that "awareness must precede action," emphasizing that the board must be provided with material information if it is to do its job.[7] Yet statistics from a national survey of nonprofits find that more than 30 percent of organizations provide no formal orientation for board members.[8] Both sectors are seeing an enhanced focus on having robust audit committees, and critics in both sectors have noted the lack of reasonable evaluation of the boards themselves.

In addition to these structural features that have been identified as important for all boards, there are other aspects of boards that should be driven by the nature of the venture and the needs of the organization. A useful way to frame the process of designing a board is as a needs or gap analysis.

Needs Assessment and Gap Analysis

An enterprise that is different enough from the parent nonprofit to justify separation inevitably needs different things from its board than the parent organization needs. Rather than use the parent organization's board as the reference point, it may be more useful to focus on the activity at hand and assess its needs. This process builds on the type of gap analysis recommended by Dees, Emerson, and Economy,[9] which considers the needs of the new venture in terms of strategy and staff. To the extent that needs are identified, this analysis can be used to identify the specific skills that board members will need to meet those needs. The new venture's business plan should guide the process, asking, What are the resources needed to make the venture work? In conducting this analysis, there are several aspects to consider.

First, consider the functional needs of the new enterprise and the current assets, including whom you already have on the existing board. Next, think through some of the issues that have already arisen in this chapter: Are you continuing to do something that you already do but to price it or sell it to new clients? If so, while you might continue to need operational expertise, you already have the product or service in hand. But do you have any expertise about the new market? For many of these enterprises it is particularly important to assess the new market. Are you competing against some for-profits? What does that mean for the "business expertise" you need at the board level?

Another aspect of need to consider in addition to skill set is roles and intensity of involvement. During the early stages of an organization's life, the board tends to be an integral part of most aspects of the organization, with board members frequently playing operational roles. During later stages of development, as the organization and the board matures, actual operational involvement by board members decreases while the importance of strategic roles increases. Nonprofits undertaking new ventures tend to be more experienced organizations, ones that have moved successfully in several arenas before considering earned-income ventures. As such, they have matured as organizations and have more mature boards in terms of these "life cycle" characteristics, such as members' roles and the intensity of their involvement. It is important for these boards to realize that the board of the new venture is likely to look more like that of a start-up than like the board of the parent organization.

Finally, a warning about creating a board whose members are too like-minded. While the members of such boards may share a common vision, homogeneous boards have been found to be low in conflict but poorly suited for handling change and problems.[10] While it may be very tempting for executive directors to cultivate such boards, such boards have specific weaknesses that you should be particularly wary of if you are considering a nonprofit venture. Such a venture is a change point for an organization, and the circumstances require a highly functioning board that is willing to question seriously the basic premise of proposals and engage in creative thinking. A homogeneous group that was created out of complete agreement on the organization's basic mission might handicap the enterprise from the start.

Combining Features and Alternatives to Create Entirely New Boards

In many cases, of course, new ventures are not separated into distinct entities but rather are kept within the parent organization. In such cases, each of the analyses just presented is still relevant. It is particularly important to have developed a distinct mission statement and to have clarified the primacy of mission or money for this enterprise if it is to be appropriately managed in your organization and by your board. But if such an enterprise is kept in-house, the current management and board will have to deal with a number of issues.

First, examine your board. Recognize that you are asking this board, which was designed around the broader mission of the organization, to do something different. Is this the right board to lead this effort? Has your gap analysis suggested some needs that will not be met by the board as it is currently composed? It is possible that the exercise of addressing the mission and developing the mission statement will in and of itself lead to some board turnover. In addition, it may be the charge of the nominating committee to work with the board on identifying new board members.

Distinct from developing the board, and with the enterprise in mind, there are other mechanisms that might improve your organization's ability to govern and manage the new enterprise. For example, you can create a board just for the venture. Keep in mind that this new board is ultimately responsible to the organization's board and that to accommodate this mission there is usually substantial overlap in membership. This overlap provides a way to focus specific board members' attention on the enterprise without requiring the board to be reconfigured.

Additional formal structures are available for accessing needed skills. Advisory boards and auxiliary boards have been used in this way. Their core function is to provide support and counsel with respect to specific aspects of the enterprise. Designed to tap external resources, they can be large, formal, or informal, but they tend to be quite focused in their efforts. In establishing any of these structures, expectations need to be clear at the start. Such entities, like boards themselves, can work either well or very poorly. Business project teams (usually a smaller group of people who are primarily although not exclusively internal to the organization) have been suggested as an additional means of tapping some necessary resources. Such teams may have more ability to deal with operational issues because they are internal, and they may be easier to manage. They may also be particularly useful during the development and early stages of a new enterprise. In addition to providing necessary expertise for the enterprise at a particular time, all of these mechanisms are also potential testing grounds for new board members over time.

Finally, as your organization undertakes an enterprise, potentially expanding its mission or range of activities, it is important to rethink the committee structure of the board. Committee structure does seem to matter in terms of board performance, presumably because it permits the organization to use the skills of the board members better—something to keep in mind as the skills needed and the focus of the board change. There is an increasing trend in organizations toward creating structures to facilitate the actual work that needs to be done, and this has also been recommended for boards.[11] As the work of the board changes, so should its committee structure. Indeed, a key take-away from this chapter is that these new enterprises are an indicator of great change, and the governance structures, of both the parent organization and the enterprise itself, need to reflect this.

Conclusion

This chapter suggests many options for structuring the oversight and support structure of your nonprofit enterprise. To help you select among these options we have devised a series of analytic steps that should help clarify which options might be most appropriate for your enterprise and for your organization. There is no one solution that is best for all.

But there is one approach that will not work for any organization starting a new venture: simply continuing along with the old governance structure as though no change has occurred. A new venture is not simply a new program; by definition you are taking your organization in a new direction, requiring clarity of mission, a detailed understanding of what is needed to get there, and the appropriate adjustments to governance to facilitate this. Avoiding the work associated with developing the best governance structure undermines all of the effort put into the venture to date and decreases your chances of success. It may be the last piece put into place, but it is a critical one to consider if your venture is to succeed.

Notes

1. Moyers, R., and Enright, K. *Results of the NCNB Nonprofit Governance Survey.* Washington, D.C.: National Center for Nonprofit Boards, 1997.
2. Steinberg, R. M. "Effective Boards: Making the Dynamics Work." boardmember.com Resource Center, Apr. 2001 [http://www.boardmember.com/network/index.pl?section=1086&article_id=10278&show=article].
3. For a summary, see Hermalin, B. E., and Weisbach, M. S. "Boards of Directors as an Endogenously Determined Institution: A Survey of Economic Literature." *Federal Reserve Bank of New York Economic Policy Review,* Apr. 2003, pp. 7–26.
4. O'Regan, K., and Oster, S. "Does the Structure and Composition of the Board Matter? The Case of Nonprofit Organizations." Yale School of Management Working Paper No. 04, 2002.
5. For information about the 2002 Sarbanes-Oxley Act, see http://news.findlaw.com/hdocs/docs/gwbush/sarbanesoxley072302.pdf.
6. Sonnenfeld, J. "What Makes Great Boards Great?" *Harvard Business Review,* 2002, *80*(9), 106–113.
7. Glassman, C. A. "Speech by SEC Commissioner: Sarbanes-Oxley and the Idea of 'Good' Governance." Washington, D.C.: U.S. Securities and Exchange Commission, Sept. 27, 2002 [http://www.sec.gov/news/speech/spch586.htm].
8. Moyers and Enright, op. cit.
9. Dees, G., Emerson, J., and Economy, P. *Enterprising Nonprofits: A Toolkit for Social Entrepreneurs.* New York: Wiley, 2001.
10. Bradshaw, P., Murray, V., and Wolpin, P. "Do Nonprofit Boards Make a Difference? An Explanation of the Relationships Among Board Structure, Process, and Effectiveness." *Nonprofit and Voluntary Sector Quarterly,* Fall 1992, pp. 227–250.
11. Taylor, B., Chait, R., and Holland, T. "The New Work of the Nonprofit Board." *Harvard Business Review,* 1996, *74*(5), 36–40.

PART TWO

FINDING AND
ATTRACTING CAPITAL

CHAPTER EIGHT

SECURING FINANCIAL CAPITAL

David Bornstein and The Goldman Sachs Foundation

One of the greatest challenges faced by an organization seeking to launch a nonprofit enterprise or to expand an existing one is finding the capital to finance the venture at various stages in its development. The for-profit world has developed an array of financing vehicles to help launch and grow businesses. In early stages, businesses are often funded by investments or loans from friends, family, partners, or "angel" investors (individuals who provide capital usually in exchange for ownership stakes). As businesses grow, they can seek secondary or so-called mezzanine financing from venture capitalists, institutional investors, or banks. Further down the road, businesses can attract large-scale capital through bond issues or public stock offerings.

Currently, the nonprofit sector has a more modest selection of financing tools available for nonprofit enterprises. As a result, managers of nonprofit enterprises have to spend more time and effort than business managers to raise significant levels of financing. (In the for-profit sector the cost of raising capital to start and expand a business is estimated at 2 to 5 percent of the value of the funds raised. In the nonprofit sector, the figure is estimated to be three to four times higher.)

All businesses, whether for-profit or nonprofit, need start-up or seed capital to finance operations until the business begins generating positive cash flows. For nonprofit ventures, that initial financing—which may be referred to as "patient capital"—typically comes from funds generated internally by the parent nonprofit or from grants from foundations or board members. Nonprofit enterprises may also be funded by government grants, loans from foundations (called program-related investments), government small business loans, and commercial loans.

Unlike businesses, nonprofit enterprises do not attract equity financing, because they are prohibited from distributing profits to owners. Some nonprofit organizations running enterprises set up for-profit subsidiary corporations or limited liability partnerships or companies to run social-purpose ventures. In addition to obtaining grant funding, these organizations often seek to attract commercial loans or, in certain cases, private equity investments, although the latter are uncommon.

Many managers of nonprofit enterprises do not seek loan financing from commercial sources, particularly for start-up ventures, because it is assumed that banks are unwilling to make such investments. While commercial bankers are indeed hesitant to lend money to nonprofit enterprises in their early stages (because they cannot demonstrate predictable cash flows and because nonprofit enterprises frequently have lower profit margins than comparable for-profit businesses), many commercial banks do have vehicles for community development or social investing once the businesses have become stable. In the eyes of a banker, "stability" typically translates into either sizable cash flow from operations or security in the form of collateral (such as real estate). One cautionary note is that bankers are often hesitant to secure a loan with collateral if collecting on that collateral—for example, taking control of a building—might force a nonprofit to cease operations. While commercial loans are by no means easy to secure, they are certainly a possible route to financing, and an option worth exploring.

On average, it takes about two and a half years for a nonprofit enterprise to break even.[1] Once the business reaches that point, it often will have to continue growing to remain viable and profitable. A business that does not grow will have trouble responding to new market opportunities or improving its products and services. In a competitive market environment, that can lead to business failure. Growth, of course, means raising more capital to finance new investments in staff, equipment, fixed assets, and inventories. A nonprofit enterprise experiencing steady revenue growth will need to build up its capacity in a number of areas, including management information systems, production capacity, performance evaluation, and financial controls. Moreover, to attract experienced financial management professionals and skilled managers, it will often have to provide competitive compensation and incentive packages.

The initial forms of financing that nonprofit enterprises usually depend on—grants and internal funds from the parent nonprofit—are in limited supply and carry high transaction costs, chiefly, the amount of time and energy expended to secure philanthropic grants and/or internal funding sources. Therefore, organizations seeking to launch nonprofit enterprises should seek to research a range of funding options early in the business planning process. As businesses mature, cash flows become more stable and it is generally easier to access debt financing. (Indeed, in their early stages nonprofit enterprises and for-profit small businesses face similar financing difficulties. It is worth exploring how the large body of knowledge about small business financing and the resources available to for-profit entrepreneurs in the start-up stage can be channeled and applied to nonprofit enterprise financing.) In the business planning stage, organizations may look to identify different categories of funders who can provide financing appropriate for the different stages—start-up, growth, and maturity—in an enterprise's life cycle. The challenge is to identify funders who are interested in nonprofit enterprise and wish to provide the type of financing that will suit your enterprise at various stages—from seed capital in the form of one-time grants to growth capital in the form of multiyear grants or renewable loans.

Different types and sizes of organizations have different options available to them, of course. Large institutional or quasi-institutional organizations, such as state- or privately operated residences for elderly or disabled people, can, in addition to seeking grants or debt, contract out services, engage in joint ventures with corporations, or establish for-profit subsidiaries and seek to attract debt financing, or in rare cases, investment capital, from commercial sources. These arrangements are often too complex, time-consuming, or beyond the financial scope of small community-based or informal organizations, such as day care programs, after-school programs, or soup kitchens.

Sources of Capital

Seed or Start-Up Capital: Grants

The most common form of start up capital for nonprofit enterprises is either grant funding or funding from internal or operational sources within a parent nonprofit that is reallocated to the nonprofit enterprise.

General Nonprofit Enterprise Resources

Nonprofit enterprise is a growing field that has attracted interest among a variety of funders. Some of the organizations that have compiled useful sets of resources include Community Wealth Ventures; New Profit, Inc.; Roberts Enterprise Development Fund; Social Enterprise Alliance; Venture Philanthropy Partners; and the Yale School of Management–The Goldman Sachs Foundation Partnership on Nonprofit Ventures.

One particularly useful resource is a 2003 report prepared by Community Wealth Ventures entitled *Powering Social Change: Lessons on Community Wealth Generation for Nonprofit Sustainability,* which provides an overview of the field of nonprofit enterprises, including a survey of organizations running these enterprises, as well as case studies and essays from practitioners that explain how their organizations have grappled with a range of challenges, including finding seed and growth capital.[2] Another resource for practitioners in this field is the npEnterprise Forum (http://www.npenterprise.net), an online forum sponsored by the Social Enterprise Alliance where nonprofit managers, consultants, and funders can discuss practices and exchange ideas and leads. Additionally, Venture Philanthropy Partners makes reports available on its Web site that provide an overview of high-engagement grantmakers, many of whom invest in social enterprise. In recent years, groups of businesspeople-cum-social investors, many of whom, such as Social Venture Partners, provide financing and technical assistance to nonprofit enterprises, have sprung up.

Nonprofit Enterprise Competitions

In addition to the National Business Plan Competition for Nonprofit Organizations organized by the Yale School of Management–The Goldman Sachs Foundation Partnership on Nonprofit Ventures, a variety of other awards and competitions are open to nonprofits pursuing a social enterprise strategies, including the Global Social Venture Competition sponsored by the Haas School of Business at the University of California at Berkeley, the Columbia Business School, the London School of Business, and The Goldman Sachs Foundation; and the Social Stimulus Nonprofit Funding Competition supported by the Keiretsu Forum Foundation and Social Stimulus.

Investigation

Additionally, there are many creative options for nonprofit development directors who are interested in doing some investigation beyond the traditional routes. One idea is to search through the various Marquis-type "Who's Who Directories" (http://www.marquiswhoswho.com/products/productlist_main.asp) to compile lists of influential individuals in businesses, or working in particular fields, who have demonstrated a potential interest or connection to your nonprofit enterprise. Another option is to attend conferences, trade shows, or gatherings where potential businesspeople or funders meet. For example, Investors' Circle, a nonprofit national network of individuals and institutional investors, foundation representatives, and entrepreneurs who seek to achieve financial, social, and environmental returns, sponsors a national conference and a number of venture fairs around the United States each year. Businesspeople in related industries may be interested in assisting a nonprofit enterprise by sitting on the board, contributing expertise, doing business, or providing funding through a family or corporate foundation. Another direction for research are networks of socially responsible businesspeople and students, such as Business for Social Responsibility or Net Impact.

Corporate Support for Nonprofit Enterprise

Another approach is to identify corporations, either local or national, that are working in industries similar to your enterprise's industry or reaching a customer base that is likely to be responsive to your area of activity. Many companies are eager to ally themselves with nonprofit associations, especially with organizations whose work bears a natural connection to their businesses. For example, one of the winners in the 2002–03 National Business Plan Competition for Nonprofit Organizations was the El Puente Community Development Corporation, based in El Paso, Texas. In launching its business—Diseños Mayapán, which markets colorful, stylish, and better-sized hospital scrubs to hospital care workers, many of whom are Mexican American, in El Paso—El Puente sought and received initial seed funding from a local hospital. In addition to making financial donations, companies may find it cost-effective (or attractive for tax purposes) to donate real estate or equipment or to provide low-cost office space.

General Grant Resources

The single most useful resource for identifying foundations that are interested in supporting nonprofit enterprises is the New York-based Foundation Center, which has an extensive library as well as a range of online research tools to help nonprofits identify potential funders in its database of seventy thousand grantmakers, including private foundations, corporate grantmakers, grantmaking public charities, and community foundations. Some of the Center's resources are available free on the Internet; more extensive searches are available for a fee. It is worth noting that for every major national foundation there are hundreds of smaller family foundations and corporate-giving offices that focus narrowly on particular geographic regions or special areas of interest.

In general, family foundations and corporate-giving offices tend to provide smaller grants than large foundations do, but their application procedures may be simpler and they may be able to respond more quickly to individual funding requests. The most important consideration in targeting a foundation is, of course, to identify the subject area of interest to that foundation.

The Chronicle of Philanthropy's Web site provides a list of links to private and operating foundations and corporate grantmakers in the United States. It also provides a list of information sources for soliciting government grants and funding from community foundations.

Associations of Regional Grantmakers and Affinity Groups

Also listed on the Chronicle of Philanthropy's Web site are a number of associations of grantmakers with regional focuses, such as the Association of Baltimore Area Grantmakers and the Donors Forum of Ohio. Another avenue for research available on this site are funding affinity groups such as Funders Concerned About AIDS or Grantmakers Concerned with Care at the End of Life. From among these groups a development director can identify a subselection of funders with an interest in a particular issue area. There are many regional grantmakers and affinity groups that are not listed on this site; they remain useful avenues for further research.

Philanthropic Tax Credits

In a number of states, corporations can claim philanthropic tax credits through state-mandated neighborhood assistance programs. These programs offer tax credits to corporations that commit long-term grant support, as well as management assistance, to nonprofit organizations working to promote economic and social development in low-income communities.

Collaborative Funds

One way that foundations achieve greater impact from their philanthropic resources is by pursing collaborative funding. By pooling resources and expertise and coordinating planning and decision making, cooperating foundations can channel a larger quantity of resources to several organizations pursuing similar or complementary strategies vis-à-vis a particular social problem. This strategy is useful for increasing the capacity of the grant recipients while advancing learning about a particular strategy among a large number of donors and practitioners. The Ms. Foundation for Women, for example, has launched two such funds, one of which has a strong overlapping focus on the field of nonprofit enterprise: the Collaborative Fund for Women's Economic Development, which pools resources from twenty-four funders to provide financial and technical support to organizations across the United States that help women start or scale-up microenterprises or cooperative businesses; and the Collaborative Fund for Youth-Led Social Change, which uses a similar strategy to support youth development organizations. The Collaborative Fund for Women's Economic Development provided support to two of the finalists in the 2002–03 National Business Plan Competition for Nonprofit Organizations: the Lewisburg, West Virginia-based organization Appalachian by Design, a home-based machine knitting enterprise that provides employment to women in the sparsely populated, underdeveloped Appalachian region; and the El Puente Community Development Corporation, which provides employment through four different nonprofit enterprises to workers in El Paso, Texas, who have been displaced by the North American Free Trade Agreement.

Sustaining Growth and Working Capital, or Loans

Historically, managers of nonprofit enterprises have been reluctant to seek loan financing for their initiatives. Generally, organizations with considerable revenues—in the millions of dollars—are far more likely to seek loan financing than those with lower revenues. It is often assumed that banks are not interested in providing loans to nonprofit ventures because the profit margins are too low, there are insufficient assets to collateralize the loans, and there are inherent risks and difficulties in doing business with low-income clients and employing tough-to-manage workers. Additionally, nonprofits often rely on third-party revenues, such as state appropriations and government contracts, which are vulnerable to budget cuts.

Perhaps the strongest obstacle to debt financing is cultural resistance within the nonprofit sector. Many people in the nonprofit sector are uncomfortable with debt because they are worried about their ability to repay loans, they don't want to incur interest expenses, they lack experience managing debt, they are more familiar with the players in the foundation world, and they are reluctant to expose an organization providing vital social services to the risks associated with debt. Most nonprofit enterprises are initially staffed by employees from the parent nonprofit organization. The management teams often lack significant experience in business. This also makes them less attractive as potential borrowers in the eyes of commercial lenders.

When considering debt versus grant financing many nonprofit organizations fail to take into account the full costs of grant financing, including the costs associated with lengthy discussions, preparation of grant applications, detailed reporting, and year-to-year renewals and refinancing. (Many nonprofit organizations do have revolving lines of credit from traditional financial institutions and community development sources.) For nonprofit enterprises to scale up significantly, however, it is likely that in the future more of their financing will have to come from commercial and below-market debt instruments.

There are a variety of sources that nonprofits can turn to when seeking various forms of debt financing for nonprofit ventures. These include commercial banks, community development financial institutions, state or municipal community-development authorities, the U.S. Small Business Administration, specially designed financial intermediaries, diversified financial services companies, and foundation or corporate program-related investments. A number of these are described here.

Bank Loans. Many banks across the United States have social investment or nonprofit financing portfolios. Banks frequently lend money, either at market or concessionary rates, to nonprofit organizations that don't meet their regular business loan qualifications. They do so both to comply with the Community Reinvestment Act and to reach out to underserved and growing markets. As a general rule, it is worthwhile for any organization seeking to launch a nonprofit enterprise to walk into a local bank and initiate a relationship. At the very least, having a conversation with a local banker about your nonprofit enterprise may provide valuable insights or contacts. Bankers are experts at evaluating financial statements and projections, and they can help you think through the question of how and when debt financing might fit in with the needs of the nonprofit enterprise. (Any organization that is considering using debt to finance its activities needs to be informed about when it should be using debt and when it should not be using it.) Bankers also tend to be tied into the economic life of a community. So even if a banker cannot offer a loan under the bank's lending rules, he or she might think your nonprofit enterprise is an intriguing idea and refer you to friends or colleagues who are in positions to help.

When a financial institution looks to make a loan to a nonprofit venture, it generally looks for three basic things: uncomplicated, reliable income streams; a set of assets that can be used as collateral; and a management team that inspires confidence. For the nonprofit organization, many payment streams can be put forward, such as government payments or contracts, sales or revenue history from the enterprise, history of fee-for-service income, proven fundraising ability, commitments of future grant support and loan guarantees from foundations.

Program-Related Investments. The term *program related investment* (PRI) was created by the U.S. Congress three decades ago to describe a particular type of investment—usually a loan—that applies in the nonprofit sector. About two to three hundred foundations in the United States offer PRIs today. Additionally, many corporations, including insurance companies, utilities, and financial services companies, are engaged in targeted social investments, providing below-market loans to groups involved in community development work. In many cases, companies seek to make investments where their employees are based.

The Foundation Center publishes a review of foundation PRIs every two years. In 1999, PRIs accounted for about $275 million in revenues for nonprofits. From a foundation's tax perspective, PRIs are similar to grants; they count as part of a funder's required 5 percent minimum charitable distribution for the year in which they are issued. When the money is repaid, it counts as an inflow of capital to the foundation. In addition to PRIs, some foundations provide *recoverable grants* to nonprofits, which function as interest-free loans.

There are three basic legal requirements for a PRI investment: it must enhance the primary purpose of the tax-exempt organization, the investment and the terms of the investment have to be such that a prudent profit-seeking investor would not make it, and no part of the funds can be used to lobby the government.

Loans are the most common form of program-related investments. PRIs can take a number of other forms, however, including lines of credit, loan guarantees, direct asset purchases, and equity investments in for-profit subsidiaries of nonprofits. The loans may be secured by real estate or other assets, although many PRIs are unsecured. The biggest benefit of a PRI is that once a foundation has gone through its loan evaluation process and agreed to issue the loan, the sums available are often considerably larger than grants tend to be.

Although PRIs carry lower interest rates than commercial loans and are provided by foundations as a form of assistance to nonprofits, they often take longer to negotiate than loans and thus involve high transaction costs. These costs need to be taken into account when seeking this type of financing. But foundations also provide benefits that commercial lenders do not: they are less demanding about collateral requirements for PRI loans and they generally provide additional intellectual or technical resources to help ensure the success of the nonprofit enterprise.

PRI Funding Example: The Success for All Foundation

The Success for All Foundation is a spin-off of Johns Hopkins University. Under the aegis of the university, Success for All developed a series of reading and math programs to help elementary schools in high-poverty areas improve the learning of their students. It charges fees for its services, materials, and training programs. As it expanded to serving more schools, its revenues increased. When revenues reached $20 million, it spun off from Johns Hopkins and became an independent nonprofit organization. Today, Success for All works with fifteen hundred schools in forty-eight states and generates close to $60 million in revenues.

When Success for All was spun off from Johns Hopkins, the organization needed to raise money to finance its operations. It identified loans as a viable source of capital. The business showed solid growth in terms of increased revenues and in the number of schools with which the organization worked. The biggest need for funding was for unrestricted working capital, particularly during the summers, when Success for All does a great deal of printing and shipping of materials in preparation for the following school year. The organization also employs staff who provide on-site trainings to schools across the country. At any time it needs $10 million to $20 million in working capital to manage cash flow and make necessary investments in inventory.

To help meet these needs, Success for All sought and received a number of PRIs—below market, long-term, unsecured loans from several foundations, including the Ford Foundation, the MacArthur Foundation, the New Schools Venture Fund, and The Goldman Sachs Foundation. The loans carry interest rates that range from 1 to 3 percent, with repayment terms ranging from three to five to eight years. The PRIs have provided a number of benefits to Success for All. They have supplied working capital at lower cost than commercial debt instruments do. They also have helped Success for All establish a diversified base of financing, which has enhanced the organization's profile for commercial lenders. The long-term loans have helped Success for All establish a revolving line of commercial bank credit, which is collateralized with its receivables and inventory balances.

Each of Success for All's funders required a business plan to start the loan negotiation process. The due diligence period ranged from six months to eighteen months for loans ranging from $400,000 to $2 million. The reviews involved detailed financial forecasting and sensitivity analyses—looking at the effects on cash flow and revenues if business growth diverged considerably from the plan. Additionally, Success for All had to provide detailed management letters explaining how the organization would address a number of internal policies and procedures.

Once the loans were authorized, the reporting requirements were not onerous. Some foundations requested annual reports, others requested quarterly reports. All funders requested reports on both financial and program results. Success for All's commercial bankers required that their loans be given priority over the PRIs in the case of default.

In the nonprofit sector, there is still relatively little awareness about PRIs. Foundations have been slow to adopt PRIs as a financing tool because in general funders are more comfortable with grantmaking than they are with debt financing, and they often lack the expertise to evaluate nonprofit enterprise's investment opportunities. As the philanthropic and investment worlds grow closer to one another, and as the field of nonprofit enterprise becomes more sophisticated, it is likely that more funders will be exploring PRIs as a financing tool. Also, because foundations have fewer resources for grant funding today, some are looking at using PRIs as an alternative.

When looking for PRIs, organizations should seek corporate, public, or private foundations that have strong program interests that parallel their own activities. PRI loans are not catch-all financing mechanisms for all nonprofit enterprises but rather another tool that foundations can use to provide support in areas in which they are already involved.

Although PRIs are often unsecured loans, foundations do expect to be paid back. PRIs can be highly useful to nonprofits in helping them build up the credit history that is necessary to establish financing relationships with capital lenders.

(Some foundations also provide loan guarantees to enable nonprofits to meet the collateral requirements of commercial or community-development lenders.) Generally, nonprofits seeking to capitalize their ventures through PRIs should invest in professional financial managers who have the skills and experience required to obtain debt financing and prepare the requisite financial reports and statements for lenders.

Community Development Financial Institutions. Community development financial institutions (CDFIs) provide various forms of support to nonprofits and for-profits operating enterprises to bring social and economic benefits to under-resourced communities. These institutions, such as the Nonprofit Finance Fund, specialize in providing low-cost, long-term growth capital to nonprofits. They are unregulated and often boast considerable assets. As such, they are well-suited to meet the financial needs of nonprofit enterprises seeking such capital. CDFIs are usually structured to serve the needs of particular markets and locations, such as real estate or business development in a particular city or state. They specialize in extending loans that commercial lenders would find too risky.

The Illinois Facilities Fund (IFF) finances nonprofit enterprises through its New Visions loan product, as well as providing assistance in financial planning and business plan development. Its loans, which carry terms as long as fifteen years, are structured to accommodate nonprofit enterprise revenue streams and provide for deferments on interest and principal payments until the ventures reach a break-even stage.

The National Community Capital Association provides an on-line CDFI locator to speed the search by geographic region. Their Web site provides an overview of CDFIs, including the following:

- Community development banks, which provide capital to rebuild economically distressed areas through lending and investment
- Community development credit unions, which promote ownership of assets and provide credit and financial services to low-income people
- Community development loan funds, which lend money primarily to nonprofit housing and business developers in economically distressed communities
- Community development venture capital funds, which provide equity and debt financing to small and medium-sized for-profit businesses that create jobs and wealth in low-income communities
- Microenterprise development loan funds, which provide loans and technical assistance to small business people who are unable to gain access to capital through traditional sources

Community Development Venture Capital. For nonprofits that run for-profit social or double-bottom-line businesses, there are many avenues for investment. For
example, Community Development Venture Capital Funds provide equity capital
rather than loans to new or expanding businesses in low-income areas. The Community Development Venture Capital Alliance (CDVCA), an umbrella group with
more than one hundred member funds, seeks to create jobs, entrepreneurial capacity, and wealth in low-income and distressed communities through venture-
capital-type investments, in amounts typically ranging from $100,000 to $1
million. CDVCA's member funds can be searched by state on CDVCA's Web site
(http://www.cdvca.org/funds_geographic.html).

The Investors' Circle channels capital to private companies that seek to address social and environmental problems through commercial solutions. An excellent new resource is the Columbia Business School's Research Initiative on
Social Enterprise, which has produced the Double Bottom Line Investor Direc-
tory, a national searchable public database of investment funds that make early-
stage equity investments in for-profit ventures whose products, services, or business
structures have positive social or environmental impacts.

Funding Intermediaries. Funding intermediaries exist to link nonprofit organizations and investors. The Community Health Facilities Fund (CHFF), based in
Stamford, Connecticut, is a funding intermediary that links nonprofits and investors. CHFF provides nonprofit behavioral care providers with low-cost, long-
term, fixed-rate loans. The New York-based Local Initiatives Support Corporation
(LISC), which works in thirty-eight cities as well as several rural areas in the
United States, provides grants, loans, and equity investments to community development corporations (CDCs)—locally controlled nonprofit organizations involved in neighborhood redevelopment. LISC, which is financed by foundations,
corporations, and individuals, works with hundreds of CDCs across the United
States, usually matching funds that the CDC has raised locally. LISC targets its
resources at organizations involved in rural development, housing, economic development, community-building, and organization and leadership development.

Considerations When Taking on Debt

As discussed, many nonprofits are averse to taking on debt. However, debt can be
thought of as just another asset that an organization is "renting." Organizations
are usually comfortable paying rent for their office space, photocopying machines,
and other assets. Taking on debt can be seen as renting money. The advantages
or disadvantages of doing so should be evaluated based on the returns that can

be expected to be generated with that particular asset. Although grants have the advantage of not having to be repaid, loans also have advantages over one-time grants. Above all, loans are often much easier to renew than grants. If a business is performing on its loans and if its market prospects and balance sheet have not changed markedly since the original loan was negotiated, renewing or extending a previously negotiated loan can be a fairly straightforward and painless process.

By contrast, one-time grants come with hidden and high transaction costs. A great deal of human resources are invested in writing and editing grant proposals and attending meetings until the grant is received, and then going through the process again the following year with each funder separately. Often this process drains considerable resources from an organization. It's always worth tracking how much time and effort it takes to actually get money in the door. If a nonprofit enterprise fits with the market for financing, it's worth thinking about the long-term advantages of debt.

The Business Social Bridge: Finding Capital for Nonprofit Enterprises Through Sponsorships, Exchanges, or Partnerships

One important and growing opportunity is to work in partnership with the business sector. In recent years there has been a great deal of bridge-building between the nonprofit and corporate sectors as both sectors have discovered common areas of interest. For example, while nonprofits have focused on social entrepreneurship, ventures, and improved management strategies, businesses have sought to become better corporate citizens, pursuing socially responsible practices and engaging in various forms of social investing. Studies indicate that MBA graduates from leading business schools today are increasingly looking to get involved in the nonprofit world and to work for companies that are known to be socially responsible. These trends hold particular promise for nonprofit enterprises seeking grant financing, business contracts, volunteer support, office space, or pro-bono management consulting or marketing assistance.

Nonprofits can raise considerable resources by forming partnerships with businesses. There are a number of different kinds of exchanges that nonprofits and businesses engage in that can increase access to resources—human and financial—for the nonprofit while providing some form of value to the corporation.

Corporate Philanthropy. Many corporations regularly donate funding or goods or services to nonprofit organizations, or encourage their employees to volunteer, serve as mentors, or provide pro-bono assistance. The field of nonprofit enterprise is well positioned to benefit from this trend because of the overlap of skill sets needed in each sector. Social organizations in the United States regularly receive thousands of dollars worth of business assistance from well-known consulting or public relations firms.

Operational Partnerships. Nonprofit enterprises can earn profits by supplying goods and services to businesses or providing training or recruitment services that help companies achieve their business goals. In exchange, the enterprises receive a reliable flow of business revenues that can help service loans and finance growth. As part of their relationships with businesses, nonprofit enterprises may also receive benefits from corporate-giving offices, pro-bono or in-kind support, assistance in product or service development, and credibility in the marketplace.

This is a strategy that has proved effective for Pioneer Human Services, an organization that provides employment and training as well as housing and counseling services to individuals in need, including recovering alcoholics, people recovering from chemical dependencies, and ex-offenders. Pioneer has created eight nonprofit enterprises in Seattle that supply products and services to such corporations as Boeing, Starbucks, Nordstrom, and Hasbro, bringing Pioneer close to $55 million in annual revenues.

Another example is the New York-based Greyston Bakery, a for-profit subsidiary of the nonprofit Greyston Foundation. The Greyston Bakery has established an operational partnership with Ben & Jerry's ice cream. Today Greyston Bakery is the exclusive provider of brownies for a number of Ben & Jerry's best-selling ice cream flavors. This reliable business relationship has helped Greyston Bakery build its customer base and raise financing, including a loan of more than $1 million from the Nonprofit Finance Fund to help construct a modern, energy-efficient bakery. Although Ben & Jerry's was eager to do business with Greyston Bakery from the outset, it took a few years for the initial partnership to take hold as the bakery built up its production capacity, perfected its recipes, and instituted systems to ensure that its products were consistently high quality.

Marketing Partnerships or Sponsorships. Many nonprofit organizations have also discovered the value of creating marketing alliances with businesses. Typically a corporation will provide some form of payment or sponsorship to a social organization in exchange for the right to associate with the organization or its cause. Such cause-related marketing can help companies develop their brand identities, differentiate themselves from competitors, and lure high-quality employees who seek to work in socially responsible corporations.

Share Our Strength, a national antihunger group, is an example of an organization that has demonstrated the potential of this strategy through its long-standing marketing partnerships with such companies as Calphalon, American

Express, and Jenn-Air. Through these partnerships, Share Our Strength has raised more than $50 million for antihunger projects. Similar marketing alliances exist between Green Mountain Coffee Roasters and TransFair USA, which markets and certifies "Fair Trade" coffee, and between Timberland and City Year, a full-time voluntary national service program that brings together young people from diverse backgrounds for a year of service.

Other Considerations

When launching a nonprofit enterprise, it is helpful to adopt the language and concepts of a business plan, separate the enterprise to create financial transparency, and plan for the long-term capital needs that come with growth and success.

The Business Plan Executive Summary: A Tool to Engage Funders

One major difficulty that nonprofits face in raising funding for nonprofit ventures has to do with language, specifically with the fact that the nonprofit and business sectors have historically looked at the world through different lenses and employed different vocabularies. As social investing continues to gain momentum, commercial investors will likely become more attuned to the needs and particularities of the nonprofit sector. For the time being, however, nonprofits seeking to tap investment capital, particularly from nonfoundation sources, will benefit by learning to apply the terminology and concepts with which investors are familiar. It is worth remembering, therefore, that one of the most powerful communication tools for thinking through the challenges of a nonprofit venture and explaining the enterprise to social investors is a business plan executive summary. The general idea of this summary is to boil down your enterprise to its essence so that the idea can be communicated in business lingo to a potential funder in about ten minutes. (See Chapter Nine of this volume, "Pitching Your Venture," by Amy Solas and Adam Blumenthal for guidelines on how to do this.)

The Financial Relationship Between the Venture and the Parent Organization

From the perspective of a financier, it is important to be able to analyze the nonprofit enterprise on its own merits, separate from the parent nonprofit. The tendency is to merge the two—to evaluate ventures and their associated risks on the basis of the parent nonprofit's capacity to absorb shocks. If the nonprofit enterprise is not sufficiently separated from the parent organization, it is likely to be reliant on the larger infrastructure or on indirect assistance that won't be fully reflected in the venture's financing. To know if the venture is truly profitable, for example, or to know if it is generating surplus cash that can be used to advance the mission, the nonprofit enterprise needs to stand alone.

From the point-of-view of outside investors, lack of separation from the parent organization will blur the financial reporting. Without separation, the parent company may also see fit to redeploy some of its resources from the nonprofit enterprise to another part of the organization. A funder may then discover that resources that had been anticipated are unavailable. It is critical to clarify the resources that belong to the parent and those that are specifically allocated to the nonprofit enterprise.

Capital Structure

One final consideration for organizations seeking financing for a nonprofit venture is to keep in mind what the capital structure of the organization is going to look like after it is fully financed. That is, what will it have in terms of assets—cash, receivables, investments, real estate, equipment—and liabilities?

Growing a nonprofit enterprise means changing an organization's capital structure—usually by acquiring more assets, particularly fixed assets, and increasing management and overhead expenses, thereby putting strain on other programs, restricting flexibility, increasing organizational complexity, and making it necessary to increase unrestricted cash balances.

It is important to think early about the medium- and long-term capital needs of a nonprofit enterprise, particularly if the parent organization has historically relied on short-term permanently or temporarily restricted revenues such as foundation grants. Organizations should not just hope for success and growth, they should anticipate and plan for it, especially for the capitalization needs of the enterprise, well before that enterprise has outgrown its parent.

Conclusion

The key to finding financing is to understand how what you want to do fits with the market. It is important to ask, *What does a particular funder understand this enterprise to be? How can your organization be presented so that it looks like what the funder or lender wants to see?* It is important to start conversations with potential funders early. Every funder has a different culture and a different set of objectives. Successful funding partnerships go beyond financing; they are grounded in common objectives and expectations, both short-term and long-term, between funders and investees.

Today the capital markets for nonprofit enterprises are still underdeveloped. The range of financing options, from grants to loans, remains limited compared to those available to traditional businesses. As the market for social financial services grows and as more organizations build up track records developing successful nonprofit ventures and repaying loans, we can expect that it will become easier to find capital for nonprofit enterprises in a cost-effective manner. As the financial barriers are removed, we can hope to see a great deal of business and social creativity unleashed toward the pursuit of social value and new solutions.

Notes

1. Community Wealth Ventures. *Powering Social Change: Lessons on Community Wealth Generation for Nonprofit Sustainability.* Washington, D.C.: Community Wealth Ventures, 2003. [http://www.communitywealth.com/Powering%20Social%20Change.pdf].
2. Ibid.

CHAPTER NINE

PITCHING YOUR VENTURE

Amy Solas and Adam M. Blumenthal

In launching an earned income venture, many nonprofits for the first time confront a new opportunity: raising capital from private investors. This new opportunity brings with it new challenges as well, for there are many ways in which private investors differ from the donors and foundations that nonprofits typically confront. In this chapter we describe some of the techniques involved in making a *pitch* to potential investors. We explore some of the typical questions that investors are likely to ask and some of the concerns they may have about a new venture.

Every time you communicate about your venture to a potential investor—regardless of the form that communication takes—it's a pitch. The goal of all of your communications is to convince potential investors to invest in your venture. An effective investor pitch guides its audience to understand why the venture will succeed and how it meets their investment criteria. This latter point is critical. Different investors have different criteria beyond the venture's potential commercial success that influence whether or not they will invest in a promising venture. It is vital to understand these specific criteria—especially those relating to risk-return trade-offs—when designing a pitch. Investors are different from grant funders in that they are interested in earning a return on their investment, not simply in doing good. With every potential money-making investment come potential risks, and the level of risk an investor is willing to assume informs the investments he or she is willing to make. That question of return on investment translates into a different risk-return profile for each investor. Before pitching any investor, it's important to understand his risk-return profile and to tailor your pitch to address how your venture fits that profile.

Finally, just as important as having the right strategy for approaching an investor is translating that strategy into an effective and persuasive pitch. This chapter suggests some techniques for developing an effective pitch, and provides an example to illustrate our points.

What a Pitch Is

The pitch is simply the answer to the question, why should I invest in this venture? It can be written, oral, or both. It can be delivered under formal or informal circumstances. It can take several forms:

Business plan. This is the pitch at the most detailed level and it is always written.

Investor presentation. This is the presentation that management gives to prospective investors. It is formal and has both spoken and written elements.

Facilities visit. When prospective investors tour the company's offices and other facilities with management and key employees as a part of due diligence, this too is a pitch.

Elevator pitch. This is the pitch that one can deliver in the time it takes to ride an elevator. It's a good idea to have two elevator pitches, one that takes thirty seconds and one that takes two minutes, so that you can use the right one for the situation.

Whatever the format, all of the *information* you provide *in* your pitch, no matter how long or short it is, should be relevant to answering the investor's central question: Why should I invest in this venture? The pitch is not simply a compendium of information assembled so that investors can draw their own conclusions. Your job is to persuade prospective investors that your venture is the right investment for them.

Shaping your information to guide and persuade the investor to see things the way you do does *not* mean leaving out potentially negative information, such as the threat of new technology or a critical capacity that you don't have. On the contrary, only if you address these issues head-on will investors be confident that you have done all of the work necessary for your venture to succeed.

Because different investors have different priorities and objectives, to develop a persuasive pitch you must in turn understand the investors you are courting and how they make their investment decisions, address everything the investor expects you to cover, and shape everything you plan to cover into a set of compelling key messages and a succinct investment story. We address each of these issues next.

Understanding the Investor's Mind-Set

Investors have very different objectives from funders. Foundations, through the grant proposal process, generally are trying to ascertain the impact that their dollars will have when directed to a specific program. They have general social objectives and are trying to select specific projects for which their limited supply of money can be used to further those general objectives to the greatest extent possible. To determine the answer to their key question, why should we fund this project? they ask questions such as the following:

- What services or activities will be provided and are they consistent with our objectives?
- Who will benefit from these services or activities, and is that a population we hope to benefit?
- How can we be certain that these services or activities will be delivered or carried out as promised?
- Will our grant help the organization raise grants from other funders?
- How can we be sure that this activity wouldn't take place except for our dollars, that our dollars will be well-utilized?

An investor has a very different mind-set because an investor's goal is not to ensure that the venture activities in themselves will further some social aim. Rather, in order to answer the question, "Why should I invest in this venture?" the investor asks, "Will the venture I am funding create economic value, and will I be able to get my money back with a return?" It is not that investors are indifferent about the benefits a nonprofit enterprise may have, but even social investors are at least in some measure interested in whether or not a return on investment is obtainable. In this sense we can think of foundations and philanthropists as focusing on *value creation*, while investors care about *value capture*. Value creation is a necessary but not sufficient condition for value capture. In the dot-com world, for example, many businesses have created enormous value for consumers but have led to very little value capture by the firms that started these businesses. A private investor will want to know not only how much your product or service is worth to recipients, but also how much it costs to produce it and how much you can charge for it. For many nonprofits, this is quite a change in mind-set.

Investor Expectations for Returns

An investor typically measures the creation of economic value by determining if she is going to get her money back plus a return on that money after a finite and specified period. A return on investment is created one of two ways. First, the business can be sold to someone else for more than it cost to launch and run it. Second, the business can produce a stable, ongoing stream of cash flows that also are ultimately greater than what it cost to launch and run that business. Of course these two ways to create value are not entirely independent of each other. In particular, it is possible to sell a business only if there is at least one buyer who believes that the business will generate returns at least some time in the future. But these two methods of recovering investment point to one key difference among investors: their expectations on the payback and on the payback period.

Different types of investors have different time horizons and tolerances for risk and are therefore looking for different rates of return. What rates of return will investors in a nonprofit venture want? There are no hard and fast answers to this question, for several reasons. First, the absolute level of returns demanded by investors changes over time, with changing market conditions. As overall interest rates on safe investments such as treasury securities fall, so too will the return investors expect to earn on more risky ventures. Second, investors may require an additional risk premium for investing in nonprofit ventures, and those premiums may vary. On the one hand, ventures initiated by nonprofits are typically privately held companies with unusual structures. The markets for investments in even conventionally structured small businesses are often both illiquid and somewhat opaque. This increases the risk to an investor because it makes it hard to exit through sale of the venture. This feature of the nonprofit venture tends to increase the risk premium required. On the other hand, at least some private investors will accept a lower risk premium in return for the social returns they expect to earn over and above the financial returns.

This discussion makes clear that it is critical to research and understand an investor's risk-return expectations before crafting a pitch to, or even targeting, that potential investor. Is this an investor who will "give you credit" for the social return you generate? How long a payback period is the investor expecting? Many venture capitalists expect to exit the investment within two to three years as ventures either go public or are sold. Nonprofit ventures typically require more patient investors. As a general guideline, it is helpful to distinguish three types of potential private investors, each with a specific investment profile.

The Socially Motivated Investor. You may come across investors who are willing to take returns that are quite low relative to what conventional sources provide.

For example, a foundation's program-related investment or a state economic development program arm may be willing to accept a 5 percent annual return on a risky venture that a venture capitalist would price at a 15 or 20 percent annual return. Such investors are getting part of their return on investment from the good they are doing or from the political benefits of their investments rather than from the money they are making. A socially motivated investor will structure her relationship with the venture to take advantage of some of the benefits of the investment culture, but the relationship still has some grantlike qualities.

The Bank. A *bank* generally has a three-to-seven-year time horizon for recouping its investment with its desired return. Banks are willing to take very little risk. As a result, a bank wants to be able to see into the future and have several options to get out of the investment if things go wrong. These options may include a lien on hard collateral (a building, an inventory, or machinery and equipment) or the personal or organizational guarantees of the venture's champions. In some cases a bank that holds real estate as collateral may have a longer time horizon. When a bank lends to small businesses it typically prices its loans relative to the prime rate, which generally can be found in the financial pages of a newspaper. Business loans could start at a point or two under prime and go to four to five points over prime, depending on a bank's assessment of risk.

The Equity Investor. An *equity investor* takes more risks than a bank. The equity investor is willing to accept much more uncertainty about how the future may unfold, or to invest for a longer or even indeterminate time. As a result, equity investors require a higher return, which they hope to generate by ownership of a portion of the stock, or equity, of the business. Equity investors include angels (private individuals who invest their own money), small business investment companies (investment funds run by individuals or financial institutions but that receive some subsidies from the government), and private equity funds (which may be managed by individuals or by banks or similar institutions). A conventional *private equity fund* that invests in pure market-based transactions is generally looking for investments that, if successful, will earn a return of approximately 20 to 25 percent per year over five years. Most of this return, of course, will not be earned as current interest. It will be earned as a result of the increasing value of the business over time.

How Investors Analyze Returns

We have suggested that potential investors' risk profiles will vary and that the nonprofit's pitch needs to be adjusted accordingly. The story is in fact more complicated, however, because investors differ not only in the returns they expect from a venture and in how soon they expect those returns, but also in the ways in which they typically calculate risk and return. In developing your pitch, particularly the financial material, it is crucial that you know how your prospective investor will analyze this material. Consider the following exemplars.

A value investor, such as Warren Buffett, looks carefully at operations and cash flow, using established metrics. Buffett looks for stability of cash flows and invests in slow-growth, old economy companies, such as manufacturers and insurers. A pitch to a value investor is therefore going to have to support the point that the business will produce stable cash flows. Someone who makes an argument about the company's great growth potential is not going to get past Warren Buffett's door.

Of course not all investors have Buffett's bias toward current, identifiable returns. A tremendous amount of money was transferred to Internet entrepreneurs by investors on the basis of proposals in which cash flows from operations were negative and expected to remain so for some time. For investors in these ventures, it was high-growth potential that justified their decisions. In pitches to investors focused on growth, the eventual size of the market and the appetite of future investors may be more relevant than careful calculations of soon-to-be realized cash flows.

Social investors have a variety of perspectives as well. Here too the key is to know the investor. When an organization with a fiduciary duty to pensioners, such as the New York City Comptroller's Office, evaluates an economically targeted investment (ETI), the pitch to potential investors must be able to make two separate arguments. First, it must demonstrate that the ETI will provide a market-based return. Second, it must also be able to make a persuasive case that the program has a social benefit. Other social investors, such as church-based investors, economic development groups, and banks driven by community reinvestment provisions, will also take a below-market return in exchange for some social return. For these investors, a *reasonable return,* rather than a *market return,* is the standard. In this context, reasonable is whatever return the investor has defined as satisfactory, given his or her social goals. Market return is that which the investor would expect to earn in the public markets given the level of risk this investment assumes.

As suggested earlier, there will typically be some trade-off in the required financial return as the social return increases. But for most social investors, a positive financial return will be required. Moreover, most social investors care not only that there is a social return but also what type of social return is being generated. In this sense, private social investors resemble foundations with specifically targeted areas of interest. Banks making investments to fulfill requirements under the Community Reinvestment Act, for example, are highly sensitive to the location of the venture. Many screened investment funds focus on projects that promote specific goals, such as peace, environmental progress, and better housing. Again, our message here is to know the audience before structuring the pitch.

Key Questions That the Pitch Must Answer

We have suggested ways in which a pitch should vary according to the characteristics of the potential investor; however, to convince any investor that the venture will succeed and generate the return he seeks, certain questions must be addressed to the investor's satisfaction as part of the pitch. Following are the six key questions that investors ask, and ways in which an organization needs to answer these questions to demonstrate its credibility to investors.

HOW DO I GET MONEY BACK, WITH A RETURN, AFTER A FINITE PERIOD?

In essence, investors want to hear how they will get their money back with a return after a finite period. The purpose of the pro forma financial statements in your business plan or investor presentation is to demonstrate this.

The financial plan is a prediction of the future that uses every piece of information you have about the past and present to support that prediction. It represents the culmination of the assumptions or assertions you have made in other sections of your pitch. All of the information in your business plan or presentation should ultimately tie into the financials.

For example, suppose your financial model assumes that the number of customers you will serve will increase by 5 percent per year while your price stays constant. In a pitch that gets down to this level of detail there should be some assertion of why you believe this. For example, you expect the overall market to grow by 5 percent per year, or you have some compelling reason to expect your venture to capture a larger share of a stable market. If your market analysis shows new rivals cropping up by year three of your operation, the financial picture should reflect this new competition either in softening prices or falling share.

A lack of connection between the financial model and information found elsewhere is one of the most common failings of all pitches by nonprofit and for-profit entrepreneurs alike. If you can't draw a connection between how a certain piece of information in your pitch ultimately shows up in a number, you should not include it. Investors want to understand why your financial model works; like you, they are busy people who are not interested in information for information's sake.

WHAT ARE THE EXPERIENCE AND COMMITMENT OF THE MANAGEMENT TEAM?

A good investor is strongly focused on evaluating a venture's management team. Many private-sector venture capitalists believe that the management team is the key to the success of a new venture. The primary question on the investor's mind about management is, who is the person in the operation responsible for creating value? The investor wants to know that someone is accountable, someone who is totally committed to the venture's success, a *product champion*. An investor wants to know that if something is not going right there is a dedicated person who is going to work around the clock until it is on track. You should be able to demonstrate this type of accountability to anyone you are asking for money. If you cannot, the investor will be led to other questions, which perhaps can be answered by demonstrating the depth of the organization and the experience of the team.

Other key questions investors want to know about management include, what is the management team's relevant experience? Have they done something like this before? What are management's incentives? How strong are those incentives? Are they aligned with mine?

WHAT ARE THE DEPTH AND CAPACITY OF THE ORGANIZATION?

Investors want to know that the organization has the depth and capacity to make the venture succeed. Beyond the management level, do people have the right skills? Have they demonstrated that they have the experience to undertake the activities? Does the venture have the right number of staff? If not, do they recognize what they need?

A key question for investors is whether or not the organization has previously successfully executed similar activities, regardless of whether these activities have made money. Frequently nonprofits that are operating business ventures have not run an income-generating venture before. In the absence of direct experience with a for-profit venture, it is helpful, for reassurance, to point out similar experiences to a new investor. Demonstrating prior use with analytical performance metrics, for example, or careful budgetary controls can help to indicate a businesslike approach to the enterprise. The case you're trying to make is that some aspect of what you do now is almost exactly like what you're going to have to do to make this business work. Similarly, investors will want to know if the proposed model has been tested by someone and already succeeded. Nothing gives investors comfort like copying a preexisting successful model, though they will of course want to know the ways in which your venture will be able to outcompete existing ventures.

WHY WILL YOUR PRODUCT OR SERVICE SUCCEED IN YOUR CHOSEN MARKET?

The market section is typically the longest, vaguest, and most discursive element of a business plan or presentation. An investor does not want you to prove that you understand the market by telling her everything you learned in the course of your research. Rather, the investor wants to know that on the basis of the various factors that go into making up a market, you have developed a strategy that copes with those elements that are relevant to your specific business environment: *your* potential customers, competitors, suppliers, and so on. Investors want to know that you have successfully identified your strategic relationship with each of these entities, and why you have chosen those entities and not others. The market section should quantify all relevant factors and provide evidence to back up your assertions. Any information that is not relevant to making these arguments should not be included.

HOW HAVE YOU DEFINED YOUR COMPETITION?

Carefully defining the competition serves several purposes:

- It demonstrates that you know what the customer wants and the various approaches to filling that need economically.
- It gives context to your strategy—how it differs from other ways of approaching the market that seem to work for someone else.
- It demonstrates awareness that others will be targeting the same customers.

"No one else is doing this" doesn't mean that there is a market for the venture. In fact, investors will assume that there is a good reason no one else is doing this—specifically, that a profit cannot be made—until you persuade them otherwise. For example, suppose you wanted to sell chocolate-covered frozen bananas from carts on the street. No one else may be doing this, but that doesn't mean there is sufficient demand for chocolate-covered frozen bananas in your community to sustain a profitable business, even if you are using an underemployed segment of the population to make and sell the product, your organization's name is on the product, and you will be selling different varieties of frozen bananas, such as with nuts and without. Similarly, "no one else is doing this" doesn't mean there is no competition. Just because no one else is selling chocolate-covered bananas doesn't mean you won't be competing with ice cream vendors or even taco vendors, as well as delis and convenience stores.

WHAT INFRASTUCTURE WILL THE VENTURE REQUIRE AND HOW WILL THE VENTURE BE OPERATED?

Investors want to know that you have sufficient infrastructure to operate the venture. If you do not, they want to know what you need and how much it will cost.

The answer to this question must include a clear description of your physical assets, or a demonstration that you have adequately taken into account in your financial plan the costs of getting the space and equipment you will need.

Investors also want to know that you have a thorough plan that takes into account all phases of how your product or service will be produced, how any raw materials or services required to produce your product or service will be purchased, how your product or service will be marketed and sold, how many people will be required to do all of these things, and how much they will produce.

Developing an Effective Pitch

Investors expect a clear, succinct pitch. If the pitch reflects a lack of clear thinking about the venture, or if the pitch is poorly articulated, most investors will look no further, regardless of the venture's merits. Investors are notorious for their short attention spans; there are simply too many investment opportunities competing for their attention to fully analyze each one. If you don't hook your audience immediately during your presentation, they will grow impatient and may ask you to skip pages. Likewise, if you don't hook your audience immediately in your executive summary or elevator pitch, they will stop reading or tune out.

When developing any pitch:

- Begin your pitch with a concise introduction in order to make sure everyone is "on the same page."
- Figure out the key reasons that the investor you are pitching to should fund your venture—your investment highlights or selling points—and how best to support these points.
- Put these points at the beginning of your pitch rather than at the end.
- Support your points logically.
- Adapt your pitch to your audience and time frame by selecting the appropriate level of detail, from the highest-level points to the most granular-level points.

In addition, when presenting to investors:

- Be prepared to spend a disproportionate amount of time on financials and the assumptions behind them.
- Close your presentation by reiterating your investment highlights.

To illustrate these principles, we turn to a hypothetical example of an investor pitch. The New City Space Museum is writing an investor presentation to attract funding for its new venture, the Space Museum Café. The Space Museum is seeking equity investors who are willing to take a below-market return.

BEGIN YOUR PITCH WITH A CONCISE INTRODUCTION.

Any pitch—not just a presentation—should start with a concise introduction. The purpose of this introduction is to make sure that you and your audience are on the same page, so to speak. The introduction establishes the story by providing basic facts about the situation. It does not sell the opportunity.

The introduction is the first page of the Space Museum Café's presentation. It reminds the audience who is seeking the money (the New City Space Museum), how much they are seeking to raise ($60,000), what they are seeking to raise the money for (start-up costs to open a restaurant adjacent to the museum), how the profits will be used (to provide funding for the museum), and who the other investment partners are (the New City government and the Space Museum). If appropriate to the audience, the introduction may also mention exit opportunities. Exhibit 9.1 shows the presentation's introductory page.

FIGURE OUT THE KEY REASONS THAT THE INVESTOR SHOULD FUND YOUR VENTURE.

The point of your pitch is the answer to the question in your audience's collective mind: Why should we invest in the Space Museum Café? Investors do not want a data dump in answer to that question. Your job is not simply to present all of the information you have and let the investor make up her own mind. Rather, your job in a presentation or any other pitch is to persuade the investor to invest in your venture by answering that question in a way that satisfies that particular investor.

EXHIBIT 9.1. SPACE MUSEUM CAFÉ PRESENTATION'S INTRODUCTORY PAGE.

The Space Museum Café Investment Opportunity

- The Space Museum is seeking $60,000 to open a restaurant adjacent to the museum.
- The capital will go to facility renovations and other start-up costs.
- Profits will fund the Space Museum's operations.
- The city government and the Space Museum are our current investment partners.

An excellent way to figure out the answer to this question is to jot down all of the reasons for investing in the venture as they come to mind, making sure that all of the investor's criteria are covered in a convincing way. As we have seen, these criteria may differ to an extent from one investor to another depending on the particular investor's objectives, but regardless of the details, you must convince the potential investor that the venture will succeed within an appropriate time frame and provide the expected return. Then work out the relationships among all of these reasons and group them in meaningful ways, making these groupings mutually exclusive. That is, the groupings should not overlap. For example, suppose you are categorizing the items on your shopping list so that you can get around the grocery store more quickly. Your list includes apples, bananas, cucumbers, and pears. "Fruits" and "produce" would not be mutually exclusive, whereas "fruits" and "vegetables" would be. In fact, you could further group fruits and vegetables under the category produce. You will find that many of the reasons you have written down have something in common with some of the other reasons you have recorded. You will also find that some of the relationships you have identified are causal and some of them overlap. You may decide that some of the answers ultimately are not relevant to the investment decision. When you have finished, draw conclusions and write statements about what these groupings indicate. These conclusion statements form the basis of your investment highlights and constitute your pitch at the highest level. They tell the investor exactly why she should invest in the venture.

MAKE YOUR POINTS AT THE BEGINNING OF YOUR PITCH.

The next step is to take these points and order them logically. If you are writing a presentation, put these points on a single page that comes after your introduction and serves as a table of contents or agenda page. This page, called a *tracker page,* gives you a logical structure on which to build your presentation and gives your audience a clear map of where the presentation is going.

Another benefit of the tracker page is that it takes away the mystery. Presentation writers are tempted to take the audience through the thinking—all of their research and analysis—to lead up to their conclusions. This is not an effective approach. It keeps the audience in the dark about how to evaluate the opportunity and forces them to ascertain how all the facts fit together. As we noted earlier, investors are impatient people. Like any other busy audience, they want you to get straight to your point. Your audience doesn't want your presentation to unfold like a mystery novel. When you set out right at the beginning of the presentation the reasons that your audience should invest in the venture, they immediately get the big picture.

Repeat the tracker page each time you move to a new section, and highlight on the page the section into which you are moving. This repetition reinforces your messages, makes transitions easier, and reminds the audience of where you are going. The Space Museum Café presentation's tracker page is shown in Exhibit 9.2.

SUPPORT YOUR POINTS LOGICALLY.

Each of the points you make to answer the question, why invest in this venture? in turn raises another question that you must answer: How do you know that? This is where all the other things you wrote down and grouped come in.

You can envision the structure of your pitch as a pyramid, with your broadest, highest-level points at the top, followed by the hows and whys that support each point, down to the lowest levels of detail. Figure 9.1 illustrates how the Space Museum Café pitch looks when mapped out as a flow chart.

For example, how does the Space Museum know that there is clear demand for a restaurant on the site? First, their research shows that many museums the size of the Space Museum have successful restaurants. Second, their research demonstrates that the restaurant is in an excellent location. Third, there was a successful restaurant on this site until it was destroyed by a fire.

In turn, each of these assertions must be backed up. How do they know, for example, that the restaurant is in an excellent location? First, there are no full-service restaurants within a mile of the museum. Second, thirty thousand people work and live within that one-mile area. And third, the museum has a captive audience of more than 23,000 visitors annually.

Continue to translate the flow chart into a presentation. Each page within the section should convey a message that supports the point of the section, and the content of each page should support the message at the top of that page. In the museum's presentation, for example, within the section on "There is clear demand

EXHIBIT 9.2. SPACE MUSEUM CAFÉ
PRESENTATION'S TRACKER PAGE.

The Space Museum Café is a unique investment opportunity.
- The Space Museum is a strong partner.
- There is clear demand for a restaurant on the site.
- We have an experienced management team.
- We have a thorough operations plan.
- The venture will provide needed jobs.
- The venture has excellent financial prospects.

FIGURE 9.1. SPACE MUSEUM CAFÉ PITCH TO INVESTORS.

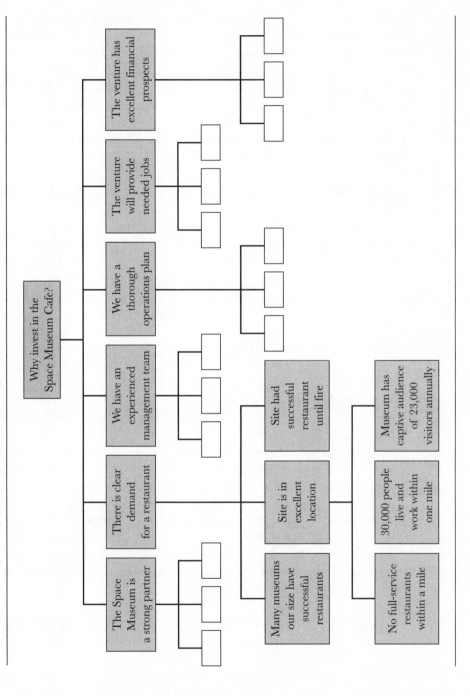

for a restaurant on this site," one page states, "The Space Museum Café is in an excellent location" and lists all of the facts from the flow chart that support that point, as well as some facts from the next level as well. (There are no sit-down restaurants within a mile of the museum. More than 30,000 people live and work within a mile of the museum, and the museum provides a captive market of 23,000 visitors annually.) It also provides some facts from the next level as well, to prove the assertion that the museum provides a captive market. First, the museum currently offers no food service, and second, most of the museum's visitors have children, and children expect to be fed frequently.

ADAPT YOUR PITCH TO YOUR AUDIENCE AND TIME FRAME.

Thinking of your pitch as a pyramid makes it easy to adapt it to your audience and time frame. You can select the appropriate level of detail and easily identify which messages to tweak for your audience. For example, your introduction and the highest-level points of your pitch form the basis for your *elevator pitch*. Here's one way to turn the Space Museum Café's investor pitch pyramid into an elevator pitch, rather than a presentation:

> The New City Space Museum is seeking $60,000 to launch a restaurant with an outer-space theme next door to the museum. The profits from the venture will be used to subsidize the museum and the café will also provide jobs in the community. We believe the restaurant will be successful for several reasons. First, the museum is more than twenty-five years old and is well-established in the community. It is contributing to the venture, and the venture also has the city's financial backing. Second, there used to be a successful restaurant on the same site and our research has identified clear demand for a restaurant there, including strong foot traffic and a lack of other options. Third, we have hired a professional restaurant manager who will oversee operations and put together a strong team. Fourth, we have a thorough operations plan and know what our costs will be and how much we plan to charge, and we have solid assumptions about how many meals we will serve. Finally, we believe that the restaurant will become profitable at the end of its first full year of operations and will generate $40,000 a year in free cash flow to support the museum by the end of year three.

PREPARE TO SPEND A DISPROPORTIONATE AMOUNT OF TIME ON THE FINANCIALS AND ASSUMPTIONS.

The financials section, which in this case opens with "The venture has excellent financial prospects," is the heart of the pitch. This is where all the arguments you have made in the other sections must come together in a credible fashion. Unfortunately, the financials section is often given short shrift when the presentation is being prepared. Many companies spend a great deal of time creating elaborate graphics for other sections and then simply cut and paste a couple of spreadsheets from their model into the financials section. But the argument you are making in your financials section is the most important one of all, so you should be prepared to spend more time on the financials than on any other part of your presentation— perhaps one quarter of the meeting. It's crucial not only to provide thorough pro forma financial statements, but also to spell out thoroughly the assumptions behind them. Investors must feel comfortable with the assumptions behind the projections, and you have to persuade them that those assumptions are reasonable. Exhibit 9.3 shows a sample presentation page on financial assumptions.

Each of the assumptions should be fully supported by explanations of their drivers, which in turn should be based on all the support and arguments in the previous sections. Only after showing the building blocks of the integrated financials will the numbers make sense and be believable. For example, the Space Museum team assumed that the café would initially serve one hundred lunches and sixty dinners each day based on all they had learned about foot traffic, museum visitors, and the demographics of the area. They decided that the average revenue at lunch would be $6, based on interviews with potential customers, on competitor research, and on selecting their menu and analyzing their costs.

CLOSE YOUR PRESENTATION BY REITERATING YOUR INVESTMENT HIGHLIGHTS.

Finally, close your presentation by reiterating your key points and repeating the tracker page.

EXHIBIT 9.3. SAMPLE PRESENTATION PAGE ON FINANCIAL ASSUMPTIONS.

We have used the following assumptions in our financial projections:
- Our capacity will be to serve 160 lunches (at three seatings) and 106 dinners (at two seatings).
- We will initially serve an average of 100 lunches and 60 dinners each day, six days a week.
- The average lunch will be priced at $6; the average dinner at $12.
- We will start the staff with one manager, one chef, two assistant cooks, three servers, and two buspeople.

Conclusion

Crafting a solid pitch requires a strategic approach, and one that is different from that of a grant proposal. The key is to know your audience and their expectations for return, including their time frame, and their appetite for risk. Regardless of the length and level of detail of your pitch, it must convince the prospective investor that your venture meets his investment criteria. Fundamentally, this means that your venture will create economic value and achieve the investor's expected return on investment within the investor's time frame. The most effective way to communicate your understanding is by logically developing your points and fully supporting them, and by communicating your points at the beginning of your pitch instead of leading up to them.

CHAPTER TEN

FORMING STRATEGIC ALLIANCES

Richard Steckel

S trategic alliances, according to the narrowest definition, are transaction based. In essence, they consist of two organizations going after the same objective and helping each other achieve their respective goals. When the relationship is between a for-profit and a nonprofit, the alliance might be, for example, a transaction-based promotion designed to increase traffic and sales at a corporate site, at a chain of retail stores, or of a particular product line or offering. Often the alliance is based on a customer purchase, and a portion of the sale price goes to the nonprofit partner. Other alliances involve the backing of events, licensing arrangements, or volunteerism. All such alliances assume that the commercial partner's competitive advantage will be enhanced and that measurable commercial gains will result from the relationship. Strategic alliances are effective because the nonprofit brand is the motivator for the corporate customer to take actions that are favorable to its self-interests. Also, although no alliance comes with a foolproof method or a money-back guarantee, the risks of not trying often outweigh the risks of failure. To increase the odds in your favor, however, this chapter presents real-life examples—real-life mistakes and real-life successes. It is my hope that you will write notes in the margins, turn down pages, highlight phrases, and ultimately use this chapter to help you form strategic alliances with corporations that make sense for your organization.

Trends, Trends, Trends

To begin, let me tell you about a number of trends. First, the number of strategic alliances, partnerships, joint ventures, and coventures—whatever they are called—between for-profit and nonprofit organizations is in fact increasing and has been over the past few decades. Second, there are business trends that include the emergence of the culturally creative consumer, the growing acceptance of reputational assets or social capital, and the increasing importance of nonprofit–for-profit relationships. Third, we find sociocultural trends that include purification, homesickness, and soft social activism. All of these are discussed in the following paragraphs.

Emergence of the culturally creative consumer. In the United States, culturally creative consumers are 44 million strong, and the majority (60 percent) are women.[1] These consumers are driven by values much more than the average person is, and they want to do business with companies that they feel reflect the people they are or wish to be. In essence, they want a personal relationship. This is why companies like Starbucks and Timberland and, to some extent, Ben and Jerry's were formed in an almost values-led way.[2] Businesses are always thinking about brands because, in essence, businesses are all about building their brands so they can market their products and services successfully. They are also thinking about how they become accepted and favored by a particular population, because their marketing strategies have the best chance of success if they target a specific demographic. So in seeking acceptance, business will try to embody the values of these target populations.

Growing acceptance of reputational assets or social capital. Reputational assets are key because businesses are now concluding that a significant amount of their true value as a company is actually intangible. In fact, in a recent speech, an executive from Coca-Cola stated that most of what Coca-Cola is as a company is ephemeral; if they miscue (which they did in Europe a couple of years ago by saying they had a tainted product only in Belgium when it was also showing up in France and Germany), the bottom line will be hit. It was. Their share price dropped about 15 percent in two weeks.[3] Unfortunately, this type of story is common: similar things have also happened to many other companies. In fact, there are Web sites dedicated to calling the public's attention to companies that are being boycotted for one reason or another, such as David Grayson's Web site at http://www.davidgrayson.net. There are even corporations that have not been able to get into communities because of perceived unethical behavior such as selling garments that are manufactured by people who are paid exploitive wages. So what we have is a growing appreciation that if a company does something foolish, its share price and reputation will be tarnished.

Increasing importance of nonprofit–for-profit relationships. Corporations know they have to be in transformed relationships with multiple stakeholders in their community and that these relationships have to be mutually beneficial. Understanding this is key because when you go to a corporation to make your presentation, they will need to see not only that you're a serious and worthy partner but also that you've done your homework. Simply put, they will want to know that you are an organization they can trust. David Grayson, consultant and noted author of *Everybody's Business,* has said that according to many private-sector companies, nonprofits do not understand their business and have expectations that are often inappropriate and unrealistic with regard to the time it takes to develop a solid working relationship and the potential revenue to be gained from a partnership (from a private conversation with David Grayson). One example cited was a company that assigned its senior vice president of marketing to manage the strategic alliance while the nonprofit assigned its summer intern to manage the project and serve as the liason to the corporation. This is a situation in which both parties need comparable decision makers in the relationship. They should have similar decision making authority, since corporations are often very hierarchical and uncomfortable with a person of "lower" responsibility and authority to make commitments. If a nonprofit does this, the corporation with which it is partnering will not trust it.

A related issue is that companies no longer perceive nonprofit partnerships as the soft side of business. Consequently, any company will have a strategic intent when considering seriously a nonprofit's proposal of an alliance. So it behooves the nonprofit to have one too, and to put forth its best people and best efforts.

So what can you, the leader of a nonprofit do? Put yourself in the mind-set of a business executive. What do executives think about every morning? They think about risks and opportunities. So, when you prepare for a meeting with a corporation's representatives, look at the risks they worry about. What is the stress on the company? How are you going to reduce or contain or in some way help manage the risks that the corporation perceives it has? Also, ask what opportunities they want to explore. What do they see as a new market, a new niche? How can you convey to them that you actually understand their corporate needs and are going to help create a new business opportunity for them?

Finally, when talking to the representatives of corporations, use their business language, not the language of your nonprofit. Use the language that's in what they read. Follow the magazines, the newspaper business section, any trend research that's being issued by the corporate world, the Conference Board, and so on. Why? Because the corporation is not going to learn the language of the nonprofits; they are not going to take the time. But if you use their language, they will gain confidence in what you're presenting and in you and your colleagues, and they will believe that you are mindful and respectful of the world in which they operate.

The kind of impacts that these business trends have on corporations can also result from three sociocultural trends. The first of these trends is called *purification,* which is often described as a life-simplification process. "My life has gotten too crazy, too out of control. My PalmPilot, my beeper, my cell phone—it's like I'm never alone. I'm just always on." If you want evidence of this trend, just take a look at Anna Quindlen's book, *A Short Guide to a Happy Life,*[4] a best-seller translated into several languages because in any country where there is a market economy and a middle class of any size, they're reading books like this. What else? *The Positive Power of No,* by Kim Demotte—it's a best-seller now, too.[5] It's not an accident that the books people are reading are in many cases business best-sellers. So, people around the world are worried about the pace of life and they're looking for connections with things that are genuine. And that's where nonprofit organizations come in—because the customers of the corporations with which you are forming strategic alliances are often involved because they care about what you're doing. They care about something in the world beyond themselves.

The second sociocultural trend is *homesickness.* Homesickness involves the nostalgic return to a period that was calmer, that seemed a bit more down-to-earth, than where we are now. We see this trend operating in a lot of different ways. For example, look at the success of highly stylized cars such as the new Volkswagen Beetle. A few years back, a commercial for the new VW Beetle showed a flower in the cup holder. The reissued Beetle with its "vase" for flowers hearkens back to a time, for babyboomers and even their children, of changing the world, improving the civil rights of minorities, ending an unjust war, and so on. It represents nostalgia for a time when society seemed to have more principles and people were more passionate about what they believed in. Another example is the return of popular candies or sweets to their original packaging. Then there are retro colors such as lime green, and foods such as meatloaf. All of these products hearken back to a time that seems to have been a bit more authentic than the present, when society felt that personal values and principles were played out in behavior toward advancing, for example, the women's movement. People did things for one another, for example they created food cooperatives (co-ops), shared babysitting, knew their neighbors, and so on. Speaking of authentic: look at the ads now in newspapers and magazines. The words *authentic, genuine,* and *traditional* pop up again and again.

A third sociocultural trend is *soft social activism.* This is the activism of the culturally creative consumer, who wants her purchasing decisions to have some social impact such as help reduce pollution or generate money for a social cause.

This desire is beneficial to you because your organization represents a cause or an issue, a way for people to do something that is driven by values and principles and passion. Also, the people who tend to become associated with nonprofit organizations through some kind of funding or volunteer relationship are often part of the market segment that's called culturally creative.

When working with corporate partners, ask them to send you their market research so you can see what factors are influencing them. You'll be amazed that there will be a high correlation between their research results and the trends discussed here. For this reason, one of the most important things a nonprofit should know before attempting a business relationship is that trends are the most significant realities driving corporate life. Research trends, thirty-year trends, social trends, cultural trends, industry trends—companies live for these, and they're all important for one reason: trends give companies comfort that there's some rationale for what they're about to hear. So, before you talk to corporations, before you say, "Let's get to the heart of the matter," before you talk about their self-interests, tell them you'd like to put everything they're about to hear around a framework by saying, "I'd like to present some trends." Saying this will pique their interest more than any facts, statistics, endorsements from other partners, or stories you could tell.

Identifying Potential Partners

There are three kinds of companies with which a nonprofit will likely do business. The first type is the *defensive business*—a company that has done something foolish that has gotten it into trouble. Such a company is looking for ways to deepen its reputational assets, and the credibility provided by the nonprofit offers the company a boost. But you, the nonprofit, have to decide if this type of or specific company is one with whom you want to work. That's your decision, and that's what's important.

The second type of company with which a nonprofit is likely to form an alliance is the *affinity business*—one that has a logical link to what the nonprofit is and does. Some years ago Bank Street College of Education in New York teamed up with Levi Strauss and provided, during a back-to-school promotional period, a chance for parents to get a booklet for their children on learning how to get dressed and an accompanying booklet for the parents. Why did Levi Strauss get involved? Well, it was an opportunity for them to differentiate their product from that of other companies. This relationship with Bank Street College of Education brought Levi Strauss a 12 percent increase in sales and 72 million favorable media impressions—the number of people reported by the company who read or heard about their advertising campaign—and Bank Street College got several thousand dollars of unrestricted income from the Levi Strauss Corporation (from a personal conversation with Jim Levine, former new product director at Bank Street College of Education). But what's most important about this alliance of Bank Street College and Levi Strauss talking with the public about issues of parenting is that it was a natural: talking about parenting was Bank Street College's core competence, and a booklet on getting dressed might encourage the purchase of back-to-school clothes made by Levi Strauss.

The third type of company that nonprofits may partner with is the *opportunistic business*. This type has two strands: *emerging* and *mature*. Financial institutions and supermarkets are mature opportunistic businesses. The best they can do, because they have a fixed number of customers, is nibble around the edges of some of their competitors. Emerging companies are just beginning to make customers. Nokia comes to mind because it markets relatively new technologies and operates on a model of fast-paced customer acquisition. Emerging companies are also, in many cases, interested in finding a differentiator, because they are always looking for some kind of competitive advantage.

In conclusion, it is important to note two points. First, the definition of corporate social responsibility is shifting. The notion of what it takes to be a good corporate citizen, to earn a license to practice business, greatly affects how and why businesses form strategic alliances with nonprofit organizations. Second, corporations are changing the way they perceive nonprofits. What's important for the nonprofit is to understand these changes and that nonprofits fit strategically into the changing mind-set of for-profit companies.

Types of Nonprofit Enterprise

There are three pathways, three categories, of nonprofit enterprise. Companies in the first category, *small businesses*, are what today and tomorrow are really about—nonprofit-instigated stand-alone business ventures. These ventures are indeed businesses, and some of them are quite substantial. For instance, Pioneer Industries in Seattle has five thousand people and is a multimillion-dollar business that develops widgets and sound baffling for Boeing Aircraft. Most ground-level employees at Pioneer are either recovering from some form of addiction or have recently been released from prison (from a conversation with Gary Mulhair, former director of Pioneer Industries). Another example is the Rivertown Trading Company, the direct marketing arm of the for-profit Greenspring Company, a subsidiary of the tax-exempt nonprofit American Public Media Group, which also owns Minnesota Public Radio (MPR), Southern California Public Radio, and the

Fitzgerald Theater Company. The Rivertown Trading Company was sold in 1998 to the Target Corporation for $120 million, and $90 million of that income went right to MPR's endowment. There was also a business, E-Source, that spun out of the Rocky Mountain Institute (RMI) and provided commercial intelligence to large energy consumers, businesses, governments, universities, and hospitals. The spin-off created a three-tier membership with proprietary products and services that members were able to access based on their specific level of membership. Eventually, the business was sold for $18 million to McGraw-Hill.

The second category of nonprofit enterprise is *earned income businesses*, which provide clever and competitively priced products and services that are sold directly to consumers for a profit, as opposed to giving them away or sold at a price that only covers expenses. Some of these products and services are sold through for-profit subsidiaries that are spun off from the parent nonprofit. An example of such a venture, Zoo Doo, was created by the Bronx Frontier Development Corporation, an organization that aids low-income neighborhoods by creating employment opportunities through development projects. Several years ago, this organization developed urban spice farms. The spices grown on these urban farms were sold to cruise ships, motels, and hotels. To cut costs, the Bronx Frontier Development Corporation sought to reduce its fertilizer expenses. It went to the Bronx Zoo and asked it to donate its animals' "doo." The zoo agreed, and the partnership was a mutual success. The zoo saved $25,000 annually and the Bronx Frontier Development Corporation was provided with the fertilizer needed for its spice farms. Then one day someone cleverly observed that the fertilizer could be packaged and positioned as a two-pound bag of Zoo Doo for at-home gardeners. The organization researched who might want to sell the product it planned to develop. None other than Bloomingdale's bought thirty thousand bags for several years, in keeping with its tradition of offering unusual products in its catalog.

The third category of nonprofit enterprise is *strategic alliances*. These are joint ventures, coventures, or mutually beneficial relationships between nonprofit causes and for-profit corporations. What is significant about them is that the nonprofit's brand is well-known, trusted, respected, and powerful enough to motivate consumers to choose this company's product over that of another company. The Save the Children Fund is one of the archetypal practitioners of these forms of relationship. Its imagery on plates, cookie jars, utensils, ties, socks, and other products helps to generate very significant net income for the organization annually from companies such as Candlewick Press, Gymboree, Hasbro, Inc., IKEA, and T.J. Maxx.[6] What this organization knows is that its brand is a sufficient motivator for a consumer looking at two competing products on the shelf and saying, "Which one will I buy?" to answer, I'll buy that one because it's connected to a cause I believe in, it gives me an opportunity to use my purchasing power to make a political statement, it says I can make a purchase that makes a difference, and it represents who I am or the kind of person I want to be.

This example leads to a point made earlier about the importance of relationships. Nonprofits are enabling corporations to create integrated strategies to reach the so-called culturally creative consumer. So, in a presentation to a corporation about a proposed alliance, one of the best ways to qualify these relationships is to quantify them. In other words, use statistics. For example, tell the company that nearly nine in ten consumers report they are "more likely to remember a company when they see information about its social activities;" that 92 percent say they have "a more positive image of companies and products that support causes;" and that 84 percent say that they "would be likely to switch brands to one associated with a good cause, if price and quality are similar."[7] These numbers are very important because they are comforting to the corporation's representatives who are listening to the presentation, who can then include them in a convincing argument to their colleagues who are in a decision-making position.

Increasing Revenue

There are four ways to generate money in alliance relationships. First, the nonprofit charges a fee to the organization that wants to use its idea. For example, Exel Petroleum, the largest black-owned South African energy company, is paying the Youth Development Trust $50,000 to use the initiative "Children Should Be Seen and Not Hurt" (conversation with Ntutule Tshenye, CEO of the Youth Development Trust in Johannesburg, 2001). Second, the nonprofit makes money from managing the project. That is, it builds a net profit in to the proposed budget with the corporate partner. It is therefore up to the nonprofit to calculate direct and indirect expenses carefully. Third, if delivery of the product or service requires purchasing materials or services of any kind, the nonprofit organization makes money by marking up the costs of these by 15, 17, even 20 percent and passing that along to the corporation. Fourth, the nonprofit organization makes money through mechanisms, which give consumers the opportunity, through the corporation's distribution network as well as its customers, to add money to the pot, which then goes to the nonprofit's cause. Eddie Bauer did this with its customers by asking if they would like to add a dollar at the time of purchase to American Forests' Global ReLeaf project, which encourages the planting of trees.[8] Four million people said yes. Posta Bank in Austria, Slovakia, and Slovenia said to its customers during a six-week period that it would donate a small amount of money to select organizations every time they used one of the bank's automated teller machines. Six million people used these ATMs in six weeks. These customers changed their banking habits so that money could go to certain designated causes (from conversations with Peace Corps volunteers working with children of the Slovakia Foundation, 2000).

The Presentation

Now that you know the trends that are affecting business, the types of companies with which you might do business, and how your organization can make money through partnerships with businesses, you now need to think about whom to target, how to get through the corporate door, and what to do when you get there.

To whom are you going to talk? In general, you want to talk to people at the very top of the company. Talk to a board person, the CEO, the CFO, or the COO. It's not that one of these people will make a decision, but if they are good at their jobs they will refer you to the marketing department with a pat on the back and a recommendation that will be hard for the head of marketing to ignore. This referral is golden because it means that somebody in a senior position says you have a good story that's worth listening to for fifteen minutes. You can also talk to people who have above-line responsibilities—those who are accountable for producing a net gain to the company. Marketing staff for sure, as well as communications directors and brand managers, are the people who make decisions. They have much larger budgets than their counterparts in community relations and public affairs and tend to talk to other people in the corporate world who make decisions that are perceived as powerful. Talk to other people who have budgets, such as those in investor relations and supply relations. Such connections are really quite strategic. If you look, for example, at why Coke makes contributions to McDonald's charities, it's because Coke products are sold in all McDonald's restaurants. The same is true for Kodak and Disney because so many photographs are taken in a Disney venue, and Kodak is a major player in the industry.

Who are you going to take with you to meet these people? First, take no more than three people, including the seniormost person in your organization (your executive director or president or CEO) and your technical or program person. The third person should be the most influential person associated with your organization that you can find—usually a volunteer for your organization with publicly recognized value or stature. This person will provide an associative credibility that will make the company you are approaching think, "Well, if so and so is involved with this venture, we should pay attention."

How are you going to get through the corporation's door? The easiest way to get inside so you can make your pitch is to ask an influential person who is known personally by your intended corporate decision maker to make an introductory call on your behalf. If you strike out there, a trick that generally works quite well is to call this corporate decision maker a half hour before the workday officially begins or a half hour after it ends. This timing improves your chances of getting past the decision maker's gatekeepers. Quickly explain that you are not making a charitable request but have a business proposition that will take fifteen minutes or less to present. Say that because of its unusual, sensitive, timely, and commercial nature, your board (always blame it on the board) has obligated you to make an in-person communication. Do not send an e-mail (which can be deleted too easily and besides, e-mails are so cold). If the person insists on receiving something, send a very general outline of expected outcomes of the meeting. Enthusiasm and persistence are your watchwords.

Before presenting your idea for an alliance to a company, there are some rules and advice you need to know that are key to surviving and thriving in such a meeting.

The Rules of the Game

Rule 1: *Do not provide the corporation with a copy of your entire presentation before a face-to-face meeting.* Even if they insist on seeing your proposal in writing before your meeting, just blame your reticence (real or imagined) on your board. Say, "We are presenting something of high commercial sensitivity that was designed to provide you with a competitive advantage in your industry. The board has therefore authorized me to present this opportunity in person only."

Rule 2: *Request fifteen minutes of meeting time,* because even the most egocentric person somehow sees fifteen minutes as OK, and if you ask for an hour you might as well ask for the firstborn child of the person you want to meet. Besides, no one ever leaves a presentation in fifteen minutes, even when that's all you've scheduled.

Rule 3: Never distribute the materials to the participants until the end of the conversation. So you must be *careful where you place your "leave behind" materials.* Simply put, if you lay out the presentation materials with the text facing up, the people entering the meeting will pick them up, read them, and be distracted. If you place the materials face down they won't pick them up.

Rule 4: *Don't initiate a conversation unless two key pieces are in place:* approval from the leadership of your organization to enter into a strategic alliance, and a guarantee that no power struggles will occur between your board and your staff. Your staff must have the authority to make decisions, otherwise there will likely be unnecessary delays that will shake the confidence of the corporation in your ability to make timely decisions and stick with agreed upon deadlines.

Rule 5: *Know how much time you will give the company after the first meeting to make a decision.* Ask them what is normal and customary within their culture. The answer "We'll get back to you" is never acceptable because it is vague and unspecified. You need a time horizon. Your response to them, in fact your comment in any case, should be, "The Board has authorized me to allow no more than two weeks because of the sensitivity, timeliness, and commercial value of this idea." On the flip side, never say to a corporation, "We'll get back to you after our board meets in nine months," because it's too long a time delay between your meeting and action. Expect no more than thirty days for decision-making.

Rule 6: *Make sure that going into the presentation you have some understanding of what outcomes are acceptable to your nonprofit.* That is, know with which companies you will work, which ones you won't touch, what money will go where, and the impact and social benefits or use of that money. Don't enter into any relationship unless you know how success, minimum and maximum, will be defined.

Rule 7: *Be prepared for some ambiguity.* You can count on there being trade-offs and tough decisions from the second meeting forward. That's life. Be prepared for having big wet stains of perspiration under your arms when you leave some of these meetings, because you just won't know where you stand. Corporate people don't have to be nice. This is not philanthropy. These are people who are calculating whether or not you meet their needs. They are potentially providing you with unrestricted income. Have a walkaway price or walkaway conditions. Be prepared to say, "It doesn't look like we're going to have a relationship." Not every relationship is made in heaven; not every relationship should take place.

First Impressions: The Appearance of Your Presentation Materials

So, I have presented some items you need to know, understand, and anticipate when you're in a presentation, but what does the pitch, or the materials that are presented, actually look like? Let's look at the pitch in more detail.

First, *the company's logo must appear on your presentation materials.* Why? Because your meeting with the company is about them, about the company's "family." It's about what their needs are, what their competitive advantage and concerns are. It's about the risks they need to contain or reduce. It's about the opportunities they need to exploit. That's why their logo should be on front.

Second, *you should present an industry analysis.* It should be one-page, sometimes two, but no more than two, and should describe the competitive stresses, strains, and opportunities defined by the industry in which the business operates. From where do you get this information? None of it comes from your own original research. It all comes from secondary sources, such as trade association publications. Trade associations are brilliant. They give you terrific information. Ask for it. It's not just online. It also comes from brokerage houses, especially ones that specialize in the industry of the company in which you are interested; and from financial institutions, business schools, the business section of the library, business Web sites, speeches, public relations packages, U.S. Securities and Exchange Commission filings (if they're public), and investor relations packets. None of this information is mystical. It comes from commonsense action research that has been done by qualified researchers. Then, be sure that your industry analysis is written by people who understand the difference between information gathering and analysis, who can analyze, not just regurgitate, what they've read, and interpret the information and its implications for your corporate presentation.

Third, *your presentation should include a company analysis.* Where should the information used to prepare this analysis come from? It should come from such sources as the company's Web site and from its annual report, which may or may not be on the Web site. Don't, however, look only at the annual report; look also at the notes at the end of the annual report or at the end of the financial statements. These notes outline the issues facing the company, such as lawsuits. They convey what the company is really doing. And call the public affairs or communications department at the company. Say, "Tell me about your . . ." (whatever you want to find out about). Clip newspaper ads and ask who approved and produced them. You want to know these people because they're spending money to put information about the company into a media venue, and that information about the company's products, competitive advantages, quality workforce, service excellence, give-back to the community relates directly to some aspect of the proposition that you are presenting. In essence, know what you want to learn about the company and ask for the information. What is the company worried about? What opportunities does it have? You want the people in the company who hear and see the presentation to say, "Oh, you've really done your homework. Where did you find that information? How did you know that?" It's like holding up a mirror to them so they can see themselves more clearly, more objectively, and ultimately more successfully than they did before. If they ask why you are asking for this information, the honest answer is that you're going to be making a presentation to the corporation and want it to be convincing. Say you want to be intelligent, informed, and accurate. Ask for help in doing that. They'll understand.

Fourth, *you should create and present a strategy that includes a value that is important to the company.* It's very hard for a company to say it is not supporting a strategy that promotes honesty, responsibility, and so on this year. It's also very hard for a company to think that one of its competitors might say yes to you, potentially placing the company at a competitive disadvantage. Tell the company, "This is an opportunity for you to have or do something that no one else has seen just yet."

Fifth, *use storyboards that contain pictures of what the product or service or event or strategy will look like in operation.* What the company has whispered as an idea, as a possibility, should be translated into pictures. In those pictures on the storyboard is what's called a *buyer's proposition.* It shows the company what success can look like. It gives the company a three-dimensional view of its idea and of your idea to do it with them. Storyboards are invaluable.

Sixth, *use mechanisms to help the company understand how its customers or consumers will be involved, and how the company will participate in the relationship.* For example, the Tesco Computers for Schools Program, which is entering its fourteenth year in England, sets aside six weeks for consumers of its retail grocery business to redeem coupons for computer hardware and software that have been given to their children's schools (from a conversation with Sue Adkins, Director of Cause Related Marketing at Business in the Community, London).

Seventh, *the presentation materials should include a one-page document listing a maximum of five bullet points that depict the most impressive things you can possibly say about your organization.* Why five things? Because after reviewing these points, if the company loves what you've presented, they will want to know who you are. If they don't love what you've presented, then they won't care who you are, so you might as well be succinct. After presenting these points, say that you've spent the time talking about the company's needs and opportunities, and about meeting those needs and exploiting those opportunities. At this point you should also talk about why you are a natural partner for this alliance.

Finally, along with the company's logo, *include your logo on the presentation materials,* because you want to show that you and the company will be equal partners in the relationship.

Conclusion

Remember that marketing is all about stories. It's about a nonprofit celebrating a company as one that has had a measurable impact on people and places, whether around the corner or around the world. The story gets woven not just into the company's fabric but also into society's fabric. That is the power of nonprofits—because, for the most part, nonprofits are viewed as moral, untainted, impartial, and incorruptible forces in society. And that is why strategic alliances are working and growing in number because people like you are moving your organization's beliefs out of dialogue and into action and tangible, bottom-line results that companies are willing not only to listen to but also to support in campaigns that benefit everyone involved.

Notes

1. Florida, R. *The Rise of the Creative Class: And How It's Transforming Work, Leisure, Community and Everyday Life.* New York: Basic Books, 2003.
2. See Garten, J. E. *The Politics of Fortune: A New Agenda for Business Leaders.* Cambridge, Mass.: HBS Press, 2002; and "Corporate America's Social Conscience," *Fortune,* May 26, 2003.
3. Marks, B. "The Real New, New Brand PR." Speech presented at a meeting of the Los Angeles Chapter of Public Relations Society of America, Los Angeles, Jan. 2003.
4. Quindlen, A. *A Short Guide to a Happy Life.* New York: Random House Publishing Group, 2000.
5. Demotte, K. *The Positive Power of No: How That Little Word You Love to Hate Can Make or Break Your Business.* Tempe, Ariz.: BRB Publications, 2003.
6. See http://www.savethechildren.org/corporate/partners.asp.
7. "Cone Corporate Citizenship Study: The Role of Cause Branding." Boston: Cone Inc., 2000. See also http://www.coneinc.com.
8. For more information, see http://www.americanforests.org/global_releaf/.

CHAPTER ELEVEN

GROWING YOUR BUSINESS WITH A HIGH-ENGAGEMENT FUNDER

Kristin Majeska

High-engagement is an increasingly common approach to funding that is particularly relevant to nonprofit enterprises. High-engagement funders are often well suited to support nonprofits in the typically fast-paced and unpredictable world of enterprise, a world that often presents a steep learning curve for more traditional funders, who have less interaction with and fewer resources to offer any one grantee. An understanding of the high-engagement approach can be useful for funders looking at ways they can increase the odds for success of the nonprofit enterprises they support. Further, an understanding of what constitutes and drives high-engagement funding is an important first step toward social entrepreneurs being able to encourage and secure these types of investments for their ventures.

High-engagement funders have explicitly chosen a strategy of working closely with the nonprofits they support financially. The intensity of these relationships varies by funder. For some, working closely with a nonprofit enterprise means meeting once a quarter to discuss progress and strategy; for others it means being

It is a pleasure to thank my colleagues Erick Jensen of Wolfe's Neck Farm, Mark Swann of Stone Soup, Nancy Robertson of Common Good Ventures, and especially Chip Warner of Common Good Ventures for their collaboration in this work, and also to recognize the Woodcock Foundation for supporting Common Good Ventures's contributions to the national dialogue on nonprofit business enterprise.

in contact weekly or more often as needed to offer guidance or provide specific assistance. While intensity may vary, researchers Christine Letts and William Ryan have defined three consistent elements of effective high-engagement relationships: alignment of interests, reliable grant money, and strategy coaching.[1] When successful, they assert, these components lead to "an accountability relationship that uses power to improve performance."[2] In even simpler terms, Letts and Ryan explain, "These funders do for grantees what sports coaches do for teams: hold them accountable for their performance."[3]

Example: Common Good Ventures

Common Good Ventures (CGV) is a high-engagement funder with the mission of improving nonprofit performance. CGV helps its nonprofit partners achieve their social goals—for example, feeding more hungry kids, putting more homeless people to work, preserving more acres of open space, and so on. CGV also helps its partners attain greater long-term financial self-sufficiency. To accomplish these goals, CGV leverages philanthropic dollars with long-lasting business consulting and coaching focused on accountability and results. CGV began with an initial portfolio of five social enterprises; that portfolio now consists of twelve nonprofits, including seven nonprofit enterprises at various stages in their lifecycle.

CGV places equal emphasis on its high-engagement model and on the philosophy of partnership that underlies its strategy for helping both social enterprises and traditional nonprofits work smarter.

One High-Engagement Model

• *High leverage opportunities.* CGV invests significant resources in a small number of organizations that due diligence has suggested can be helped by its assistance to achieve significantly greater social impact.

• *Management and strategy coaching.* CGV provides strategic coaching, asking tough questions and encouraging its partners to step back and justify their decisions with numbers. But CGV also provides tactical, hands-on assistance, whether helping to set up a cash flow statement, reviewing a job description, or critiquing a funding proposal. This approach helps CGV's nonprofit enterprise partners become stronger organizations and develop new skills in-house.

• *Top-notch resource people.* CGV maintains a strong network of talented individuals from the for-profit, nonprofit, and government sectors. CGV draws on this network to provide its partners with targeted, expert assistance, such as the opportunity to participate in a one-time strategy session, a discount rate on best-in-class professional services, or a board member recommendation.

- *Strategic capital investments.* CGV invests capital in the long-term success of its partners, helping them define how these unrestricted dollars can be used for greatest impact. CGV's dollars often go toward funding management and staff time, but they may also be used to invest in marketing, operational improvements, or whatever else creates more bang for the buck. These investments vary in size but are timely and flexible.
- *Focus on results.* CGV's interactions with its partners are characterized by a focus on the nonprofit's end goals. CGV staff and partners regularly consider the question, How does this step move us toward accomplishing our vision? Because CGV is accountable to its own donors, resource people, and board, staff are constantly asking, Is this group using its resources and is CGV using its resources for the best possible results?
- *A partnership philosophy.* CGV takes its partnership approach very seriously. Partnerships are long-term relationships based on trust and mutual benefit. Each nonprofit enterprise contributes to the partnership and both CGV and the nonprofit enterprise must benefit for it to be successful. CGV's philosophy is based on the following elements:

> *Mutual accountability.* Funders need to be as accountable for the time they expect from nonprofits to dedicate to the funding relationship as nonprofits need to be accountable for accomplishing the outcomes for which they are striving.
>
> *Respect.* The unique skills and perspectives of each partner and CGV are recognized and valued.
>
> *Progress toward partners' goals.* CGV doesn't assume that everything will go exactly according to plan—it won't. But the ongoing relationship is contingent on a partner's making sufficient progress toward mission outcomes and, more importantly, on the expectation of continued progress.

Understanding Potential Nonprofit Enterprise Investors: What Drives High-Engagement Funding?

High-engagement funding is usually driven by two beliefs: that nonprofits can do more good if they receive tailored assistance as well as money over multiple years, and that focusing on good performance and results while providing intense assistance to help achieve those results ultimately means that the funding dollars will go further. Many funders also choose a high-engagement model because they have had experience with an investment approach in the for-profit world and feel comfortable applying the same logic to their nonprofit passions. They want to increase their odds of having a big impact, whether that impact is in terms of scale, depth, or sustainability, by putting not only dollars but also people toward this goal. High-engagement funders understand that significant, lasting results usually require discipline, long time horizons, and timely and strategic investments of financial and human resources.

The Potential Appeal of Nonprofit Enterprise to High-Engagement Funders

High-engagement funders want to work with organizations that are focused on performance and sustainability. Although relatively few high-engagement funders fund nonprofit enterprises today, with a little preparation nonprofit enterprises should be able to make a strong case that resonates with funders who claim to be motivated by results and accountability.

First, the bottom-line mentality that high-engagement funders want to see is literally built into the operations of a nonprofit enterprise through its income statement. If the accounting is done right, financial sustainability is directly related to performance—to how well the business is run rather than to how much grant money the organization raises. This experience with transparent results should make it easier to similarly track and measure success against the enterprise's stated social mission goals.

Enterprises also force nonprofits to develop a customer focus and the capacity to respond quickly to a changing environment, again with an emphasis on results. If the enterprise is not performing, customer response lets the organization know quickly, and if the organization doesn't respond, the enterprise won't survive. Because of these market pressures, nonprofit enterprises are a natural place for nonprofit leaders to test new management techniques and tools, such as making speedy decisions, with minimal resistance from traditional program staff. Also, these management experiments—whether tracking financials by business unit, rewarding outstanding performance, or learning how to market a new service aggressively— are nonthreatening ways to introduce new results kinds of thinking to the whole organization. Success in one division is likely to drive imitation by another division. As suggested by researchers Cynthia W. Massarsky and Samantha L. Beinhacker, successful nonprofit enterprises build the confidence and reputation of their entire organizations, making those organizations likely to try more risky, high-reward strategies in their programmatic work, as well as increasing the odds that the organization will be around for the long haul.[4]

Finally, a nonprofit enterprise's ability over time to fund some or all of its work through the revenue from its products or services, and its flexibility to invest any profits in developing a healthy organization, should appeal to these funders who preach sustainability.

What's Really Involved in a High-Engagement Relationship

A high-engagement relationship involves mutual trust and accountability that are built over time through consistent actions, not rhetoric. Although it is important to set expectations up-front, this type of relationship is hard to explain before living through it. Every funder will structure it slightly differently and will provide different levels and kinds of resources, but there are a few commonalities.

Strategy and Tactics

Savvy high-engagement funders realize that in order to provide high-value guidance on strategic decisions, they may also have to address the nonprofit enterprise leader's highest existing priorities through tactical assistance. They may roll up their sleeves themselves, access volunteer resource people, or hire consultants, but this type of funder will usually find a way to help the manager with a pressing personnel issue, new financing deal, or critical marketing decision.

When assisting at the tactical level, at least three things set a high-engagement funder apart from a typical technical-assistance provider. First, most high-engagement funders think strategically, and their advice about any given task considers the organization's overall mission and financial goals. Second, the high-engagement funder identifies and prioritizes tactical areas of assistance from a medium- to long-term perspective rather than as a series of discrete projects. Third, a level of personal accountability that rarely develops with a contracted technical assistance provider comes out of this side-by-side work over time.

The even more important strategic coaching that goes on with a nonprofit enterprise often takes place in regular, structured meetings as well as in designated strategy sessions. Equally likely, however, this strategic coaching happens during discussion of a mundane operational issue or in informal conversations over lunch. Good high-engagement funders do this work by asking honest questions and by gently testing implicit or explicit assumptions rather than by coming up with a strategy themselves on the nonprofit enterprise's behalf.

Limits

Although there are usually no off-limits areas for high-engagement funders, even the very hands-on funders of nonprofit enterprises tend to focus their advice on the management and operations of the venture itself. They certainly analyze social outcomes and want to know what is working, but they rarely provide advice on pure mission areas. For example, a high-engagement funder may recommend a good boilerplate human resources manual but would not likely provide useful input on the best type of diagnostic tests to give to ex-offenders before offering them work in a business venture. At the end of the day, the nonprofit enterprise's management team must own each decision, whether program or management related, and the board of directors always has ultimate authority.

A High-Engagement Relationship Life Cycle

High-engagement funders' relationships with their grantees change over time. Figure 11.1 illustrates the evolution of a typical high-engagement partnership. It takes time and the right attitude on both sides for the funder and enterprise relationship to become a partnership.

Engagement begins during the due diligence phase. This period of mutual scrutiny either benefits the relationship or suggests that the parties are not a good fit for each other. Naturally the first big boost to most relationships is a grant, usually sizeable enough to get the nonprofit enterprise's attention. In a sense, this significant *investment* buys the nonprofit's ear before the nonprofit has enough experience and confidence to value the funder as a trusted adviser. The relationship often moves forward rather quickly through the funder's hands-on *tactical work* with the nonprofit enterprise's manager, particularly when the tactical work responds to the manager's priorities.

A nonprofit enterprise further values the relationship with the funder once it expands its network of resource people through funder *introductions*. Unlike as in most funding relationships, the funder's first receipt of *bad news* from the nonprofit usually propels the relationship further ahead because rather than punish the enterprise for not succeeding, the high-engagement funder values the honest revelation and provides useful assistance. A more common first dip in the relationship comes from *miscommunication*. The relationship can get back on track with a *speedy response* from the funder when the enterprise next needs a hand.

Over time, as the management team develops more and more confidence in the high-engagement funder, the funder is likely to play a role in *strengthening the*

FIGURE 11.1. EVOLUTION OF A HIGH-ENGAGEMENT PARTNERSHIP.

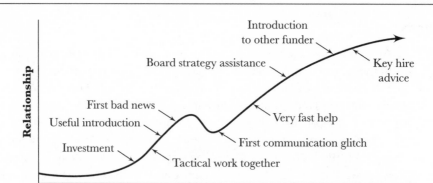

nonprofit's board. This may mean suggesting board structure, identifying needed skills, recruiting new members, and so on. Access to introductions that result in additional funding can happen at any time in the relationship, but is more likely to occur as the high-engagement funder feels more comfortable about his or her recommendation to other funding sources and clearly helps cement the partnership in both directions. Although the relationship evolution curve undoubtedly flattens out over time, a healthy partnership relationship continues to grow thanks to a wide variety of interactions that may occur, many of which may not require either significant time or resources.

Exit Strategy

A for-profit investor will exit a funding relationship when she or he is able to cash out, but a successful exit strategy for a nonprofit enterprise funder is less clearly defined. One natural exit strategy is to pull out when the nonprofit enterprise hits certain profitability targets and is able to be self-sustaining. Unlike the for-profit investor, however, the high-engagement funder of a nonprofit enterprise is unlikely to be indifferent about the venture's success after the funder's exit. If further growth would enable even greater social and financial returns, is the enterprise a success if it does not grow? When is growth enough? It's important to understand upfront the high-engagement funder's anticipated exit plan. When will the funder consider the venture to be a success? Will the funder want to get out in three or five or seven years? Is the funder likely to be interested in providing capital to finance ongoing growth? If so, what does that assistance imply for the nonprofit enterprise?

Of course, the funder's exit strategy may include broader considerations than simply financial concerns. For example, CGV defines its exit strategy as helping to build an organization that is financially sustainable and that has access to the skills it needs to deliver on its social mission without assistance from CGV, whether those skills reside in-house, on the board, or in the enterprise's own network of resource people.

Example: Wolfe's Neck Farm

A founder's perspective, by Erick Jensen, CEO of the nonprofit Wolfe's Neck Farm Natural Meats

Wolfe's Neck Farm (WNF) is a nonprofit organization that operates a nonprofit enterprise with the mission of preserving open space and family farms by developing economically viable models for sustainable agriculture. The enterprise's goals are to increase the income of cattle producers, increase the presence of Maine-raised beef in the national market, and preserve open space through sustainable working farms. The branded natural meat distribution business that is accomplishing these goals is a complex one that has grown to $2.5 million in revenues in fewer than two years.

When Wolfe's Neck Farm started out, we had the same dilemma that farmers do—lots of great ideas and the determination to make our demonstration farm profitable, but no idea how to do it. Then I borrowed an idea from a producers' cooperative in Oregon, and CGV got involved in helping us start it up. I'll admit that initially I had no clue what CGV was talking about when we met—I don't think they were using the term *high-engagement* but the idea was the same. My response was, "Well, just give us the money—that's all I need." But you know, it wasn't just getting money; we did get a small grant initially from CGV, but it has gone way beyond that.

Managing Complexity. Although WNF "owns" its beef only during one brief moment between the calving barn and the supermarket shelf, it orchestrates and controls the quality of every step in a complex process. Figure 11.2 illustrates the multiple relationships that WNF must closely manage every day.

For example, WNF controls the feeding protocols used by more than eighty farmers, works with the feedlots to determine which animals to harvest each week, coordinates the transportation, and works with the packer and distributor to ensure that the right product is on the right shelves at the retailer. We manage store- and chain-level sales, and complex marketing and customer service relationships. This is why farmers can't put this thing together themselves. They are too busy producing and it's just too complicated.

FIGURE 11.2. WOLFE'S NECK FARM'S KEY RELATIONSHIPS.

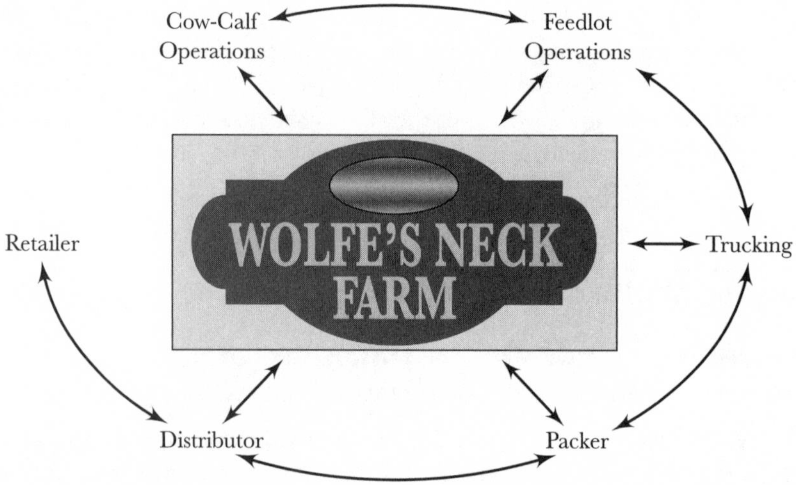

Source: Used by permission of Wolfe's Neck Farm Natural Meats.

Advice. CGV has brought us business expertise. I knew how to raise cattle, but I didn't have any business background. CGV helped me write the original business model, and today they know more about my business than my board does because they are thinking about it every single day. They are involved in every step and are invested partners in this process. CGV is a sounding board. I probably call them two or three times a week, at least, with ideas or questions. We're growing very fast, so I meet with CGV at least every other week. They help me with the analytical perspective. They are the devil's advocate, saying, "Have you thought about this, have you thought about that?" Me, I want to just do it! But they bring me back to thinking carefully about the ramifications of a potential action. They also help me with very specific things. For example, CGV helped me identify that our previous sales and marketing person was not the right person for the position. They even help me communicate to my board of directors some of the challenges I'm having.

Resource People. There are so many pieces in our process. CGV really helps us to access folks who are experts at each piece. We're a small staff, so this access is very useful. For example, when Wolfe's Neck Farm was trying to get its product onto the shelves of a major retailer in the area, CGV brought in the store's vice president of marketing to sit down with us and talk about our brand and how to position ourselves in the marketplace. That was invaluable. Similarly, we know we need capital to continue to fuel our growth. CGV has brought in a senior analyst from a local venture capital firm to help us evaluate the business and set up a model to help identify and proactively manage our need for cash infusions. We've also had several business school interns come in and develop management tools specifically for our program, and they even evaluated a related business we were running, which they thoughtfully told us to shut down. At the other extreme, CGV has helped us recruit people to our board of directors who have been great additions. And not only did CGV put in some money initially, they've also helped us identify other funding sources and helped us when we have written other grant proposals.

Results. We've learned that in a new business everything takes time and that we have to adjust constantly. The exciting thing is, it's really working! We will have shipped 4,500 head of cattle in 2002–2003. Over the past twenty months that translates into more than half a million dollars of new revenues we've put into the Maine livestock industry. Farmers are reinvesting in their farms, creating jobs for their kids, and seeing some light at the end of long tunnel. And more than thirty thousand acres of open space are being used in sustainable agriculture production rather than being turned into tract housing or sprayed with pesticides. We've even inspired the creation of a nonprofit enterprise that supplies some local institutions with local produce and meats. CGV is using what they've learned with us to help that group too. And Wolfe's Neck Farm can now be a strong voice for sustainable agriculture in the Maine public policy arena. We're having a big influence.

How a High-Engagement Approach Can Benefit a Nonprofit Enterprise

As the Wolfe's Neck Farm example suggests, a high-engagement funding approach can bring substantial benefits to nonprofit enterprises, and at least some high-engagement techniques should be considered by more traditional funders when they are investing in nonprofit enterprises. A new nonprofit business venture is intrinsically high risk and unpredictable. The committed, flexible, and timely funding and assistance provided by a funder with a long-term investment mentality may better match the enterprise's needs than most traditional forms of project-based funding. Because high-engagement funders are up-to-date on what's happening and understand management's thinking, they are also likely be more responsive when the business plan changes, when results aren't exactly as expected, or when more investment is required to subsidize a loss—all to be expected with any new venture.

This same mentality is important because investment in a nonprofit enterprise takes a little longer to bear fruit in terms of financial sustainability—several years is quite normal. The transparency and view of interim results that a high-engagement funder enjoys means that it is more likely to be comfortable with this longer time frame. Similarly, dramatic shifts in tactics are more likely to be tried in nonprofit enterprises when management information developed at the behest of a high-engagement funder quickly reveals what's not working. A high-engagement funder may even help ensure this kind of rapid course adjustment, because they are actually looking at the numbers every month (or even every week) and have an informed outsider perspective.

Nonprofit enterprises also are completely new territory for most nonprofit managers and board members. The coaching, access to experts, potential customers, suppliers, flexible capital, and so on that a high-engagement funder can provide reduces the risk involved in a new venture. In the words of Mark Swann, founder of Stone Soup, a nonprofit enterprise that operates a retail soup business and trains homeless people in the culinary arts, "I would be sleeping a lot less if it weren't for Common Good Ventures."

Finally, Letts and Ryan observe that high-engagement funders tend to encourage their grantees to make tough decisions, to grow aggressively, and to take risks to accomplish a bigger vision—traits that strengthen a nonprofit enterprise.[5] In the words of one of CGV's enterprise partners, "Common Good Ventures has provided us with growth in management skills, an appreciation for management tools, and a sense of urgency."

Example: Stone Soup

A Founder's Perspective, by Mark Swann, executive director of Preble Street Resource Center

Before our launch, we did our first business plan, and I thought it was a real plan, that step A would happen, then step B, and step C would follow nicely. When Stone Soup opened, business was incredible for about a month—then it stopped; foot traffic where our stand was located went way down. The related culinary arts training for chronically homeless people, however, was going wonderfully. It was at about that time that Common Good Ventures showed up. It was incredibly validating for us to sit with someone who knew the struggles we were going through and could offer, if nothing else, support and validation. Our relationship grew from there.

Learning New Territory. Starting a nonprofit enterprise is a very messy and complex effort. It felt different from what we've always done as a social service agency. We needed different skills, different advice, different kinds of people involved in the whole effort than we have on our parent board at Preble Street Resource Center, where our work is making sure that homeless people get access to the services they need. I know how to run a social service agency, but I don't know how to run a restaurant, even when it has a social mission. We have gotten our advice and support and networks by relying on Common Good. We have had times when the CGV portfolio manager and I have met every week, looked at time sheets, and figured out how to reduce the restaurant's labor hours in a very hands-on way. There has even been very tactile consulting. You know, taste this smoothie, tell me if it's any good, then we'll figure out how much it would cost to make it.

Bringing Connections. Both Stone Soup and our parent organization have raised money and found new friends through relationships with Common Good Ventures. Our parent organization has just completed its first capital campaign, quite a large one, and some of the key folks who have helped us with the campaign we met through Stone Soup and Common Good Ventures.

Building Confidence. We've gotten tremendous exposure through Stone Soup. Without that and without Common Good Ventures' role in seeing Stone Soup through, I don't think for a minute we would have had the kind of confidence we needed to do our capital campaign and be so aggressive in this economy.

Through Ups and Downs. Stone Soup has had an expansion phase and a downsizing phase. We really suffered through a few years on the business side even though the training continued to go well. Now this year we're proud to say we're making a little money at the bottom line and are putting it into the training program. The largest partner we've had to help us all along the way has been Common Good Ventures.

Trust and Support. I've been doing nonprofit work for twenty years and I've never worked with a funding source in the way that we do with Common Good Ventures. With them there's an incredible honesty, an incredible partnership. It's warts and all. We've definitely had bad times, and we haven't masked them. In fact, we've just said, "We're losing money here month to month and we need help." The key is that the funder is actually engaged with you and doesn't think they know all of the answers. With Common Good Ventures it's a conversation.

Leveraging More Dollars

Like any investor, high-engagement funders want to reduce their risk and increase their odds of success. This is particularly true for potential first-time funders of nonprofit enterprises because success and failure are very hard to hide. Providing dollars to a business venture that is already backed by a high-engagement funder reduces this risk. First, the risk is shared because multiple funders are involved. Second, high-engagement funders tend to work with nonprofit enterprises only after intense scrutiny, including a hard look at both the business's viability and the capabilities of the management team. Third, and perhaps most important, the high-engagement funder stays closely involved throughout the life of the investment and often beyond, and frequently puts in additional resources to ensure the success of the enterprise. Although an enterprise may fail even with support, a high-engagement funders' involvement can reduce the odds of that happening.

Over time, a high-engagement funder is also likely to enable a nonprofit enterprise to bring in more funding because of the funder's focus on achieving and measuring tangible results. A nonprofit enterprise that has carefully tracked its social and financial outcomes can make a much more compelling fundraising case to other funders. For example, Stone Soup now points to statistics documenting that a higher percentage of its training program graduates (60 percent) stay in jobs than the national average (32 percent), at a lower per-person cost.[6] Wolfe's Neck Farm keeps a running count of the new revenues going to family farms and feed-lots ($600,000 in its first twenty-two months) and of the multiplier effect this has on the local economies of northern Maine (an impact of $1.8 million). Donors who funnel their dollars through the high-engagement funder can expect to see the same credible financial and social impact numbers that the high-engagement funder itself sees.

Making It Work: Before You Engage

High-engagement funding can sound too good to be true, but it is not for all nonprofit business ventures. Nonprofits should think carefully about the potential risks for their enterprise of a high-engagement relationship and weigh these risks against the likely benefits before entering this type of partnership. Once a nonprofit enterprise has begun truly to take advantage of the high-engagement funder's assistance, replacing in-kind resources and expertise will likely be quite challenging. Also, because relationships with high-engagement funders tend to be visible, a short-lived relationship that ends because of poor fit can implicitly act as a red flag to other funders.

Are You Ready?

The first step in assessing whether a high-engagement relationship is right for your enterprise is to ask what you are really looking for. If it's just reliable money you want, a high-engagement relationship is unlikely to work. A high-engagement funder will ask lots of questions; look for ways you can do things better, faster, or cheaper; and expect you to be interested in frequent dialogue with those goals in mind. This process will undoubtedly challenge your organization's status quo, and the funder's careful scrutiny may even improve the viability of your venture. Most funders just don't look too closely, so they won't help you avoid bad investments; but because they are not invested in your organization's historical way of doing things, high-engagement funders will likely encourage you to make changes that will increase your enterprise's ability to accomplish its goals. Over time that may involve bringing in new staff with new skills, learning from private sector experience, and adopting a more aggressive attitude—and it will mean moving out nonperformers relatively quickly. As a leader, you need to be able to see these suggestions as opportunities for improvement rather than as questioning of your competence.

You will also need to feel comfortable with not having full control over the funder's access to your organization. Rather than attending carefully orchestrated annual site visits, these funders will likely be interacting with multiple people at all levels of your enterprise, perhaps including the parent organization, frequently and at unpredictable times. Similarly, the funder's tracking of financial results will invite comparisons and suggestions for improvement, and because of its networks in the community, the highly engaged funder is much more likely than traditional funders to get direct feedback from the customers of your venture.

Furthermore, in a high-engagement relationship, the nonprofit leadership no longer answers only to its board; it also answers to the funder, for helping to accomplish the vision put forth as the funding relationship began. While this accountability may seem uncomfortable for some organizations, it can be very useful in prompting change and experimentation, thanks to most high-engagement funders' obsession with measurable results and most nonprofits' valuing of both the funder's money and its time. For example, rather than saying that a program is "going very well" and has twenty-five participants, an update to a high-engagement funder is more likely to include the number of participants who finished the program relative to those who started, their average job readiness on a scale of one to three, and the percentage still in jobs after six months. This type of reporting alone usually translates into staff putting greater pressure on themselves to meet the objectives they have set. Both management and the board should be prepared for this new level of accountability.

Finally, when evaluating your organization's readiness for a high-engagement relationship with a funder, it's important to ask whether management has sufficient time to dedicate both to the relationship and to the recommendations that will come out of discussions with the funder. If the organization has other major initiatives under way, a merger or major capital campaign for example, it will be difficult to begin a high-engagement relationship simultaneously. Once a relationship is established, it is a little easier to manage this ebb and flow, but initially it can be quite time-intensive. In addition, the organization should consider how many high-engagement funders it wants to work with at one time. Most nonprofits find that one is plenty.

Is There a Fit? Assessing the High-Engagement Funder

Letts and Ryan suggest that successful high engagement is based on a foundation of alignment between the funder and the nonprofit, reliable money layered on that foundation, and a culmination of strategy coaching.[7] In many ways, money is the easy part; nonprofits should also carefully consider alignment, the funder's ability to be an effective strategic coach, and equally important, the funder's attitude. Doing your own due diligence on the funder is crucial—you should ask pointed questions about time expectations, reporting required, and so on, but you should also talk to the funder about its current nonprofit partners. Talk to these partners as well. High-engagement dollars come with significant expectations for the nonprofit and it's important to understand these expectations up front. In the words of Stone Soup's executive director, Mark Swann, the relationship "should be worth more than the money you get."

Alignment. Any high-engagement funder will talk about goals with a potential nonprofit partner. Because a shared vision of success is critical for a long-term relationship, clearly defining these goals early on is very useful for both parties. For example, it's important to clarify whether a funder's view of furthering women's economic independence would include building their self-esteem and political leadership skills or just wanting to see new jobs created and more wages earned. Changes in agreed-upon strategy and goals can then be discussed with the high-engagement funder. Such a funder is too close to the organization not to perceive such changes, and not having these conversations can undermine trust. It's also important to know in advance what changes in mission or strategy would prompt a high-engagement funder to exit the partnership, so those expectations can be considered before major decisions are made.

As Letts and Ryan point out, funders focusing significant dollars and involvement in one program or aspect of a nonprofit, such as the business enterprise, can create an inequality of resources within the organization.[8] This focus is particularly likely for nonprofit enterprises because of their visibility, their potential to generate income, and their urgency to ensure they are not losing money. It may be entirely appropriate and welcome for an enterprise in which management can really use additional support. However, it may also siphon senior management time and energy from other parts of the organization that may be equally high priority from the nonprofit's perspective. Of course, over time the support of a high-engagement funder may also free members of the parent board to invest their energies in the organization's more traditional programs because the enterprise is in good hands.

Ability. It is strongly recommended that prospective grantees assess the actual expertise and experience that a high-engagement funder will bring to the table. The funder must be able to contribute relevant expertise to the endeavor. What is its track record in advising successful ventures? How applicable is this funder's experience to advising a nonprofit enterprise? Does it have experience running a business? Does it understand where its expertise lies and in what areas it should not get involved? Is it familiar with the nonprofit sector and comfortable with the constant margin-mission trade-offs that characterize nonprofit enterprises?

Advice that comes from a major funder but is not grounded in experience is much worse than no advice at all. This is particularly true for a nonprofit enterprise because a management team that doesn't have deep private sector experience may be tempted to listen carefully to any outside advice coming from those considered to be experts, regardless of the appropriateness of their counsel.

Attitude. Nonprofit practitioners are the first to say that not all high-engagement funders operate the same way. They recommend carefully considering the funder's personality, operating style, and fit with the organization before going too far.

Regardless of the quality of its advice, a high-engagement funder who claims to have all the answers should be avoided. Even if it brings great sums of money to the table, the relationship will not be effective. As one nonprofit enterprise veteran has said, "There's a big difference between a partnership in which we figure out the answer together, even if the funder ultimately gets us to their point of view, and a partnership in which the funder just talks at you—and believe me, they are out there!" Other nonprofits warn against funders who, flush with success and dollars from the for-profit world, swoop down on an organization, demand many changes, and throw things into turmoil, without respect for the organization's processes or having taken the time to build the relationship that will lead to the most constructive recommendations.

Responsiveness from high-engagement funders is also important: outside evaluations conducted by Christine Letts and William Ryan find that nonprofits place a premium on high-engagement funders' willingness to be responsive.[9] Effective nonprofit enterprise funders understand the value of a timely response to a request for assistance with a human resources issue, a networking connection to an important supplier, or a cash flow bridge loan. Even more important, however, is simply the funder's attitude. Do people from the funder's office call back? Are they willing to jump in when they are needed, not simply when it's scheduled and convenient? In an effective partnership, nonprofits know they can find and get an answer from the funder when they need it.

Attitude is also reflected in the willingness of high-engagement funders to tailor their programs, assistance, and even types of funding to meet the needs of the nonprofits in their portfolios first rather than the needs of the foundation. Although some standardization is efficient for the funder, incredibly busy nonprofit enterprise managers are better able to absorb assistance and training that are delivered with their specific needs in mind. Effective high-engagement funders also tailor reporting requirements to consist of measures that are important to both the nonprofit and the funder.[10]

Finding the Right High-Engagement Funder

If all of this sounds right for you, how do you begin to partner with a funder-partner-coach? Unfortunately, one of the hallmarks of high-engagement funding is placing large bets with a relatively small number of organizations. Most high-engagement funders have identified specific issue areas and other relatively clearly defined selection criteria that are beyond the control of potential nonprofit partners. Furthermore, few high-engagement funders solicit grant applications, a traditional means of ensuring that the opportunity is open to any group that might be interested. Nonetheless, it may be useful for you to let a local high-engagement funder or one interested in your issue area know what you do and look for an introduction or an opportunity to sit down with one of the funder's decision makers. Rarely are criteria written in stone, and there may just be a click that sparks an interest in exploring the idea of working together.

CGV's nonprofit enterprise selection process is fairly typical for a high-engagement funder. CGV identified its broad goals, then began talking to community leaders, nonprofits, and other funders to identify nonprofits that were doing some form of enterprise work and had a reasonable reputation. During its market research phase, CGV talked to groups running a total of almost forty ventures, both big and very, very small. It looked for the following characteristics:

- A strong entrepreneur and management team with an intuitive understanding of business
- A viable business idea
- A business model that could accomplish the desired social mission
- An eagerness to benefit from the range of additional resources that CGV could offer

An initial in-person or telephone conversation revealed whether each group had the basics to be able to benefit significantly from a partnership with CGV. A next round of interviews focused on the viability of the organization's business model and, most important, the management team's likelihood of succeeding with the venture given additional resources. CGV simultaneously evaluated the likelihood that each nonprofit would fit into a high-engagement relationship and into CGV's own operating style. Through this process CGV initially developed partnerships with five organizations.

Increasing Your Odds

Focus first on doing good work rather than on trying to tailor your organization to be what you think a funder will like. High-engagement funders want to invest in something that will work, and nothing breeds success like success. They will look at your track record as a predictor of what you can do in the future. High-engagement funders are also more likely than most funders to ask around rather than rely on what you might write in a proposal. They will quickly shy away if what they hear from your constituents and colleagues in the community is inconsistent with your rhetoric.

Once you've established that a potential high-engagement funder is serious, responsible, and trustworthy, be honest in your conversations. You'll want to present your best side and your big vision, but don't whitewash all that will need to happen before you get there. A good high-engagement funder will recognize your up-front honesty as boding well for a future relationship and will be glad to know there are opportunities to put their resources to good use. Because such partnerships are a new kind of relationship, it can be particularly useful to brainstorm beforehand ways that you might be able to benefit from outside assistance. But again, think first about what you need rather than about what you guess they might want to fund.

To the extent that you have considered the pros and cons of getting involved with the funder, share that as well. The funder will appreciate your recognition that it isn't merely another source of dollars, and your understanding of the time and openness the partnership will require. In the same vein, it is very useful to involve key board members in these discussions. Experienced funders know that strong boards are instrumental to any organization's success and that the funder's own impact will be greater if the organization's board is aligned with the goals of the partnership.

Making It Work: Engaging as Partners

Although grant dollars clearly translate into power for the funder, it's important to remember that any funder is only as successful as the groups it supports. For high-engagement funders, this connection is even more visible, creating more potential for partnerships in which grantor and grantee succeed or fail together. The following recommendations can help nonprofit enterprises create successful partnerships:

Ensure that expectations are clear. High-engagement relationships are difficult to grasp fully until you're already involved in one, but it's worth trying. Ask peers for concrete examples of how the relationship with the funder really works on the ground, including both what has worked well and what hasn't. An explicit initial conversation with the funder and written follow-up documentation will help get things started on the right track and provide a useful vehicle for check-ins. For example, CGV drafts a customized memorandum of understanding with each partner that lays out expectations for the relationship. The memorandum is reviewed periodically—at least annually—to make sure that CGV and the partner are meeting agreed-upon obligations. Involve at least one or two board members at key points in your discussion (the board chair must also co-sign the memorandum with CGV) so they understand that a new stakeholder will be coming to the table and agree on the role the funder might play in the organization.

Be honest. In the words of Mark Swann, Stone Soup has had a successful relationship with CGV because "it's warts and all." Truly high-engagement funders will uncover the organization's reality regardless of its attempts to share only good news, and if they don't know about problems beforehand, they won't be able to help. And like for-profit investors, most high-engagement funders respond much better to bad news than to surprises.

Communicate. Managing a high-engagement relationship requires vigilant communication, particularly for a fast-moving nonprofit enterprise. Overcommunicate when in doubt, especially at the beginning of the relationship. Many partners find it helpful to have both regularly scheduled formal updates and frequent e-mails, phone conversations, and working sessions as needed. In addition to strategizing about the venture, communication should include honest feedback about the relationship as soon as problems or potential improvements are identified.

Take advantage of more than the dollars. The costs of satisfying a high-engagement funder are too high if you're not getting value beyond the stable dollars it provides. Nor will a high-engagement funder be satisfied with just giving away money. If you are not using its other resources effectively, you are leaving money on the table, and over time it will likely reallocate its grant dollars to another nonprofit. You might not choose to heed a particular piece of advice, but for both your own potential learning and the health of the relationship, it's important to consider the suggestion thoughtfully.

Stand your ground. As Erick Jensen of Wolfe's Neck Farm describes it, he gets lots of ideas from his funders, but at the end of the day, "I'm driving the bus." You must use your judgment to determine what's best for your enterprise and organization—keeping in mind that often what is best (firing someone, trying a brand new approach, and so on) is neither easy nor comfortable. No high-engagement funder knows it all, and you'll want a relationship that accommodates respectful differences of opinion. One of CGV's nonprofit partners talked about this balance: "It's like we're a team and they're the coaches. We take 80 percent of the advice they give us but don't feel obligated to take all of it if it doesn't fit."

Think big. Most high-engagement funders want big impact, whether that is defined as scale, depth of impact for beneficiaries, or the ability to pilot a replicable model. Focusing, however, on delivering on the specific results defined up front can get you stuck making incremental improvements and ignoring higher-leverage opportunities to accomplish your mission. Take the time periodically to assess what your organization really wants to accomplish—and what you would do if resources (dollars, staff time, know-how) weren't a barrier. Share this vision with the high-engagement funder and you might find that some of those barriers could disappear.

Celebrate the successes together. In the constant push to accomplish measurable results and strive for greatest impact, it's easy to look constantly for the next area for improvement. Yet chances are you're glossing right over many amazing feats. Stop at every monthly meeting to recognize and give credit for all that's going well. And celebrate outside of the routine. Invite the funder to internal events that you have planned to celebrate your accomplishments—a new store opening, trainee grad-uation, or a volunteer thank-you dinner. For example, Preble Street Resource Cen-ter, the parent organization of Stone Soup, has a long tradition of holding an informal annual dinner for staff, its board, and a few close friends that celebrates the staff's success and hard work during the year. CGV's participation in these events has helped build the relationship and provided opportunities both for CGV to applaud Stone Soup's successes and for Stone Soup to recognize CGV as part of "the family."

Conclusion

At its best, a high-engagement funding relationship can be a partnership that helps take a nonprofit enterprise to new heights and independence. Building this rela-tionship implies a significant commitment for all parties and is not without its risks and trade-offs. Yet with the right fit, attitude, and ability on both sides, a high-engagement relationship can be an investment that generates remarkable returns for the nonprofit enterprise, for the funder, and for the community.

Notes

1. Letts, C. W., and Ryan, W. P. "Filling the Performance Gap: High Engagement Philan-thropy." *Stanford Social Innovation Review,* 2003, *1*(1), 26–33.
2. Ibid., p. 29.
3. Ibid., p. 30.
4. Massarsky, C. W., and Beinhacker, S. L. "Nonprofit Enterprise: Right for You?" *Nonprofit Quarterly,* 2002, *9*(3), 50–55.
5. Letts and Ryan, "Filling the Performance Gap," p. 28.
6. National Results Council, *Occupational Skills Training, Stone Soup Summary Performance and Na-tional Comparisons Report,* 2001.
7. Letts and Ryan, p. 29.
8. Ibid., p. 32.
9. Ibid.
10. Ibid.

CHAPTER TWELVE

SUPPORTING NONPROFIT ENTERPRISE IN EMERGING MARKETS

Lee Davis and Nicole Etchart

As both the number and size of nonprofit, civil-society organizations (CSOs)[1] in emerging market countries and the so-called developing world increase and CSOs begin to expand and diversify their activities, there is an increasingly urgent need to address the basic question of how to sustain their valuable efforts financially. The question of how to achieve sustainable financing has always confounded CSO professionals, fundraisers, donors, and policy analysts. It represents perhaps the single greatest obstacle for the nonprofit sector. CSOs are eternally faced with the limitations of public and private philanthropy and with the limitations of both their institutional form and their capacity to gain access to adequate resources. The problem becomes particularly critical if one considers the fundamental role that CSOs play in the democratization process in the emerging democracies of the developing world. As countries move to consolidate their democracies, CSOs are central to the representative and distributive goals held by

This chapter draws heavily on Nonprofit Enterprise and Self-Sustainability Team publications, including *Profits for Nonprofits: An Assessment of the Challenges in NGO Self-Financing* (1999), the *NGO-Business Hybrid: Is the Private Sector the Answer?* (1997), and *Risky Business: The Impacts of Merging Mission and Market* (2003). An abbreviated and adapted version of this chapter was also prepared for *International Perspectives on Social Ventures/Enterprises*, a collection of papers from the International Social Venture/Enterprise Forum hosted by the Alcoa Foundation at Wingspread in Racine, Wisconsin, June 19–21, 2003.

democratic regimes. The need to strengthen and sustain CSOs becomes key, therefore, to these consolidation efforts.

Historically, many CSOs in the developing world have been sustained (or even established) with international donor assistance funds. During the decades of authoritarianism in Central and Eastern Europe and Latin America, for example, local CSOs emerged as partners of foreign governments, international private foundations, and international organizations, often as independent voices of change and solidarity against repression or political persecution. Many of these CSOs proceeded to formulate projects, account for their finances and serve as conduits for international funding to support the work of grassroots organizations, solidarity movements, and other civil or human rights groups. Little if any attention, however, was given to the financial sustainability of these efforts. Today the situation is exacerbated as some foreign governments and private funding institutions have begun to reduce—or altogether eliminate—their foreign assistance to certain countries and regions. Particularly in the more developed (that is, emerging market or second world) countries of Central and Eastern Europe and Latin America, the commitment of resources to CSOs is waning. In other countries of the developing world (that is, the third world countries of Africa, Asia, and parts of South America), foreign support continues to play an active role. Even when combined with limited local charitable giving, however, these international funds remain insufficient to meet growing needs. One operating assumption of many donors working in the international arena has been that country indicators of economic progress (such as gross domestic product) translate into increased philanthropic support for the nonprofit sector. This assumption is categorically false. Yet many international donors have exited some of the wealthiest countries of the developing world and left behind a vacuum of funding that has left a fledgling nonprofit sector underresourced and vulnerable.

The types of resources that are typically available in the current nonprofit financial market for CSOs in the emerging market and developing world are limited in three primary ways:

Limited availability of resources. Typically, the support provided by international donors and international intermediaries accounts for the single largest source of CSO funding in the developing world overall when compared with support from national private donations, membership dues, government grants, fees for services, and so on. This support is diminishing and shifting toward other regions of the world. Meanwhile, the domestic sources of funding for the nonprofit sector, whether state or private-sector sources, public charitable giving or locally based endowed philanthropies, in many countries have not yet developed to a level sufficient enough to meet demand.

Limiting restrictions on existing resources. CSOs in the developing world have historically faced an additional limitation in donor project-based funding. Many of the resources from abroad that have found and continue to find their way to local CSOs are often made available only for prescribed themes or restricted to project-related expenses. This leaves little opportunity for CSOs to find adequate support for their ongoing operational expenses. Project-based funding has had a dramatic effect on the institutional capacity of CSOs. It has led to uncertainty and inconsistency in the activities of many CSOs, limiting the long-term impact of their work and their ability to think and plan strategically.

Limited duration of resources. Time restrictions are also placed on most grants from donors to CSOs due to donor-defined project cycles (typically of one to three years). The short-term nature of most funding contributes to the inability of CSOs to plan long-term strategies and sustain donor-funding projects beyond a terminal project cycle.

The withdrawal of many international foundations and agencies from countries in Central and Eastern Europe and Latin America, coupled with the continued focus of many of these organizations on project-based funding, have left CSO leaders searching for alternatives. Efforts to assist CSOs in achieving financial sustainability have typically relied on educating CSOs to diversify their donor resources and decrease dependence on any single donor. Many CSOs are forced to go where the money is, however, regardless of whether the project priorities identified by a prospective donor fit the CSO's long-term strategic plans. This approach has led CSOs into an endless cycle of resource dependency. Mounting frustration with the current funding status quo has increased attention among developing world practitioners, donors, and others to the concept of nonprofit enterprise. Over the last decade, interest has increased among CSO leaders in finding the means to strengthen their own capacity to generate new sustainable sources of revenue for their work. They believe that local philanthropy, although very important, will not by itself solve the sector's financial problems because it is a long time in coming and tends to focus on certain types of activities and programs.

While this activity may be relatively new in the developing world context, earned income or self-financing has been an ongoing practice for years. In fact, some of the most innovative and entrepreneurial cases of nonprofit enterprise can be attributed to nonprofit organizations operating under the most dire circumstances. We have seen many small social-change CSOs from all fields across Central and Eastern Europe and Latin America employ innovative, entrepreneurial approaches to generating income for their work, such as the following:

Environmental CSOs employ creative and potentially lucrative eco-enterprises both to further their mission and to generate surplus income. Open Garden Foundation in Gondollo, Hungary, operates a home-delivery organic food service to finance its sustainable agriculture and education programs.

Social welfare CSOs such as Betlem and P-Centrum in the Czech Republic are operating businesses to generate revenues and employ their constituents. Betlem operates a construction company as a means of financing its support to the severely mentally and physically disabled. P-Centrum operates a woodworking shop as a means of creating job training and employment opportunities for at-risk youth while also financing other outreach programs to support the youth, many of whom are overcoming severe drug addictions.

Cultural CSOs, including such organizations as Tamizdat in Prague, Czech Republic, have turned to self-financing strategies to finance their work in alternative cultural activities. Tamizdat operates an online CD store, selling music from Central and Eastern European artists as a means of maintaining a more independent, pluralistic voice in society.

Community or rural development CSOs such as Vydra in Cierny Balog, Slovakia, and CIEM Aconcagua in San Felipe, Chile, have also succeeded in increasing local employment opportunities and increasing tourism, while generating significant income and furthering their missions. Similarly, CIEM operates a café, gallery, cinema, and printing company to generate income in support of its programs to promote local culture, education, environmental conservation, and employment.

These are just a few of the many examples of creative nonprofit enterprises in emerging market regions. They confirm that many—even very small nonprofit organizations—have already succeeded in using entrepreneurial strategies both to generate income and to further their mission.[2] These and many other cases like them illustrate that when used effectively and responsibly, nonprofit enterprises can provide significant benefits to their parent nonprofits, including increased income; a diversified funding base; greater flexibility in allocating income; improved organizational planning, management, and efficiency; improved financial discipline and oversight; increased and improved benefits for stakeholders; improved relations with philanthropic donors; and increased self-confidence and value placed on work.

However, nonprofit enterprise is not a panacea, nor is it possible to derive an equation for success or a formula for replicating positive experiences among other CSOs of diverse experience, stages of development, and so on in the developing world. Our experience since 1997 running the Nonprofit Enterprise and Self-Sustainability Team (NESsT), an international organization dedicated to supporting social enterprise in emerging market countries in Central and Eastern Europe and Latin America, illustrates significant challenges for nonprofit enterprise practitioners at all stages of enterprise development.

Key Obstacles and Opportunities for Nonprofit Enterprise in Emerging Market Countries

In 1997, NESsT launched an effort to document the experience of nonprofit enterprises among small social-change organizations in emerging market countries in order to determine the primary obstacles they faced in enterprise development and to define a strategy for supporting such entrepreneurs. After documenting more than one hundred practical examples, NESsT synthesized the key obstacles into two main categories: internal (that is, those related to the management of human and financial resources and organizational capacity) and external (that is, those related to the surrounding policy, regulatory, and general public environment in which the organizations function).

Internal Obstacles

Many of the key challenges that emerging-market CSOs face in operating nonprofit enterprises arise regarding support and commitment within the organizations themselves.

Conflict Between Mission-Related and Profit-Making Cultures. One internal obstacle common among nonprofit enterprise cases is the philosophical clash between nonprofit and for-profit cultures. Many CSO staff possess a set of values and principles that may be fundamentally at odds with an entrepreneurial approach. Many who have chosen careers in development or social change have done so for the purpose of linking their work to a greater good. Accepting private sector, market-oriented approaches to generating CSO resources may therefore seem simply unethical—the veritable antithesis of CSO values. The introduction of formal corporate management styles into a CSO for the purpose of maximizing profits through greater efficiency not only may disengage the CSO and its staff philosophically from their organizational vision but also, on a very practical level, may lead to an irreconcilable contradiction between two organizational objectives: mission and resource generation. This is particularly an obstacle for those who maintain that reliance on the market is the cause of, not the solution to, global inequity.

Lack of Business Planning and Management Skills. It is more the exception than the rule that CSO practitioners in emerging market countries have business expertise. As a result, the majority of nonprofit enterprises suffer from lack of sufficient preparation and planning, insufficient knowledge of a particular market or industry, and difficulties with product development, pricing, marketing, and competition.

Insufficient Organizational and Staff Capacity. Lack of sufficient human and organizational resources also impedes the nonprofit enterprise efforts of many CSOs. New burdens are foisted onto already overworked CSO staff or volunteers, internal financial management systems are often inadequate, and CSOs find it difficult to attract and retain qualified staff or to access outside expertise. Meanwhile, although the social change field often attracts creative and strategic thinkers as well as natural and dynamic leaders who found new CSOs; develop and implement new programs, services, and problem-solving approaches; and empower and organize individuals and communities, these people are not necessarily motivated or skilled in enterprise development or management.

External Obstacles

The challenge of undertaking nonprofit enterprise in emerging market countries also requires coping with a number of key potential external obstacles, realities, and threats.

Access to Start-up and Working Capital. Almost unanimous among CSOs operating nonprofit enterprises in emerging markets is concern about undercapitalization. Financial limitations hinder the efforts of many nonprofit enterprises to take their activities beyond the start-up stage and stabilize, expand, and diversify. Prior to launching their enterprises or in the process of expanding an existing enterprise, many CSOs lack the seed capital required to research and develop their ideas sufficiently. Furthermore, due to limitations in their legal status, lack of assets and collateral, or credit history, CSOs typically do not have access to mainstream capital resources, whether for start-up, expansion, or cash flow, or simply to compete with better-financed competitors. Instead they rely heavily on piecemeal strategies such as gathering resources from individuals within or close to the organization or diverting other project-related funds.

Unclear Regulatory (Legal and Tax) Environment. While the legal environment varies from country to country, a general lack of clarity in the law about the legality and tax treatment of CSO economic and commercial activities in emerging market countries results in a variety of practical and ethical challenges for many CSOs. Even those CSOs with the best of intentions find insufficient, inconsistent, or inaccurate information; burdensome reporting requirements; and inadequate tax incentives for nonprofit enterprise. Furthermore, lack of clarity in the law presents ethical dilemmas for CSOs as they struggle to promote and preserve a reputation of transparency and accountability to their constituents, donors, and the public-at-large while also trying to identify for themselves the most favorable tax treatment for their nonprofit enterprise activity.

Ambivalent or Negative Public Perception. In addition to the ethical dilemmas just mentioned, CSOs in the developing world also face the challenge of communicating effectively their motivations and goals for employing entrepreneurial activities while maintaining their nonprofit organizational status. Many CSOs in emerging market countries find that the public response to nonprofit enterprise can be at best ambivalent or skeptical public perception and at worst negative and potentially damaging. CSOs must work hard to maintain the public's trust and ensure transparency regarding the use of income from enterprise activities. This has implications for preserving not only the individual organization's reputation but also the public's perception of the nonprofit sector at large.

A Philanthropic Investment Strategy to Support Nonprofit Enterprise in Emerging Market Countries

Most CSOs in emerging market countries develop nonprofit enterprises in relatively ad hoc ways, with little or no previous experience, planning, or support to help them flourish and avoid some of the pitfalls of their peers. In some ways this situation reflects the general lack of infrastructure and support for nonprofit enterprise in emerging market countries—where local philanthropic giving and public and private support for the nonprofit sector remain small relative to growing need. For practitioners seeking funding for nonprofit enterprise in emerging market countries, this is not optimistic news. Having said this, however, cases of nonprofit enterprise within emerging market countries remain some of the most entrepreneurial and ingenious of all nonprofit ventures. Unlike their peers in developed countries, nonprofit enterprise managers in emerging markets face a slew of obstacles (beyond simply capital); yet perhaps due to a lack of other options or out of absolute necessity, these enterprises are flourishing.

The capital marketplace for nonprofit enterprise in emerging market countries has yet to catch up on this trend, however. Established in 1999 and launched in 2000, the NESsT Venture Fund is currently the only financing mechanism designed specifically to serve these enterprises in emerging market countries. The model is built on two primary goals that run simultaneously and parallel to one another: to build the leadership and institutional capacity of CSOs to implement nonprofit enterprise strategies effectively, and to provide access to partial financial resources for CSOs to start or expand nonprofit enterprises (see Table 12.1).

The NESsT Venture Fund strategy also recognizes the very different needs of (typically smaller) business ventures at varying stages of the enterprise development process. NESsT has therefore developed a two-tier process for supporting nonprofit enterprises:

1. It provides support to an early-stage portfolio of nonprofit enterprises through rigorous feasibility study analysis and business planning.
2. It invests in and adds value to a late-stage portfolio of nonprofit enterprises through multiyear financing and capacity-building assistance.

TABLE 12.1. NESsT VENTURE FUND MODEL.

Capacity-Building	Capital Investments (Venture Financing)
Goal: To build the leadership and institutional capacity of CSOs to implement nonprofit enterprise strategies effectively.	Goal: To provide access to partial financial resources for CSOs to start or expand nonprofit enterprises.
Assumption: Without sufficient capacity and skills, CSOs cannot efficiently manage nonprofit enterprises and could potentially threaten their mission-related activities.	Assumption: CSOs lack access to mainstream financing sources to capitalize their nonprofit enterprises. Without such support, nonprofit enterprises will fail.
Strategy: Provide multiyear, targeted, and tailored capacity-building and consultation support to a portfolio of nonprofit enterprises to build their expertise, skills, and knowledge of enterprise development and management.	Strategy: Provide a multiyear, targeted, and tailored package of financing to a portfolio of nonprofit enterprises to capitalize their start-up and growth.

The NESsT Venture Fund Early-Stage Portfolio Strategy

The early-stage portfolio of the NESsT Venture Fund receives assistance from NESsT through a three-stage process of prefeasibility, feasibility study, and business plan development for nonprofit enterprise ideas (see Figure 12.1). NESsT has a set of portfolio selection criteria and the NESsT Venture Fund due diligence process, in addition to the submission of briefing papers from prospective enterprises, includes an extensive process of personal visits by NESsT staff to the prospective enterprise, completion of financial and program information about the organization, a checklist of accompanying documents, references, and so on.

Prefeasibility Study Development. From the venture briefings NESsT receives it selects promising nonprofits to complete prefeasibility studies of their proposed enterprise start-up or expansion. The purpose of the prefeasibility analysis is to assist nonprofits in assessing their enterprise ideas against criteria they have established (such as financial, mission-related, values, or other criteria) to determine whether the ideas deserve further study. NESsT provides organizations with a

FIGURE 12.1. THE NESsT VENTURE FUND EARLY-STAGE PORTFOLIO.

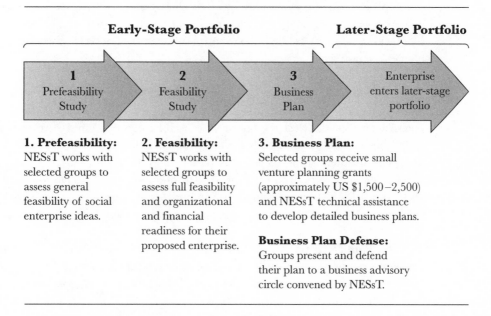

Early-Stage Portfolio   **Later-Stage Portfolio**

| **1** Prefeasibility Study | **2** Feasibility Study | **3** Business Plan | Enterprise enters later-stage portfolio |

1. Prefeasibility: NESsT works with selected groups to assess general feasibility of social enterprise ideas.

2. Feasibility: NESsT works with selected groups to assess full feasibility and organizational and financial readiness for their proposed enterprise.

3. Business Plan: Selected groups receive small venture planning grants (approximately US $1,500–2,500) and NESsT technical assistance to develop detailed business plans.

Business Plan Defense: Groups present and defend their plan to a business advisory circle convened by NESsT.

prefeasibility study template and consulting assistance to guide them through a series of questions and research on the viability of their enterprise idea and to help them determine which (if any) deserve further exploration.

Venture Feasibility. NESsT then selects from among completed feasibility studies those enterprises that illustrate the greatest potential for success and assists them over a three- to six-month period to go through a rigorous feasibility analysis with the assistance of NESsT enterprise development staff. This support is provided through a combination of personal visits by the NESsT enterprise development staff and e-mail and telephone coaching from NESsT Enterprise Development Associates who are responsible for day-to-day communication with NESsT Fund Portfolio members. NESsT has a feasibility study template that has been tested and used by more than several hundred nonprofit enterprises participating in NESsT trainings or receiving individual consulting. Using a template along with individual consulting and guidance from NESsT, the feasibility process assists nonprofits in exploring their venture ideas in more detail, including the potential market, competition, income projections, break-even analysis, and so on. The exercise also helps social change organizations to be more realistic in estimating the time, expertise, and resources that enterprises require. NESsT believes strongly that self-financing is not for all nonprofits and that many nonprofits are unrealistic in estimating the time, expertise, and resources their enterprise will require. NESsT therefore starts the process of assessing venture feasibility with a larger pool of prospective fund members, with the knowledge that in the process some will come to realize that their enterprise idea may not be feasible or may endanger the nonprofit.

Venture Planning. From the completed feasibility studies NESsT then selects organizations whose feasibility studies indicate that their enterprise ideas possess the potential for success. Selected groups receive venture planning grants (approximately U.S.$1,500 to 2,500) and individual consultation to help them develop detailed business plans for their proposed ventures. Over the subsequent months NESsT staff provide technical support and mentoring through tailored consultations and site visits to develop the business plans, providing advice on product and service development, legal and tax issues, financial management, marketing, and so on.

Business Plan Defense. At the end of the venture planning period, each entrepreneur is required to present and defend its business plan to the NESst Investors Circle, a group of roughly ten people (NESsT staff, business advisors, and selected outside donors and investors) assembled by NESsT. The Investors Circle provides direct feedback to each entrepreneur and evaluates each business plan. The business plan defense serves two important purposes: it develops entrepreneurs' ability to present and defend their enterprise plans to potential investors, and it leverages additional financial investments for starting or expanding their nonprofit enterprises.

Organizations that complete the business plans and defense are then assessed for potential entry into the NESsT Venture Fund's later-stage portfolio.

NESsT Venture Fund Later-Stage Portfolio Strategy

Organizations accepted into the NESsT Venture Fund's later-stage portfolio receive multiyear support for the development of their nonprofit enterprises. NESsT seeks diversity within its portfolio in terms of social change issue (environment, human rights, and so on), type of nonprofit enterprise, level of risk, and stage of enterprise development (early or later stage). There is no guarantee that all organizations completing and defending their business plans will be invited into the later-stage portfolio. Organizations that have developed viable business plans and demonstrated capacity and leadership will be invited to join. Criteria used by NESsT to determine whether the enterprises are compatible with its investment strategy include potential for high positive impact on nonprofit mission; potential to generate untied, sustainable resources; proven leadership and a realistic and ambitious plan; commitment and attention to quality; potential to create local role models and replicable models of nonprofit enterprise beyond the individual enterprise itself; ethical, environmental, and social responsibility; and opportunity for NESsT to add value.

Each portfolio member receives an individually tailored, multiyear venture financing and capacity-building package from the fund to help start or expand its enterprise (see Figure 12.2).

Capital Investments. Nonprofit enterprises in the portfolio are eligible for the equivalent of up to U.S.$10,000 in venture grants per year for a three- to five-year period, determined on a case-by-case basis and contingent on success in reaching enterprise development benchmarks. Each portfolio member receives an initial investment upon entering the portfolio, depending on the size of the organization and its enterprise and on the nature and scale of its venture activity. Investment will be earmarked for one of two purposes:

> *Organizational capacity investments.* Used to focus on development of the nonprofit parent organization's core capacity to manage the enterprise (for example, staff development, financial systems development, upgrading equipment, software or office space, and so on)

FIGURE 12.2. THE NESsT VENTURE FUND
LATER-STAGE PORTFOLIO.

Capital Investments
Package of financing tailored to
organization and enterprise needs

Capacity-Building
Close, tailored technical assistance
from NESsT and strategic partners

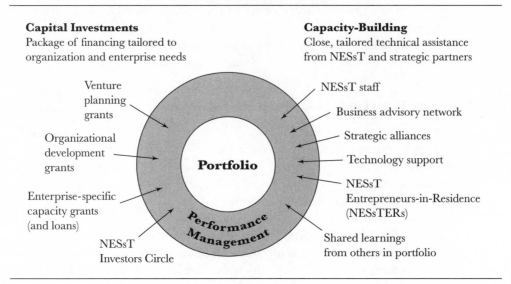

Venture
planning
grants

Organizational
development
grants

Enterprise-specific
capacity grants
(and loans)

NESsT
Investors Circle

Portfolio

*Performance
Management*

NESsT staff

Business advisory network

Strategic alliances

Technology support

NESsT
Entrepreneurs-in-Residence
(NESsTERs)

Shared learnings
from others in portfolio

Enterprise capacity investments. Used for self-financing start-up expenses as
identified in the business plan (for example, product or service development, marketing, enterprise-specific equipment purchases and upgrades,
and so on)

NESsT capital investments provide only partial financing for the enterprises
in the portfolio and must be matched by each organization's own resources
(financial, human, and other in-kind, at a level appropriate to each CSO's size
and capacity); by resources from other investors, donors, or local financial institutions; or by both. At the end of each organization's first year in the portfolio,
the progress of its enterprise is evaluated (relative to the value drivers and benchmarks established at the start of the relationship), at which time NESsT deter-
mines if and when further investments will be made.

The fund also serves an important brokering role for the CSO enterprises in
the portfolio. The Investors Circle helps leverage additional sources of financing
for the portfolio of enterprises. Starting with the business plan defense, NESsT
continuously helps prepare portfolio members to present their business ideas and
plans clearly to other potential donors and investors.

Capacity-Building. NESsT and its team of local and international partners serve
as an incubator for mentoring each enterprise in the portfolio by continuing to

provide planning, management, and other technical assistance to help make the enterprises self-reliant and, it is hoped, profitable. NESsT helps all portfolio members develop a set of core enterprise development skills in addition to providing a capacity-building assistance strategy tailored to the individual needs of each nonprofit enterprise.

Regional Quarterly Portfolio Meetings. A central part of this model is the benefit of regional sharing of lessons learned among portfolio members themselves. NESsT's experience since 1997 has been that this regional exchange of information and experience is invaluable because CSOs struggle with similar challenges and can learn from one another's mistakes and successes. NESsT therefore hosts quarterly meetings (one to two days each) that bring together members of the portfolio.

Regional Enterprise Development Workshops. All portfolio members also participate in a regional curriculum of core enterprise development skill-building workshops organized by NESsT at the quarterly regional portfolio meetings. One full day of each meeting is reserved for providing portfolio members with training in business planning and management, financial planning and management, accounting and social-cost accounting, marketing, product and service development, organizational and staff development, fundraising, and so on from NESsT staff, partners, business school students, and outside trainers and consultants.

Enterprise Development Meetings. NESsT, its partners, and the business advisory committee provide ongoing individual consultations to portfolio members through on-site visits and online and telephone advice.

Business Advisory Network (BAN). The BAN is a group of business, finance, investment, and nonprofit advisors with skills in accounting, business development, law, management, finance, accounting, investment, risk analysis, and so on. The role of the BAN is to provide individual advice and guidance on strategic fund decisions, review fund briefings and drafts of business plans, and review progress of the fund portfolio and provide advice to portfolio members.

Technology Support. NESsT provides advice to individual portfolio members on effective ways to use technology to further their enterprise development, to use technology to market the portfolio's products and services, and to monitor portfolio performance.

NESsT Entrepreneurs-in-Residence(NESsTERs). NESsT often places students and graduates from leading business schools with members of the Venture Fund portfolio to assist with distinct projects (such as marketing plans, product development, financial systems, and so on).

Cases from the NESsT Venture Fund Portfolio

The following cases represent how the NESsT Venture Fund strategy of capacity-building and financial support is adapted to the needs of both early-stage and later-stage enterprises in emerging market countries.

Early-Stage Portfolio Case: La Morada, Santiago, Chile

La Morada Corporation for Women's Development is committed to "confronting patriarchal power relations and public policies in Chile in order to overcome gender discrimination, change sexist practices, and improve the quality of life for women," according to the mission statement on their website (http://www.lamorada.cl). The organization grew out of the feminist movement of the early 1980s, during the military dictatorship, and became legally incorporated as a private, nonprofit organization in 1994. La Morada operates several programs in citizenship and humans rights, communications, culture, and education, and a psychological services center for low-income women. The center is staffed by six psychologists and provides individual psychological therapy; produces publications; hosts seminars, lectures, and workshops; and offers training internships for university students. The center opened in 1993 with services addressing family violence and was for many years resourced through financial support from international donors. By 2000 the center was in a financial crisis as resources to Chile from abroad evaporated. For the next three years the center operated in survival mode with fee income mainly coming from individuals requiring psychological services and from universities for student training internships. Consequently, La Morada was forced to scale back the center's outreach activities, reduce the team from eight to six professionals, reduce the number of women serviced, reduce the center coordinator's salary, and request a loan from La Morada to cover its overhead (fixed costs). The center's team began to disintegrate.

As a result of reductions in grant funding, La Morada began to explore the enterprise potential of its psychological services center. Seeing an opportunity in the Chilean market for paid psychological therapy services to women, La Morada began to work with NESsT on a feasibility study to explore this idea as a real money-generating opportunity. La Morada first established its mission and financial objectives for the enterprise:

- To strengthen the team
- To improve quality and professionalism of service

- To increase public awareness
- To position the center as a high-quality training facility for psychology students
- Financial objective: to reach the break-even point in a reasonable term

La Morada worked closely with NESsT to develop a feasibility study for extending its psychological services to paying clients in the Chilean capital of Santiago.

Defining the service. The first step was to define and refine its service: individual psychological therapy to address general problems, motherhood issues, violence, and sexuality. The sessions—typically forty-five minutes in duration, twice a week over a maximum two-year period—would be offered in rooms in La Morada's building.

Defining the target market. Initial market analysis (through individual surveys and focus groups with potential patients and through interviews with independent professionals and those working in other centers) indicated that the profile of potential clients would be both male and female, between twelve and fifty years of age in the metropolitan area of Santiago. La Morada's target market included a primary segment of approximately 735,000 individuals, including females between fifteen and thirty-nine in the higher-income sections of metropolitan Santiago. These females were primarily university students and professionals, secondary school students, technical career students, and graduates. La Morada would focus attention on positioning itself to capture a projected market share of .005 percent of this primary segment. The second market segment included 1,265,000 females between fifteen and thirty-nine years of age in the lower-income sections of metropolitan Santiago.

Defining competitive advantage. La Morada considered its greatest competitive advantage over other psychological service providers in Santiago to be its affiliation with a nonprofit organization focused on improving women's quality of life. Furthermore, it was thought that the professionalism of La Morada's psychological staff, a competitive and flexible fee structure for clients with varying income levels, the center's strong relationships with Chilean universities, and so on would place it well ahead of other service-providers in the marketplace.

Defining price and fee structure. A particular challenge in La Morada's feasibility study was the initial financial analysis and the effort to establish a differential fee structure allowing for flexibility based on clients' income levels. La Morada calculated that the average fee per session would be 8,400 Chilean pesos (approximately U.S.$12). To break even, La Morada would need to have 418 billable hours with clients per month. Some potential clients would be unable to pay this amount. Therefore, continuing to serve lower-income women through a cross-subsidizing fee structure for higher-income clients was an important mission-related decision for La Morada in developing its nonprofit enterprise.

Overall, the feasibility study that La Morada completed with NESsT indicated a positive mission impact for the organization: paid services would still benefit individual clients in need and help promote the overall mission of La Morada while, it was hoped, consolidating and energizing the psychological services team. As with the enterprises of many small nonprofits, however, La Morada's feasibility study raised several concerns. Of particular concern was the issue of compensation for the center's psychologists, especially in the start-up phase prior to reaching break-even, when the center would be losing money. Concerns also arose about pulling staff away from La Morada's primary constituent—low-income women—to provide services to paying clients. Some La Morada staff were also concerned about the potential risk of promoting a commercial image or perception of La Morada.

La Morada staff identified a strategy for mitigating the potential risks they identified, including developing a remuneration strategy based on equity among staff (rather than based on the number of or income from clients), revising the division of responsibility and accountability among staff, and developing clear guidelines in the business plan about enterprise goals, exit strategies, and so on.

As with all feasibility studies, La Morada ended with a few outstanding questions requiring additional research and planning: How can we predict and mitigate fluctuations in the proposed enterprise? How and when do we capitalize a reserve fund for La Morada from enterprise income (rather than reinvesting in the business)? How and when do we move from hourly salary calculations to salaries based on functions and responsibilities within the team? What methods shall we use to apply a sliding fee scale? What marketing methods shall we use to attract clients from higher-income segments? Ending a feasibility study process by having a CSO ask well-defined priority questions such as these is a key part of helping to guide it through the early-stage process of refining an enterprise idea, and if necessary, helping it realize whether or not its idea is worth pursuing.

Later-Stage Portfolio Case: Vydra, Slovak Republic

Vydra in Slovakia is an example of an organization that has completed the comprehensive early-stage preparation process of feasibility study analysis and is prepared to start a business enterprise. In fact, in the first year that NESsT worked with Vydra on its feasibility study, NESsT staff rejected the approach proposed by Vydra to start its venture. Determined, Vydra staff went back to the drawing board and completed a second feasibility study and business-planning process. Only then was it invited into the NESsT Venture Fund portfolio. It is this early process of critical analysis and planning that prevents CSOs from taking on what may be very risky or unfeasible enterprise ideas.

The mission of Vydra, established in 1997, is the "preservation of local traditions, cultural and natural values" and the sustainable development of the rural microregion Cierny Hron of Slovakia (http://www.vydra.sk/). Vydra is a national association of young people (140 members in 2002) that grew out of a fifteen-year-old Slovak youth movement that had been started to preserve the historic Ciernohronská Forest Railway (CHZ). After restoring the CHZ, Vydra began a rural tourism effort to contribute to the broader community development of Cierny Hron. With an annual budget of approximately U.S.$75,000, Vydra's priority programs include volunteer and leisure-time activities for children, consulting and information services, and development of rural tourism in the microregion.

The NESsT Venture Fund currently supports the development of Vydra's tourist camp designed to encourage tourism, create local employment opportunities, and sustain Vydra's nonprofit operations. The camp includes a buffet near the new Museum of the History of Forestry that offers refreshments and meals (regional specialties) to tourists, cultural events on an outdoor wooden stage. environmental education programs for schools, and recreation areas for tourists (children and adults).

Defining the enterprise's goals. The business plan developed by Vydra for the tourist camp identified multiple objectives for the enterprise: to provide supplemental services for tourists, to meet the growing demand for rural tourism, to offer new activities to attract new customers, to support local suppliers, to help the local community, to provide long-term financial stability to Vydra, and to promote ecofriendly business.

Defining the target market. Vydra recognized a market opportunity for the camp both outside and within the region. Outside the region, the tourism industry is growing fast in Slovakia. It is predicted that Central Europe is going to be among the most visited places in the next ten years, and Slovakia is still an undiscovered country among tourists to the region. Meanwhile, inside the region Vydra calculated that domestic tourism is growing annually by approximately 7 percent. In 2002 there were roughly sixty thousand visitors to the historic railway. The primary target market for Vydra's tourist camp is families with children, who, according to Vydra surveys, constitute 65 percent of the visitors to the region. School groups constitute a significant part of visitors during May and June every year.

Defining the competition. Vydra's market research found that despite the growing rates of tourism, there remained a shortage of accommodations facilities and leisure-time activities for tourists in the village. There was also no sufficient catering facility serving visitors to the railway. The three existing restaurants were not visited by Vydra's identified target market. The station restaurant did not offer a sufficient menu of meals to tourists. The nearby boarding house served meals only to its own guests. And a cottage next to the nearby ski lift offered only more expensive meals. This left a gap in the market for tourist food services. Vydra developed a plan to open its own facility in the area where all other tourist activities (such as music, entertainment, recreation, museums, and so on) are situated to make it easier for tourists to get low-cost food. Vydra developed a joint agreement with the railroad, the Slovak Forestry Department, and the municipality of Čierny Balog to cooperate on the venture, leaving no other potential for direct competition.

Identifying and mitigating risk. Vydra's business plan for the tourist camp identified a few remaining potential risks for the venture. To mitigate these concerns, Vydra took several preemptive measures, shown in Table 12.2.

In the end, the tourist camp represents a real opportunity for Vydra to fulfill both mission and financial goals. The camp offers an opportunity to develop a

TABLE 12.2. IDENTIFYING AND MITIGATING RISK.

Potential Risk	Mitigation Strategy
The nearby forestry museum is still under construction, raising concern about tourist traffic to the site.	Vydra projected its enterprise income based on a conservative assumption of a 40 percent occupancy rate for its services.
Vydra's dependence on a few key local suppliers raised concern about their closing or failing to provide timely quality service.	Vydra identified at least two suppliers for each needed product.
Vydra had concerns about potential changes in regional tourism rates.	Though a risk generally beyond Vydra's direct control, a focus on professionalism and quality among Vydra employees would hopefully encourage return customers.

profitable, environmentally sound, and sustainable venture; it brings benefits to local inhabitants and the local economy; it helps to develop sustainable rural tourism in the region; it offers alternative ways for people to spend their free time; it contributes to the financial stability of Vydra; and it helps to fulfill the mission and goals of Vydra.

Key Lessons Learned in Supporting Nonprofit Enterprises in Emerging Market Countries

NESsT has learned some key lessons over the last few years of operating the NESsT Venture Fund for supporting nonprofit enterprises in emerging market countries:

• *Tools and strategies of support need to be tailored to the local realities and specific needs of business ventures at various stages of the enterprise-development process.* Both in terms of the tools it develops and the process for providing support, NESsT has learned that flexibility and adaptability to local realities is paramount. While materials and case stories from abroad may stimulate creative thinking, pointing to local lessons that function within the same realities is far more relevant and valuable for local nonprofit enterprise leaders. "That may work in New York, but it won't work here" is a commonly cited concern, and despite the fact that many of the management challenges that enterprise managers face are universal, pointing to local cases is a far more powerful lesson. Adaptation and production of local-language versions of many of NESsT's tools, including local case examples, has been one important part of this strategy. Clearly, when it comes to particular regulatory (legal and tax) issues related to nonprofit enterprise, information and support need to be completely local in order to be at all relevant. The NESsT Legal Series is one example of this.[3] Moreover, NESsT has learned that predefined timelines for supporting nonprofit enterprises do not recognize the very different needs, realities, and stages of development of different CSOs—thus the support for two types of nonprofit enterprise portfolios: early-stage and later-stage, described earlier.

• *Many of the challenges that nonprofit enterprises face (and the mistakes they typically make) are in the earliest stages of their enterprise development process.* This is why NESsT developed its early-stage portfolio approach. Few nonprofit enterprises are launched with a full business plan completed. The early-stage portfolio approach is a valuable means of helping CSOs clarify their core values and set mission and financial goals for nonprofit enterprise and of selecting enterprises that are consistent with these values and goals to help preempt or prevent many of the cultural obstacles discussed earlier and to prevent mission drift. It is also a means of helping prevent CSOs from making risky mistakes or launching a business with many unanswered questions, thus helping to anticipate or prevent many of the costs, management challenges, and potential risks of the proposed enterprise.

NESsT has noticed a marked difference in success between nonprofit enterprises who have completed rigorous feasibility and business planning processes and those who have not. For example, Pachamama, a CSO that creates employment opportunities for low-income women in Chile, never went through a feasibility and business planning process for its nonprofit enterprise, Flores del Sur, a flower production and export company. As a result, the organization faced many problems that would likely have been prevented through greater planning and preparation. Now within the NESsT early-stage portfolio, Flores del Sur is completing a full feasibility study for its enterprise expansion. Vydra in Slovakia (presented earlier) underwent its first rigorous business-planning process with NESsT, only to realize that its proposed venture was not feasible. After completing another planning process for a revamped enterprise concept, it has now entered NESsT's later-stage portfolio and is expanding its enterprise with tremendous potential. Some nonprofit enterprises require guidance only in the planning and start-up phases, while others face greater challenges in the later stages of management and enterprise development. The Centre for Community Organising in the Czech Republic, for example, needed assistance only to develop a comprehensive business plan for its consulting enterprise. Once it had a better understanding of costs, break-even analysis, start-up costs, and so on, it needed only minimal financial and consulting assistance before the enterprise was well on its way to profitability.

- *The feasibility study development and business planning need to be rigorous and demanding.* First, this process can be incredibly empowering for CSOs as they capture and understand the concept of business as a tool to further their social mission goals. For example, simply observing the difficult but rewarding process can be rewarding—for example, seeing the staff of Fundacion Chol Chol in Chile completing the planning process for a textile business (selling local artisan products made by indigenous women) and conducting market research to assess the size of its target market and the ideal pricing scheme and export potential of these products; or seeing the psychotherapists of La Morada (discussed earlier) beginning to understand and apply the valuable calculations and terms of break-even analysis to their enterprise concept.

Second, the rigor of the process helps to test the commitment and capacity of a CSO to undertake the enterprise it is proposing to undertake and is thus an integral part of the NESsT due diligence process for selecting nonprofit enterprises to enter the later-stage portfolio of the Venture Fund. NESsT plays the role of enabler and coach as well as critical observer in the process; a balance of incentive and high expectation is necessary. Therefore, while it provides templates and one-on-one coaching and consulting to help organizations complete the process, NESsT does not complete work for portfolio organizations. The process is increasingly demanding and rigorous, but NESsT also provides increasing levels of incentives along the way to help keep organizations committed, engaged, and focused. For example, the NESsT venture planning grant mentioned earlier provides a small amount of resources to offset some of the costs incurred by CSOs in completing a full business plan for their nonprofit enterprise, but it can also serve as an important reward for a strong feasibility study and as an incentive for completing a rigorous business planning process.

- *Truly engaged capacity-building support can far outweigh the value of financial investments in determining nonprofit enterprise success.* Each of the individual organizations in the NESsT later-stage portfolio has faced a unique set of challenges in developing its nonprofit enterprises. NESsT has learned that an engaged process with the members of the portfolio requires that a certain level of flexibility be maintained to address challenges and opportunities as they arise. The tailored one-on-one coaching and consulting provided by NESsT staff, NESsTERs, and the BAN are by far more valuable in both financial and nonfinancial terms than NESsT's direct financial investment in the portfolio of nonprofit enterprises. Although the financial support is incredibly important, in the absence of corresponding consulting support it lacks the added value of the NESsT engaged investment approach. Goals and benchmarks are set out in a signed investment memorandum. NESsT enterprise development staff maintain regular and close relationships with the managers of nonprofit enterprise portfolio members to troubleshoot problems and address opportunities as they arise and to monitor progress. The basis of the working relationship is win-win (that is, NESsT's performance as a fund is dictated by the success of the nonprofit enterprises in the portfolio) and designed to promote honesty, transparency, and mutual respect. NESsT and portfolio members are therefore honest about learning as they go along. For example, P-Centrum (mentioned earlier), a Czech organization operating a woodworking enterprise to employ at-risk youth overcoming drug addiction, learned that the projections in its business plan needed to be adapted once it launched its enterprise. Support from NESsT helped expand the product line and the woodworking shop in order to employ more youth. This success became a potential liability as it became clear that increased sales placed unrealistic production demands on the youth. The enterprise thus needed to be carefully managed with the addition of full-time (non-youth) employees to ensure that employed youth received the benefits of therapy and job training while clients were also ensured of reliable production quality and fulfillment. Meanwhile, the Centre for Community Organising, mentioned earlier, in the Czech Republic, required assistance in developing a more appropriate human resource system for its consulting enterprise. Rapid growth of its enterprise had exceeded business plan projections, but at a toll, to managing staff in its five regional offices. Energy Centre Bratislava, however, faced other challenges in its consulting enterprises. The loss of an expected corporate partner for its Energy Advisory Services led to a major revision of its business strategy and to challenges in managing a growing demand for its consulting services with a very limited in-house staff.

Likewise, the relationship that NESsT has developed with the local BAN helps to build direct links between portfolio members and local area business leaders. BAN members have provided hundreds of thousands of dollars worth of pro bono advice and consulting to the portfolio members, opened doors and networks, and assisted portfolio organizations with very specific challenges, from product development to marketing, accounting to law. Furthermore, many of these pro bono relationships have also translated into additional financial support to the portfolio. Local BAN members who become engaged on a volunteer basis with individual members of the portfolio are increasingly becoming involved as financial supporters. This engagement thus becomes an important part of a wider strategy to increase local giving from local individuals and corporations (indigenous philanthropy) to nonprofit enterprises in their community, and to build a local network of support around each nonprofit enterprise portfolio member.

- *Nonprofit enterprise success is a means, not an end, to financial and organizational sustainability.* While nonprofit enterprise is the entry point of NESsT's investment in the portfolio members, this involvement is within a broader context of enabling CSOs to be more organizationally strong and effective overall, and thus to further their social change missions. However, while nonprofit enterprise can be a valuable tool, some organizations have lost sight of the forest for the trees. NESsT has learned that nonprofit enterprise itself does not necessarily lead to greater financial or organizational sustainability for CSOs. Some of the best-performing nonprofit enterprises (in terms of financial return) have contributed little to the overall organizational health and effectiveness of their CSO parent organizations. In fact, some have drained valuable resources (human and financial) from their CSO parents; others have succeeded in generating net income, but at the cost of losing sight of the original mission; still others have generated net income in support of the nonprofit mission in the short-term but have contributed little to the long-term stability of the organization. NESsT has learned that an important part of fostering nonprofit enterprise is ensuring that it helps to increase effective organizational financial and management systems, untied or unrestricted income, a diversified funding base, accumulation of assets, and long-term financial stability.[4]

• *Issues of ethics, transparency, and accountability are particularly important in countries in transition.* Nonprofit enterprise managers have a responsibility to preserve and protect one of their greatest assets—their reputations as independent voices of social change. Particularly within the emerging market context, where corruption can be a way of life, nonprofit enterprises must be particularly prepared to articulate their purpose and illustrate transparent behavior. NESsT has learned that it is therefore an important part of the nonprofit enterprise development process to help managers understand the ethical dimensions of nonprofit enterprise activities and to manage their business activities as transparently and fairly as possible, always placing the nonprofit mission and values first. In 2000, NESsT therefore launched an effort to address the unique ethical issues of nonprofit enterprise by working with practitioners, business ethicists, donors, and others to develop the first code of ethics on nonprofit enterprise.[5] All organizations entering the NESsT later-stage portfolio are required to agree to the principles outlined in this code and to commit to putting them into practice in their enterprise management strategy.

Notes

1. NESsT uses the term *civil-society organization* to refer to the wide diversity of not-for-profit, nonstate organizations as well as to community-based associations and groups that fall outside the sphere of the government and business sectors. These organizations are often also referred to as nonprofit organizations, nongovernmental organizations (NGOs), charities, voluntary organizations, and so on.
2. See such NESsT publications as *Profits for Nonprofits: An Assessment of the Challenges in NGO Self-Financing* (1999), *The NGO-Business Hybrid: Is the Private Sector the Answer?* (1997), *Risky Business:*

The Impacts of Merging Mission and Market (2003), and the NESsT Case Study Series for further case examples (http://www.nesst.org/furthering_publication.asp).

3. The NESsT Legal Series consists of country-specific guides to help CSOs understand the legal and regulatory framework for nonprofit enterprise in their country—how such activities will affect their nonprofit status, how such income should be reported or how it is taxed. With extensive input from lawyers, accountants, nonprofit practitioners, tax specialists, and others, the guides provide assessments of what the current law states about CSO commercial activities, of how the current law is and has been interpreted, and of the effects of the law on the nonprofit sector, and recommendations for improving the law.

4. NESsT's new book, *Risky Business: The Impacts of Merging Mission and Market* (2003), looks at these issues in greater detail by looking at the impact of nonprofit enterprise on more than forty-five social-change organizations around the world.

5. *Commitment to Integrity: Guiding Principles for Nonprofits Entering the Marketplace* was first published in 2000 and is now available in English, Czech, Slovak, Hungarian, Slovene, Spanish versions. NESsT expanded its work on ethics in 2002 by launching the Nonprofit Enterprise Ethics Initiative (see http://www.nesst.org/SEEINIT.htm).

PART THREE

THE BUSINESS PLAN IN ACTION

CHAPTER THIRTEEN

FUNDAMENTALS OF IMPLEMENTATION

Patricia Caesar and Thomas Baker

Which is more difficult: to develop a business plan or to implement one successfully? Anyone who has actually put a business plan into practice knows the answer to that question.

Developing and writing a plan, gaining agreement, and getting the plan approved are certainly an enormous accomplishment. But the job of implementing the plan is very different. For most nonprofits, it takes a whole new set of skills, and perhaps an entirely different set of people, to make a business plan a success. Everyone is used to hearing that what lawyers learn in law school is completely different from what they actually practice. That same contrast between the abstract world of theory and the realities of day-to-day business applies in the world of business planning.

Why do business plans fail? In some cases it is simply because the plan was based on a bad strategy in the first place—a product or service for which there is no market, a new venture that doesn't fit with the organization's brand or capabilities. Far more often, however, the idea and the strategy are good enough, but the organization fails to follow through on and execute the plan. In some cases nonprofits put in place people who do not have the required skills or cannot make necessary course corrections; in other cases they set unrealistic goals; in still other cases they have no mechanism for getting immediate marketplace feedback or measuring their own performance. These details of execution are not details at all—in many cases they make the difference between a plan's success or failure.

Foundations of Implementation

This chapter focuses on a checklist of six major business plan implementation issues that must be addressed in order to achieve success. Before presenting the checklist, however, we want to emphasize that in order to implement a business plan effectively you will first need to pay special attention to what we consider the most critical—and most often shortchanged—elements of the plan: market drivers, strategic imperatives, the business model, and performance metrics. These are the four points on the road map you will use for implementation—the constant benchmarks you will use to stay on course.

Inevitably many details of a business plan will change once the process of implementation has begun. Your plan's pricing structure may prove, in real marketplace experience, to be too high; demand may be higher for one product or service than you expected and lower for another. Changing the plan to reflect these realities is normal, prudent, and necessary. However, the four elements discussed in the following paragraphs are the unchangeable assumptions that underlie the plan, and when the realities of implementation suggest that these assumptions may be wrong, it is appropriate to question them and to react quickly by making more fundamental changes in the plan's strategy and direction.

Market Drivers

We define market drivers as the key trends in the marketplace that will stimulate the demand for the product or service you are planning to sell. These drivers may range from broad demographic or economic trends, such as the aging of the population or changes in technology adoption, to documentable changes in consumer or institutional buying habits, to specific trends within an industry, such as the exit of a competitor from the marketplace or the emergence of a new customer segment.

Many organizations think they know the market drivers for their product or service. Our experience suggests, however, that many of these market drivers are based on trends that are too broad and often do not reflect a real knowledge of the specific customer behavior and attitudes that will enable your plan to succeed. Many Internet-era business plans, for example, were built on the assumption that rapid Internet adoption alone was a sufficient market driver. In fact, such companies often found that while Internet adoption was in fact as rapid as they had expected, what really counted was whether consumers used the Internet *in the way their plans assumed*.

Make your list of market drivers as specific to your business plan and customer environment as you can. During implementation, if you find that your assumptions about these drivers are incorrect, address them immediately. Failing to do so may well result in the demise of your business.

Strategic Imperatives

What *absolutely must happen* if this plan is to succeed? The items on this list can be as simple as getting the money to carry out the plan. But in other cases the plan may require some key alliances or distribution relationships to be put into place, or regulatory or government action; in other cases you may need to develop a sales or marketing competency in an entirely new area; in still other cases you may need to change the way your institution or its brand is perceived. Every plan has key dependencies, both internal (things you have to do well) and external (relationships or actions that need to take shape in the world around you). In either case, if they do not happen, the plan fails.

A strong, clear list of strategic imperatives makes it clear to everyone working on plan implementation where they must concentrate their energies, and it may prevent them from being distracted by nonessential projects—or worse, ignoring some clear evidence that one or more of the plan's key dependencies simply is not happening.

Business Model

Our definition of the term *business model* centers on defining what business you are in and on how you are going to make money. Sound simple? It is not. We are constantly surprised at how few business plans in either the for-profit or nonprofit sector are able to articulate their models in a way that a funder or a potential partner can understand quickly and, just as important, pass along to others.

Most descriptions of the business model end up being too grand or vague (or sometimes both). Remember that a model is not the same as a mission. A mission can define the broad changes in society or culture that you are hoping to bring about; a business model, however, describes the product or service you are producing, who will use it, and how the business will manage to pay for itself.

If you cannot define the end result of your work—your product—in a specific and practical way, then perhaps your idea is too complex or has too many unsupportable assumptions to be ready to move forward. A business model should be succinct so that everyone in the organization can recite it like a mantra. One image that some venture capitalists like to use when evaluating business-plan concepts is the *elevator pitch*—that is, the story you would tell if you had thirty seconds in an elevator with someone who could be instrumental to the success of your plan. If you cannot answer the key questions about your business plan (what it is, which customers it is for, and how it will make money) in that short a time, keep at it until you can.

Performance Metrics

This issue will be dealt with in more detail later in the chapter, so at this point we will mention only that this is perhaps the most often neglected element of any nonprofit business plan. Far too many plans presume that the real results of their efforts will be immeasurable improvements and benefits to society as a whole. That may well be part of your goal, but without real benchmarks to shoot for—whether a legislative agenda, a target number for revenues, or program participation—businesses and even entire organizations have a tendency to drift and even out-live their usefulness, simply because no one has asked the question about what tangible change or results they are hoping to see. You can develop performance metrics both for your earned-income business and for your entire organization. These will require you to develop a new way of seeing your nonprofit organiza-tion and its interaction with and impact on the world.

Implementation Checklist

Implementing plans is a complex process and every plan has its own timetable and implementation milestones, which differ widely among organizations de-pending on organizational readiness, the competitive environment, and market-place realities. There is, however, a checklist of critical issues that you should address in any launch. It contains some of the most common implementation er-rors and pitfalls and is a reference that you may use both at the beginning of the implementation process and throughout the process of taking the plan forward.

HAVE YOU VALIDATED YOUR IDEA IN THE MARKETPLACE?

Your first reaction to this item might be that this question sounds like it ought to be asked a lot earlier in the process, while you are actually writing your busi-ness plan, rather than during the implementation stage. You would be right. Un-fortunately, in the real world people get to the implementation stage all the time without having been through the process of defining their set of customers and talking with them. That is the bad news. The good news is that it is not too late, even if your plan has already been approved. In fact, if you have not taken this step already, it is the very next thing you should do.

The rationale for validating a product or service idea before real investment and building have started is simple: it is a lot easier and cheaper to fix a problem with a product or service when it is still in the factory than when it is out on the road and has encountered a problem because of something you could have anticipated if you had thought to ask.

The goal of this validation process is not to slow you down. With all the excitement about getting started that occurs when a plan is approved, you may be tempted to think that launching your idea is far more appealing than subjecting it to some serious customer scrutiny. Instead, you should be thinking of the product or service validation process as actually a way to move faster—to get to the right product or service soon rather than have to make major repairs well after you have gone through the launch process.

Be careful not to label what we are proposing "market research." In the market research you may be imagining, you go out and ask people questions about their needs, desires, and attitudes, and about how they might react to products or services that do not yet exist. You may also be thinking that you are going to need to spend a lot of money on professional researchers, focus groups, and major studies. We propose that instead you make what are in effect *sales calls*, and that the only people who can make those calls are the people who are going to be running your business. You need to be willing to invest some key people's time rather than lots of money; more important, you need to be willing to risk hearing some things that you simply do not want to hear.

Validating your product or service idea means taking it, perhaps long before you think it is ready, to the customers who need to say yes in significant numbers in order for your business to work and getting them to say yes. You are not looking for them to say "I like it" or "That's a neat idea." You want them to say, "I'll do it. You come back here to me having done this and I'm in." Just as in a real sales call, you are trying to close the sale—and that provides a very different focus to the discussion, and hopefully a more realistic one, than a traditional research interview would. Do not be stalled by the concern that your offering is not ready or that not enough details of its operation have been decided or built. In a way, that is the point of the validation process: to force you to show your operating assumptions to customers early, before you make an expensive error that could have been corrected.

This process adds a double advantage to your plan's implementation: not only are you confirming that the business model you have is a good one, but even more important, you are also confirming your assumption about the people who will be buying it. Good business plans and strong implementations depend on a thorough knowledge of both the product or service and its market, in very specific terms. Many nonprofit organizations find it easy to be very specific and enthusiastic in their business plans about the product or the service they are going to launch, but they have a much vaguer idea of who is going to make the magic happen in terms of actually buying it. Revenue projections get made all the time in business plans, but they often don't include a supporting page that says, "These are the customers underlying the numbers. And not only that, we have talked to them, and six out of the ten we talked to said that if we started our business tomorrow they would be on board." Implementation plans start with customers, and if you do not know who they are going to be and how they are going to behave, it's time to get started on finding out.

How do we recommend you go about doing this? There are two possible directions. The easy way, although not every product or service lends itself to this kind of exploration, is real test marketing through *direct marketing*. If your product or service will ultimately be sold by mail or e-mail or telemarketing, then the way to confirm the assumptions in your plan is simply to do a test run of the real thing—long before you even have the product or service. Many executives and managers resist this idea, but in fact in many industries it is an expected and valued way of testing products and services. Magazines, for example, are tested in direct mail long before final commitments have been made to actually publish them. Before there is a magazine, in the direct mail piece the potential customer sees a cover and gets a sense of the magazine's editorial personality, the kinds of stories it would have, and how much it would cost. For many magazines this is all a prospective buyer would have on which to base a decision. Also, direct-mail tests can show publishers which variations in positioning, language, personality, and price seem to be the key drivers of success for the product or service. They can also verify that the response-rate projections they have made in their business plans are the right ones.

In most cases, however, direct marketing will not be the ultimate sales channel for your product or service. Nevertheless, you need to undertake the same process that the magazine publisher uses to test a magazine concept. You should take your idea into the marketplace well before you have invested so much money in your business that mistakes are expensive to repair. You may not have a real product or service yet, but you likely have enough material to test whether someone can completely understand your business proposition. Begin by setting up ten to twenty appointments with people who may buy your product or service, and ask them to buy it. Take with you on this virtual sales call a list of specifications, a menu with prices, a Web site prototype, and the sales materials you would actually be using to sell your product or service if you had to distribute those materials today. Pack up these items, and sell whatever aspects of your product or service are available. Then, do not be content with the usual polite acceptance that such interviews usually generate. You are not asking people whether they like your idea; you are asking them whether they would change their behavior and use your product or service and write you a check. You won't get a clear yes or no; instead you will find out, if you listen carefully, what these customers really need compared to what you are offering them. In some cases their unwillingness to commit may mean that your interpretation of their needs was correct only in part. It is not uncommon, for example, for interviews like this to reveal that the product or service being proposed is far more complex, or overdesigned, than what the potential customers really need; and if you listen carefully right up front, you will avoid a lot of investment and a lot of disappointment that would have been generated if you had never asked.

Of course, despite the urgent recommendation, this process of customer interviews is not a guarantee of market success. Like any test, it can deliver *false positives*—people who say they will buy your service and then later, in practice, actually do not. You can also get *false negatives*—products or services that fail miserably in testing but somehow, because of the imagination or skill with which they are positioned and marketed, end up succeeding. However, while the occasional false positive does occasionally happen, false negatives rarely do. If your product or service does not pass muster in a brace of serious customer interviews, the odds that it would succeed in a real launch, without real changes, is very low.

The main pitfall of setting up a business without first making a serious effort at market validation is that significant investment dollars and management time can be spent supporting unproductive directions. In one nonprofit start-up with which we have been involved, a talented leadership team made significant investments in technology, staffing, and marketing to build a Web site that would attract consumers to donate more to nonprofits. While the organization did pursue some research among consumers, its interviews did not disclose that individual donors rarely use the Internet to give online, but they do use it often to research specific nonprofits and their work. Through a new market validation effort, the organization discovered that the technology investment it had made could be repurposed successfully as a product sold to nonprofit institutions rather than to individual consumers, and in the process it was able to develop a business plan that was much more dependent on recurring earned income than on philanthropic dollars. This ultimately successful process might have been shortened, however, with an earlier, more thorough validation effort.

ARE YOUR PRICING AND REVENUE ASSUMPTIONS CORRECT?

While revenues are the key issue for most nonprofit enterprises, it is not always the case that pricing is a complex variable in a successful implementation.

For example, you may be entering a marketplace where what you have to charge given the other competitors on the scene may be a little higher or a little lower, but the ballpark is well established. In other product or service categories, such as professional services, consulting, and even parts of the information business, pricing can go all over the lot. Many different pricing levels can work well if the product or service delivers the right perception of value. How can you make sure that the price you launch with is the right price?

First, and this cannot be said too often, pricing often is not the issue in product or service failure. Many more business plans fail because people overestimated the demand that existed at any price than failed because they set the wrong price. In many, many categories of product the demand is relatively price-insensitive. If you were to cut the price by half, you would not sell twice as much, and if you doubled the price, the quantity you would sell would not be cut in half. The first pricing issue to review at an early stage of implementation is where you are on that continuum: Will price make a key difference to the success of your product or service, or will it simply be a distraction from the issue of whether your product or service is finding marketplace acceptance?

The key moment in which to address this issue, and really any issue involving price, is early in implementation, ideally as part of the product or service validation process just described. Simply put, *never test your product or service concept without price as part of the discussion*. Never show people the product or describe the service without the price, because that is not the way it is generally going to be marketed in the real world. You may be reluctant to do this at an early phase of implementation; nevertheless, pick a number, put it down, and get a reaction. Price is an integral part of how any product or service is positioned in the marketplace, and yours, no matter what it is, cannot be evaluated without one.

How do you come up with the price? There are many methodologies that work well but few that work well in every situation. The only tried-and-true way of checking out your price assumptions is to use several methodologies and see if they all point you in the same general direction. For example, evaluate your pricing on the basis of all of the following approaches:

- *Cost-driven.* What does it cost you to deliver each unit of your product or service, and what does that cost imply about the pricing level you will need to support production? Do not be fooled here by the idea that some products or services serve as effective loss leaders—that is, they don't cover their own costs but somehow have benefits for other products or services that do make money. The number of situations in which this works out in practice is far lower than the number of situations in which loss leaders produce the loss but not the leader.

- *Market-driven*. What are customers telling you about the price you have shown them for your product or service? As we discuss in a moment, there are always obstacles to getting potential customers to address prices with you honestly and productively, but customer reaction to pricing levels and to what customers expect from you at various pricing levels are critical input to the pricing decision.
- *Competition-driven*. If there are clear alternatives in the marketplace for what you are planning to deliver, you will need a thorough understanding of how those prices are perceived and of the opportunities there might be to undercut marketplace pricing—or just as common, to come in over existing pricing and deliver a service that is perceived as a strong step ahead of what competitors currently have.

In many cases, looking at all three of these pricing realities will enable you to vector in on a price that makes sense from all three perspectives. If they do not, your plan is not ready to be implemented, because there is a disconnect between your business model and your marketplace assumptions. For example, in many cases pricing that appears in business plans is driven far more by the necessity of generating enough revenues to cover expenses than by a sense of the customer environment. In those cases, if prospective customers are telling you the price is too high, you may need to reexamine your expense assumptions thoroughly. Perhaps what customers are telling you is that they would rather have a simpler, lower-cost solution than the higher-end product or service (and expense structure) you have imagined.

Unfortunately, just as product validation itself is not an exact science, price discussions with prospective customers—even after a product or service has been launched—are prone to misunderstandings. It is very hard, in many cases, for people to tell you how much money they will pay for something. At lower price levels, such as for products that sell for less than $25, people can be extremely generous in hypothetical discussions, and product managers frequently leave a customer meeting thrilled with the customers' willingness to buy a $20 product that in practice will not be bought at all. (There are occasionally situations on the low end of the pricing spectrum in which people err in the opposite direction and underestimate how much they will pay for something; who knew that coffee could sell for $4 a cup?)

At higher prices, it is much more common for people to underestimate what they would really pay if a product or service met their needs exactly. People are reluctant to tell you what in fact they would pay for what you are purporting to give them—partly because they fear you will actually apply that price. This is what leads to the fallacy of multiple-choice questions about pricing—such as, "How much would you be willing to pay for the product we described to you?"—on all sorts of market-research surveys. It is not uncommon for the next-to-lowest category among five possible prices to win, regardless of the levels of the actual pricing. It is as if people think to themselves, "I won't pick the lowest one because that's not fair, but why should I pick one of the higher ones? It might only encourage them to price it higher." So just as you should take the news with a grain of salt when customers accept your price a little too easily, do not fail to be aggressive with pricing when you have confidence that you are delivering something that will ultimately be seen as a clear market leader.

One last pricing issue that comes up frequently in nonprofit earned-income plans is making the transition to charging for a product or service that formerly was provided for free. This is hard for two reasons. First, and most obvious, you have an audience that is used to getting this product or service for free and you need to move them from seeing your product or service as a giveaway to seeing it as something they perceive as having a higher value. Not all of your customers will make that transition—it will only be the ones who genuinely use and value what you are providing. By studying usage patterns, survey results, and customer interviews you will come to understand exactly what proportion of your "free" universe values your product or service enough to get over the initial hump of paying for it.

The second, less obvious obstacle to making this transition is that giving a product or service away for free deceives you, the provider of the service. In such a case the organization's manager is often fooled into looking at the overall number of customers, which often grows rather well over time, but fails to measure real usage and commitment, which are what will translate into the ability to charge a price. So it is critical, before moving too far down the path of implementation, to be honest about your data and customer behavior trends, because they will have an enormous impact on the success of your pricing decisions.

In the transition from free to paid services, there is simply no substitute for actual customer discussions to confirm hunches and gut-level reactions to significant changes in pricing policy. In one business plan we helped prepare for a national nonprofit service organization, there was significant internal reluctance to begin charging membership fees to the nonprofit organizations that benefited from its services, even though a rapidly changing funding environment made this change obvious and necessary. Years of providing these services for free had conditioned management to believe that members would resist this seemingly dramatic change. However, a series of customer interviews with these members confirmed a high willingness to shift to a paid membership model, at dollar levels significantly higher than the national organization had imagined. Just as important, the interviews helped confirm the nature and level of membership services that the organization needed to focus on delivering in order to make a successful transition. (For more detail on pricing strategies, please refer to Chapter Five in this volume.)

HAVE YOU PUT THE RIGHT PERFORMANCE METRICS IN PLACE?

Performance metrics are a difficult issue for managers in the nonprofit sector. Nonprofits are inundated with demands for evaluations and results reporting. Expectations in this area from funders of every description are higher than ever.

What are performance metrics? In a good business plan they are simple, clear, measurable, and quantifiable. Many organizations are fearful about clarifying and quantifying their goals—the fuzzier and broader the metrics are, the more the organization thinks it can get away with. But in reality, the fuzzier and less quantified your metrics are, the weaker your business plan is going to be in implementation, because you will be unable to know when your plan is off target and when you need to change and adapt to the conditions you are actually experiencing.

There is no one magic performance metric for every business; instead there is a dashboard of metrics, of different measurements that can illuminate different aspects of a venture's performance, in the same way that the performance of a car's disparate components can be monitored easily on its dashboard. On a dashboard you see in one place what has to happen to keep a car on track: you need fuel, you need electricity, you need to watch your speed. Such a dashboard should exist, in a very real sense, for every aspect of the plan being implemented—a regular report in a single place on the key metrics that everyone agreed at the outset were critical to the success of the enterprise.

This dashboard should reflect the two basic kinds of metrics familiar from many nonprofit evaluation processes: short-term (or process) measures, and long-term (or outcome) measures. Inevitably, many of your short-term measures will (and should) focus on money, and the process of quantifying goals and benchmarks can be a straightforward one.

- Are we getting on a timely basis the resources we need to create product so we can make money?
- Is our cash flow proceeding as expected?
- Are revenues, unit sales, customer growth, and customer retention proceeding as expected?
- Are we reaching critical mass as quickly as we need to for the plan to operate?

Longer-term metrics are frequently most inclined to drift, and to show that a nonprofit thinks that the real long-term success of its business is too difficult (or too intangible or too far in the future) to measure. What this reluctance to measure can

easily lead to is an environment in which everyone accepts on faith (or via anecdotal evidence) that a business is a success, whereas in fact its long-term goals are
not being achieved. For example, if an earned-income venture is intended to increase the operating cash flow of an entity, has it done so? Without such long-
term metrics, a business venture often can continue to operate because it has
internal constituencies that support it, rather than because it is genuinely contributing to the overall mission. Similarly, if the goal of a new business is to expand the universe of people with whom the nonprofit has a service relationship,
has it done so? Or has it simply reached the same audiences or constituencies that
the organization was reaching before? Here too the goal of the metrics is to ensure that the venture's future is determined by the organization's need for mission
and focus, not by the popularity or sentimental value of the business within the
organization.

In addition to determining the metrics that matter, new ventures need to establish, before implementation, how they will set up systems to produce the numbers and indicators they need to measure. In some cases, improved or increasingly
frequent financial analysis or customer data will be needed early in the implementation; in other cases, the organization will need to take some prelaunch
benchmark measurements of its audience or of the organization's effectiveness or
visibility in order to make a valid postlaunch comparison. In either case, do not
accept the argument that measurement systems are a distraction from the real
business of launching your enterprise; without measurement, the problems you
inevitably encounter postlaunch will remain invisible to you until it is perhaps too
late to respond to them effectively.

An example of a venture that succeeded on some of its most visible metrics
but failed to meet an equally important but less visible metric is an earned-income
venture started several years ago by God's Love We Deliver (GLWD), a New York
City-based AIDS support organization. GLWD initiated a catalog marketing program offering food, holiday ornaments, and other merchandise and set clear metrics for revenue from the business and increases in public visibility for the
organization. On those two metrics, the venture was a success, and the catalog
venture expanded significantly over the next several years. A less visible but equally
critical metric established at the outset, however, was a longer-term goal of
strengthening the organization overall and enabling its staff to undertake even
more work central to its mission. On this metric, the venture was proving less successful, because the catalog's success had placed unexpected strain on existing staff
and had increased rather than alleviated internal resource constraints. Recognizing the importance of this seemingly less quantifiable metric early in the venture's
life enabled GLWD to make changes in the catalog's scope and product mix, and
to maintain its revenue flow while making the workload and organizational investment associated with it more manageable.

DO YOU HAVE THE RIGHT TEAM?

In most nonprofit earned-income ventures, it is likely that new staff with specific skills for the new project will have to be hired on a temporary or permanent basis. It is very rare that staff members already in place will be able make the transition to a new marketplace or a different set of management skills. In any event, you will need to undertake an honest, thorough, fair process that helps everyone in the organization understand what decisions about staffing are being made and why.

To do this effectively, early in your implementation you need to develop a *skills gap chart*. Take a complete inventory of all of your staff members' skills, including skills they do not currently use in their jobs, and also inventory the kinds of businesses and industries in which they have specialized knowledge. Then make a separate, honest list (put together with expert advice, when needed, from people in the business you are entering) of the skills and competencies and knowledge sets you will need to make the business plan a success. Looking at the two lists together, you will quickly see the key areas in which your existing staff cannot reasonably be expected to perform at a level that can help make the business a success.

In many cases, organizations are intimidated by the prospect of finding (and paying for) the people who can close the skill gaps they have identified, and they feel pressured to make do with existing staff. But nonprofits should also recognize that increasingly funders who are active in earned-income projects will be open to providing the funding to bring on board the skills you need. This is, after all, as integral an ingredient to your business's ultimate success as any other element. Having in place the wrong people, who simply are not experienced enough to respond to marketplace realities and day-to-day problems, causes the failure of far more business plans than flashier issues of product design, naming, advertising, and pricing.

Do not automatically imagine that the outside talent you may need will come from the for-profit sector, even though it is an earned-income business you are seeking to launch. Despite what many people in the business world would have you believe, not every business person with blue-chip corporate experience actually has the real-world savvy and ability to react quickly that a start-up venture in any sector requires. Very often nonprofit managers have more of the flexibility and ability to improvise that are the hallmarks of strong entrepreneurial managers. So, while new blood may be needed in your organization, be prepared to base your decision about where it will come from on the skills gap assessment rather than on any prejudices about the types of corporate and business experience that will be helpful.

In some cases, these personnel needs will extend to many levels of your organization, not just project and business leadership. For example, revenue from the National Council on Economic Education's earned-income program, which focuses on selling kindergarten through high-school teacher training and class-room materials related to the study of economics, has more than doubled over the past seven years, thanks in part to a strong investment in online sales technology. The NCEE realized early on that successful e-commerce sites require a high degree of specific experience and expertise related to customer service, inventory management, database engineering, and online catalog display and maintenance. NCEE's skills inventory of its existing four-person information technology staff suggested that over time this area would need significant strengthening, and its hiring and training decisions in the early years of its plan supported this clearly identified need.

ARE EXPECTATIONS IN YOUR ORGANIZATION
SET AT THE RIGHT LEVEL?

Many nonprofits do not have a business culture, and many nonprofit managers and board members nurture a disdain for business terminology, business practices, and what are perceived as business attitudes. In some cases, the very idea of a business plan is disturbing enough to prevent organizations from preparing one. This attitude may, when you least expect it, create an internal aversion to your venture that can derail it and damage its chances for success. In some cases, staff members strongly disagree with the very idea of nonprofits making a profit, and their active or passive resistance can prove to be a serious long-term issue.

Another challenge faced by nonprofits falls at the opposite end of the spectrum—that is, staff or board members who believe that the earned-income venture will be the salvation of the organization or become the major source of revenue for it. This misguided perception usually reflects a naiveté about business in general, and especially earned income projects and the effects they generally have on a nonprofit organization and its financial picture. The history of revenue-generating businesses inside nonprofits tells us that, except in special circumstances, earned income ventures rarely become more than an ancillary part of the overall income picture. Most often they make a healthy addition to the broad mix of funding that most nonprofits require. They are not silver bullets.

Whether you face one or both of these circumstances, it is critical that you communicate with your internal constituencies, as clearly and fully as possible, your real expectations for the venture. What will the business earn? How long will it take to achieve this goal? What will its effect be on organizational culture and functioning? Try to make sure that everyone is on the same page before you start, and that significant changes in your expectations or in marketplace realities are also communicated honestly throughout the organization.

In another way, your board of directors can be either a help or a hindrance when it comes to implementing your plan, and everything depends on the extent to which you have involved them, informed them, and planned to manage their participation. Many nonprofits do not have the money to hire all the talent they really need to implement the plan, but they do have board members, some with tremendous business skills. Suggesting that board members participate in the launch of a new business is one of the most exciting and interesting opportunities you can offer; in many cases, this kind of project can get your board more engaged with you than they have ever been before. People who work on launching businesses end up with a personal stake in the success of those businesses to an extent that traditional forms of board involvement can rarely generate.

Obviously, just as with any management project, involving a board member in day-to-day help on a project involves risks. In some cases, board members' enthusiasm and energy lead them to overinvolvement and micromanagement to an extent that undermines and frustrates the paid staff; in other cases, board members eager for a critical role turn out to have less expertise or real hands-on experience than was at first supposed. Here too you can subject your board members to the skill gap assessment we recommended earlier, and you can make sure that the nature of their involvement is suited to the project, written down, defined, and agreed to.

WHAT IF REALITY DOES NOT FOLLOW THE PLAN?

You may as well accept it right up front, before you take another step toward implementation: reality will not follow your plan. Inevitably some of the assumptions your plan makes will wind up being wrong, perhaps sooner rather than later, with the inevitable result that at the bottom line your expenses will be higher than you expected, or revenues will be lower than you imagined. What do you do to react, and when do you react?

The first piece of advice in this area is *do not overreact*. Revenue problems do not always mean a fatal flaw in your product or service concept or your understanding of the market. Do not immediately imagine that when revenues are slow you have a disaster on your hands. For example, if you were depending on direct mail to generate the response you need and you do not get it, perhaps it is simply that direct mail will not work as the primary channel for your service. Maybe enough explanation or introduction is required for it to be sold in person or on the phone; perhaps Web-based marketing will be more cost-effective. The problem in some cases is not the product or service but the channels through which the product or service is being sold, the way it is being explained and positioned, or some other element of the marketing strategy that may be just wrong enough to be causing a larger-than-expected problem.

Similarly, it is important not to overreact positively. Admittedly it is hard to do otherwise, once the phone starts ringing, e-mails start arriving, and there seems to be some excitement and interest building around your new business. Most businesses, however, stand or fall not on interest and inquiries but on orders; even more so, they thrive not on initial orders but on repeat purchase, subscription renewal, and word-of-mouth recommendations from satisfied customers. Remember that in your internal communications and planning you should always keep focused on the longer-term measures of customer acceptance and success. While it is fine to be happy with a good initial response, keep everyone prepared for the challenges and uncertainties that are still coming.

While warning you not to overreact, however, we also encourage you to react *quickly* once you have identified the potential root causes of the results you are seeing. How do you know where to turn first? Your first reaction to any revenue shortfall should be to go back to step one of this checklist and talk to customers—potential, current, and former. Talk to people who have received your information and sales approaches and have not responded; go back to everyone who said before launch that they would be on board and find out in detail why they are not. Ask everyone in the organization, even those who normally would not interact with customers, to call, visit, and e-mail customers. The answer to revenue problems lies in only one place: with the people who are supposed to be giving it to you.

Finally, there is the greatest implementation caveat of all, the pit that, more than any other pit, managers of troubled product and service launches fall into: If and when your product or service results are disappointing, do not assume that it is somehow the customer's fault. The always unjustified lament of product managers in this position focuses on the customer's lack of understanding: *if only they understood*. Unfortunately, a lack of understanding on the part of your proposed customer is always your fault, not theirs, and it either is the fault of your own messaging and communications or even more often reflects some way in which your product or service concept just is not as compelling or relevant to customers' lives as you convinced yourself it was. So, if at any point in the implementation process you hear yourself blaming the customer, not your product or service, for your results, it is time to step back to the foundations of implementation and the checklist and make sure that your focus is always on the realities of your marketplace.

Conclusion

When you begin implementing a business plan, the day-to-day operational and logistical activities and decisions bring both exhilaration and exhaustion—reactions that coexist in even the best-conceived ventures. But one can get caught up too easily in the minutia and crises of the moment. What we hope to suggest by providing you with this higher-level view of the issues at stake in any earned-income launch is that you refocus your attention on the larger issues that are the genuine reality questions surrounding your launch process. Every launch will have mistakes, scheduled mishaps, unexpected customer reactions, and even rejections. But none of those need be fatal if the larger issues of your business—its customer focus, business model, performance metrics, and management team—are firmly in mind throughout the process. If you jot down the six items on our implementation checklist and keep referring to them as your own reality check during the good and the bad times of the launch of your venture, you will be better able to stay on track and to be confident that your earned-income venture will make the significant difference to your organization's future that you hope it will.

CHAPTER FOURTEEN

REAL-WORLD CHALLENGES OF IMPLEMENTATION

Kim Alter

Nonprofit business plans, like their for-profit counterparts, are management tools intended to inform decision making. For this reason, a business plan is only as useful as it is used. A good business plan doesn't just lie in the bottom of the drawer; it is an instrument of daily business.

A common analogy for a business plan is a road map, but possibly a more accurate analogy is a war plan. "Once the first shot was fired, the whole war plan was out and we had to start over," Tommy Franks said during an interview on CNN in May 1, 2003 about the war in Iraq. In other words, a new venture can demonstrate rather quickly that reality rarely reflects expectations. Contingency planning should prepare you for surprises, but a silent phone or an empty store can shake even the most confident nonprofit entrepreneur. Or perhaps your immediate business success exceeded your expectations and consequently your capacity or capital as well. Experienced venture practitioners have learned to expect the unexpected, to adapt their plans accordingly, and to have plans B, C, and D in hand.

For their invaluable contributions to this work, appreciation is owed to Daniel Helfman, principal of Social Venture Consulting and former director of business development and marketing for Greyston Bakery, as well as to John Brauer, executive director of NW Works and former CEO of Community Vocational Enterprises. These are two of the warmest, most qualified, and talented implementers of nonprofit business plans that I know. Their ideas, experience, stories, and words are in this chapter, and without them this work quite simply could not have been written.

The reward for the hard work of developing a business plan is the even harder work of implementing it. So what happens when you create a road map and still aren't getting where you want to go? This chapter introduces tools and strategies to help you maintain the agility, flexibility, and confidence required to implement your business plan in a living, dynamic environment. It focuses on how to manage by a business plan, using it as a decision-making tool and a guide, a map or a war plan, for your nonprofit venture.

Implementation from the Trenches: The Nonprofit Entrepreneur

Ultimately, business success rests on the people behind the plan. An adage from the for-profit world is that venture capitalists invest in people, not just in good ideas. High team risk, defined by the lack of a strong leader and talented management, is a deal breaker for most investors. Good ideas come relatively easily, but the champions who make them happen are in short supply. With or without external pressure from donors, nonprofits must be at least as vigilant, if not more so, about hiring the right people to run their ventures. Low human resource capacity to deliver social service programs is a recurring theme in nonprofit management; in a business it can determine whether the company makes or loses a lot of money.

Nonprofit ventures need great leaders—savvy, energetic entrepreneurs with business smarts and imagination—to implement their business plans. Most important, nonprofit entrepreneurs are flexible and willing to do what it takes to make the business a success. During start-up, the job is twenty four hours a day, seven days a week, and full of oddball responsibilities never anticipated in a job description. For example, the driver at the nonprofit enterprise Greyston Bakery once was unable to deliver a five-thousand-pound shipment of brownies to its customer. Its marketing director rose to the occasion, getting up at 4 A.M. and driving the truck from New York to Pennsylvania, arriving at the ice cream factory at the designated time—7 A.M. (interview with Daniel Helfman, former marketing director at Greyston Bakery). In this situation, a make-it-work attitude preserved the customer relationship.

The best entrepreneurs also aggregate talent. Like the Pied Piper, they attract other talented people. In the early 1980s, Ben Cohen of Ben & Jerry's attracted an amazing team to his fledgling ice creamery. Two of Ben & Jerry's former employees, Perry Odak and Chico Lager, became the CEO of Wild Oats and (now former) chair of Whole Foods, respectively. If you want a venture that grows to scale—a $5 million annual business, for example—you need an excellent CEO who can also bring in a great director of marketing, business development person, and so on.

An industry expert is another essential component of the venture team. If your business model is not centered on commercializing the organization's social services but is moving into a new industry, you will especially need that know-how in-house. For example, a human services organization that, instead of selling counseling services that are part of its core competencies, chooses to start a landscaping business to employ its clients will need a landscape architect with commercial experience. Your nonprofit may contract out for technical expertise to inform the development of your business plan, but by launch time this person should be on staff. Find a candidate familiar with the industry value chain who can advise on suppliers and marketing channels for your business as well as ensure saleable services. Additionally, industry representation should sit on your organization's board or advisory committee.

Bootstrapping during start-up may entail cobbling together a functional team from other organizational departments, such as marketing, information technology, and finance, as well as from the board of directors. During this time your industry specialist may also play the role of operations manager, and your CEO might be the "sometimes receptionist" and answer phones. As the venture grows, however, you will have to hire qualified functional talent at the right time in order to achieve targets, manage growth, and meet financial goals. Timing is key. Most plans call for staggered implementation, bringing on new staff when work volume, functional needs and revenues warrant it. The unfortunate marker for adding staff is the breaking point, when someone is doing two jobs. Here you will have to be careful to test assumptions and revisit projections to ensure that your plan's timeline is consistent with implementation doability and capital.

Like the Back of Your Hand: Know Your Customer and Market

Traditional nonprofit social programs are designed for clients' needs rather than for their wants and willingness to pay. Nonprofit customers are clients, donors, and stakeholders such as the public. In a double-bottom-line business it's important to be clear about customer levels and to discern social customers from financial ones. On the venture side, financial viability depends on the person who's buying your goods and services. Once demand—the willingness and ability to pay—enters the equation, the formula for success is drastically different than the formula in traditional nonprofit management. Without intimate knowledge of the particular customer's wants and desires, likes and dislikes, there is no business. In one case, customers of a soap company operated by a nonprofit organization kept asking for glycerin soap. The company did some market research on the manufacturing process and costs and then introduced a few sample products. They sold out instantly, which prompted the company to create a glycerin soap product line. The company found immediate success, and all it took was listening to its customers.

The El Puente Community Development Corporation operates affordable housing, provides child care, and develops job training programs and jobs for the largely Hispanic population living in an area of El Paso designated to receive government assistance. When major jeans manufacturers exited El Paso, many of El Puente's clients were laid off from jobs where they made jeans and other garments. The abandoned factories offered infrastructure for a venture, but what would El Puente manufacture? El Puente's clients noted a small but perplexing problem that would become the basis of their business. Nonsurgical scrubs were too long and too narrow to fit the average Latino, who is shorter and stockier than the average American. El Puente discovered that standard scrub sizes were created in the 1950s and never updated, and it saw a niche for a product in a market that it knew very well (interview with Cindy Arnold, executive director of El Puente).

El Puente created Diseños Mayapán, a for-profit venture, to produce the nonsurgical scrubs. The target market was clear, yet questions remained about whether sufficient demand existed for the products to make the business idea viable. Disenõs Mayapán needed to find out who was interested in the scrubs, who would buy them, why they would buy them, what prices they would pay for them, and with what frequency they would buy them. Frequency is critical because it is a determinate of sustainability. When you forecast frequency you are projecting potential customers' buying habits—whether they are going to purchase your products with enough regularity to make your venture a going concern.

Try It, You'll Like It: Test Marketing

The best way to learn about your market is to create a prototype and try out your concept. Test marketing—selling a small sample of a product or service to a targeted audience—is an excellent method for validating, or invalidating, business plan assumptions and informing implementation early on. Although it seems counterintuitive, for many organizations the best time to develop a business plan is after selling something. In practice, many entrepreneurs open their businesses with no plan in hand, and only when they have a little experience in the market and a few raps on the chin do they go to the drafting table. Informally these entrepreneurs are test marketing their products and services. Test marketing is a low-risk way to try your price, product, and business model, and a strategy that allows you to build your business slowly, making adjustments as you go along. Disenõs

Mayapán tested its scrub idea with a prototype model and in twelve months sold $40,000 worth of scrubs. Now management knew there was a market for the product, and they could make their enterprise a multimillion-dollar business.

The Never-Ending Story: Market Research

One nonprofit working on a business plan for its venture asked, "When will we finish market research?" The answer is never. Market research is a perpetual and relentless process, not a task to be neatly scratched off a to-do list, especially once you're open for business. The reason is that markets are moving targets. Conditions change constantly—a new competitor enters the market with a lower-priced or higher-quality product, the economic situation causes your customers to change their purchasing habits, or new fashion trends make your once-popular product out-of-date—and that can affect your business. Staying focused on the external environment is challenging because it requires nonprofits, accustomed to functioning in reactive mode, to be proactive and forward thinking.

Many nonprofit entrepreneurs are wary of the time and costs involved in market research. It is important to discern the difference between the kind of market research you do before starting your business and what you do afterward. In prelaunch business planning you may invest a lot of time in formal market research: surveys, focus groups, questionnaires, and statistical data. Once you've launched, with the exception of introducing new products or penetrating new markets, market research can become less informal. This type of market research means paying attention to your industry—spotting new opportunities, emerging risks, or shifting customer habits simply by talking to your industry peers, suppliers, and customers; studying your competitors' moves—reading trade publications and market reports, and surfing the Internet. Informal market research is instinctive. Most entrepreneurs are born with a sixth sense; for these people, analyzing the market is like breathing. For many nonprofits, however, the cultural shift to internalizing ongoing market research is a leap, necessitating time and energy to build the organization's capacity to do what entrepreneurs do naturally.

In a venture, some things can't be prepared for in advance. Regardless of how much time and energy are spent on market research, some things must be experienced firsthand. For example, Save the Children studied the seasonality of agricultural inputs for its peanut butter enterprise but would not know the full impact on its business until it entered the market. It took Save the Children a full two years of self-study (without extreme weather conditions affecting peanut production) to understand the ebbs and flows of its food-processing business (conversation with Heather Shapter, technical advisor to the Save the Children project in Haiti). In this way, market research is also internal. As demand grew for Save the

Children's products, enterprise managers analyzed the market as well as their organizational capacity before making decisions to add storage and diversify with new product lines to facilitate manufacturing year round. It's easy to get bogged down in the day-to-day details of running a business; it takes a lot of work to constantly appraise the market and assess it in relation to your internal operations.

Change Is the Only Constant: Be Ready to Adapt

Nonprofit practitioners are accustomed to preparing proposals as planning documents. A proposal's logical framework projects costs and impact over a specific period; its construct is rigid, however. Its main purpose is to communicate a program plan and outputs to a potential donor and ask for funding. The proposal's structure does not lend itself to adaptations that correspond to a changing environment or unexpected obstacles and new opportunities.

A business plan, by contrast, is flexible. It's likely that you will start with a vision and end up somewhere totally different during implementation. In the process you will learn a lot of things that you didn't intend to learn at the outset. John Brauer, executive director of NW Works, warns, "Don't get married to a business just because you put a lot of time, energy, and effort into it. It's going to be dramatically different after you start your business" (conversation with John Brauer, executive director of NW Works, a nonprofit that provides training, support, and employment opportunities to individuals with disabilities). A business plan serves as an excellent guide for making adjustments. Sit down with your team and review your business plan every few weeks to appraise what's really happening. Assess whether you are reaching your targets and, if you are not, why not? How are markets acting differently than you expected? In what way are you selling more or less than projected? What modifications do you need to make to your plan? Are your targets over- or understated? As soon as you start selling goods or services, many of your original assumptions will become null and void.

Search Development Center (SDC), a $10 million organization that serves developmentally disabled people in the Chicago area, was approached by Horny Toad Activewear (HTA) about a partnership opportunity. HTA wanted SDC to manufacture camping pillows that were stuffed with and covered by leftover fabric from producing Horny Toad's existing clothing line. Horny Toad would then sell the camping pillows through its network, including Title 9 Sports (an online and direct mail catalog for women), REI, and other retailers and wholesalers. Wow, thought SDC, what luck: a gift-wrapped contract sealed with a bow. It sounded perfect, and it was, until SDC received its first order for five thousand camping pillows. Suddenly SDC had some problems. One was that commercial sewing was a difficult skill for its clients to master. It was also a challenge to produce pillows of consistent quality and with sufficient speed to earn a profit. Everyone was frustrated: the clients, the staff, and the sporting goods company. Making camping pillows was not the right business for SDC.

Today SDC's multimillion dollar business has nothing to do with camping pillows; instead, it operates a third-party logistics company called Planet Access Company. The only similarity between the camping pillow business and Planet Access Company is the sector it serves—the outdoor sports and recreation industry. SDI manages contracts such as adhering instructions to flashlights from China, then boxing, packaging, labeling, and shipping them off to REI (conversation with John Lipscomb, executive director of SDC).

When a Good Business Plan Goes Bad: Planning for the Impossible

One of the first ventures started by Community Vocational Enterprises (CVE) of San Francisco was called CVE Bakery. If you were to look up CVE Bakery today you wouldn't find it, because it doesn't exist. Before launching its bakery, CVE spent time developing a working business plan. It contracted experts to help analyze the market, measure the risks, and project financials. CVE's managers asked all the right questions: What is the market? Who is the customer? What volumes will we sell? How much capital will we need? And so on. CVE thoroughly examined everything that could possibly go wrong and developed contingency plans.

At that time, CVE was a part of a larger hospital chain, California Pacific Medical Center. One of the key success factors of the CVE Bakery business model was gratis use of one of the hospital's commercial kitchens. The free space, offered as an open-ended lease, enabled CVE to save a significant portion of its fixed costs, which dramatically lowered its business risk.

The CVE Bakery and Café was an immediate hit. The business plan called for a gourmet menu, which was tested successfully. During the market analysis for the business plan, CVE noted that many busy San Francisco professionals preferred to order in rather than eat out. Hence, a market for catering existed. So the bakery now had two successful businesses. Catering operations quickly expanded from the bakery's immediate neighborhood to serve businesses throughout the city.

After operating the bakery for roughly six weeks, with much better sales than CVE had anticipated, it was time to revise the business plan. CVE Bakery managers needed to figure out how to meet demand and how fast to grow the nascent bakery, and how to do so while using a labor force of disabled people. The risks were twofold. On the business side, rapid growth could result in CVE being unable to maintain product quality for its customers; and on the social side, the extra volume of work could stress its clients. CVE developed a plan to manage the growth of the bakery's retail and catering businesses and started to ramp up slowly. It all went so well—at first.

When you work with people who have mental health disabilities, things sometimes go wrong. In this case, a client was preparing toasted almonds for one of the bakery's salads. Normally almonds are placed in a pan in the salamander oven, where they get nice and toasty, and then are sprinkled on salads. This time the pan was not quite as clean as it might have been and it caught on fire. The client panicked, and rather than pulling out the fire extinguisher, he pulled the alarm. Flame retarding chemical foam was released throughout the building, and in the kitchen area it was waist deep. As one can imagine, this terrified the hospital's patients and left a terrible, costly mess behind. That afternoon, CVE's CEO received a call from the president of the hospital, who said, "We really love the café, but you can't have it here anymore."

CVE began a search for new space for the bakery, which in San Francisco is horribly expensive. The key assumption behind the business plan projections was that CVE would not have to pay for space. CVE did eventually rent space for about six months but was never able to fully recoup the costs; without the free kitchen, the business didn't work. How do you plan for that? The hospital had said, "It's yours for life," and then the phone call came and everything changed. So go the best laid plans.

Be Patient: Growing a Business Takes Time

In the same logic as "a watched pot never boils," executing a business takes longer than one expects, especially if one is pining for customers. Nonprofit entrepreneurs underestimate with amazing regularity the lead time to get their businesses up and running. Take the case of Greyston Bakery's expansion. In 1998, Greyston Bakery was literally bursting at the seams, badly overcapacity. The company resorted to using freezer trucks parked across the street as an extension of its refrigerator to store brownies as they were baked. When it was time to grow, Greyston planned to build a new bakery. The company had already acquired the land, so it wrote a business plan for expansion and started working on raising investment dollars. The business plan timeline projected that the bakery would move into the new space by the following summer, 1999. Yet it was 2003 before Greyston moved into its new home. It took a lot longer than had been expected. It always does, so be patient.

A business plan provides a timeline for execution. Serious problems can arise if you're wildly off the mark in your estimations. Yet acute optimism is one of the most common characteristics of the nonprofit entrepreneur. If your venture takes four times longer to roll out than anticipated yet your burn rate and capital are consistent with your projections, you will be out of money before you even set up shop. It's important to recognize that implementation starts well before you sell, meaning that you have prelaunch activities and costs for which you must account, plan, and budget during the start-up period. As you write your business plan you might think, "I'm going to get my space, then hire my staff, start an inventory—

that should take about three months." On paper, three months seems like a long time, but realistically it will probably be more like six.

A business plan that lacks operational details, as many do, will require a separate implementation plan. In short, you should plan everything and revise your plans regularly as you implement. What are the capital requirements? Where is money coming from and when will you get it? Was the equipment order shipped on time and when will it arrive? How long will it take to renovate the space? What about construction permits? Who's responsible for what? Is this a new business? If so, how long is it going to take to learn it? How will you plan for inefficiencies and learning curve? Break the plan into increments of weeks or months, put it on a Gantt chart, and have a budget for each stage of implementation. Construction projects, especially buildings, are notorious for experiencing delays. Raising capital often takes more time than predicted, and estimations for any activity involving bureaucratic processes should be doubled or tripled. In a new business, setbacks, mistakes, and surprises happen, so plan liberally for the start-up period. A general rule is to be conservative and build in a generous amount of time to accommodate delays.

New Nonprofit Math: The Numbers Keep Changing

Running a new enterprise is never easy. While the good news is that you may have secured financing for your business, the bad news is that by the time your business plan is fully financed, it is likely out-of-date and the numbers probably are no longer valid. Successfully operating your business venture will depend on your knowledge and management of key financial indicators, including expenses, costs of goods sold, amount of inventory in stock, your cash flow, and more. Several decision-making and information tools exist to help you track the expenses of your nonprofit enterprise on a daily basis:

Cash flow management. This is an eighteen-month projection that clearly tallies and categorizes the inflow and outflow of cash (all revenues and expenses) on one comprehensive spreadsheet. The spreadsheet can be used as the basis for setting budgets, planning for management of lengthy receivables and payables, and more. The cash flow projection includes an analysis of net income and highlights the often-missed difference between positive cash flow and losses in the income statement.

Cost accounting. Cost accounting proponents typically say that cost accounting models depend on your assumptions, including what you're measuring, what you're looking for, and why. Cost accounting is a method of allocating operating expenses to specific products and services. Cost accounting makes it simple for an operations manager or purchasing agent to analyze how slight changes in the cost of inputs can change the cost of the product. For example, consider the price of cocoa for the production of brownies. A war in the Ivory Coast—where most high-quality cocoa is produced—may seem like a minor detail, but it can have devastating results on the brownie bottom line.

Allocating resources. Shifting resources from a nonprofit structure to a business enterprise is often harder than you expect. It can be difficult to release funds for a new project. The managers of a profit center within a business may be reluctant to share critical resources (people, space, finances) with a cost center. These scenarios and others suggest the importance of developing a practical formula for allocating resources within your organization.

Accounting systems. At a minimum, the accounting system for your enterprise must be separate from that of your parent organization. Thus your accounting system will need to mature beyond simple spreadsheet programs and move from fund-based accounting, which is common for traditional nonprofits reporting on grants and charitable giving, to standard business systems that follow Generally Accepted Accounting Principles. These systems—the profit and loss statement, balance sheet, and cash flow statement—generate the key financial reports that management typically uses for decision making, for financial reporting to funders or creditors, and as communication tools to stakeholders. Numerous low-cost, quality off-the-shelf software accounting packages exist in today's small-business-friendly market. Most are suitable for businesses with income in excess of a million dollars and can be customized easily to accommodate the particulars of your venture or industry. For product-based enterprises it is strongly recommended that you use software that integrates inventory management and control with accounting.

Plan use of revenue. Include in your business plan how you will use the profit generated by your venture. Running a sustainable enterprise requires investments in the business; for many nonprofits, however, the purpose of the business is to funnel money into its social programs or parent organization. Although generating a profit may be your ultimate goal, internal strife over how it will be directed can cause considerable discord. As with allocating resources, it is also important to have a plan for distributing profit.

Shrugging off Misperceptions: Nonprofits Can't Run Businesses Well, and Other Fallacies

A challenge for nonprofit enterprise is overcoming the perception that nonprofits cannot provide the same level of quality and consistency as their for-profit counterparts. Additionally, there's the conundrum of entitlement, the blanket belief that nonprofit services are free and hence somehow "owed" to the public. How do you handle these misperceptions?

A short time ago a nonprofit hosted a series of "pizza days" as a way of thanking its loyal customers for their continued support and acknowledging their patience with disabled clients who provided a particular service. On pizza days, the nonprofit charged a dollar for a slice of a pizza, a price that cost the organization money but was considered a public relations activity. Instead of expressing appreciation for the cheap eats, several customers complained, saying, "Why don't you just give the pizza to us? After all, you're nonprofit!"

Breaking out of the so-called nonprofit box demands either public education or a disguise. Save the Children uses the latter strategy in its microcredit programs to surmount venture-hampering perceptions in the minds of the public and its clients, and to differentiate its business from its nonprofit activities. Save the Children is so well branded as a children's charity that its name has proved a liability in marketing and running its credit ventures. Clients who have taken loans from Save the Children have rarely felt an obligation to pay them back. Today Save the Children establishes its financial services businesses as separate entities operated under different names, or business pseudonyms, and housed in separate locations from the parent.

Another nonprofit, NW Works, decides when to focus on its business services or social mission during new contract discussions. The approach used in its janitorial company is dependent on the customer. If the potential customer is interested in NW Works's mission of workforce development, then contract negotiators begin from that angle. If, however, the potential customer expresses concern that its previous contractor didn't get the job done or that its price was too high, NW Works pitches cost-effective quality services first and raises the issue of social mission later. There is a perception, sometimes rightfully so, that nonprofits can't or won't perform to prevailing standards. A potential customer may or may not have had a positive experience working with a nonprofit enterprise in the past; therefore, NW Works goes into any new sales situation prepared to discuss commonly asked questions, gives the potential customer a list of major customers who can be contacted for references, and talks about how they review and inspect each contract on a monthly or quarterly basis. This strategy seems to satisfy the potential customer's concerns (conversation with John Brauer, executive director of NW Works). Nevertheless, it's important to recognize that once your enterprise secures a contract or sale, you have to deliver on it, or all the marketing in the world won't make a difference.

Bring the Board on Board: Stakeholder Buy-In

Management 101 tells us that no initiative can succeed without leadership's blessing. Many nonprofit leaders are uncomfortable integrating business into their practices; however, most understand the need for money—a good motivational starting point. Building stakeholder support is an ongoing process, one that seems to take hold more vigorously once the venture moves from the boardroom to the marketplace and generates greater visibility. Your public, donors, clients, community, and board members will have various issues with your venture at various times. Stakeholders' overriding concerns generally correlate with resistance to change and with fear that the organization will lose sight of its mission. Board members and executive directors may be apprehensive about harming the public trust or tainting the organization's reputation, jeopardizing funding sources, or assuming financial risk and tax liability. Staff who are comfortable with the status quo are most likely to be concerned about implications of the venture on their jobs.

In its janitorial business, NW Works anticipates that sales will continue to climb, resulting in a generous amount of net revenue for the parent organization. Money from the business will fund organizational priorities such as increasing the staff-client ratio and hiring professional occupational therapists. Additionally, it will be used for some innovative "wish list" items, such as creating a resource center with a computer lab, something that NW Works has wanted to do but for which it has never secured the funding. Now that NW Works actually has generated net revenue, one would think that the board and staff would be ecstatic, but this is not the case. Instead, some staff think that making money in the janitorial field takes the organization off target and have been overheard to say, "I didn't sign up to be a janitor; I don't want to work in a facility. I'm a social worker; why do I care whether a janitorial company makes an extra 15 percent profit?" NW Works learned that stakeholder buy-in is not an inevitable outcome of a profitable business but rather is achieved by creating a tight link between the venture and the mission and selling that over and over and over again. Change can bring out strong emotions for those who did not sign on to be a part of a nonprofit enterprise.

Sabotage and resistance can also happen whenever people feel threatened, not just when introducing a new venture. Getting buy-in requires maintaining open and ongoing communications with both internal and external stakeholders. John Kotter's advice in "Leading Change: Why Transformation Efforts Fail" is sage: "A classic error in change management is to undercommunicate the vision by a factor of ten."[1] What he means is that you must constantly articulate the motivations and plans for your venture to your public, staff, clients, and donors. Informing stakeholders of what to expect helps them understand the venture's impact both on the organization and on them personally. Venture activities and intentions should be transparent to everyone, because people fear what they don't know or understand. A good communications strategy quiets rumors and abates interference by educating stakeholders on how the business benefits the organization and contributes to accomplishing its mission. To move stakeholders from "talking the talk" to "walking the walk," a venture's business planning needs to be integrated and coordinated with other organizational planning, such as strategic and program plans. Finally, a sense of ownership of the venture is essential to building support. To achieve this, include everyone who needs to be involved in venture discussions, especially the resistors and skeptics. Ultimately you must live by your word, demonstrating consistent values across the venture and the organization, as well as producing the promised benefits.

Managing Expectations: Balancing Money and Mission

Balancing money and mission comes down to purpose and priorities. How much business revenue will you funnel back to your parent organization and how much will you retain in the business? How many jobs, and what kind, will you create? Money and mission are strange bedfellows, and balancing these two objectives in a nonprofit venture is no easy task. Sometimes they are complementary and other times they're contradictory, calling for tough choices and trade-offs. Are you going to serve fewer people but make more money? Provide more services but lose some market share? Will you increase consumer awareness of socially responsible purchasing but decrease support from long-time constituents in doing so? What is the social impact you're trying to achieve, and how much money do you want to make?

Running a nonprofit venture is a balancing act. Before you can reach equilibrium you must have an unambiguous understanding of what you want to achieve. When you first prepared your business plan, you set social and financial objectives; now, during implementation, you must manage according to these objectives. If the main objective of your venture is to generate revenue for your parent organization, then presumably you've selected a business for its profit potential. When operations are under way, your business plan projects a profit margin and targets to meet its financial obligations to the parent. Business decisions revolve around how much can you realistically put back in the parent organization without draining your ability to grow the business. As you strive to reach financial objectives, you must constantly scrutinize whether market opportunities are coming at a cost to your mission and to what extent that is acceptable.

The corollary is also true: many nonprofit ventures never earn a penny for the parent organization, nor do they intend to. A common assumption is that the financial objective is always profit. Not true: in many nonprofit ventures, social programs and ventures are integrated, and financial objectives are aimed at recovering a percentage of the operating costs or diminishing program subsidy. From the outset, for example, the ventures of the nonprofit that hosted pizza days were not destined to be money-making vehicles, and they may in fact never make any significant contribution to the parent organization. But they employ a lot of people with disabilities, provide them with transferable skills, and serve to educate the community as well. The organization's mission is "to create employment opportunities for people with psychiatric disabilities and other underserved individuals through innovative practices and distinct choices." Relative to mission accomplishment, the objectives of this organization's enterprise center on the number of quality jobs created and on recovering all or a large percentage of its operating costs. This organization has many enterprises and each has its own business plan. While some have as their raison d'être the ability to make money, others are geared solely toward clients gaining valuable experience in the food service industry. No matter what the business, the minimum criterion for this nonprofit is that in the end its clients win.

Balancing social mission with the business is a recurring theme in implementing nonprofit ventures. Trade-offs are involved at almost every decision juncture. Consequently, it is critical to understand and articulate where you draw the line in the sand. For example, more than 85 percent of Greyston Bakery's workers are classified as "hard to employ" (conversation with Daniel Helfman). Prior to beginning at Greyston they were homeless and on welfare and had numerous obstacles to employment. Consequently, many of Greyston's workforce lacks both technical skills related to producing baked goods and social skills such as showing up on time, being reliable, wearing the proper uniform and the right shoes, and so on. Developing these skills requires more training and supervision than what's required in other businesses. Obviously this increases costs and weakens margins. At the same time, Greyston is concerned about profits, and that can create a conflict. More profit means more money for social programs, though ironically if sales stagnate or contract, there's the temptation to work with fewer clients or spend less on staff development to increase margins. Greyston, like other nonprofits, must constantly manage social and financial tensions and trade-offs in its business.

Enterprise success or failure can threaten to change your organization's mission. NW Works's janitorial company will likely double in size again, reaching $3 million in annual revenue. Customers are flocking to the company, and NW Works is placing clients on its waiting list in janitorial jobs. Clients earn wages up to $12 an hour—a living wage in small-town Virginia (conversation with John Brauer, NW Works). At some point, however, market demand for janitorial services is going to outgrow NW Works's workforce capacity (the number of clients who want janitorial work). What will happen then? NW Works could hire other disenfranchised people in their area, but that's off mission. The board of directors signed on for creating job opportunities for this particular population of disabled folks. Expansion would bring more revenue to the parent organization, but would it be worth it? What would be the payoff? How can it be identified?

Conversely, if your nonprofit venture is unsuccessful, how will your stakeholders deal with failure? When CVE closed its bakery and cafe, people were very disappointed. The customers liked the baked goods and the salads. The clients liked the work. The board liked the income and social benefits. The stakeholders were angry. CVE learned that it must have a plan in place to handle stakeholders if its venture goes south.

In-Facility Work: The Bird Seed Fiasco

In the early days of CVE, the organization concentrated on job placement services for its clients. At the same time, CVE management realized that some of its clients were not equipped to work in full-time jobs yet could benefit from work and were capable of doing a task for four or five hours a day. To fill the employment gap for these clients, CVE decided to investigate contract opportunities for piecework, assembly, and clerical jobs, such as stuffing direct mail envelopes. It began with a holiday contract to glue bay leaves to Styrofoam balls to make decorative, nice-smelling trinkets to be sold in upscale shops. Next, CVE's clients fulfilled a contract to drill holes in nutmeg seeds, and another to embed dried rose petals and lavender in concrete blocks.

The next contract was to make birdseed balls, or stress balls—squishy rubber balls that people squeeze to relieve their tension. Before accepting the contract, CVE ran a trial with samples to determine whether the clients could conduct the activity, which consisted of filling balloons with birdseed. The test went smoothly, so the company delivered supplies to assemble the stress balls. The turnaround time was two weeks.

CVE was astonished to discover that the balloons the company supplied for CVE to fill with birdseed were not the ones used in the trial. Neither CVE's clients nor staff could blow them up. During the trial one person was able to make up to thirty balls per hour. However, with the new balloons the best that some CVE clients and staff could do was one stress ball per hour. To remedy the situation, CVE purchased three air compressors for twenty clients who wanted to work, but this created an immediate logjam. Moreover, with the new air compressor system, most of CVE's clients could no longer do the job, because using the machinery increased the complexity and skill level required. To make matters worse, the only space that could accommodate the buckets of birdseed, boxes, and compressors was the CEO's office. To fulfill the terms of the contract, the CEO's office was emptied and transformed into a temporary production facility. Programs were closed down for ten days and the phone was put on night mode while the entire clinical staff and the CEO made stress balls. CVE did not make money on this contract.

The proverb "There's no great loss without some small gain" was not lost on CVE. Although the birdseed ball experience was a bitter pill, it forced the organization to reexamine venture opportunities in the context of mission. Assigning staff time to contract employment was not only contrary to finding jobs for clients; it also meant that program staff were unavailable to clients. Therefore, even if the job had generated net revenue, it was not in keeping with CVE's mission. CVE also learned that contract workflow is difficult to project due to its sporadic nature, and that tight turnaround times often did not agree with the pace clients wanted or were able to work. For CVE, the stress ball contract was a milestone toward aligning business activities with mission.

Today CVE has a number of successful enterprises, including two coffee bars, a messenger service, a full-service janitorial company, and a mailing and packaging business. The agency has grown to more than 70 employees, 350 disabled trainees, and a budget of more than $3 million annually.

Contingency Plans: Preparing for Worst-Case Scenarios

No law applies to starting a nonprofit enterprise better than Murphy's "Anything that can go wrong will go wrong." Troubleshooting potential situations that can negatively impact your venture enables you to make contingency plans to prepare for and avert crisis. One of the best ways to do this is to use what-if scenarios to play out cause-and-effect relationships of possible situations—"If this happens then that"—to arrive at plans B through Z. Focus on the financially vulnerable points of your venture (often the categories where the largest expenditures occur). Ask questions such as, "What will happen to enterprise profitability if the costs of raw material increase by 10 percent? What if the sales forecast is realized at only 80 percent? What will happen to our cash flow if a major piece of equipment conks out before its projected usable life?"[2] Undoubtedly you will need to outline several options for major decisions in areas of your business where risk exposure is the highest.

Most changes in the operating environment do not drop from the sky but can be predicted to some degree if nonprofit entrepreneurs continually appraise the environment and the enterprise's strengths and weaknesses in relation to various risk factors. For example, Save the Children's food processing (peanut butter and jam) enterprise is mainly a variable-cost business, highly susceptible to changes in the price of raw materials. Bad weather affects crop yields, causing peanut prices to go up. Seasonality is another factor; when peanuts or fruits are out of season, their prices increase. Therefore, Save the Children makes its financial projections on the basis of different peanut costs, beginning as low as 10 cents a pound up to as much as 25 cents, to see how price fluctuations affect the bottom line and to think through decisions it will need to make on the basis of different peanut price levels.[3]

When you write a business plan, your revenue projections and estimated expenditures are based on numerous assumptions. While the assumptions are probably verified by primary and secondary market research, it is possible, if not likely, that the assumptions will change due to economic forces, customer demand, and many other situations that are out of your control. Survival and success are found with creative solutions, often generated on a daily basis.

The Greyston Bakery has strong revenues with nearly $5 million in sales. The majority of this revenue is generated by one customer, during the ice cream season. To lower the level of risk associated with dependence on one customer account, the bakery management team explored three main strategies. First, it identified additional ice cream manufacturers as customers. Second, it developed new products for new markets that have a complementary peak season—Halloween to New Years' Eve—to that of the ice cream business, which occurs in summer. Finally, product developers within the food sector were approached in order to assess interest in the bakery's product line and to determine if bakery research and development capability had value in other sectors. Such contingency plans evolve and do not happen over night; it took two to three years for Greyston to acquire additional ice cream manufacturers as customers. No one account was as big as the primary customer, but each account lowered the overall risk.

The budgetary side of contingency planning also means building in a buffer for unplanned expenses. For new enterprises this is usually a slower-than-expected start-up and inefficiencies due to learning a new industry. Contingency money can range from 3 to 20 percent of the budget depending on the level of financial conservatism applied and the number of unknowns and risks your enterprise faces. Having a safety net will be useful after you've exhausted each contingencies because you will undoubtedly stumble upon another of Murphy's truisms, "If you perceive four possible ways in which [your venture] can go wrong, and circumvent these, then a fifth, unprepared for, will promptly develop."

Common Business Planning Pitfalls to Avoid

Keeping all this in mind, it is well worth mentioning a number of common business planning pitfalls to avoid. These include the following:

Failing to Market the Mousetrap

Writing a business plan is such an intense internal process that it's easy to get carried away and think that your customers will be as enthusiastic about your business as you are. But what happens if you open the door and nobody comes?

Marketing is a dramatic cultural shift for nonprofit organizations. The marketplace for social services is fixed. The target market (clients) is evident and the desire for services generally overwhelms supply. Typically nonprofits provide services that their clients need, not necessarily those they want or are willing and able to pay for. Clients don't usually have trouble finding nonprofits; they are likely directed to the organization by another social service agency, government agency, or peer network. Rendering free services puts the onus on the client to find the organization, not the corollary. It's not surprising therefore that a nonprofit would expect a deluge at its venture's ribbon-cutting ceremony while having completely overlooked the marketing function.

Incorporating a marketing function requires a cultural reorientation from "build it and they will come" to "build it and advertise like crazy and they will come." In implementing ventures, nonprofits are challenged to focus on the benefits that paying customers want, and on how to attract them. Competing with the private sector, as nonprofit ventures do, means using the same marketing vehicles and tactics that are used by private-sector businesses to draw customers. One mental health organization developing a business plan for a private-pay counseling and play therapy venture limited its marketing budget to a small amount of money for a Web site. Its justification was that as a nonprofit the primary vehicle for publicity would be public relations. But there are at least three problems inherent in this: first, there is no guarantee that a press release will be published; second, even if it is published, the organization has no control, as it does with paid advertising, over what will ultimately appear in print (which could be damaging); and third, the media audience is not necessarily the target market. Bad plan.

Marketing doesn't have to be expensive; there are lots of viable low-cost or even no-cost options. It simply has to be appropriate for the target market. Developing a solid marketing plan requires selecting vehicles and tactics based on their appropriateness—its fit, frequency, and reach to the targeted market or segment. Failing to market has been the epitaph for many a nonprofit venture.

Trying to Be All Things to All People

Bill Cosby said it well: "I don't know the key to success, but the key to failure is to try to please everyone."[4] In this case, the venture is a small, socially conscious organic market with a big agenda. The concept is to educate the neighborhood about nutritious food, sell 100 percent organic produce purchased from local farmers, employ economically disadvantaged and mentally disabled people, and throw off profit to the parent, a community-development organization—all from the get-go.

Would you eat in a restaurant that had sushi, tacos, and pasta on the menu? Trying to be all things to all people is a classic mistake that many new businesses make. It's a lack of positioning. Having a vision is great, but nonprofit ventures, like other businesses, need to start small and focus on a niche and a handful of products as they enter the market. Who specifically is your target market and how is your venture differentiated from others? What products will you sell first and how will you test them in the market? Can you wait to employ disadvantaged people until after your venture stabilizes? Otherwise you run the risk of ending up like the organic market—out of business, replaced by a weekly farmer's market, which fills the market need but does not render the social benefits.

Marketing the Mission Instead of the Message

Using social mission as a sales tactic is a nonstarter if you don't have a quality product or an economical price. Customers may buy a product for its social mission once or maybe twice, but you can't build a business solely on doing good. Sustainability rests on repeat business and on developing a loyal clientele. Save the Children's venture tried to market its products made by poor rural women on the premise of community impact. They found that this strategy didn't sell products. To satisfy customers and build patronage, they needed consistent, high-quality products, and to be a reliable supplier to their retail customers. Mission may be the defining factor in the purchasing decisions of the socially conscious shopper, but only if the price is similar to and the customer perceives the product to be the same as or better than that of the competitor. For some products, selling on social mission may be a deterrent. Another food-related business staffed by formerly homeless clients struggled with how to use mission to market its products. Venture managers believed the image of homeless people preparing food would not attract their customers. In the end they chose to use mission as a marketing strategy, specifically targeting socially responsible shoppers, and in doing so they referred to their clients nebulously as "disadvantaged." Another disabilities organization in Massachusetts focuses on rendering excellent service in its motel business but chooses to leverage its mission to solicit charitable contributions from guests upon checkout.

Operating an Enterprise Without Sufficient Capacity

So what happens when you plan your venture, build it, and hope they'll come, and not only do they come, but they come in droves? Success creates its own set of problems, especially when you don't have the capacity to deliver, the infrastructure to handle such growth, and the support of key players for your enterprise's increase in size.

NW Works, the six-year-old janitorial business, grossed about $450,000 per year. One of the first things the new executive director did was to analyze the business, assess its strengths and weaknesses, and determine its future within the organization. He determined that it was a viable business and one that could grow significantly given better management systems, increased training, and a concentration on core competencies. A new business plan was developed that addressed the training and infrastructure issues and projected growth of 50 percent over eighteen months. Next NW Works hired an expert in the janitorial field, one who had both a social service and a janitorial business background. The industry expert was the right hire at the right time; the janitorial enterprise was poised to meet all its internal and external goals and expectations.

What happened next surprised everyone. By the end of the first eighteen months of the implementing the business plan, janitorial contracts had increased to almost $1.6 million per year, or roughly 350 percent growth. As you might guess, this presented any number of challenges, including recruitment, hiring, training, and retention of personnel; cash flow issues; and board and staff confusion and consternation that the janitorial business was taking over the organization. At the time, janitorial contracts constituted more than half of the annual budget and drained human and financial resources from other areas of the organization— exactly the opposite of the initial expectations.

Ultimately the janitorial infrastructure caught up with its growth and NW Works dramatically slowed down the pace of that growth for a six-month period. Since then, management has reworked the business plan to address these new-found issues and their impact on the organization. NW Works now has a more realistic picture of the future growth of this enterprise and how it will be accommodated and serve the organization's larger mission-related goals.

Operating an Enterprise Without Sufficient Capital

Starting or recapitalizing a business nearly always happens under a different timetable than you expect. Numerous for-profit dot-com ventures were capitalized far too early, resulting in untested business plans and a fast cash burn–rate. In traditional economic conditions, most businesses bootstrap to achieve success (that is, they hold to tight budgets, no overhead, and no pay). This also applies to nonprofit ventures. Capitalizing a nonprofit enterprise may take four or five times longer than optimistic business projections forecast. In addition to the capitalization challenge, most nonprofit ventures burn cash at a faster rate, placing the venture in danger of running out of cash before it really gets going. The funding cycle of foundations—an important source of capitalization for nonprofit ventures— is typically slower than a manufacturing or production cycle—a further challenge to cash flow.

The Enterprising Kitchen (TEK), a nonprofit social venture in Chicago that trains and employs low-income women, has a moderate burn rate, but the time it takes to turn raw ingredients into finished goods (high-quality cold-process soap) is twenty days. As a result, it is quite possible that $50,000 can be tied up in inventory or work-in-process at any one time. If TEK's top three customers took longer than twenty days to pay, a cash crunch would be created in a hurry. Considering TEK's reliance on foundation and government funding, the venture survived first on debt and later on cash flow generated from grants.

What We Know Now

Here are a few questions to ask yourself and approaches to take at various points during your business planning and implementation.

Before the Launch of Your Business

Ask the hard questions up front. Who owns the venture? What happens when you make money? How will revenue be used? What happens if you don't make money? How do you manage failure? What happens if you're successful? In the event of either success or failure, who's responsible? What's the legal structure of the venture and its relationship to the parent organization? What's the exit strategy?

Bring negative people to the table and let them hit you with their best shot. Invite your worst critics to tire-kick your plan. Honestly, you want to know upfront what you're up against (it's either there or behind your back). You want to know what they think the potential problems will be. You want everyone on board before you start the venture; otherwise you run the risk of nonsupporters poisoning your business.

Get support from stakeholders and the community behind your venture. You want support lined up to help you through future problems, because they will occur. In the event of a setback or surprise, you should be able to pick up the phone and call in the troops.

Once you've done your research and planning, don't be afraid to just begin. No business plan will cover all the potential issues, but if you know that up front you will be ready to tackle the unknowns. The truth is that once you're in business you will work long hours to make it successful. Write the business plan first so you can do the fun part.

To the extent possible, set realistic targets. Unrealistic targets set everybody up for failure, which is not a good way to start. It's best to be conservative until you get a practical feel for your business's operational ebbs and flows. Take the advice of most marketers and underpromise and overdeliver, and stakeholders and customers alike will be delighted.

After the Launch of Your Business

Get your negative critics to shush. The critics have had their say, now it's time to be supportive. The last thing you want to do is build this business while people attack it. No matter what, you won't be able to please everyone; don't be surprised if some of your worst critics choose to opt out by finding other jobs when the venture launches.

Become an expert. Learn your venture's industry backward and forward. Is your business a coffee shop? Then you should know the price ratio for a cup of coffee and whether cardboard is better than Styrofoam for the environment. As a nonprofit entrepreneur you will become a specialist at things you never imagined.

Be flexible. Even if your new plan looks completely different than the original, the important thing is that it meets your goals. If the venture isn't working, find a way to fix it, or let it go.

Expect the unexpected. In business as in life, stuff happens. You may think you have a bulletproof business plan, but you may learn otherwise as you move to implement it. Unfortunately, nonprofit entrepreneurs don't have crystal balls; one thing is certain, however: the unexpected will happen.

Ask for help. Business planning is no small task, and you'd be amazed at those willing to help if you ask. Board members, consultants, industry experts, or qualified volunteers can be summoned to roll up their sleeves and pitch in. Even great business plans are subject to blind spots and can benefit from another pair of eyes.

Keep your sense of humor. There will be plenty of times when you feel pushed to the edge. For the nonprofit entrepreneur, humor is not only a coping method, it's a survival strategy. Try to make light of the bumps, scratches, and raps on the chin that you will encounter while building your business; they will make great stories later, like so many in this book.

Conclusion

"In a difficult business, no sooner is one problem solved then another surfaces—never is there just one cockroach in the kitchen."[5] This quote by Warren Buffet captures the experience of many nonprofit entrepreneurs. It's important to recognize that, for most of us, introducing a venture in our nonprofit will undoubtedly rock the organizational culture. The business will likely collide with the mission of the organization, and vice versa. Remember that the successful integration of a venture is a transformative process, and a business plan will help guide the evolution toward becoming an entrepreneurial organization. However, like a map, a business plan isn't helpful if you don't use it. You should see it as a working document, and as you implement your venture, your business plan should become dog-eared, underlined, written on, and accented with coffee rings. It should be referenced at every management meeting, and constantly revised to reflect market realities that you can know only after you start selling something. Think of your business plan not as an end product but as a milestone that marks the launch of your new venture. Bon voyage!

Notes

1. Kotter, J. "Leading Change: Why Transformation Efforts Fail." *Harvard Business Review*, 1995, *73*(2), 59–67.
2. Alter, S. K. *Managing the Double Bottom Line*. Washington D.C.: Pact, 2001.
3. Ibid.
4. Cosby, B. http://www.quotedb.com/quotes/161.
5. Buffet, W. "Chairman's Letter to the Shareholders of Berkshire Hathaway Inc.," 1989. See also http://www.berkshirehathaway.com/letters/1989.html.

CHAPTER FIFTEEN

DEPLOYING RESOURCES EFFECTIVELY

Dennis R. Young

Undertaking new ventures within the context of nonprofit organizations requires careful attention to using scarce and valuable economic resources efficiently. Start-up resources are often difficult to secure and limited in quantity. Also, the early years of a venture are frequently characterized by bare bones operations and the necessity to establish a track record that will ultimately lead to a more secure flow of revenues. Given these conditions, new ventures, whether in the for-profit or the nonprofit sector, often fail. Many are undercapitalized, that is, they have insufficient resources at the start to carry them through to a state of longer-term stability.

Claims of undercapitalization can also, however, be a facile excuse. Undercapitalization occurs when an enterprise uses its start-up and operating resources as efficiently as possible and still fails, for lack of additional resources, to reach a state of financial stability. There are two key presumptions in this diagnosis: first, there must be a stable state that can be reached; second, resources must have been used as efficiently as possible in attempting to reach that state. The first assumption hinges on a proper analysis of the demand and cost conditions under which the venture is designed. If these are incorrect, the venture may fail no matter how efficiently it deploys its resources. The second assumption has to do with whether the venture is given a maximum chance of succeeding by putting its limited resources to the best use. The latter assumption is the subject of this chapter.

The theme of this chapter is that fundamental principles of economic analysis, applied in a commonsense way, can help you make resource-related decisions efficiently. Such decisions include production choices among combinations of different kinds of inputs that can be used to produce the intended goods or services, personnel decisions associated with deploying alternative combinations of people to carry out the work of the enterprise, decisions associated with the venues in which the work takes place (inside or outside your organization), programming decisions focusing on the combinations of goods and services provided by the venture in order to achieve the largest mission impact, resource development decisions that focus on the mix of different sources of revenues that will support the venture, and marketing decisions that determine which market segments and marketing strategies your organization will engage in order to generate demand and financial support for its services. The foregoing constitutes a broad spectrum of resource-related decisions that challenge nonprofit ventures—ranging from day-to-day operational decisions to longer-term strategic choices.

Despite their diversity, all of these decisions are framed here in a particular way—less as binary choices between one alternative and another than as choices of appropriate combinations of these alternatives. This framing reflects how such decisions are analyzed in this chapter—as *trade-offs* between one or more alternative choices, noting that the best choice is often a particular mix. There are conceivably several rationales for such an approach. One rationale is that utilizing more than one alternative at a time—whether classes of personnel, revenue sources, or marketing strategies—provides a hedge against risk (avoiding putting all of one's eggs in one basket). Another rationale is that combinations of alternatives often take advantage of synergies, sometimes called economies of scope, that allow more efficient resource usage than singular alternatives would yield. Economies of scope reflect the popular notion of synergy, in which resources (say plant and equipment) employed for one use create economical conditions for another use. For example, a museum with facilities and staff that support fine arts lectures can offer musical concerts more efficiently than another organization that uses those resources for musical concerts alone. Hence, the combination of musical concerts and arts lectures may be more efficient than either one alone.

A third rationale argues that combinations may be more efficient than singular choices where there is a limited resource budget that must be allocated among alternative uses. This situation occurs when two or more inputs—instructors and computers, for example—are employed to produce a certain result—say skills training. The likelihood is that using either of these inputs alone would be less productive than using them in some combination. Moreover, continually expanding use of one input without increasing use of the other is likely to yield diminishing returns in terms of the additional results produced. The object of effective decision making in this case is to find the combination of inputs that yields the desired quality of skills training at the lowest overall cost, or that produces the largest volume of such training within budget limitations.

The latter type of situation is especially amenable to analysis using a fundamental idea from economics—namely, *analysis at the margin.* In the next section, this concept is explained in commonsense terms. Subsequent sections of the chapter apply this principle to various types of resource-related decisions that may arise in your nonprofit venture. For purposes of concreteness and to provide a common thread through the chapter, a hypothetical nonprofit venture—a nonprofit library in an urban community that is considering undertaking a tutoring program—is used for illustration. The chapter concludes with a summary of the principles, based on thinking at the margin, that you can apply to a wide spectrum of possible existing or new enterprises.

Thinking at the Margin

Analysis at the margin is one of the most basic conceptual tools that economists use to understand how rational decision makers can make efficient choices. The concept is deceptively simple. Starting from some status quo, you ask, *What if an additional unit of some resource is allocated to a certain use?* If such an incremental change leads to an improvement, the principle of marginal analysis stipulates that the change should be made and then the question should be asked again. The process is continued until an incremental change no longer leads to an improvement. At that point, the resource is said to be allocated efficiently so as to have its greatest impact. (There are certain technical assumptions that underlie this logic, but these leave open a wide spectrum of practical situations to which it can be applied. Please refer to any basic microeconomics textbook for appropriate caveats.)

While the logic of marginal analysis is simple, it is nonetheless profound. Indeed, it is grounded in differential calculus, which was invented by great minds such as Isaac Newton and Gottfried Leibniz and adapted by sage economist Alfred Marshall. It is also fundamentally intuitive and easily grasped and applied by busy, practical managers trying to do their best with limited resources.

Traditionally, economists have applied analysis at the margin to decisions in the commercial sphere. For example, how does a business maximize its profits? Economists provide the following analysis: Suppose a business is producing a certain quantity of a product (say toothpaste) and is able to sell the product at a certain price, yielding a given level of profit. The business manager can then make two (marginal) calculations: What would it cost to produce another unit of the good (the *marginal cost*) and what would that unit sell for in the marketplace (the *marginal revenue*)? If marginal revenue exceeds marginal cost, then the expansion of production by another unit is worthwhile because it will increase net profits. The business decision maker can continue to make these marginal calculations at increasing levels of output until marginal cost starts to exceed marginal revenue, at which point profits will be maximum. That is, any further expansion would yield incremental losses.

Actually, the foregoing logic is just a little more complicated on the revenue side if the product is being sold into a market in which the business decision maker is a major player. In this case, the price may have to be reduced in order to sell additional units. Thus, marginal revenue must account not only for the increased revenue from selling the additional unit, but also for reduced revenue on units that could previously have been sold at the current level. Still, the basic principle is the same: compare marginal cost with marginal revenue and determine whether to take the next step.

Clearly the foregoing logic applies directly to a nonprofit venture that is purely commercial, that is, designed solely to generate net revenues for the organization without reference to any direct impact on the organization's social mission. Most nonprofit ventures, however, have both mission and revenue impacts. Hence, while the logic of analysis at the margin still applies powerfully, its parameters must be suitably modified to determine the appropriate price and volume levels. In particular, account must be taken of the social benefits produced at the margin, and of the additional costs incurred for the sake of these benefits. These benefits may accrue both to direct service recipients and to others in society who benefit from having the recipients receive the service. For example, recipients of inoculations to prevent a disease benefit directly, and others in society also benefit from the lower probability of contagion. The art of marginal analysis in this case is to figure out what an additional unit of service is really worth—clearly more than just what those who will be inoculated are willing to pay for it—so that a decision can be made to produce the service at a level that will maximize net social benefits.

The concept of analysis at the margin applies to many other types of nonprofit business decisions as well. As suggested at the beginning of this chapter, many venture decisions involve choices among alternative inputs, outputs, or strategies. The basic idea in these decision contexts is to ask what impact is felt on your organization's mission when a little more of one alternative is used, holding other things constant. Economists have a term that characterizes this incremental impact—they call it the *marginal product*. So, for example, in the context of a fundraising campaign, you could ask about the marginal product of making an additional telephone call versus the marginal product of sending out an additional letter in the mail. In this case, these marginal products can be measured in terms of the additional funds expected to be raised from each increment. The logic of analysis at the margin stipulates that you should find that combination of mailings and telephone calls that yields marginal products of these alternatives that are *equal*. Why equal? Because if one product were greater than another, it would be sensible to shift resources (incrementally) toward the alternative with the greater marginal product—and that logic would persist until the two marginal products were equal.

Note that the likely outcome of this analysis is that some *combination* of mailings and telephone calls will be chosen. While it is possible that (within budget constraints) one of these alternatives will always be more productive than the other (in which case the whole budget should be spent on that alternative), the more likely situation is that each alternative will at some point experience diminishing returns. If, for example, as you invest more and more money in phone calls the productivity of another phone call drops below what would likely be garnered by sending a letter, then you should begin to allocate additional monies to mailings.

The prospect that combinations of alternatives produce the most efficient results lies at the heart of what analysts call *trade-offs*. Given that resources are limited, you can ask what you lose and what you gain by moving resources incrementally from one use to another. When you can no longer achieve net gains by making such incremental trades, then you have found the optimal combination, reflecting the most efficient use of resources. The following sections consider a number of such trade-off situations that arise in the context of nonprofit ventures.

A Prototypical Nonprofit Venture

The Bookbinder Public Library is a hypothetical nonprofit organization that serves Reading County, an urban community of low- to moderate-income residents on the North Coast. Historically, Reading has served as a transitional community for immigrants and lower-income families who are working their way up the economic ladder. Bookbinder Library is financed by an allocation from the Reading County budget as well as by private contributions raised by an affiliated group of library patrons, Friends of the Bookbinder Library. Recently, however, the library has come under financial pressure due to cutbacks in government funding and a slowing of private contributions associated with a stagnant economy. To address the need for additional revenues and to help community residents improve their prospects for gainful employment, the management staff and trustees of the library are considering undertaking a new tutoring program that would increase the English reading and speaking skills of recent immigrants and the level of literacy of younger residents.

The proposed venture would exploit economies of scope in Bookbinder's operations. Through its conventional book-lending and community lecture programs, Bookbinder already generates a substantial flow of potential consumers for the new service. In addition, the library's building has various nooks and crannies in which tutoring can be comfortably accommodated, and it has an educated staff and volunteer corps capable of working in the program, especially when traffic for other activities is slow.

One question for Bookbinder is how to set prices for its proposed service so that the venture meets its objectives. If the service were intended solely to generate as much net revenue as possible, the logic of price setting and the consequent volume of service would be clear: continue to expand the service as long as additional revenues cover the additional costs incurred—a straightforward application of analysis at the margin. As a nonprofit organization concerned, however, with producing social benefits associated with its mission to serve the community, and with accommodating clients with limited capacity to pay, Bookbinder must use a more nuanced logic to determine its pricing and volume of service. In particular, it may wish to set a minimum profit goal and then to maximize net social benefits within that constraint. Making this kind of calculation is not an exact science and technically requires assigning a dollar value to each unit of service (hour of tutoring) provided. But the logic of analysis at the margin still applies: design a fair pricing schedule that accommodates clients with limited ability to pay and then expand the service as long as marginal social benefits exceed marginal costs and profits are growing or continue to exceed the profit goal. Obviously this may require some experimentation in order to find the price level and service volume that meet these conditions. (For further guidance on pricing, please refer to Chapter Five in this volume.) For purposes of this chapter, however, it is assumed that these parameters can be successfully worked out so that the library is able to meet its profit goals and provide a substantial volume of service at a quality level that it deems desirable. This assumption will allow us to focus on the various trade-off decisions that the library must make in order to deploy resources in as efficient a manner as possible.

Of course this is a chicken-and-egg process, because the efficiency of resource use affects costs, which in turn influence pricing and production decisions; but we need to start somewhere. To begin, then, we need some description of the output of the proposed tutoring program. Furthermore, we need to approach this question at several different levels, depending on what particular trade-off questions are being examined. At one level we want to know how best to use resources to produce units of tutoring as efficiently as possible. At a second level we want to know what level of resources to devote to the tutoring program compared to other programming alternatives. At a third level we can ask about alternative ways to develop revenues to support the program. Each of these trade-off decisions requires different ways to characterize output.

In the first instance, we can think of output as an hour of tutoring provided within certain parameters of desired quality (reflecting the qualifications of the instructor, content of the curriculum, physical conditions under which the service is delivered, and so on). Call this unit a *quality tutoring hour* (QTH). Obviously QTHs will vary in their social and mission-related impacts depending on the student's ability, personal circumstances, and future choices. The program itself, however, produces QTHs per se and the object of trade-off decisions is to produce them as efficiently as possible. Recall that trade-off-type choices using the logic of marginal analysis require thinking in terms of a marginal product associated with an additional unit of some input. In this case, the marginal product can be characterized in terms of additional QTHs generated by additional units of whatever input resource we are examining. Later in this chapter this logic is applied to production, personnel, outsourcing decisions, and marketing decisions.

At the second level, we want to ask about the intended impact of the tutoring program and the degree to which this venture contributes to the mission of the organization compared to alternative programmatic investments. For this purpose we need to look beyond QTHs to ask how we would assess their contribution by using a common metric to compare their impact with the impacts of other library programs, such as circulation of books and videos, community lecture programming, reference services, and the like. In a full-blown cost-benefit analysis we would try to put a dollar value on QTHs and on the direct outputs of these other activities using various techniques such as comparing them with similar services produced in the private marketplace or calculating what they should be worth to their recipients. For example, in the case of the tutoring program, in order to put a dollar value on a QTH, one might estimate what comparable private tutoring services would cost or the degree to which the tutoring increases the future earnings potentials of the recipients.

Short of the ability to estimate the dollar value of social benefits associated with alternative outputs of the library, we can try to think more generally about what the library as a whole produces. Along these lines, we can conceive of the library's various program outputs as inputs to this larger organizational output. Presumably, everything that the library does is intended to serve the educational and informational needs of the community in some way. Hence, even if we can't measure it, we can think of the library as producing *community service units* (CSUs); hence the trade-off question becomes how to produce these CSUs through the most efficient combination of programs. At this level of thinking the marginal product is the additional CSUs produced per additional dollar spent on any given library program, such as the additional CSUs produced by another dollar allocated to the tutoring project.

Finally, at the third level, the library is concerned with generating revenue to support its various programs, including the tutoring venture. As already noted, the library will want to price this service so as to balance revenue needs with the social objectives of the program. Thus it is likely that it will seek various sources of philanthropic or governmental support to (at least partially) underwrite the program. Within this context, the library will want to be as efficient as possible in generating these sources of revenue, recognizing that revenue development requires the expenditure of resources and that some combinations of revenue development strategies will be more efficient than others. Here again is a trade-off situation involving alternative ways to produce a desired output. The output in this case is revenue, the inputs are alternative ways in which funds can be raised, and the marginal product of any given revenue strategy is the additional dollars generated per additional dollar spent on that strategy.

Production Decisions

The production of outputs such as the tutoring program's QTHs usually requires that a number of inputs be combined through a certain technology. Economists characterize this process as a *production function*. In the case of the Bookbinder Library, QTHs are produced by combining instructors, facilities and equipment, educational materials, and management support through a technology of instruction. In other nonprofit ventures, the inputs will vary. For example, a food service venture combines labor of various kinds, equipment and facilities, food and drink, furnishings, and so on. The logic for combining such inputs to achieve efficiency, however, is basically the same: use thinking at the margin to find the combination of inputs that produces the stipulated level of output at least cost—or alternatively, to find that combination of inputs that produces the most output within the constraints of the available budget.

As suggested earlier, the logic of analysis at the margin requires that the combination be found in which all inputs are making equal incremental contributions to output. For the library's tutoring venture this requires asking how many additional QTHs could be produced by adding another tutor relative to adding another computer station relative to adding some additional space, such as by installing another library carrel. And because additional units of these various inputs have different costs, the question needs to be asked on a per-dollar basis. That is, where will an additional dollar of expenditure have the most impact on output—by spending it on a tutor or on a computer or on a carrel? The marginal dollar is best spent on the input that produces the greatest return in output. Hence, if certain inputs are yielding greater return per dollar than others, resources should be shifted from one input to another until the impacts are roughly equal.

Of course these kinds of decisions are "lumpy"—that is, one must spend a lot more than a dollar (or even a hundred dollars) on additional space or a computer station and equipment. One must purchase a whole computer or an additional carrel or none at all. But even within these constraints one can still ask whether a marginal unit of expenditure is best allocated to one input or another. For example, suppose our library has nominally set up its tutoring program with one tutor, one computer workstation, and one library carrel—all presumably necessary components to producing some reasonable level of output (say five hundred QTHs) with these resources. Now suppose that tutors cost $500 each, computers cost $1000, and carrels cost $1,500, and that the additional output (marginal product) gained from another unit of each of these inputs (without varying the amount of the others) is the following:

- Another tutor yields a modest additional fifty QTHs because sharing an existing carrel and computer limits what the tutor can do.
- Another computer yields an additional one hundred QTHs because students can now work independently (at the same carrel) while the tutor is occupied with another student.
- Another carrel yields an additional two hundred QTHs because this allows the tutor to work simultaneously with more than one student under comfortable conditions.

Suppose now that the library is trying to decide how to spend the next $1,500 of its budget allocation. The possibilities are the following:

- Three additional tutors yielding at most another 150 QTHs. (Given the crowding that will occur it is likely that the second and third additional tutors would have lower marginal products than the first.)
- Another computer and another tutor, yielding at least 150 QTHs. (Indeed the addition of the computer might increase the marginal product of the additional tutor.)
- Another carrel, yielding an additional 200 QTHs.

In this case, it appears that purchasing another carrel is the most efficient thing to do. This depends of course on the full $1,500 being available. If only $500 were available, another tutor might be in order, and if $1,000 were available, another computer would seem best. In these latter cases, however, the library should also assess whether adding to the budget is the more sensible course of action. Finally, the library must recognize that once the new carrel has been purchased, the marginal products of all three inputs will probably change and the next budget increment would probably be best spent differently. Exhibit 15.1 outlines the steps for conducting a marginal analysis of production.

EXHIBIT 15.1. MARGINAL ANALYSIS OF PRODUCTION: A ROUGH AND READY APPROACH.

1. Specify a measure of program output.

2. Identify the alternative inputs that contribute to program output.

3. Start with a minimal budget allocation and an additional sum to be allocated.

4. Choose a nominal combination of inputs by allocating the minimal budget and estimate how much output this combination produces. (If the venture is already up and running, start from the status quo.)

5. For each input, estimate separately how much additional output (marginal product) would result from spending another $10,000 on that input.

6. Allocate the $10,000 to the input with the highest marginal product. If two or more inputs are tied for the highest marginal product, allocate the $10,000 to any one of them.

7. Return to step 5. Continue until the additional sum to be allocated is exhausted or until it is determined that the benefit from additional output (marginal benefit) is less than the additional (marginal) cost to produce it.

8. Check to see if the marginal products of each input are now roughly the same. If they are not, experiment with shifting the budget in $10,000 (or smaller) increments from inputs with lower marginal products to those with higher marginal products.

Personnel Decisions

The foregoing logic of production decisions extends to choices that nonprofits involved in new ventures must make in engaging and deploying human resources. All organizations have to decide what kinds and combinations of people to employ, but nonprofits often have a particularly wide range of choices that may include volunteers as well as paid workers, clients of the organization's services as well as candidates from the open labor market. The range of choices naturally depends on the circumstances. In some areas of service—professional counseling, for example—reliance on volunteers may be unlikely. In other areas, employment of clients may contribute directly to mission, as in sheltered workshops that produce goods for sale to the public or a restaurant established by a nonprofit to help train disadvantaged workers with marketable skills. Nonprofits (and other organizations) also need to consider other categorical personnel decisions as well: To what extent should the venture employ experienced senior personnel rather than junior staff? And in what proportions should it engage administrative rather than direct program staff? In the case of the Bookbinder Library's tutoring venture, management has several personnel resource choices to consider. For example, what combination of volunteer and paid tutors should it engage? And how much library supervisory staff time should it devote to the project?

The logic of these choices is much the same as the logic for making other input combination decisions. You must ask what a unit of each personnel category adds to output at the margin, and how much each costs. Incremental allocations to equalize the marginal contributions of expenditures for each category are then prescribed. Consider the issue of volunteers versus paid tutors in the Bookbinder Library case. Volunteers and paid workers are likely to differ in terms of both productivity and cost, and different combinations of these workers are likely to be more productive than others. For example, an all-volunteer tutoring staff could suffer from reliability problems and unfamiliarity with professional standards of teaching. Alternatively, an all-paid tutoring staff could be very expensive and might lack the special motivation that a cadre of volunteers could bring. Under these conditions, some combination of volunteers and paid staff is likely to produce a better result.

One tricky issue is the assessment of the marginal cost of adding a member to the tutoring staff. If the individual is paid, then obviously his or her salary and benefits must be included in the marginal cost. In addition, the supplies that such an individual would use and the additional cost of supervision that he or she would require constitute other components of the marginal cost. For volunteers there is no salary component, but like almost everything else in life, volunteers are not free. For a paid worker, market wages represent the opportunity cost associated with the value of work that individual could be doing if not employed in the present position. Volunteer time also has an opportunity cost, though it may be more difficult to estimate. You must ask what else the volunteer would have been doing if not volunteering on the current project, and then estimate a value for that forgone activity. In the case of the Bookbinder Library project, for example, a volunteer for the tutoring project might otherwise have been employed behind the desk in the reference section. An estimate of the opportunity cost might be obtained by determining what it would cost to replace the volunteer in the reference function with a paid worker or another volunteer.

In addition to such opportunity costs, employment of volunteers entails the costs of supplies they will use, possibly the costs of reimbursable meals or travel, as well as the cost of supervision. Also, volunteers must be rewarded in some way that usually requires resources, even if only a certificate of appreciation and perhaps an annual reception. Additional costs associated with administration may be particularly important for volunteers, particularly if they require substantial training. In any case, the opportunity costs of volunteer time and the additional costs of recruiting, training, supervising, evaluating, and rewarding volunteers constitute various components adding up to the marginal cost of adding a volunteer.

Given a nominal mix of volunteers and paid tutors, the Bookbinder Library will want to make additions or adjustments to its staffing to ensure that its staff members are deployed in the most efficient manner. Again, it is convenient to start with a given personnel budget and to ask in incremental steps whether the next addition to staff is best allocated to a volunteer or paid position. Suppose the marginal cost of a volunteer hour is $10 and that of a paid staff person is $40 (taking into account all of the components just discussed). Further, suppose that these costs remain constant as additional staff members are added. Now suppose that paid staff are also somewhat more efficient in delivering QTHs: for example, volunteers need to devote more hours than paid workers to prepare to deliver a QTH. Finally, suppose that as more volunteers and paid staff are employed it becomes more difficult to find excellent workers, so the marginal product of an additional volunteer or paid worker declines as the scale of the staff increases. With these conditions, the calculation might go something like this: Given a budget of $500, what combination of volunteers and paid staff should be employed? Suppose at the outset (with no staff yet engaged) the marginal products of an additional staff hour are 0.5 QTH for a paid worker and 0.25 QTH for a volunteer. Then we can calculate that a paid worker delivers 0.5 QTH per $40 or 0.0125 QTH per dollar, while a volunteer delivers 0.25 QTH per $10 or 0.025 QTH per dollar. So it seems sensible to engage a volunteer first. Suppose a volunteer is so engaged for, say, ten hours of work, producing 2.5 QTHs at a cost of $100. In this situation, however, a second volunteer might not be as productive, perhaps producing only 0.1 QTH per hour of work. That volunteer would deliver only 0.01 QTH per dollar compared to 0.0125 for a paid worker, so the next allocation should be for a paid tutor. At ten hours of work, a paid tutor would cost $400 and produce another 5 QTHs, yielding a total output of 7.5 QTHs for the $500 budget. (If that $400 had been spent on volunteers, it would have purchased forty additional volunteer hours, producing 40 × 0.1 or 4 additional QTHs, for a total of 6.5 QTHs.)

At this point, suppose another $100 becomes available for tutors. How should it be allocated? It depends again on the new marginal products of volunteer versus paid tutors, given that there is already one of each on board. Suppose the marginal productivity of another volunteer remains at 0.1 QTH while the marginal productivity of a (second) paid worker drops to 0.4 QTH. Then both paid and volunteer workers would deliver 0.1 QTH per $10 = 0.4 QTH per $40 = 0.01 QTH per dollar of additional cost. Hence, the additional funds could be allocated to either category with equal effectiveness, or perhaps split (say one paid-worker hour and six volunteer hours). The fact that the marginal products of additional expenditure on either volunteers or paid tutors are equal indicates that the original $500 budget was efficiently allocated.

The foregoing example is instructive not because of its particular numbers or mechanics but rather because of the principles it illustrates. To find the most efficient mix of staff for your venture, you need to focus on the margin, asking whether incremental changes in one category of staff versus another category increases productivity and whether equal productivity per dollar is being received from each personnel category. Exhibit 15.2 outlines the steps for conducting a marginal analysis of personnel.

EXHIBIT 15.2. MARGINAL ANALYSIS OF PERSONNEL: A ROUGH AND READY APPROACH.

1. Specify a measure of program output.

2. Identify the alternative types of staff that contribute to program output.

3. Start with a minimal personnel budget and an additional sum to be allocated.

4. Choose a nominal staff combination by allocating the minimal personnel budget (possibly the status quo) and estimate how much output this combination produces.

5. For each personnel type, estimate separately how much additional output (marginal product) would result from spending another $10,000 on that category.

6. Allocate the $10,000 to the category with the highest marginal product. If two or more categories are tied for the highest marginal product, allocate the $10,000 to any one of them.

7. Return to step 5. Continue until the additional sum to be allocated is exhausted or until it is determined that the benefit from additional output (marginal benefit) is less than the additional (marginal) cost to produce it.

8. Check to see if the marginal products of each personnel type are now roughly the same. If they are not, experiment with shifting budget in $10,000 (or smaller) increments from personnel categories with lower marginal products to those with higher marginal products.

Outsourcing

As a nonprofit venture manager, you need to ask similar questions about how particular activities or components of the venture are executed. In particular, is it more efficient to employ and supervise your own staff or to hire an outside contractor to do the work? Unlike production or personnel decisions, however, outsourcing decisions are often binary (in business terms, there are only two choices: "make" or buy"). That is, you have to decide whether to carry out a particular activity in-house or out-of-house rather than through a combination of these two options. For example, the Bookbinder Library could outsource the tutoring program to an external contractor or run it in-house. Though a combination of the two is possible, and may even have some merits (for example, the benefits of competition between program components), it is unlikely to be efficient unless the program grows to a large scale. Still, nonprofit venture managers do commonly face decisions about combinations in outsourcing. In particular, there is the overall portfolio decision—the decision as to what combination of activities should be contracted out and what retained in-house. That is, what combinations of in-house and out of house activity are most efficient?

Several factors affect outsourcing decisions: the core competencies of your organization, its mission and identity, economies of scope, and the competitive advantage of your organization relative to other organizations that are capable of carrying out the work. One way to think about the issue of outsourcing is to conceive of your nonprofit organization as having a core of activity that you should not consider outsourcing for fear of losing your public identity or abandoning your core competencies. The Bookbinder Library should probably not consider outsourcing its book-lending or reference service functions, for example. Nonetheless, careful thought needs to be given to what really constitutes an organization's core, because that cluster of activities may be relatively small compared to the organization's full array of functions. Organizations can even contract out key parts of their management without losing their integrity.

Certainly when you consider undertaking a new venture you should consider the possibility that it might be more efficiently undertaken on a contract basis. This is particularly true for ventures intended primarily to generate net revenues rather than to address essential mission-related objectives. In such cases, the venture can be thought of as a financial investment for the organization, a function that is often delegated to a competent agent.

So how does marginal analysis enter the picture in making efficient outsourcing decisions for a nonprofit venture? Starting with the in-house core of activity, you can think of each additional function as a margin along which you can ask, Is this best done in-house or outside? The answer in each case will depend on what is already done in-house (existing internal capacities and competencies) as well as on the competencies of potential outside suppliers and on the organization's relative abilities to supervise in-house production and external contractors. For example, suppose the Bookbinder Library wants to publish a newsletter to publicize its activities and let people know about its new tutoring venture. The marginal costs of starting up and running a newsletter in-house might be high compared to engaging a company or consultant that is experienced with such projects and already carrying them out on an efficient scale. In addition, the costs of supervising an external contractor may be relatively low in this case. (You can approve the product by proofreading it before it goes out, and you can negotiate a fixed-cost contract to control the cost.) Thus, the marginal product (measured in terms of additional QTHs that could be produced for a dollar spent) may be greater for expenditures on a contractor than for in-house production of the newsletter.

Conversely, the library may be best advised overall to administer its tutoring venture in-house rather than have it run by an outside agent. First, the venture may fall close to the library's core competency of helping students and community members with their informational and educational needs. Educated staff with strong literacy and reference skills may comfortably accommodate this addition to their professional responsibilities and work assignments. Moreover, the venture may be able to utilize space already available to the library. Third, the venture may be intended to contribute directly to the library's mission of community service—a perception that may be obscured by involvement of a contractor. Given the nature of the library's core functions, the marginal cost of the tutoring venture may be relatively low compared to what the cost might be for an external contractor; equivalently, the marginal product of the in-house alternative, gauged in terms of additional QTHs per dollar, may be greater at a given level of operation than if a contractor were engaged. It is always possible, of course, that at some scale of operation the library will find it efficient to contract out for additional capacity for the tutoring venture. Again, focusing on the margin will help with this determination. As the program grows, the margins of cost and productivity will change, and the outsourcing of additional capacity should be considered at each stage of growth.

Within the context of the tutoring venture, other outsourcing decisions may also be considered. It may be unlikely, for example, that the library will want to design its own software programs or perhaps even undertake an in-house promotional campaign to recruit clients or volunteer tutors. Analysis of the margins for these functions may indicate that contracting out is more efficient. That is, more QTHs can be produced per additional dollar spent on the tutoring venture if the contracting option is used for certain functions. Overall, review of organizational and venture activities, margin by margin, is likely to result in a mix of decisions, with some activities being outsourced (those for which there is no special in-house competency and for which there are strong outside alternatives) and others being retained (those for which the competitive advantage goes to the organization itself). Thinking at the margins in this way gives you the advantage of pursing maximum efficiency wherever it is best secured—sometimes in the external marketplace and sometimes by doing it yourself. Exhibit 15.3 outlines the steps for conducting a marginal analysis of outsourcing.

Marketing and Resource Development Decisions

The ability of a nonprofit organization to maximize the output of a venture and the efficiency with which it uses its resources will depend in part of how well that venture is marketed to its potential clients. Moreover, the level of resources available to the venture will depend on how well the venture is marketed to potential donors and financial sponsors. Each of these cases requires thinking at the margin to determine what combination of marketing strategies is most efficient.

EXHIBIT 15.3. MARGINAL ANALYSIS OF OUTSOURCING: A ROUGH AND READY APPROACH.

---

1. Specify a measure of organizational output.

2. List noncore functions that can be considered for outsourcing.

3. Estimate total organizational output assuming that all functions are carried on in-house.

4. Estimate the cost of each noncore function assuming it is carried on in-house.

5. For each noncore function, estimate how much output would increase or decrease if that function were outsourced and allocated the same amount of funds as the other functions.

6. Consider contracting out those core functions for which outsourcing is estimated to increase output.

7. Experiment with different combinations of outsourced functions to see if certain combinations yield greater increases in output than others. For example, start by projecting that those functions that have the highest marginal additions to output from contracting out will be outsourced, and then sequentially test which other functions might add further to output.

There are several dimensions along which marketing strategies can vary. One dimension is *methodology*: What means will be used to promote the program and disseminate its information to potential clients or supporters? Possibilities range from word-of-mouth to conventional mailings to media advertisements to Internet strategies such as e-mail and Web site utilization. Another dimension is *targeting or market segmentation*: To which groups of potential clients or sponsors will marketing strategies be directed? Possibilities include alternative socioeconomic groups and alternative geographic clusters. Again there are likely to be trade-offs as alternative combinations are considered at the margins.

In the case of the Bookbinder Library's tutoring venture, alternative combinations of marketing strategies are likely to be differentially productive in generating demand for the venture. Equivalently, given levels of demand can be generated at more or less cost by pursuing alternative combinations of marketing strategies. Hence, the additional QTHs generated per dollar spent on media advertisement, on direct mailings, and on a campaign of community outreach through local speaking engagements are likely to differ substantially from one another in any particular instance, and these strategies are likely to be more efficient in certain combinations than if one or the other strategy is adopted alone. For example, the local speaking program may be most efficient up to a certain point, after which its returns are likely to diminish and be exceeded by engagement in an advertising campaign.

Similarly, any given combination of marketing techniques is likely to be more or less productive when directed at particular market segments rather than at other segments. A local community focus on immigrants and high school seniors may be most productive to a point, after which additional market segments may contribute more additional QTHs per dollar of investment in marketing. Also clearly, these two dimensions of marketing strategy are interdependent. Certain methodologies may work better for certain market segments—for example, speaking programs probably work better for local groups and media strategies probably work better for more widely dispersed target populations. Each of these margins should probably be analyzed simultaneously in order to find the right combinations to maximize QTHs within a given marketing budget.

Similar analysis applies to seeking contributions to support the tutoring program. Here, however, the appropriate marginal product is the additional dollars raised per dollar spent on alternative means of promotion and on marketing strategies directed to various potential donor populations. Potential donor population segments may include library users, local residents, parent groups, members of ethnic communities, and so on. Alternative methodologies may include personal or telephone solicitations by library management, staff, and board members; a mailing campaign; or a Web site enhancement. Again, the most efficient approach is likely to be some combination of market segments and methodologies.

The latter argument can of course be extended to the Bookbinder Library's overall revenue-generation strategy. To what extent should the library rely on donor contributions rather than on government grants, and so on? Each of these sources involves investment in marketing, special accounting capacities, cultivation of certain relationships, and other aspects of fund administration—requiring varying levels of expenditure according to the particular type of revenue source. In the end, however, the library wants to find that combination of revenue sources by which another dollar spent on any one of them would yield the same return. Exhibit 15.4 outlines the steps for conducting a marginal analysis of market and resource development.

Programming Decisions

Nonprofit venture decisions must invariably fit into the context of overall programming decisions of the sponsoring organization. As such, the decision to undertake a new venture implicitly suggests that the marginal contribution of such a

EXHIBIT 15.4. MARGINAL ANALYSIS OF MARKET AND RESOURCE DEVELOPMENT: A ROUGH AND READY APPROACH.

1. Specify a measure of output for the marketing or development program.
2. Identify the alternative strategies that could contribute to this output.
3. Start with a minimal budget allocation and an additional sum to be allocated.
4. Choose a nominal combination of strategies or methods by allocating the minimal budget and estimate how much output this combination produces. (This might reflect the existing marketing and development plan.)
5. For each strategy, estimate separately how much additional output (marginal product) would result from spending another $10,000 on that strategy.
6. Allocate the $10,000 to the strategy with the highest marginal product. If two or more strategies are tied for the highest marginal product, allocate the $10,000 to any one of them.
7. Return to step 5. Continue until the additional sum to be allocated is exhausted, or until it is determined that the benefit from additional output (marginal benefit) is less than the additional (marginal) cost to produce it (for example, until another dollar spent on development fails to raise at least a dollar in return).
8. Check to see if the marginal products of each strategy are now roughly the same. If they are not, experiment with shifting budget in $10,000 increments from strategies with lower marginal products to those with higher marginal products.

venture to the existing portfolio of programs is greater than what you could achieve by incrementally expanding an existing program. A difficulty, however, is determining the nature of the marginal product that allows you to compare the additional outputs of alternative programs. For production, personnel, outsourcing, and marketing decisions applying to a particular project venture such as the library's tutoring program, we have the luxury of comparing contributions using a homogeneous output metric particular to that venture (QTHs). And for marketing and resource development decisions associated with generating revenue for the organization, we have the luxury of focusing on revenue dollars per se as the appropriate marginal product. Alternative programs, however, are characterized by alternative output measures, so the QTHs for the tutoring program are not directly comparable to, say, circulation measures for the book-lending program, the number of clients assisted in the reference program, or the number of presentations made in the community lecture program. (These juxtapositions would be akin to comparing the proverbial apples and oranges.) Moreover, in choosing among such programs we are as much interested in the relative impacts of these programs in terms of the value they produce for society as we are interested in how efficiently they use their resources internally.

Comparing program outputs is a common issue for nonprofits, because it is the rare organization that confines itself to a single variety of service. Museums host concerts and lectures as well as display fine art. Social and mental health organizations offer multiple treatment programs for widely varying populations and pathologies. Colleges and universities provide different courses of study, engage in research, and offer community service as well as degree programs. Nonprofits are more like bazaars and supermarkets than specialized vendors selling apples, oranges, bananas, and cereal, but without the advantage of being able to gauge all that they do in terms of financial profit. Still, the logic of analyzing alternative programs at the margin in order to determine the combination of input programs that will allow your organization to achieve the greatest possible mission impact for its available resources remains the same as we have explicated for the other types of venture trade-off decisions. The issue is how to characterize the impact with a metric common to alternative programs.

There is no easy solution to this problem. However, as suggested earlier, you can still think in the proper terms even if outputs and marginal products are quantitatively elusive. For example, the concept of a CSU allows you to put alternative programming options on common ground. In the case of the Bookbinder Library, all of its programs are directed to serving its community's educational and informational needs. Venture leadership should therefore ask, for every additional investment in one of its programs, What is added in terms of community service? and Is that addition superior to what would be achieved if the expenditure were made instead in another program? Naturally the same question should be asked of all existing programs, and at every scale of operation, as programs are considered for expansion or contraction.

It is important to note that this logic applies in two ways to a new nonprofit venture, such as the Bookbinder Library's tutoring program. Clearly it applies to the scale of the program: At what scale will this program's contributions to output at the margin (in terms of CSUs) be equal to the contributions of other programs in the library's portfolio? The question also applies, in a more complicated way, to the venture start-up decision itself. On the one hand, it would be prejudicial to require that the initial investments in the new venture exhibit a larger marginal product than those of existing programs. Typically, new ventures require considerable investment before they produce much of anything. On the other hand, it is not unreasonable to require a business plan to demonstrate, once it is up and running, that there is a scale of operation at which the new venture will successfully compete with existing programs in terms of the marginal contributions it makes to the organization's output. Indeed, there must be some range of venture scale within which its marginal contributions to output will exceed those of other programs. Otherwise, it would make little sense to undertake the venture at all. Exhibit 15.5 outlines the steps for conducting a marginal analysis of programming.

Conclusion

To have the best chance of succeeding, new ventures undertaken by nonprofit organizations must make the best possible use of their inevitably limited economic resources. To do so, trade-offs must be made at several levels of decision making. To efficiently produce a new service, the right combination of input resources must be used—supplies, equipment, staff, physical plant, and so on. Within this context, appropriate choices must be made among important categories of personnel in order to find the best combination of volunteers and paid staff, junior and senior staff, and so on. Trade-offs must also be made in terms of the venue for different aspects of the work that must be done in order to produce and deliver the new service: some aspects of the work may best be carried out in-house while other aspects may be more efficiently executed by contracting with outside suppliers. Marketing decisions also involve trade-offs in order to find the best combination of methodologies and target groups for consumption and support of the venture's services. Finally, the venture itself must fit appropriately into the portfolio of its host organization's programming. Hence, trade-offs among alternative programs must be examined in order to determine the most efficient combinations for this portfolio and the appropriate scale and contribution of the new venture within that portfolio.

EXHIBIT 15.5. MARGINAL ANALYSIS OF PROGRAMMING: A ROUGH AND READY APPROACH.

1. Specify a measure of organizational (mission-related) output.

2. Identify alternative existing and potential programs and services that can contribute to output.

3. Start with a minimal budget allocation and an additional sum to be allocated.

4. Choose a nominal portfolio of these programs by allocating the minimal budget and estimate how much output this combination produces (status quo).

5. For each program, estimate separately how much additional output (marginal product) would result from spending another $10,000 on that program. If the program also generates revenue, assume that the added revenue is reinvested in the program to generate further output and add this to the estimate of the marginal product.

6. Allocate the $10,000 to the program with the highest marginal product. If two or more programs are tied for the highest marginal product, allocate the $10,000 to any one of them.

7. Return to step 5. Continue until the additional sum to be allocated is exhausted or until it is determined that the benefit from additional output (marginal benefit) is less than the additional (marginal) cost to produce it.

8. Check to see if the marginal products of each program are now roughly the same. If they are not, experiment with shifting budget in $10,000 increments from programs with lower marginal products to those with higher marginal products.

Basic concepts of economic analysis, especially analysis at the margin, can help you think through these sometimes complex and difficult trade-off decisions. Analysis at the margin is a way of thinking that directs you to consider the results of incremental changes in the combination of resources used or strategies employed. As such it is a useful framework even if some of the measurements required to do exact calculations are elusive. Even with rough estimates and assumptions, analysis at the margin can give you a clearer picture of how your resources can best be deployed.

Analysis at the margin requires conceptualization of output measures associated with different levels of decision making. Decisions strictly involving alternative ways to generate financial resources are straightforward in this respect: output can be characterized directly in dollar terms. Production decisions can be somewhat more difficult, because venture output must be characterized by some unit of service production that accounts for quality and other parameters. Overall, programming decisions are more difficult still, because they require some common metric with which to compare the outputs of diverse programs. Still, with creativity and realistic assumptions, such outputs can be conceptualized to enable comparisons of marginal products associated with alternative incremental choices.

With marginal analysis, the focus of resource decision making moves from a singular focus on particular alternatives to the idea of finding the right combinations of resources and strategies. In this way you are more likely to find the balance of resources and strategies that will allow your venture to have its maximum social impact by addressing your organization's mission as efficiently as possible.

In short, analysis at the margin is a way for you to think small (by increments) in order to achieve big results (maximum mission benefits). It can be a helpful guide to you, as a nonprofit manager and entrepreneur, in a world of many choices and limited resources.

Recommended Reading

Chandler, A. D. *Scale and Scope: The Dynamics of Industrial Capitalism.* Cambridge, Mass.: Harvard University Press, 1990.

Heilbrun, J., and Gray, C. M. *The Economics of Art and Culture.* New York: Cambridge University Press, 1993.

Oster, S. M. *Strategic Management for Nonprofit Organizations.* New York: Oxford University Press, 1995.

Young, D. R. (ed.). *Effective Economic Decision Making by Nonprofit Organizations.* New York: Foundation Center, forthcoming.

Young, D. R., and Steinberg, R. *Economics for Nonprofit Managers.* New York: Foundation Center, 1995.

CHAPTER SIXTEEN

USING PERFORMANCE METRICS TO ASSESS IMPACT

Stephanie Bell-Rose

In recent years, as competition for resources in the nonprofit sector has intensified and as the nonprofit sector has grown more professional and strategic in its approach to social change, many organizations have sought to develop better ways to demonstrate the social and financial impacts of their programs.

In today's environment, funders, nonprofit managers, social entrepreneurs, and policymakers are all looking for impact and efficiency, as well as for double-bottom-line returns. Nonprofit organizations that are prepared to measure and demonstrate their own effectiveness will increasingly enjoy an enhanced ability to raise funds, communicate their values, and manage their own organizations.

The issue of performance assessment is fraught with difficulties, however. The nonprofit sector does not enjoy the relatively straightforward market signals that the for-profit sector enjoys. There are no generally accepted standards for capturing or enumerating social value that are analogous to the methods used by businesses in reporting profits or shareholder value. Nevertheless, extensive experimentation is carried out in this area as organizations work to improve their management ability and to develop systems and tools to evaluate impact. From the standpoint of society, the long-term goal of these changes is to increase both the effectiveness of individual social organizations and the quantity of resources available to the nonprofit sector as a whole.

Reasons to Measure Performance

For any organization, the most important reasons to measure performance are to improve effectiveness and to acquire information that will allow the organization to drive its agenda forward. If the motivation for doing evaluation remains outside an organization, the evaluation will have limited impact. To do performance assessment effectively, an organization must commit to adopting a culture of measurement, because acceptance must come from senior management, staff, funders, and board members alike.

It is one of the ironies in the nonprofit sector that while many organizations are already collecting performance measurement information and expending considerable resources preparing it for funders, they often fail to use it to inform their own management processes and marketing appeals. Many of the performance measurement tools that have been developed in recent years are designed to be useful for assessing impact, improving management, and communicating results to others. These tools can be extremely useful in helping nonprofit managers think through, in a step-by-step fashion, what they must accomplish in order to excel at their core mission.

Without a method of assessing impact, many organizations simply do not know if they are actually achieving their missions. They may be successful in some areas and less successful in others, but they may not know where, specifically, things are working well and where they are not. As a result, they may be missing opportunities to improve their programs.

Because not all funders have the same reporting requirements, nonprofit organizations may need to gather different kinds of information at different points in time and arrange it in different formats for different audiences. When thinking about instituting performance assessment systems, organizations should begin by evaluating how much time and energy they will need to spend gathering information. Additionally, they should test how well the data gathered actually serve internal information needs. In short, organizations ought to determine proactively the kinds of outcomes their assessments should measure.

Consider the example of Jumpstart, a national organization that recruits and trains college students to mentor preschoolers. One of Jumpstart's funders is Boston-based New Profit Inc., a high-engagement grantmaker that, in addition to providing scale-up capital, links its partner nonprofits with management consulting services and provides them with tools and training to do performance assessment. Through its association with New Profit, Jumpstart adopted a popular management and performance tool called the Balanced Scorecard, which was developed by Harvard Business School professor Robert Kaplan and David Norton, founder of the Balanced Scorecard Collaborative.[1]

The Balanced Scorecard is an analytic tool that New Profit believes can be applied to businesses, traditional nonprofits, and nonprofits running nonprofit enterprises. It is designed to provide an organization with timely feedback about both internal processes and external outcomes. The analysis breaks down an organization's activities and goals into several categories, such as social impact, finances, operations, growth, and learning and partnerships. Jumpstart's managers have found that the Balanced Scorecard has helped it to clarify goals and strategies, identify opportunities, and assess results. The process has been instrumental in spurring change within the organization, and the Scorecard itself has become a focal point for management discussions.

Jumpstart's mission is to prepare children aged three to five to succeed in elementary school. It seeks both to increase the number of children it works with and to improve the quality of its work with each child. To achieve these goals the organization needs to know what kinds of tutoring work best, how to recruit tutors cost-effectively, how to ensure that the tutors are having a measurable effect on the skill levels of the children, what each tutoring hour costs, and many other factors.

Jumpstart's staff contend that the Balanced Scorecard helps them, funders, and other stakeholders understand the drivers of the organization's mission and allows them to see their own work in the context of the whole. The process of completing the Balanced Scorecard's strategy map helps to ensure that information that is held in different people's heads in different areas of an organization will be committed to paper. This leads to greater understanding about how all the parts of the organization interact to fulfill the mission.

When Jumpstart has to balance considerations such as lowering the cost per tutor hour per child and increasing the impact per child, for example, the Balanced Scorecard does not provide easy answers about how to negotiate the trade-offs, but it does facilitate productive discussions among staff, board members, funders, and other stakeholders that allow the organization to make informed decisions. Many nonprofit enterprises face these kinds of trade-offs as they seek to maximize both social and financial returns.

This type of detailed performance information, whether it is used to guide internal processes, describe outcomes, or translate impacts into dollar figures, can be valuable for a social-purpose organization. Such information can inform management about how to improve the program, spot new opportunities, identify emerging problems, and communicate a program's values to a range of stakeholders, including the media, funders, staff, volunteers, clients, government agencies, and board members.

Challenges and Obstacles

Many nonprofits approach with trepidation the issue of measuring performance. There are structural reasons for this. Collecting and processing this kind of information requires organizational capacity, and funders have not always shown themselves to be willing to finance the creation of this capacity. In the short-term, performance measurement frequently entails taking resources away from other parts of the organization. Because of day-to-day pressures, ongoing resource constraints, and other unforeseen emergencies that inevitably arise, undertaking a process of systematic self-evaluation often falls to the bottom of the list of priorities.

Additionally, measuring performance is an inherently difficult and imprecise process. There are no standard methods to measure social value creation. When one considers that nonprofit organizations are involved in everything from environmental protection to health care to disability to the arts to economic development, it is easy to understand the difficulty. There are no universal bottom lines. Also, in addition to measuring impact, nonprofits can be assessed on the basis of the long-term importance of their strategy, their capacity to grow, and their political durability.

Indeed, one of the biggest problems is the difficulty of attributing an outcome to a particular cause. Many organizations work on issues that overlap. They may have no easy way to gauge their contribution to social change. Additionally, certain kinds of social value—such as short-term assistance and emergency services, prevention programs, advocacy, research, and so forth—are particularly difficult to assess.

There are also a variety of cultural factors that come into play. Some organizations are averse to adopting practices that seem too corporate in spirit. People working for social service organizations are not usually trained as social scientists or analysts. They have different skill sets and motivations for working in the nonprofit sector. They are often motivated by passion or a sense of mission and they may believe very strongly that their work is clearly making a difference so its importance shouldn't have to be justified.

In addition to the fact that few organizations collect performance information, those that do collect it frequently focus on *outputs*—the number of homeless people in their job-training workshops, for example—rather than on *outcomes*, or indications of impact—such as the number of clients who, after going through the trainings, landed jobs and moved out of poverty.

There is a natural tendency to measure what you are doing well. If an organization has full classrooms, it will report on the number of students it is serving.

It may not actually know how many of those students have landed jobs. In general, focusing on outcomes—indicators of genuine impact—will shift the emphasis from *activities* to *results*, from how a program operates to what it accomplishes.

Nonprofit Enterprise Considerations

For nonprofits, the task of assessing impact is similar whether the impact delivery mechanism is a nonprofit enterprise or a traditional program, although the costs associated with delivery may differ. For nonprofit enterprises, however, performance measurements are more important than they are for traditional nonprofits, simply because managers of nonprofit enterprises and their funders, or investors, generally are influenced by practices, experiences, and expectations in the private sector, where measurement of results is standard practice.

In the field of nonprofit enterprise, funders and managers need to know whether the nonprofit enterprise is generating revenues and profits and whether it is growing. They will also want to know whether the operation of the nonprofit enterprise is demonstrably providing cash to the parent organization and whether it is achieving a social impact that can be measured and, if possible, quantified— or at least described with clarity. Two primary areas of interest, therefore, are transparency and accountability in the use of funds and bottom-line results.

Nonprofit enterprises often need to implement systems that accurately capture the full costs and cash outlays involved in their work. This is necessary because it is impossible to gauge profitability without understanding the cost structure of an enterprise. Every nonprofit enterprise needs to know how much it really costs to provide its services (including hidden costs such as overhead and fundraising expenses that may be absorbed by the parent nonprofit). Otherwise, the enterprise team will have no basis for pricing, calculating profits, and planning for growth. Beyond considering the business's basic financial performance, managers of nonprofit enterprises generally have to think creatively about how to demonstrate, or enumerate, the social value that the business creates.

A number of the finalists from the 2002–03 Partnership on Nonprofit Venture's National Business Plan Competition for Nonprofit Organizations included social return on investment (SROI) assessments in their business plans. For example, the Centre for Women of Tampa, Florida, created a nonprofit enterprise called Ramps & Retrofits, which hires low-income women to build home wheelchair ramps for elderly people. The Centre for Women calculates SROI by adding its gross profits from Ramps & Retrofits to estimates of the amount of money the government saves through reductions of public assistance to the Centre's employees and through reductions in nursing home costs made possible by allowing elderly residents to remain living in their homes longer than would otherwise be possible.[2]

The Rochester Rehabilitation Center's nonprofit enterprise, Parrett Paper, provides employment to disabled people who manufacture greeting cards. Parrett Paper calculates SROI by adding up the wages its employees receive and the associated cost reductions in outpatient mental health care services. The latter represents about 80 percent of Parrett Paper's SROI calculations, or about $13,800 per participant per year.[3]

In the nonprofit enterprise sphere, managers are often faced with tough decisions about how to balance competing needs between the nonprofit enterprise and the pursuit of the mission. If a nonprofit organization seeks to reach ten thousand people with a particular service through a nonprofit enterprise, the organization may face a fundamental question: Should it reach out to the easiest-to-serve clients (with the lowest cost per individual)? Or should it reach out to the most needy clients (with the highest cost per individual)? The former strategy may prove more profitable, but the latter may produce higher social returns based on some subjective or quantifiable assessment of the value of the services to this particular customer segment. To make these kinds of decisions responsibly, organizations need good data about both financial costs and social impact assessments.

Consider the example of Rubicon Enterprises, a nonprofit organization that runs a number of nonprofit enterprises, including a bakery and a landscaping business in the San Francisco Bay Area. Rubicon Enterprises provides employment, vocational rehabilitation, and training to low-income workers, many of whom were formerly homeless.[4]

One of the difficulties that Rubicon Enterprises ran into several years ago was meeting the information needs of its funders. The organization was devoting extensive human resources to collect information for funders and for government agencies, yet the information was not maintained in a format that could be readily analyzed. To compound the problem, each funder typically requested an individualized report. As a result, there was a great deal of redundancy of effort. Moreover, the whole process didn't even serve the informational needs of Rubicon.

Seeking a solution, Rubicon Enterprises decided to restructure its information-gathering system so that data would be captured more efficiently and would both feed the needs of its programs and satisfy the needs of funders and regulators. Rubicon found a supportive funding partner in the Roberts Enterprise Development Fund and the Surdna Foundation, both of which recognized the value of performance information and also sought to develop systems to evaluate social impacts for its other programs. The result was an outcome measurement system that Rubicon developed called CICERO (Consumer Information Collection, Entry and

Reporting for Organizations), which became the basis for the Roberts Enterprise Development Fund's OASIS (Ongoing Assessment of Social ImpactS) system.

Unlike a for-profit enterprise, Rubicon Enterprises absorbs the additional costs associated with helping homeless people make the transition into stable employment situations. These additional costs are part of the price tag for creating the social value that Rubicon seeks in addition to profits. Rubicon therefore decided to measure, in addition to its normal financial performance, the value of such things as providing employment to a homeless person through its bakery (a nonprofit enterprise) and the value of helping a client find housing through its more traditional social service arm.

In each case, the challenges of assessing the social impact were similar. The key questions were, What happened to the client? How important was the change? And what level of resources was devoted to accomplish it? This information was deemed crucial in enabling Rubicon to evaluate the effectiveness of its social change model.

Today Rubicon has developed a variety of techniques to measure changes in the quality of life of its clients by looking at factors such as income, wage progression, job advancement, substance abuse, housing stability, economic self-sufficiency, and other indicators. The organization is able to estimate how many people it has helped to make the transition out of homelessness, and how much this saves public systems in terms of reduced costs associated with hospitalization, incarceration, housing needs, and public assistance.

This information is not just for funders. It is widely shared across the organization in order to fine-tune programs, diagnose problems, and identify new opportunities. At the same time, if a foundation or government agency requests information about services or impacts, the information is readily available in the formats that Rubicon has deemed most useful and sensible for its own purposes.

In developing CICERO, Rubicon had the benefit of a supportive and enthusiastic funder. It was therefore able to invest considerable resources in building the organizational capacity to implement its performance measurement system. Other organizations seeking to pursue similar strategies should consider engaging their funders early in the process—before their funders approach them—to propose similar co-development partnerships.

Performance Evaluation: A Growing Field

Performance measurement is gathering momentum. The nonprofit sector can now draw on an interesting body of work that has accumulated over the past twenty-five years in the field of nonprofit performance evaluation. Some of this work involves the creation of management and measurement tools to track operational processes to assess the capacity development of organizations. Some of it involves the creation of tools to quantify (not necessarily in dollars) social value creation through the use of *metrics*—numerical proxies that correlate with the achievement of desired outcomes. Some of the work involves methods of monetizing impact—generally asserting a dollar-value contribution to society in the form of revenues or cost reductions of social services or financial resources. (The latter has been done most often in vocational training, workforce development, microcredit, and environmental auditing.) Some of these tools and processes require considerably more resources than others to implement.

A number of organizations have done work in this area and can serve as starting points for research. They include Acumen Fund, Coastal Enterprises, Columbia Business School's Research Initiative on Social Entrepreneurship (RISE), Community Wealth Ventures, Independent Sector, New Profit Inc., Public Private Ventures, Roberts Enterprise Development Fund, Venture Philanthropy Partners, and the United Way.[5]

In the field of microcredit, Global Partnerships has studied and analyzed a range of capacity-building and assessment tools.[6] In the field of nonprofit enterprise, one new resource is the Methods Catalog of Social Impact Assessment Tools, created by the Double Bottom Line Project and commissioned by the Rockefeller Foundation. The project has evaluated a range of social-impact assessment tools for early-stage social-purpose businesses and nonprofit revenue-generating organizations—also called double-bottom-line ventures. The Methods Catalog describes various approaches and tools used to assess social impact for double-bottom-line ventures, offering criteria for comparison and guidance regarding their use. It is available at Columbia Business School's RISE project Web site (http://www.riseproject.org).

The challenge in developing metrics is to blend the best techniques of social science evaluation with the results orientation that is being demanded increasingly by funders and social investors and by social entrepreneurs for their own organizations. To date, much of the work—particularly beyond employment programs—remains experimental. Where numerical tools are used to gauge social return, the results tend to be applicable to specific fields of activity and highly sensitive to the assumptions made in the calculations.

Performance Evaluation and Theory of Change

How should organizations begin to think about creating metrics? One helpful process is to set forth the internal (often unspoken) logic that informs the organization's activities and mission. The process demands that an organization think through all the steps that must occur for its mission to be accomplished, while identifying along the way the assumptions and rationale that underlie each step. It is often easier to assess the intermediate steps on the way to outcomes than to assess the outcomes themselves, particularly if the change occurs over the long term. An organization that goes through this process of articulating its so-called theory of change may find it easier to identify the kinds of progress measurements that make sense.

A job-training program, for example, may be predicated on the assumption that helping to create employment stability is one of the most powerful ways to help people become self-sufficient. Therefore, an indicator of success would be the number or percentage of people who find jobs and remain employed for a given period after the program. The organization may also calculate the estimated cost of delivering its services and compare those costs to the benefits, or look to identify the factors that correlate with success. It may discover that certain factors are frequently associated with success, such as whether a client has earned a high-school equivalency degree or received mental health care. These intermediate indicators can be tracked and used to understand other impacts.

In the case of Jumpstart, everything the organization measures is directly related to the specific items on its strategy map, which are all aligned with Jumpstart's core mission to ensure that young children are prepared to succeed in elementary school. The organization tracks items such as the number of children served by tutors, the assessment gains made by each of the children, the systemwide cost per tutor hour, the retention of core members, the number of quality interactions with governmental agencies, the number of national features about Jumpstart in the media, the number of new university partners, and the percentage of revenues received from government sources.

Many nonprofits have the capacity to develop measurement tools to serve their missions. These tools can help identify bottlenecks, hidden opportunities, or mistaken assumptions. They can be helpful to managers who seek to improve programs, motivate staff, and create a shared vision of the organization's mission.

A Brief Comparison with the Private Sector

Given that private-sector businesses have more experience measuring their performance than do nonprofits, it is worth briefly considering the difference between the two sectors with regard to this challenge. Much of the attraction of the private sector comes from the fact that businesses typically know clearly when they are succeeding and when they are failing. A successful business can measure its performance, gauge itself against competitors, and make necessary adjustments based on information gathered as part of its daily operations.

But performance measurement in business is not as simple as this description implies. There are many indicators of success in business—some are short-term, some are long-term; some focus on finances, some on organizational quality, some on management effectiveness, and some on market strength. Indeed, too much of a focus on certain kinds of performance measurement—say, market share or short-term profits—can cause a company to lose sight of other measurements, such as employee satisfaction or new-product development.

In practice, gauging the performance of a business is as much art as science. When valuing a company, for example, in addition to considering the financials, investors and rating agencies typically take into account many subjective variables, such as the effectiveness of the management, the value of proprietary information or expertise, the trustworthiness of the financial reports, the ability to cope with new competition, the ability to form partnerships with other firms, the capacity to develop and promote staff, the potential to grow the market, and so forth.

Even with the heavy reliance on financial data in the business world and the generally accepted standards with which these data are analyzed, there is still a great deal of judgment that comes into play. In this regard, the challenge of evaluating the performance of a nonprofit organization bears similarity to the challenge of accurately evaluating a business.

From the standpoint of performance, significant differences between the business sector and the nonprofit sector have to do with who pays for products and services and how resources are allocated by markets. In the for-profit world, customers pay for the services they want. Payment is a self-affirming activity. If people are willing to pay for a product or service, it is a strong indication that they receive value from that product or service. (The reverse does not necessarily apply. People are often reluctant to pay for goods that confer value to all of society.)

In the nonprofit arena, the person who uses a service is often not the person who pays for it. Sometimes society pays for the service. It is necessary therefore to develop another mechanism to evaluate the value of services, particularly with respect to the costs associated with the delivery of those services.

The Connection Between Performance Assessment and Capital Allocation

The business sector enjoys financial markets that offer fast and consistent feedback. Despite imperfections and the possibility of deception, in general money flows toward high-growth, high-profit companies. Capital markets, which represent the outcome of centuries of industry building in the for-profit sector, have the beneficial effect of both lowering the cost of capital for effective companies and redeploying resources quickly, thus accelerating innovation and market adaptation.

By contrast, it can take decades for a market leader in the nonprofit sector to achieve anything approaching the level of growth that a top-performing business can achieve in a few years. This is because in the nonprofit world the best-performing organizations do not necessarily attract the most funding.

Conclusion

It is critical to approach performance measurement with imagination and a sense of openness. A rigid approach that seeks to mimic the private sector will likely prove discouraging and potentially damaging.

It is difficult to compare organizations that have different missions and different cost structures (far more difficult than making comparisons in the financial world). The nonprofit sector will never have a bottom line as universal as profit. Even so, the focus on performance measurement and assessment remains a fundamental step toward building a platform by which resources in the nonprofit sector can be more rationally allocated—a step closer to a time when the best-performing organizations can indeed "capture" the benefits of their performance and innovation.

It is worth considering the following:

- The most important reason for measuring performance should be to improve services and effectiveness.
- A useful frame of comparison for any organization is the organization's stated performance goals.
- Organizations seeking to engage in systemic performance measurement should commit to it at all levels.
- To get working, the process may require outside assistance at the outset and a long period of experimentation. Initially it may be more important to gather information than to set hard targets.
- It is helpful to work with a funding partner who supports the process and is willing to finance the capacity build-up.
- It is important to share practices, ideas, lessons, and if possible resources with other organizations pursuing similar goals in order to accelerate the learning process within the sector.

As more nonprofit organizations get better at measuring what they are doing—looking at their own goals and evaluating their own success at meeting those goals—it may be possible to begin developing a framework in which one can speak of industry standards and frames of comparison. Today, however, there is an opportunity to increase the efficiency—and impact—of the nonprofit sector by developing improved systems to align performance and rewards.

Notes

1. Kaplan, R. S., and Norton, D. P. *The Balanced Scorecard: Translating Strategy into Action.* Cambridge, Mass.: Harvard Business School Press, 1996.
2. Business plan submitted to the Yale School of Management–The Goldman Sachs Foundation Partnership on Nonprofit Ventures' First National Business Plan Competition for Nonprofit Organizations, April 2003.
3. Business plan submitted to the Yale School of Management–The Goldman Sachs Foundation Partnership on Nonprofit Ventures' First National Business Plan Competition for Nonprofit Organizations, April 2003.
4. See http://www.rubiconpgms.org/pages/bizEnterprises.html.
5. See http://www.acumenfund.org/; http://www.ceimaine.org/; http://www.riseproject.org/index.html; http://www.communitywealth.org/; http://www.independentsector.org/; http://www.newprofit.com/; http://www.ppv.org/; http://www.redf.org; http://www.venturephilanthropypartners.org/; and http://national.unitedway.org/outcomes/library/pgmomres.cfm.
6. See http://www.globalpartnerships.org/.

CHAPTER SEVENTEEN

TAKING YOUR VENTURE TO SCALE

Rick Aubry

Bringing a business venture to scale has proved to be one of the most difficult aspects of nonprofit enterprise in the United States today. Though some ventures are created to start small and stay small, many have aspirations to become large enterprises. Yet time and time again those that try hit a glass ceiling, unable to reach their goal. Apart from the healthy hubris of the entrepreneur, there are many good reasons why nonprofits look to bring their earned income ventures to scale. These include the following:

To meet a particular social purpose. This may take the form of providing additional jobs for targeted employees or simply creating greater impact to advance the parent organization's mission.

To bring additional capital to the parent organization. The ability to grow to a significantly larger size, particularly in terms of net profit from the venture, supports the financial and mission goals of the organization.

To support the long-term sustainability of the venture. Larger ventures are frequently less susceptible to market vicissitudes than small ones. The growth to scale of the business venture may strengthen the nonprofit venture.

To benefit from the economies of scale that often accrue to larger ventures. Larger ventures often enjoy significant operational and competitive advantages.

To augment the field of social entrepreneurship by creating a venture that grows to what by all accounts would be considered a significant scale. A nonprofit venture that reaches such a significant scale can validate nonprofit enterprise for the general public and then serve as a shining example and catalyst for greater growth in the field. This may be a goal of greater interest to funders of nonprofit enterprise than to the particular organization, but being recognized as a model enterprise would surely be of interest to most nonprofits.

A significant number of nonprofit ventures aspire to grow to a larger scale. A recent major survey of the field conducted for the Pew Charitable Trusts by Cynthia W. Massarsky and Samantha L. Beinhacker, deputy directors of the Yale School of Management–The Goldman Sachs Foundation Partnership on Nonprofit Ventures found that "many nonprofits aspire to see their ventures grow and replicate. Forty-seven percent say they have developed a strategy to move their venture "to scale" or next stage. Another 42 percent say they have not yet developed a strategy to replicate their venture, but plan to do so. Forty-six percent say they have already implemented their scale-up strategy, and many (56 percent) of these organizations say they feel their scale-up strategy has been successful."[1]

Despite these aspirations and the self-assessments of many that they have achieved their desired scale, this author's review of the field concludes that in general nonprofits have a long way to go before they're able to grow their ventures to scale. While no explicit market exists to signify definitely the point at which nonprofits achieve an optimal scale, it is this author's contention that the breakthrough of one or several ventures in going to scale will encourage others to follow suit.

This chapter focuses on providing a working definition of what going to scale means for nonprofit enterprises, the significant challenges that need to be addressed in getting to scale, and recommendations of steps to take to attain scale for existing and new nonprofit ventures.

Definitions of *Going to Scale*

There are many ways that *going to scale* is currently defined within the scope of nonprofit enterprise. In almost all definitions it means getting bigger. The concept of *rightsizing* is not inherent in the term; this euphemism for reductions in an organization is also an attempt to create the correct scale for an organization. In general, however, the meaning of *going to scale* and the predominant challenge for nonprofit ventures is to get larger.

Perhaps the most important aspect of going to scale involves the practical steps required to grow a business. While there are numerous ways that businesses grow, the strategic questions that most nonprofit ventures face if they want to grow are as follows:

- How to expand geographically
- How to grow the number of customers locally
- How to move a product or service into new distribution channels or into new markets in the same geographic area
- How to broaden the range of products or services
- How to affect a combination of any or all of these items

The *Familiar* Definition: Getting Very Big

In its imprecise but typically construed meaning, *going to scale* connotes growing a nonprofit enterprise large enough so that it achieves general brand awareness and so that its activities are commonly accessible. This definition may be connected to the aspirations and possibilities created by the "new economy" era, in which *going to scale* meant converting an idea into a universal way of doing things. This is perhaps best exemplified in the business models of companies such as eBay, Google, and Amazon.com. None of these companies existed ten years ago; they all represent ventures with high brand recognition and wide distribution. This hyperbolic definition of *going to scale* defines the outside boundaries of the concept and has an effect on discussions of going to scale. The familiar or perceptual definition of *going to scale* is thus that something is big if enough people perceive it as big.

To those who think that such scale is attainable only in for-profit business, particularly in the high-tech new economy model, it is important to point out that many nonprofit activities have achieved this same kind of scale and universal awareness. The following two examples are reminders of the scale a nonprofit can potentially achieve quickly, and they provide indicators of both the opportunity for *going to scale* and the distance that nonprofit enterprise must travel to get there.

The Red Cross was a social invention of one person, Henry Dunant, who in 1859 viewed the battle carnage in Northern Italy and established an organization to bring aid to the war-injured. Wars had been going on forever, battlefields were historically inhumane places, and the injured and prisoners of war had received scant attention throughout humanity's history. The confluence of the extreme carnage of modern warfare, the advances in medicine, and the social compacts of the "modern" industrial world created a time ripe for a new worldview. Within five years of Dunant's first efforts on behalf of the injured and the captured, the First Geneva Convention was issued. It dealt with how the injured and prisoners of war should be treated (humanely) and identified the nonprofit Red Cross as the agency to administer fairness. Within twenty years the Red Cross had become an international organization that changed fundamentally the ways of providing for people in distress.

Habitat for Humanity is a nonprofit started in 1976 by Millard and Linda Fuller. Within its scant thirty-plus years of existence, Habitat has built more than 150,000 houses in three thousand communities throughout the world. Affordable housing was not a new concept back in 1976, and neither was the idea of self-help community barn raisings and other such activities. In those days the Fullers did not have the Internet available to them to create a market for Habitat. Nevertheless, because of the personal vision of the founders, their ability to tell the story in the right places, and the embodiment of the story in former President Jimmy Carter, Habitat has reached a real and perceptual scale of tremendous international awareness since its founding.

By reflecting on the importance, power, and breadth of these two nonprofit organizations we can understand what true scale can mean. Those who aspire to grow their nonprofit venture to such a scale have great examples in the nonprofit world to hold up as both icons and opportunities for learning.

The *Precise* Definition: The Proper Calibration of Value Creation, Organizational Capacity, and the Market Environment

Perhaps a more precise definition of what it means to *go to scale* is in order. For our purposes, then, let us say that it is the proper calibration of value creation, organizational capacity, and the market environment. The ideal scale or size for a nonprofit venture is as follows:

- It corresponds to the aspirations and mission of the organization.
- It has the ability to create a sustainable business model in the absence of unusual short-term subsidies.
- It makes appropriate use of initial, current, and potential investments of financial capital.
- It fits the current and future capacity of the venture and organization.
- It matches the value created by the venture for its customers.

According to this definition, scale is

- The value that the product or service creates for potential customers that is greater than the competition or substitutes
- Constrained in its ability to attract resources by the capacity of the organization
- Either constrained or enhanced by the aspirations, mission, and strategy of the enterprise and the nonprofit organization of which it is a part.

This is perhaps the most rigorous and realistic definition of what scale is for non-profit enterprise.

In such an analysis, a nonprofit venture must grow to a certain point so that the nonprofit parent can both have sufficient impact and create a sustainable business to justify its initial and ongoing investment and the investments of outside funders. A realistic business model can help identify the best scale for an organization to strive for to accomplish these purposes.

This is where a scaling analysis most closely resembles a return-on-investment analysis of a private-sector venture. In its business venture, the nonprofit must of course also take into account the social return-on-investment that the venture creates (if no social value is created, the venture is strictly an investment on the part of the organization), but such social-value creation can be sustainable only if the venture has a clear path for financial sustainability.

Many nonprofit organizations embark on creating an enterprise without fully analyzing all the costs and risks associated with such an endeavor. Such "innocence" is an inevitable part of the early stages of any activity. Before starting its venture, however, a nonprofit may not be able to gauge, or even fully understand, how much money, time, and other resources are going to be invested in the enterprise, and what the gross margins and cash flow needs are (that is, how much business has to be done for the activity both to become profitable and return the initial investment).

The classic problems of undercapitalizing the start-up of a small business are not as threatening to the health of an organization as when it considers taking its small venture and bringing it to scale. These challenges are in fact magnified during the growth stage, when the nonprofit venture's capital needs must compete with the nonprofit's mission-based programmatic activities for the use of cash.

Whatever challenges there are in the cash crunch of the start-up phase, cash is particularly more challenging during the nonprofit enterprise's periods of growth. The amount of resources needed to grow a venture is often much greater than the amount needed in the early start-up period. Further, nonprofit ventures usually have a much more difficult time in the nonprofit capital markets during the midstage, mezzanine financing period of growth than they have obtaining start-up funding from foundations and other sources. This is a particular vagary of nonprofit social markets, where capital often flows more easily when a venture is on the drawing board than it does when the business is up and running.

For the venture in a nonprofit environment, *scaling* capital is often needed for and spent on items that are invisible to most members of the organization. Yet using limited resources to pay for new capacity-building equipment and for the marketing of a venture rather than on the primary mission of the organization can create significant internal challenges for the venture and its champions. While the initial launch of the business may have been very appealing to the organization and its financial supporters, the continued investment in the business may seem counterintuitive.

Specifically, the organization is frequently challenged by internal and external questions such as Wasn't the business started to provide capital for the other parts of the organization? Why is significantly more cash, reputation, and executive time being spent on the business five years out? The start-up was grant funded and thus a very limited risk to the organization. The expansion has significantly more internal risk capital at play; so what happens if it doesn't work?

One need only imagine the internal strains on an organization when the investment to grow means, at least in the short run, that a program investment cannot be made at the same time. Take the example of an organization serving homeless families that operates a social venture. To grow, the venture may have to invest in a critical but expensive inventory-control system, but that investment will limit the nonprofit's ability to support its food-donation program for homeless families. Thus, the limits on growth for the nonprofit venture are governed by the marketplace, the desired effect on the organization, the capacities of the organization, and the unique capital challenges inherent in the nonprofit sector:

- The marketplace challenge requires the venture to perform an analysis of the competitive advantages the venture has in the industry in which it will compete, remembering that the good intentions and name recognition of the parent nonprofit are not necessarily competitive advantages.
- The growth of the business is constrained by the underlying purpose of the organization. If the organization's mission is to create jobs for people who live in a particular neighborhood, then unless the mission changes, the business potential is governed by the number of people who could possibly be employed.
- Raising capital for nonprofit ventures places certain limits on growth. A nonprofit cannot offer equity to investors, cannot go public, and has limited exit strategies under normal circumstances. So this threshold of moving to for-profit status may be a step that nonprofit ventures will increasingly consider as they attempt to grow significantly. Of course there are many intended and unintended consequences of such a move, and we shall consider them carefully in the sections that follow.

A Working Definition for *Going to Scale*

I would argue that in order to become a more significant social movement nonprofit ventures must meet both the precise as well as the familiar definitions of going to scale. In other words, a few ventures have to get really big, and many have to become truly successful. The field is still in need of ventures that achieve the name recognition, status, and scale of a Microsoft, Google, Ben & Jerry's, Red Cross, or Habitat for Humanity.

There are some circumstances in which quasi-nonprofit ventures have become big: the greeting card operations at UNICEF and the World Wildlife Fund are two widely known and successful businesses that generate wealth for their parent organizations. Some nonprofit health and hospital organizations, such as the Kaiser hospital system and Blue Cross, are or have been quasi-nonprofits, but these are not what people generally mean by nonprofit enterprise, although clearly there is something to be learned from these organizations.

Further, with the emergence of a significant number of nonprofits in the nonprofit enterprise arena, there are many candidates ready to reach the second and grander definition of achieving scale. In the United States, the Social Enterprise Alliance's annual meeting of nonprofit entrepreneurs, called the National Gathering, has met since 1998, with representatives from an increasing number of small start-up and growing ventures participating. In just two years of soliciting entrants to its National Business Plan Competition for Nonprofit Organizations, the Yale School of Management–The Goldman Sachs Foundation Partnership on Nonprofit Ventures has received more than a thousand submissions from nonprofits interested in creating or expanding their ventures.

For nonprofit enterprises to be truly successful, out of this increasing number of nonprofit ventures must come a handful that should attain the familiar definition of scale. The field needs icons that create a common awareness and understanding of nonprofit ventures, much in the same way as Google helped everyone quickly understand the concept of a search engine. The success of a handful of nonprofit enterprises may prove to be the tipping point for many more organizations in altering the structural challenges now facing nonprofits. These challenges include access to capital and talent, and willingness for organizations to grow.

In the last several years, many social ventures have taken steps to seek a larger scale. Some may take exception to the central argument here that the great breakthrough has not yet occurred. But because this is a perceptual rather than an absolute concept, those who feel that scale has been achieved have an equal claim to such a position.

In this chapter, some of the issues that such successful nonprofit ventures have faced and overcome are discussed as guidance for those organizations that are ready to meet the challenge of growth. The chapter also looks at what may be required for the organization that breaks through the glass ceiling on growth.

One final note is in order before we proceed. The primary focus of this chapter is on nonprofit enterprise in the United States. There are international examples of ventures that have achieved significantly greater scale than has been achieved in this country. The Grameen Bank and phone company in Bangladesh, the Cabbages and Condoms Chain in Thailand, Approtec in Kenya, and enterprises in other African countries are international examples of exceptions to the arguments presented in this chapter. The primary difference between these organizations and those in the United States is that these ventures have succeeded in environments where there is no traditional market or the market has failed, and they are providing something of value to consumers in places where traditional business has not. Most nonprofit ventures in the United States must compete in industries where there is intense competition from the traditional business community. Although U.S.-based nonprofit ventures may have parent organizations whose primary mission is a response to a market failure, their nonprofit enterprise is rarely such.

The Status of the Field Today

The field of nonprofit enterprise is definitely growing, even if most individual ventures are not yet moving to scale. Reaching greater scale is now more likely, and perhaps more necessary, because many other aspects of the nonprofit enterprise movement have matured. Programs such as the Partnership on Nonprofit Ventures' National Business Plan Competition for Nonprofit Organizations have brought additional people and greater attention to the field. Their first annual conference and awards ceremony brought more than four hundred people to New York City in the spring of 2003. Another competition, Social Stimulus, welcomed four hundred nonprofit entrants. The membership group Social Enterprise Alliance has also become a bellwether for the rapid rise in interest in and entrants into the field of nonprofit enterprise. This organization now includes six hundred members, 65 percent of whom are practitioners, and there are more than four thousand people on the mailing list. Some four hundred representatives of nonprofits, funders, and other interested parties attended the organization's fourth annual national gathering in Minneapolis in December 2002.

Philanthropic leaders such as Ed Skloot of the Surdna Foundation and Melinda Tuan of the Roberts Enterprise Development Fund (REDF) have made a specialty of funding nonprofit enterprise. In fact, REDF has created portfolios of organizations involved in nonprofit enterprises. Supporting organizations such as New Profit Inc. and New Schools have been created to apply a venture investor approach to making scale more attainable. Research in the field is maturing rapidly, led by the seminal work of J. Gregory Dees of Duke's Fuqua School of Business, and numerous universities now offer programs in nonprofit entrepreneurship in their graduate programs. All of these efforts have brought a greater number and variety to the field, and there is every indication that nonprofit enterprise is quickly becoming part of the jargon of the sector.

This blooming of interest and early-stage activity may well be a critical step in bringing individual nonprofit ventures to scale. A free-market quasi-Darwinian analysis might conclude that there needs to be a plethora of early-stage ventures from which a few large ones eventually evolve.

The nonprofit marketplace, however, is very different from the commercial sector in many ways. There are numerous reasons that the ability of an individual nonprofit venture to grow to scale may be particularly constrained. In fact, nonprofit ventures may be smaller than their free-market capacity because of the very nature of the nonprofit sector itself. Jeff Bradach, cofounder of the Bridgespan Group and an expert in the area of franchising in the for-profit world, has devoted significant time to researching the constraints to growth in the nonprofit world. Bradach has found the following:

> With few exceptions the nonprofit sector in the United States is comprised of cottage enterprises—thousands upon thousands of programs, each operating in a single neighborhood, in a single city or town. Often, this may be the most appropriate form of organization, but in some, perhaps many, cases it represents a substantial loss to society overall. Time, funds, and imagination are poured into new programs that at best reinvent the wheel, while the potential of programs that have already proven their effectiveness remains sadly underdeveloped.[2]

Nonprofit ventures operating on a larger scale will have the ability to leverage more social capital because they will solve the reinventions of the wheel problem and will spread their effectiveness to greater numbers of people. To achieve this scale, however, these ventures will have to overcome the traditional cottage-industry bias in the field. This bias is often held by funders, particularly local governments and place-based funders; by the communities served, which are loath to allow "outside" ventures onto "their" turf; and by the organizations themselves, which often feel it would be a betrayal to leave their home community.

We may in fact be approaching a tipping-point phenomenon in nonprofit ventures, where some of the enterprises now working to achieve more significant scale may achieve a breakthrough that radically alters the ecology of nonprofit enterprise. If so, an examination of the steps taken by others along the pathway to growth will be useful for current and future practitioners.

Challenges to Growing the Nonprofit Venture

There are significant impediments to growing nonprofit ventures. These challenges are structural because of the very nature of nonprofit ventures, and operational because they are exacerbated by the culture clash of running a business within or connected to a nonprofit organization. Several of these challenges are described here.

The Mission Fit Challenge, or What Business Are We in Anyway?

Most nonprofit ventures are subsets of a larger parent organization that has a mission that is often not inherently connected to the venture's business plan. These businesses are usually started to support the organization's mission but are typically not the reason the organization was founded. This creates significant structural problems in the areas of mission, strategy, industry, and scope of the parent organization and its business. This very basic challenge to growth raises the fundamental question, What business are we in anyway?

In her groundbreaking work on nonprofit management,[3] Sharon Oster described the six forces that a nonprofit must consider in its industry when developing an effective strategy.[4] A critical first step for such an analysis is for the organization to define more clearly its scope.[5] The nonprofit venture, however, has additional strategic challenges because in most cases the venture is a subset of a larger nonprofit. For many nonprofit ventures, the question of what industry they are in is often a challenge. The manufacturing plant, the catering company, and the sheet metal plant are usually in different industries than their parent organization, and the competitive analysis of the parent and the nonprofit venture do not always align. To succeed, a corporate strategy must be developed that allows the particular business to compete specifically in its industry and that also aligns the resources of the parent as a competitive advantage for the venture. Such a complex analysis and focus for the parent organization is a daunting task for most nonprofits.

Further, there are often contradictions. To succeed, businesses must contain their costs of goods, often translated as labor costs. One of the most common goals of nonprofit enterprises is the creation of jobs that pay decent wages, often for a workforce not valued in the competitive labor market. To be as productive as the workforce of its competitors, nonprofit ventures often have to pay (or develop indirect subsidies to pay) for the inherent productivity cost of training, supporting, and employing a workforce that has structural challenges. This problem is obviated in the affirmative business model of nonprofits that hire severely disabled workers under a sheltered workshop license and pay them less than the prevailing wage. This sheltered workshop model does not work for those organizations that want to pay wages that can move people out of poverty.

The Measurement Challenge

What is the organization trying to achieve and how can potential investors know if the organization merits the investment? Measurement in the nonprofit enterprise arena brings us to both the structural challenge of the double bottom line and to the significant operational challenge of how you measure the impact of the nonfiscal benefits and costs of the venture. Businesses know what they need to measure: top-line growth, cost of goods, bottom-line return, return-on-investment, market share, and so on. These are all universally accepted concepts that help determine the relative success or failure of a business venture and can be used by investors, managers, banks, and others to determine where capital should and should not go.

By design, nonprofit ventures are trying to accomplish more than just bottom-line returns. Leaving aside for a moment for-profit subsidiaries of nonprofits, whose only social benefit is the cash they generate for the nonprofit parent (gift stores for museums are perhaps the best example of this), almost all nonprofit ventures have as a goal a second bottom line. Frequently this bottom line is job creation for the community that the organization is designed to serve (examples of these kind of ventures include agencies doing job creation with low-income communities, working with disabled citizens, and so on). Many times the purpose is to promulgate the information the organization thinks is valuable; organizations that are doing education reform, for example, often create teaching materials and other collaterals to help change the educational environment that is aligned with their mission. Some nonprofit ventures are attempts to develop a revenue source from these materials.

The challenge of measuring the nonfinancial returns has been one of the most important and vexing issues for the nonprofit enterprise movement. Through the efforts of Jed Emerson and Melinda Tuan, REDF has done pioneering work in the area of social return on investments.

> In the past few years, foundations across the country have placed increasing emphasis on evaluation and social outcome measurement for the nonprofit programs they fund. Yet many of these same foundations are providing little funding to build nonprofit organizations' capacity to measure their social outcomes. As a result, most nonprofits are unable to deliver accurate social outcome results required by the funding community, and foundations are increasingly frustrated about the low quality of the social outcome reports they receive.
>
> From 1997 to 1998, we worked with our portfolio members to increase each organization's capacity to measure, track and utilize business information and social outcome information about their enterprises and the more than 600 individuals employed in their enterprises. We were interested in whether employment in a social purpose enterprise resulted in improved outcomes for individuals across areas such as income, barriers to employment, housing stability, social service usage, self-esteem, and social support. We were also interested in connecting the social outcomes of enterprise employment with the financial investment required to create that employment opportunity—to calculate a social return on investment (SROI) for each enterprise.[6]

This measuring of social return provides another way of valuing the worth of the endeavor. Perhaps at some future date the nonfinancial value creation of nonprofit ventures will be monetized and will provide a significant way of sustaining the nonprofit business model. Jed Emerson, in his current work at Stanford University and with the Hewlett Foundation, has developed what he calls the *blended value proposition*, which argues that since all businesses are inherently creating (or destroying) value in the financial, social, and environmental areas, investments in and the true worth of the businesses should be based on the total value creation or their blended value proposition.

Unfortunately, the time horizon for Emerson's reward for the value creation beyond the financial bottom line is quite long. Further, the commitment of time and resources necessary to create social return measurement systems are significant. The Ongoing Assessment of Social ImpactS (OASIS) system supported by REDF provides organizations with an invaluable tool to evaluate their effectiveness with the people served, but this value is worth more to the mission portion of the business than it is to the profitability of the nonprofit enterprise. In a narrow analysis of the industry, the venture's investment in complex social return measurements is a competitive disadvantage. The ability to document the cost of job creation, the retention costs, and the long-term social saving of putting someone into a job rather than their remaining on welfare is of limited help to a bakery in selling more cakes compared to buying a new state-of-the-art oven. It may provide the business with some greater access to social capital from foundations and investors who value this service, as well as give the parent nonprofit information about the effectiveness of its venture in addressing the mission. In these arenas it can influence which investments create the best social return. Because a system like OASIS can improve the overall organization's capacity, it is a very good investment of time and effort. It helps the organization identify the value of a particular program or business in advancing its mission. It can also help them differentiate themselves from their competition. And it can help overall in the capacity of the organization to manage better. It may thus help support the growth of the nonprofit, but less directly bring the business to scale.

Measuring social return as a cost over and above the typical costs needed to compete in a given venture's industry requires attention away from the core issues of the business and is thus an additional challenge to the growth of the business. Although measuring social return may be a good and possibly essential challenge for the nonprofit venture to take on, the key point here is that in doing so the costs of going to scale are likely to increase significantly.

Challenges in Securing Social Capital

The social capital market is not in any way analogous to traditional capital markets in terms of rational use of resources, efficiency, and so on. Jeff Bradach,[7]

William Ryan, and others have written about the structural challenges in the capital market, identifying such issues as the primary interest among foundations in funding new projects, the absence of analogs for "mezzanine financing," and the inability of most nonprofits to provide equity for investors. Because of the challenges of the social capital market, many of the nonprofit ventures that have grown to any scale have an "angel" investor or special circumstance that made their initial growth possible. The limits of such angels may account for the current limits to growth of the field.

Social capital market is a term widely used to describe grants, loans, program-related investments, equity, and other financing tools to support nonprofit ventures that are made available by foundations, government agencies, corporations, and individuals that are operating independently of one another. The relative size of the social capital market is usually seen to be much smaller than traditional capital markets. Further, the fundamental functioning of this market does not have the innate efficiency or discipline or "invisible hand" of the traditional market because the social capital market does not have the underlying free-market forces that reward good investments with good returns. The investors in the polio vaccine may have saved countless lives and billions of dollars, but the foundations that paid for it got less of a financial return than the investors in novelty Pet Rocks.

A seminal study on the current state of the social capital market was presented by William P. Ryan in a 2001 report for the Fannie Mae Foundation and the Rockefeller Foundation.[8] In his report, Ryan wrote:

> The current nonprofit capital market is disorganized and not clearly segmented, which imposes high transaction and opportunity costs on managers, who are forced to spend huge amounts of time fundraising. And, argues Jed Emerson of the Harvard Business School, the funding they do get is often packaged and conditioned—in small amounts, with many restrictions, and without regard to the developmental stage of the nonprofit—in unhelpful ways. "The disorderliness and complexity of the philanthropic funding environment," according to Allen Grossman of the Harvard Business School, "distracts nonprofit management, shifting focus away from organizational performance."[9]

Ryan goes on to cite some of the specific capital challenges facing nonprofit organizations that are considering growing their ventures:

> Social enterprises aimed at self-sufficiency solve one type of capital problem, but generate another. A nonprofit that succeeds in offering a service in the market can gain the enormous benefit of unrestricted income, the surplus of which becomes working capital. But in order to develop the capacity and scale to reach that point of self-sufficiency, social enterprises, like any enterprise, normally require upfront or working capital.

An assessment of social-purpose businesses funded in six cities as part of the Venture Fund Initiative suggests that social-purpose businesses often face the same kind of capital crunches as traditional nonprofits. (Many of these were formed on the sheltered-work model, which creates a business for the purpose of employing and training people who need intensive support before they are ready to compete in the open labor market.) The study found the capital problem was especially acute when a social-purpose business begins to grow and needs to expand its facilities, equipment, staff, inventory or some combination of these, in order to keep up with demand. By this point, many nonprofit organizations are effectively "tapped out"—they have already invested whatever discretionary funds might have been available when they created the business. And whereas potential sales growth might easily justify a loan, there is little or nothing left to collateralize that loan.[10]

The capital challenge lies not just in the external problems in the social capital markets, but also in the nonprofit organizations' internal issues around the use of capital. For the business venture to grow, a significant amount of the overall nonprofit's resources must be devoted to the effort. This includes internal investments that take resources away from activities devoted directly to the mission. This means that fund development efforts, or fundraising, are focused more on the business and less on the programs. This can add significant debt, which can affect the entire organization. This also means that senior management—the executive director, chief financial officer, and other organization leaders—are spending increasing amounts of time on the nonprofit venture rather than on the core services of the organization.

Further, nonprofit ventures are innately higher risks than typical mission-based programs. The risk tolerance among managers of the nonprofit's core activities is not generally as high for running a business as it is for running the organization's programs, because putting the programs at risk for a venture that might not succeed may have a negative effect on the entire organization. Everyone loves the business when it is "throwing off" excess cash to support the organization; yet these same people are ready to abandon it in the inevitable cycles when the business absorbs more cash than it provides.

Much of the risk mitigation in the more successful nonprofit ventures has occurred because a major "angel" investor has made the startup phase possible. Boeing Aircraft helped kick start one significant nonprofit venture, Pioneer Industries of Seattle. Ben & Jerry's made the growth and stability of Yonkers-based Greyston Bakery possible. The REDF made the initial growth stages of its groups such as Rubicon Enterprises and Juma Industries a reality, and the federal set-aside programs created a system that supported the growth of "affirmative businesses" such as Skookum Educational Programs, a Washington State nonprofit that markets vehicle maintenance, recycling, janitorial, and light manufacturing services.

Angel investors or set-aside situations can limit options for growth significantly. While all of the aforementioned nonprofit ventures have grown beyond the investment provided by their angels, for the most part the angel investors are still a significant part of the business model. A new competitive advantage to replace the angel phase will be needed for a major breakthrough in scale.

Challenges in Providing a Market Return to the Innovator

One the biggest structural challenges in *going to scale* is the motivation of the innovators of the program. Nonprofit ventures have to succeed in competing markets while going head-to-head with companies that reward their innovators and initial risk takers with significant financial return. Financial return to the innovators of nonprofit enterprise is still considered anathema. While there are certainly many who do it for personal, altruistic, or purposeful reasons, this inherently limits the pool of social innovators, especially when you require someone with industry-specific expertise in a field that typically has difficulty attracting entrepreneurs and innovators who are not financially motivated.

The reality of this constraint can be seen in the appeal and challenge of finding managers and social innovators from business schools. Many classes on social and nonprofit entrepreneurship are now taught in the best business schools, and many motivated and bright MBA students are expressing interest in nonprofit enterprise. Numerous internship and fellowship programs bring MBA students into nonprofit ventures for a limited period. The differing pay scales in the nonprofit and corporate sectors remains one of the biggest constraints in bringing in people with MBAs on a more permanent basis into a field in which they say they would love to work, underscoring the underlying motivational challenge for the field. For example, Stanford University operates one of the nation's premier centers on the work of nonprofits, the Center for Social Innovation (CSI). Students identify CSI as a motivating factor for coming to Stanford, and they participate heavily in its numerous nonprofit activities, including summer internships, nonprofit board fellowships, classes on social entrepreneurship, and so on. Nevertheless, typically only 2 to 5 percent of graduates go on to work in nonprofit organizations.

This financial reward challenge is not just for new entrants but is constant throughout the professional careers of leaders of nonprofit ventures. To paraphrase a comment by social enterprise scholar Greg Dees, "Society and the newspaper will applaud the inventor of the Pet Rock and will delight in his earning millions of dollars for creating something of no value, but if a nonprofit leader creates an innovation that solves a universal social challenge and works diligently in the field for years, he will be excoriated on the front page of the newspaper if his compensation is [one-tenth] the pay of a CEO of a failing mid-sized telecom company."[11]

The "scandal" that emerged in 2003 over the creator of the highly successful nonprofit Nehemiah Corporation clearly lays out this dilemma. An investigative article in the June 15, 2003 edition of the *Sacramento Bee* reported the following:

> In 1996, Don Harris, a young preacher and lawyer trying to develop senior housing in south Sacramento, had a vision.
>
> He would create a nonprofit company that would give hard-working Americans with good credit but modest incomes and little or no savings the down payments they needed to buy homes. The company then would recoup those down payments, plus a small service fee, from sellers in slow markets happy to get qualified buyers willing to pay full market price.
>
> Nearly 150,000 families—5,000 of them in Sacramento—have realized the American dream of home ownership with the help of Nehemiah's down-payment "gifts." Some 40 percent are people of color.
>
> The company, which now grosses $160 million a year, has made Harris a millionaire—and therein lies the problem.
>
> The charismatic Harris, whom friends and even foes have likened to Martin Luther King Jr., is locked in a brutal legal struggle with Nehemiah over his stake in Invision, a for-profit firm Nehemiah hired to market the pioneering home-buying program nationwide.
>
> In double-barreled lawsuits, Nehemiah accuses Harris and Invision of fraud, self-dealing, breach of contract, theft of trade secrets and misappropriating $42 million in service fees.
>
> The bruising legal dispute seems partly the result of Nehemiah's runaway success. In 1998, Nehemiah's board of directors—hand-picked by Harris, who was chairman—voted to give him a bonus of $40,000 in stock in Invision on top of his $120,000 annual salary. Four years later, Harris says, his Invision stock had made him $4 million.
>
> Harris left Nehemiah a year ago and now runs a for-profit company that is one of its fiercest competitors. He claims his hand-chosen successor, Nehemiah President and CEO Scott Syphax, turned Nehemiah's board against him.
>
> "The bottom line is, was my compensation reasonable or unreasonable?" says Harris, 38. He insists it was reasonable: "I created the business model that's become a $30 billion industry replicated throughout America."[12]

It's hard to imagine a for-profit company of that size and success suing its founder for a compensation package of this magnitude. Without taking sides in the Nehemiah debate, high compensation in the nonprofit world does require deeper consideration and scrutiny than payments in other arenas. At a minimum, this is an additional constraint for the nonprofit business venture.

The Governance Challenge

Nonprofit organizations are governed and run by people who believe in the missions of their organizations. The relationships, skills, and orientation of these people when they are on the board are better suited for the social mission of the organization than for the business needs of the venture. While there may be many highly successful business men and woman on the board, they often wear their charity hat rather than their business hat when serving on the board, focusing on the needs of the consumers and clients the organization is trying to solve rather than on the constraints and competitive issues of the business.

Many organizations address this problem by building advisory committees or venture committees to oversee the business venture, and there can be much to gain from such a structure. The integration, however, of the venture oversight and the organization governance remains an inherent structural issue with which all nonprofit ventures must deal and that traditional businesses do not have to address.

The Management Culture Challenge

Most social ventures are embedded in organizations with staff that are trained to focus on the social problems confronting the community, not on the competitive realities of running a business venture. This situation is most acute at the management team level, where social worker and community organizing types are often uneasy with the "ruthless" coldhearted analysis undertaken by business managers, and business managers are at odds with the "softheaded do-gooder" approaches taken by program managers.

Organizational Culture Wars on the Homefront

Nonprofit ventures must compete side-by-side with for-profits in their specific industry, and not as nonprofit organizations that are doing good in the world. The managers are part of a management team within the nonprofit that is usually in a different industry. Further, the colleagues of the general manager of the venture are usually trained in other areas (such as public management, social work, the arts, and so on) and often have decidedly different ways of conceiving the nature of the work to be accomplished.

The problems that occur in these culture wars become an issue when the business is introduced into the nonprofit environment and the "business types" and the "mission types" have to work together. For those organizations that make the cultural changes necessary for this to succeed there may then be a period of relative harmony among these various managers, once the business stabilizes. When the business wants to scale up, however, these issues may arise again.

There are certainly many benefits that can result from these healthy tensions. Getting managers to work together can protect the mission of both the venture and the parent organization. The trade-off, though, is that the venture manager has an additional set of challenges in considering the concerns and culture of the nonprofit management team, and vice versa.

Beyond the Challenges: What Organizations Can Do to Reach a Greater Scale

In spite of all these challenges, nonprofit enterprises are continuing to push forward and reach an even greater scale. What follows are guideposts that your organization should consider as your venture plans to cross this new frontier.

How do you know if your venture is ready to grow to scale? Your organization and venture have the internal capacity to manage the demands of growth. You have the administrative, financial, management information, and other core systems necessary to support rapid growth. You are prepared for the financial and other risks that are necessary and inevitable parts of growing a business venture.

Your nonprofit has learned to successfully integrate your venture into the normal course of doing business. Your business venture is integrated into the culture of the organization. Your enterprise and program managers have developed methods to integrate their work in support of each other and the mission. The board of your nonprofit has embraced its role of governing the business and has incorporated the necessary sets of skills to provide effective oversight for the business. Your venture has a venture champion, deep support from the senior leadership of your nonprofit, and a guarantee that this support will continue if the champion leaves.

The nonprofit organization is prepared for the potential that the "tail will wag the dog," and that if the venture is allowed to grow it may dwarf the organization. Your nonprofit's identity can benefit from, or at least withstand, such a tail-wagging change. Your internal managers are prepared to allow the "tallest poppy" to flourish, and they will support its ascendancy. The mission of your nonprofit will be advanced, not lost, if the business succeeds on a very large scale.

Your nonprofit organization is prepared for, and capable of, withstanding a major failure. Because business ventures are inherently risky propositions, and because the best business plans and the best managers can fail, you are aware of the social good that is being put at risk by taking the business to scale. Internally closing down a program is always hard. Closing down a failed business venture within a social program, particularly one of large scale, is a greater challenge in a nonprofit that is not used to ending activities for financial reasons alone. Nonprofits are used to building things, to defending them, and to terminating activities only when an external funder pulls the plug. Closing a business venture is usually an internal decision of management and the board, and such self-inflicted closures are hard to sell in nonprofit environments. Your nonprofit organization and venture team understand these realities, and are prepared to face them should they come to pass.

What will we need in order to grow to scale? You will need to understand that growing to scale will require a significant amount of money, likely up front. Undercapitalization is almost always the greatest challenge for growing businesses. It always takes more money and more time to reach the "sweet spot" of large-scale profitability. Further, *going to scale* implies breaking through the smaller local-market level of business, which usually means significant time to learn new markets to build brand equity. But nonprofit ventures don't have access to typical financing. Unless you incorporate as a for-profit subsidiary, you will not have equity to sell. There is no initial public offering. Lenders don't like to go at high risk or overly leverage a nonprofit because of the pain of closing down such an activity.

Since your venture may well be embedded in your nonprofit, the alternative to having significant working capital is to use funds from other parts of your organization. Given the fact that business ventures seem always to take a long time to reach profitability, and because achieving positive cash flow for a growing business is sometimes even a further horizon than profitability because of the costs of reinvestment, the potential for tremendous internal pressures and resentments are a major risk to the success of the venture, even in reasonably secure nonprofits.

You will need a clear concept of the competitive advantage of the business. The bigger the bet is, the steeper the competition is going to be. A very thorough industry, mission and strategy, and competitive analysis must be done to make certain that there really is something of value that you can offer, and that there are customers who are willing to choose your product or service.

Once you've identified your competitive advantage and strategy, your nonprofit venture will most likely attempt to expand its markets. As mentioned at the beginning of this chapter, this will mean focusing on one of the following:

- Expanding geographically
- Growing the number of customers locally
- Moving a product or service into new distribution channels or into new markets in the same geographic area
- Broadening the range of products or services
- Affecting a combination of any or all of these strategies

You will need a breakthrough approach in using the natural competitive advantage of being a nonprofit venture. While nonprofits naively feel that they will get business because they are the "good guys," there has been a very limited but major benefit to date of the social value of the parent organization. There have been some major breakthroughs in cause-related marketing, but this typically affiliates a large corporation with a social cause. Cause marketing can serve as the centerpiece of a corporate marketing strategy, but nonprofit-owned business ventures have not yet leveraged this advantage to its full potential.

The organization will need to give the business all the room it needs to grow. A business is typically a faster mover than the nonprofit of which it is a part. Managing these dual paces can be very hard.

Conclusion

The number of nonprofit organizations that operate business ventures as a part of their strategy is expanding rapidly. Many of these nonprofit business ventures have been operating for many years, and some have attained a relative degree of scale, with a handful generating in excess of $10 million dollars in gross revenue and a smaller cadre somewhat more.

Without slighting the incredibly hard work and diligence necessary to achieve such success, it is important to put these achievements in perspective. The goal for most of these enterprises is to support the parent organization's mission: the creation of unrestricted revenues to pay for the mission-related programs of the organization. In general, a nonprofit venture that generates $10 million in sales will be a success if it has a 10 percent net margin and thus has $1 million in unrestricted income to support the mission aspects of the organization.

Nonprofit enterprises are an important part of a diversified funding strategy for many nonprofit organizations. When they can also create jobs for people who are the mission constituencies of the organization, these businesses provide more benefits to the organization. When the perspective and business discipline of the nonprofit venture are properly blended with the perspective and social goals of the organization, the organization benefits even more.

For nonprofit ventures to achieve a significant place in the economics of how social problems are addressed, the next step is for capable ventures to grow to scale. For the overwhelming majority of nonprofit enterprises, this step has not been reached and remains an important Rubicon for the field to cross.

There are many structural constraints that make reaching such a scale more daunting for nonprofit ventures than for the for-profit sector. These constraints are relative rather than absolute, and we may soon see the emergence of one or a handful of nonprofits that attain a size that by anyone's standards will be defined as truly having *gone to scale*. As is often the case, once the first group makes it, many others may follow.

Notes

1. Yale School of Management–The Goldman Sachs Foundation Partnership on Nonprofit Ventures. "Enterprising Nonprofits: Revenue Generation in the Nonprofit Sector." Survey conducted by Cynthia W. Massarsky and Samantha L. Beinhacker for The Pew Charitable Trusts, 2002. (http://www.ventures.yale.edu/docs/Enterprising_Nonprofits.pdf).
2. Bradach, J. "Going to Scale: The Challenge of Replicating Social Programs." *Stanford Social Innovation Review*, 2003, *1*(1), 19.
3. Oster, S. M. *Strategic Management for Nonprofit Organizations*. New York: Oxford University Press, 1995.
4. As Oster points out, this is an adaptation from the five forces work that Michael Porter developed for the corporate sector. For more information, see M. E. Porter, *Competitive Strategy*. New York: Simon & Schuster, 1998.
5. Saloner, G., Shepard, A., and Podolny, J. *Strategic Management*. New York: John Wiley, 2000.
6. Tuan, M. "A Letter from the Roberts Enterprise Development Fund." In *An Information OASIS: The Design and Implementation of Comprehensive and Customized Client Information and Tracking Systems*. San Francisco: Roberts Enterprise Development Fund, Spring 2002, pp. 4–5.
7. Bradach, J. "Going to Scale: The Challenge of Replicating Social Programs." *Stanford Social Innovation Review*, 2003, *1*(1), 18–25.
8. Ryan, W. P. "Nonprofit Capital: A Review of Problems and Strategies." Washington, D.C.: Fannie Mae Foundation and New York: Rockefeller Foundation, 2001, p. 14.
9. Grossman, A. "Philanthropic Social Capital Markets: Performance-Driven Philanthropy." Working Paper. Boston: Harvard Business School, 2000.
10. Proscio, T. *A Double "Bottom Line": Lessons on Social-Purpose Enterprise from the Venture Fund Initiative, a Summary of The Venture Fund Initiative: An Assessment of Current Opportunities for Social-Purpose Business Development, and Recommendations for Advancing the Field*. San Francisco: Roberts Economic Development Fund, 1999, p. 17.
11. Presentation by J. Gregory Dees at Stanford Social Entrepreneurs class, Stanford, Calif., 2002.
12. Magagnini, S. "Vision a Victim of Own Success—While the Nehemiah Housing Concept Grew Like Wildfire, Its Big Profits Brought a Legal Fight." *Sacramento Bee*, June 15, 2003, p. A1.

INDEX

Boston Philharmonic, 104
Bottom-line focus, 14–17
Bradach, J., 289, 292
Brauer, J., 224, 229, 237
Bronx Frontier Development Corporation, 153
Bronx Zoo, 69, 70
Brown, J. C., 34
Bundling memberships, 72–74
Bundling product packages, 72, 74–75
Business entities: choosing the right, 84–91; corporation structures, 85–89; general partnership, 85; limited liability companies, 90–91; limited partnership, 89; sole proprietorship, 84–85
Business plan: adapting, 221–222, 229–230; allocating costs, 10, 232–233; assessing organizational openness/readiness, 7; for avoiding pitfalls, 240–244; balancing "how can" mind-set with objective, 14; being clear about objectives, 7–8; contingency plans as part of, 239–240; defining, researching, testing value propositions, 8–9; identifying suitable venture opportunities, 6–7; implementation of, 209–210; low cash flow justified by direct social impact, 12–13, 15; questions to ask when preparing, 244–245; road map analogy for, 224–225; for staged launch to test assumptions/uncertainties, 13–14; timeline provided by, 231–232; using cash flow as financial measure, 11–12. *See also* Implementation; Marketing plan; Nonprofit business ventures
Business planning pitfalls: failing to attract customers, 240–241; marketing the mission instead of message, 242; operating enterprise without sufficient capacity, 242–243; operating enterprise without sufficient capital, 243–244; trying to please everyone, 241–242

Business for Social Responsibility, 117
Buyer's proposition, 159

C

C corporation, 86–87
Cabbages and Condoms Chain, 288
Caesar, P., 207
California Pacific Medical Center, 230
Candlewick Press, 153
Capacity. *See* Organizational capacity
Capital funding. *See* Financial capital investment
Carter, J., 284
Cash flow: management of, 232; as measure of financial impact, 11–12; social impact justification of low/negative, 12–13, 15
CDCs (community development corporations), 124
CDFIs (community development financial institutions), 123–124
CDVCA (Community Development Venture Capital Alliance), 124
Centre for Community Organising, 199, 201
Centre for Women, 273
CGV (Common Good Ventures): benefits to nonprofit business ventures, 170; characteristics of good, 177; clear expectations of, 178; described, 162–163; honesty in relationship with, 178–179; selection process for, 176–177; Stone Soup example of, 171–172, 178; Wolfe's Neck Farm example of, 167–169, 179. *See also* High-engagement funders
CHFF (Community Health Facilities Fund), 124
Chief Executive Leadership Institute, 30
Chronicle of Philanthropy's Web site, 117, 118
CHZ (Ciernohronská Forest Railway), 196

CICERO (Consumer Information Collection, Entry and Reporting for Organizations), 274–275
CIEM Aconcagua, 184
City Year, 127
Cliff-edge effects, 65
Coastal Enterprises, 276
Coca-Cola, 148, 155
Cohen, B., 225
Collaborative Fund for Women's Economic Development, 118
Collaborative Fund for Youth-Led Social Change, 118
Columbia Business School, 116
Columbia Business School's Research Initiative on Social Enterprise, 124
Columbia Business School's RISE project, 276
Community CSOs (civil-society organizations), 184
Community Reinvestment Act, 135
Community Wealth Ventures, 22, 115
Competitive analysis, 53–54
Connolly, P., 19
Consulting, 27
Contingency plans, 239–240
Controlled subsidiary organization, 87
Convening, 27
Corporate nonprofit-for-profit relationships, 149
Corporate philanthropy, 125–126
Corporate structure: advantages of, 85–86; C corporation, 86–87; creating good board for, 104–108; directorless, 86; income tax rates for, 87; S corporation, 87–89
Cost accounting, 232–233
Costs: decision-making/information tools to track, 232–233; planning process for allocating, 10
Crosby, B., 241
CSI (Center for Social Innovation), 295
CSO investment strategies: identifying and mitigating risk, 198; NESsT example of, 187–196, 198–202; overview of, 187–188

U

UBTI (Unrelated Business Taxable Income), 79–80, 85, 87, 88, 102
UNICEF, 287
U.S. Small Business Administration, 119
United Way, 31, 36, 39

V

Value capture, 132
Value investor, 135
Value propositions: articulation of, 56–58; blended, 292; developing, 54; testing, 8–9
Venture Philanthropy Partners, 115
Venture team: assembling the, 225–226; implementation checklist on, 219–220
Versioning, 71–72

VNAs (Visiting Nurse Associations), 52–53
Vydra (Slovak Republic), 184, 196–198, 199

W

Warner, C., 161
Web sites: CDVCA (Community Development Venture Capital Alliance), 124; Chronicle of Philanthropy, 117, 118; Columbia Business School's RISE project, 276; company analysis using information from, 158–159; David Grayson's, 148; on financial capital sources, 116–117; industry analysis using information from, 158; La Morada, 194; National Community Capital Association, 123; Vydra, 196
Whole Foods, 225

Wild Oats, 225
Winston, G., 69
WNF (Wolfe's Neck Farm), 167–169
Wolfe's Neck Farm, 167–169, 179
World Wildlife Fund, 287

Y

Yale School of Management–The Goldman Sachs Foundation Partnership on Nonprofit Ventures, 115, 116, 273, 282, 287
Yale University, 69–70
Young, D. R., 247
Youth Development Trust (Johannesburg), 154

Z

Zimmerman, D., 69
Zoo Doo, 153